Introduction to International Human Rights Law

Pietro Pustorino

Introduction to International Human Rights Law

ASSER PRESS

Springer

Pietro Pustorino
Department of Law
Luiss University
Rome, Italy

ISBN 978-94-6265-562-1 ISBN 978-94-6265-563-8 (eBook)
https://doi.org/10.1007/978-94-6265-563-8

The fully revised text of this book is based on the translation of the book originally published in Italian: "Lezioni di tutela internazionale dei diritti umani" by Pietro Pustorino, © Cacucci Editore, Bari 2020.
Published by T.M.C. ASSER PRESS, The Hague, The Netherlands www.asserpress.nl
Produced and distributed for T.M.C. ASSER PRESS by Springer-Verlag Berlin Heidelberg

This T.M.C. ASSER PRESS imprint is published by the registered company Springer-Verlag GmbH, DE, part of Springer Nature.
The registered company address is: Heidelberger Platz 3, 14197 Berlin, Germany

Foreword

In a relatively limited number of pages, this book offers a lot to the reader. In my view, the author is quite modest when he says in his preface that the volume provides a general introduction to international human rights law. In fact, there is more than that. In the following pages, the reader will find quite a complete, updated and critical picture of the *status* of the matter. This *fresco* is preceded by concise but extremely precise and well-documented elements and remarks on the historic evolution of human rights on the one hand and on their theoretical foundations and general characteristics on the other hand, two fundamental aspects for those willing to approach the topic of human rights not in a superficial way.

The scientific rigour of this work is not an obstacle to its invaluable merits as a didactic tool. I am quite well acquainted with the Italian version of this book, which is used by the students of the course on *International Protection of Human Rights* (*Tutela internazionale dei diritti umani*), the responsibility of which I have the privilege to share with Prof. Pustorino at the Law School (*Facoltà di giurisprudenza*) of the Luiss University in Rome, and I can witness to which extent it helps those—a huge majority—who are successful at the exams. Professor Pustorino and I are quite happy about the enthusiasm of our students, which is sizeable. Maybe a part of it is due to our efforts during the lessons and other personal contacts with the students, but I have no doubt that a large part of the merit belongs to the attractiveness and the reliability of the textbook.

The contents of the book are extremely rich. All the relevant areas are explored: customary international law, including jus cogens, international treaties, mechanisms—binding and non-binding—for the protection of human rights both at the universal and the at the regional levels, the domestic level, with great attention paid to the jurisprudence of national courts, which is undoubtedly an added value of this work.

The rights are presented in an original and extremely effective way, i.e. somewhat independently from the various sources in which they are enshrined. This does not mean that the sources are not considered. On the contrary, they are precisely and rigorously described, but this methodological approach permits a transversal look which is extremely valuable.

In fact, this method permits to look at the extremely complex network of norms protecting human rights as an *ensemble* of communicating vessels. There can be no illusion—and Prof. Pustorino is extremely clear about that—that human rights could be the same for everybody in the world, but the fact all these norms aim at defending human dignity creates the premise for a mutual influence between norms and system which, at the end of the day, goes in the direction of a progressive better protection.

This is also valid when it comes to the relationship between the international and the national level, a dimension which is very much present throughout the book. Individual rights have been protected at a national level well before they become a concern for the international community, and an object of regulation by international law. There is obviously a risk that the national supervisory bodies, especially supreme and constitutional courts, see the international protection of human rights as a dangerous competitor and tend to oppose national solutions to the conclusions of international supervisory bodies. This is why when national supreme and constitutional courts show openness vis-à-vis the international law of human rights, this is to be saluted as a very happy development. I refer, in this connection, to an important judgement of the Italian Constitutional Court, judgment no. 388 of 1999. This is a very important decision. Before it, the case law of the Constitutional Court was firm in saying that the reference to fundamental rights contained in Article 2 of the Italian Constitution was confined to the rights already covered by the Constitution, i.e. a very nationalistic approach. In judgment no. 388, the Constitutional Court said, conversely, that the various international charters on human rights are relevant and that "the different formulas that express them integrate, complementing each other in their interpretation", which paved the way for a new season of the Italian constitutional jurisprudence, which has now a definite open orientation.

My last point would be joining Prof. Pustorino in his firm opinion that when it comes to the relationship between human rights and international law, one cannot speak of fragmentation of international law. International law of human rights is an integral part, and a very vital one, of general international law. I refer to his preface, which describes in detail the impact of the first on the latter.

It comes into my mind, in these sad days which are seeing the evil of war back in Europe, that at the end of the day international law is an instrument of peace, and this is particularly evident for the international law of human rights. So, spreading the knowledge on human rights law, as this book masterfully does, is also spreading the word of the peace.

Rome, Italy
July 2022

Guido Raimondi
President of the Labour Section
of the Italian Supreme Court
of Cassation; Professor of International
Protection of Human Rights, Luiss
Guido Carli (Rome); Former Judge
and President of the European Court
of Human Rights (2010–2019)

Preface

This book provides a compact but general introduction to international human rights law. It is aimed primarily at undergraduate students, not just in law but also in any other programmes where the topic of human rights may be studied, including but not limited to political science and social science courses. But it could also be useful for consultation by scholars and practitioners in the fields of international law and human rights.

The book aspires to provide a complete depiction of the most important and current issues of the international protection of human rights. The theoretical foundations of the subject are analysed rapidly (Chaps. 1 and 2), as always with a concrete approach in terms of application of human rights theories or the general features of the legal framework (as in the case of both the relationship between universalism and relativism and the opposing conceptions of culture: see Chap. 2, Sects. 2.4–2.5). Great attention is devoted to the practical and professional aspects concerning the application of human rights at both the universal (including the UN system: Chap. 5) and regional levels (Chaps. 3–4), and above all to the detailed analysis of the specific individual and collective human rights (Chaps. 6–12). The analysis of the specific human rights includes the rights which have recently arisen as a result of scientific advances in the field of biomedicine and biotechnology (medically assisted procreation, surrogacy, euthanasia, etc.), have been formed through a very extensive application of other fundamental rights (e.g. the right to hope: see Chap. 7, Sect. 7.3.1), or have arisen on the basis of the application of some rights to new pressing needs, as in the case of the application to climate change of the right to a healthy environment (Chap. 12, Sect. 12.4).

In regard to the concrete application of human rights, I considered it necessary to take into account not only the international law rules and case law but also some relevant national case law and non-binding decisions of human rights committees, especially in the UN context (including interesting cases in which national supreme courts applied non-binding decisions of these committees: see for instance Chap. 5, Sect. 5.2.6 with regard to a decision of the Committee on Enforced Disappearances). These decisions often integrate the international case law and sometimes even offer new and courageous interpretations of fundamental human rights, with the aim of improving the general level of their protection.

A further objective of this book is to put the study of human rights in the more general context of international law. This is premised on the idea that international human rights law should not be considered as a legal environment autonomous from the broader system of international law. Rather, it is a regime that is fully integrated into the international legal order that, at the same time, has a very significant impact on it. This impact may be described as threefold. First, it concerns the structure of the international community: for instance, as regards the issue of international personality of natural persons (Chap. 13, Sect. 13.3) or the strong importance of minorities, indigenous peoples and multinational corporation in current international law (Chap. 13, Sects. 13.4–13.5). Second, it affects the content of many primary rules of contemporary international law, especially when human rights can collide with the principle of sovereignty of States: for instance, as regards the issues concerning the immunity of States and of state organs (Chap. 7, Sects. 7.6.1–7.6.2). Third, it has to do with the content of secondary rules of international law, thus in the context of the regime on the responsibility of States to which a specific part of the book is devoted (Chap. 14). Against this backdrop, the book frequently offers a comparison between what is provided by customary international law, what is established by special conventional regimes and what are the newest trends in international law.

I am deeply honoured that Prof. Guido Raimondi, former President of the European Court of Human Rights, has accepted to write the foreword of the book.

I would like to thank my colleagues Andrea Insolia, Manfredi Marciante and Pierfrancesco Rossi for their very useful suggestions on the structure and some contents of the book as well as for checking the case law references. Of course, I am solely responsible for any errors and omissions.

I also would like to thank Richard Boyce, who demonstrated great patience and competence in revising the English form of the book.

Rome, Italy
July 2022

Pietro Pustorino

Contents

Abbreviations

ACHPR	African Charter on Human and Peoples' Rights of 27 June 1981
ACHR	American Convention of Human Rights of 22 November 1969
ACommmHPR	African Commission on Human and Peoples' Rights
ACtHPRA	African Court on Human and Peoples' Rights
ACtJHR	African Court of Justice and Human Rights
ArCHR	Arab Charter on Human Rights of 22 May 2004
ASEAN	Association of South-East Asian Nations
AU	African Union
CAT	Committee against Torture
CED	Committee on Enforced Disappearances
CESCR	Committee on Economic, Social and Cultural Rights
CFI	Court of First Instance of the European Communities
CFREU	Charter of Fundamental Rights of the European Union
CMCoE	Committee of Ministers of the Council of Europe
CoE	Council of Europe
CommEDAW	Committee on the Elimination of All Forms of Discrimination against Women
CommERD	Committee on the Elimination of Racial Discrimination
ECHR	European Convention for the Protection of Human Rights and Fundamental Freedoms of 4 November 1950
ECJ	European Court of Justice
ECommmHR	Commission on Human Rights
ECOSOC	Economic and Social Council
ECSR	European Committee of Social Rights
ECtHR	European Court of Human Rights
ESC	European Social Charter of 18 October 1961
ESCrev	European Social Charter revised of 3 May 1996
EU	European Union
HRC	Human Rights Committee
HRCoun	Human Rights Council
IACommHR	Inter-American Commission on Human Rights

IACtHR	Inter-American Court of Human Rights
ICC	International Criminal Court
ICCPR	International Covenant on Civil and Political Rights of 16 December 1966
ICESCR	International Covenant on Economic, Social and Cultural Rights of 16 December 1966
ICJ	International Court of Justice
ICTR	International Criminal Tribunal for Rwanda
ICTY	International Criminal Tribunal for the Former Yugoslavia
IHL	International Humanitarian Law
ILC	International Law Commission
ILO	International Labour Organization
ITLOS	International Tribunal for the Law of the Sea
NGOs	Non-Governmental Organizations
OAS	Organization of American States
OAU	Organization of African Unity
OECD	Organization of Economic Co-operation and Development
OSCE	Organization for Security and Co-operation in Europe
PCIJ	Permanent Court of International Justice
SCSL	Special Court for Sierra Leone
STL	Special Tribunal for Lebanon
TEU	Treaty on European Union
TFEU	Treaty on the Functioning of the European Union
UDHR	Universal Declaration of Human Rights of 10 December 1948
UN	United Nations
UN Charter	Charter of the United Nations
UNCommHR	United Nations Commission on Human Rights
UNESCO	United Nations Educational, Scientific and Cultural Organization
UNGA	General Assembly of the United Nations
UNHCR	Office of the United Nations High Commissioner for Refugees
UNSC	Security Council of the United Nations
UNSG	United Nations Secretary-General
UPR	Universal Periodic Review
VCLT	Vienna Convention on the Law of Treaties of 23 May 1969

Chapter 1
Historic Evolution of Human Rights Law: From National to International Protection

Contents

Abstract This chapter briefly analyzes the transition from the protection of human rights in national legal systems to the international protection of human rights and the consequent erosion of the domestic jurisdiction of States. It also examines the relationship between the human rights pertaining to every human being and the rights of foreigners, examining developments in the field of diplomatic protection. Particular attention is paid to the growing importance of the individual at the international level, notably to the position of the individual as holder of rights under international law.

1.1 The Overcoming of the Domestic Jurisdiction of States

Until the establishment of the United Nations ("UN"), the system of protection of human rights was weak and based almost exclusively on a number of national legal systems that were particularly advanced in terms of protection of human rights. In the English legal system, for example, reference can be made to the *Magna Charta Libertatum* of 1215, the *Habeas Corpus Act* of 1679 and the subsequent *Bill of Rights* of 1689.

Human rights were sometimes considered as *innate* rights of the human being, in line with the theories that identify natural law as the foundation of the human rights system,[1] but they found limited roots both in national law and in the actual application of domestic rules. Judicial scrutiny of the respect of human rights was even weaker.

[1] See Chap. 2, Sect. 2.1.

P. Pustorino, *Introduction to International Human Rights Law*,
https://doi.org/10.1007/978-94-6265-563-8_1

Among the best known national acts dating back in time in which the foundation of human rights in natural law was emphasised are the detailed *Declaration of Rights* adopted by the State of Virginia on 12 June 1776, the United States *Declaration of Independence* of 4 July 1776 and the French *Declaration of the Rights of Man and of the Citizen* of 26 August 1789.

In the matter of the international protection of human rights, the most important general limit was represented by the well-known principle of the domestic jurisdiction of States over their own territory and over the community of persons settled therein, as reiterated by Article 2(7) of the UN Charter, which however specifies that this principle shall not prejudice the application of enforcement measures adopted by the UN Security Council under Chapter VII.

The result was the existence of an almost absolute power of the State to regulate relations with both its own nationals and stateless persons. There were thus no limits imposed by international law on the power of the State to regulate as it wished the activities and rights of its own citizens, including the question of the attribution of nationality.[2] This was affirmed by the Permanent Court of International Justice ("PCIJ") in the advisory opinion of 7 February 1923 on *Nationality Decrees Issued in Tunis and Morocco*, countries in which France exercised a protectorate at the time.[3]

A citizen was thus considered as a *property* of the national State, which exercised over him or her a "real right of sovereignty", in the framework of a substantially private concept of relations between the State and its citizens. The State was therefore free to exercise any power over the national population, without the international community being entitled to intervene in any way.

That said, the contribution of national protection of human rights to the progressive development of the process of international protection of individual and collective rights should not be underestimated. The element of connection between internal and international protection in the matter of human rights is rather generously highlighted in the *Déclaration des droits internationaux de l'homme* adopted in 1929 by the *Institut de droit international*: the preamble notes that national constitutions envisaging rules applicable to human beings and hence not limited to citizens constituted the first legal foundations in the matter of the protection of human rights, expressly citing the American and French Constitutions of the 18th century.

1.2 The Origins of International Human Rights Law—The Protection of Foreigners

In the past, international law required the protection of rights belonging to foreigners. The international obligations regarding the protection of foreigners, though modified over time and largely absorbed by the general legal framework governing human rights, still exist. The obligations in question can concern individuals or groups

[2] On the right to citizenship and other political rights, see Chap. 10, Sects. 10.2–10.3.

[3] See PCIJ 1923, p. 24.

of them as confirmed by the conclusion—from the mid-seventeenth century and even earlier—of international treaties for the protection of religious minorities, both between European countries of different religions and between the latter and non-European states, for example, the Ottoman Empire. These treaties established respect for the faith and religious opinions of the respective citizens living abroad. Above all, the aim was to prevent conflicts between States caused by the need—or rather the pretext—of protecting their own citizens abroad, sometimes actually discriminated and even persecuted for religious reasons. These requirements, in the context of relations with non-European countries, gave rise to the so-called "regime of capitulations" whereby foreign citizens were judged abroad, both in civil and sometimes in criminal cases, by special courts that applied their own national law.

With regard to the content of classic international norms on the protection of the rights of foreigners, first of all, the territorial State is prohibited from making them subject to some specific measures in the absence of a sufficient *territorial attachment* of the foreigner. For example, the possibility for the territorial State to require a foreigner to perform military service is not justified in the absence of a bond of citizenship between the individual and the territorial State. On the other hand, the imposition of fiscal and administrative burdens based on the fact that a foreigner works in the territory of the State is legitimate.

A further obligation of the territorial State is to adopt measures preventing and suppressing conduct that puts a foreigner at risk. These measures must be tailored according to the importance of the foreigner and any functions performed by the latter abroad, so that they must be particularly significant if the foreigner performs public functions of great importance on behalf of the national State. The evaluation of the real risk of violations against a foreigner will be another important factor in determining measures of a preventive nature designed to protect that foreigner. In this regard, international law has long since provided for independent and additional rules to protect certain particular categories of foreigners, such as the rules on personal and functional immunity of the State organ, which protect the officials of foreign States operating abroad.

A more recent substantive obligation derives from observance of the principle of non-discrimination, whose content under general international law is however limited to the prohibition of serious discriminatory acts against foreigners on the basis of their nationality or other grounds (linguistic, racial, religious, etc.). That discrimination may target either natural persons or legal persons, for example, in relation to assets owned by foreign companies operating abroad.

To these obligations of a substantive nature must be added some of a procedural nature, such as the obligation to afford access to national courts to foreigners whose rights protected by international law have been infringed. This obligation provides more specific guarantees than the general ones deriving from the principle prohibiting the denial of justice to foreigners.[4] The right of access to national courts—which implies the availability of effective judicial remedies under domestic law—is to be

[4] On the right of access to national courts, which is part of the guarantees inherent in the right to a fair trial, see Chap. 8, Sect. 8.2.1.

distinguished from the right of access to international courts, which is protected in a more limited form by specific international rules.

1.3 The *Old* and *New* Holders of Foreigners' Rights

In the past, the *ownership* of the rights of foreigners belonged exclusively to the national State of the foreigners and not to the individuals who were the direct victims of the injury. Consequently, the international responsibility of the infringing State could be enforced only by the national State of the foreigner, which was the sole holder of the substantive right infringed. The national State was in particular entitled to take countermeasures—at the time called reprisals and considered lawful for the purposes of settling interstate disputes—and to afford diplomatic protection to its citizen or national legal person through exercising "its own rights", as stated by the PCIJ in its judgment of 30 August 1924 in the *Mavrommatis Palestine Concessions* case.[5]

Thus, only interstate relationships existed at the level of substantive rights contained in primary international law provisions and in the context of international responsibility regulated by secondary provisions.

This conception is now to be considered outdated. In fact, it is a rather well-established view, in the literature and in practice, that the individual may be directly entitled, on the basis of international norms, to substantive and procedural rights, such as the right to apply to international courts, and may also be bound by international obligations, in particular those prohibiting international crimes.

This evolutionary trend in international law, which implies a strengthening of the legal *status* of the individual in the international sphere, even to the point of considering his/her international legal personality,[6] would seem to be recognisable, albeit in a lesser form, in the context of international responsibility. In fact, it cannot be ruled out, as some scholars assert, that individuals are now entitled, also on the basis of general international law, to directly sue the responsible State to obtain damages for the harm suffered, at least in cases of serious violations of human rights and international humanitarian law.[7]

The existence of international rules providing substantive rights in favour of individuals has been confirmed in international case-law. In particular, the International Court of Justice ("ICJ"), in its judgments of 27 June 2001 and 31 March 2004, respectively in the *LaGrand*[8] and *Avena* cases,[9] stated that Article 36 of the Vienna Convention of 24 April 1963 on Consular Relations contemplates both a State and an individual right to inform the consular authorities of the national State of the arrest,

---

[5] *Greece v. Great Britain*, in PCIJ 1924, p. 12.

[6] On this issue, see Chap. 13, Sect. 13.3.

[7] On this issue, see Chap. 14, Sect. 14.3.

[8] *Germany v. United States of America.*

[9] *Mexico v. United States of America.*

detention and trial of its nationals. In the *LaGrand* case, the Court held that Article 36 of the Convention "creates individual rights" which, through the jurisdiction clause contained in the Optional Protocol to the Convention, may be invoked before the ICJ by the national State of the person whose rights have been infringed.[10]

The above position of the ICJ has been further confirmed, thus becoming well-settled, in the most recent judgment of 17 July 2019 issued in the *Jadhav* case concerning the arrest, detention and trial of an Indian national, suspected of having conducted espionage activities in Pakistan and who had been denied the exercise of the right of access to consular authorities under the aforementioned Article 36 of the 1963 Convention. Reiterating that the provision in question also covers rights of an individual nature, the Court held that compliance with Article 36 is not conditional on the cooperation of the national State of the individual in question in the legal proceedings instituted in the territorial State, with the result that, in the present case, the alleged lack of cooperation "does not justify Pakistan's denial of access to Mr. Jadhav by consular officers of India".[11]

1.4 Diplomatic Protection and Its Development

Human rights developments have also influenced the concept of diplomatic protection mentioned above. However, it must be acknowledged that this impact is limited in two respects. Firstly, it regards the reduction of the national State's discretion as to the decision to exercise diplomatic protection as well as to the content of the possible State action. Secondly, the impact is mainly limited to certain serious human rights violations.

In fact, there is a tendency, not entirely consolidated in national case-law, to provide for the obligation of the national State—based on an extensive and coordinated interpretation of domestic law and international human rights law—to exercise diplomatic protection in cases of serious violations of human rights committed abroad against its citizens. To this effect is the judgment of 6 November 2002 of the UK Court of Appeals (Supreme Court of Judicature), in the *Abbasi v. Secretary of State for Foreign and Commonwealth Affairs* case, which established the obligation of the United Kingdom to adopt a reasonable and non-arbitrary decision in the matter of diplomatic protection, which can be subject to judicial review in the event that its own citizen has suffered human rights violations in a foreign country.[12]

Even more significant in this regard is the judgment of the Constitutional Court of South Africa of 4 August 2004 in *Kaunda and Others v. President of the Republic of South Africa*, interpreting certain South African constitutional provisions[13] in the

[10] In ICJ 2001, p. 494, para 77.

[11] *India v. Pakistan*, in ICJ 2019, p. 450, paras 116–117.

[12] See para 106 of the judgment.

[13] The relevant constitutional provisions on the subject and relating to the protection of human rights are Articles 10–12 and 35. Particular weight, in the context of the Court's arguments on diplomatic

light of international human rights law. It was found that the government had a duty "consistent with its obligations under international law" to act in order to protect its citizens who have suffered a serious violation of human rights. In this case, according to the Court, the citizen's request for protection is unlikely to be refused, but if it is, the refusal decision may be subject to judicial review and the court may compel the government "to take appropriate action".[14]

The judicial assessment of the obligation of the national State to act in diplomatic protection of its citizens can lead to far-reaching diplomatic action for the protection of a very significant number of individuals. This occurred, for example, following the judgment of 30 August 2011 made by the Constitutional Court of the Republic of Korea, which found that the attitude of inertia assumed by the Korean government against the thousands of Korean women kidnapped and forced into prostitution by the Japanese army during World War II was contrary to the Korean Constitution. Following this decision, the Korean and Japanese governments concluded an agreement in 2015 concerning the presentation of an official apology by Japan as well as the establishment of a fund for the victims or their relatives.[15]

The national case-law of other countries on this matter would appear to be less advanced. For example, the Italian Council of State, in a decision of 29 May 2014, no. 2792, stated that it is up to "the holders of political power to decide, within a high margin of appreciation" whether to exercise diplomatic protection.[16] In a subsequent decision, the Lazio Administrative Regional Court, in a judgment dated 4 December 2017, confirmed the restrictive approach on diplomatic protection, rejecting the appeal of an Italian citizen who invoked protection by the government for the alleged persecution he suffered in Albania and which consisted of numerous criminal and tax proceedings brought against him in the courts. According to the Regional Administrative Tribunal, "the State exercising diplomatic protection is exercising a right which is held at international level by the State itself and not by the citizen. And, in fact, the State does not act as a representative of the individual because diplomatic protection does not concern cases in which the individual acts or is accountable directly at the international level". On the basis of these assumptions, the Regional Administrative Court held that the decision on diplomatic protection was a political one, and as such not subject to judicial review. It thus declared that the administrative courts had no jurisdiction in the matter.

A further limited development in the matter of the connection between diplomatic protection and human rights law is the tendency to exercise diplomatic protection in favour of an individual with dual nationality who has been injured by one of the national States. In such instances Article 7 of the non-binding Draft Articles

---

protection, was also attributed to the provisions of Article 3(2)(*a*) and (*b*) of the Constitution, further to which every citizen is "equally entitled to the rights, privileges and benefits of citizenship" and "equally subject to the duties and responsibilities of citizenship".

[14] See para 69 of the judgment.

[15] On the issue of the jurisdictional immunity of Japan in proceedings relating to this matter before the Korean courts, see Chap. 7, Sect. 7.6.1.

[16] See *Il Tuo Viaggio s.r.l. v. Presidency of the Council of Ministers and Others.*

on Diplomatic Protection adopted by the International Law Commission ("ILC") in 2006 provides for the criterion of the "predominant" nationality in order to evaluate the legitimacy of an exercise of diplomatic protection by a national State towards other national States.

Although it is questionable whether that criterion reflects general international law, some States do tend to exercise diplomatic protection in respect of individuals of their own nationality for the purpose of seeking redress for serious human rights violations by another national State. For example, in March 2019, the question arose in relation to the UK's use of diplomatic protection in respect of a woman (Zaghari-Ratcliffe) who had Iranian and UK citizenship and who had been subjected, according to the UK, to a number of human rights abuses in Iran (including lack of access to the treatment necessary for her health condition and failure to observe the rules of due process in relation to the legal proceedings against her) on the grounds that she was allegedly engaged in subversive activities and espionage on Iranian soil.

Comprehension Check and Tasks

1. For a long time, the principle of domestic jurisdiction governed relations between States and their citizens in international law. What did this principle envisage? (Sect. 1.1)
2. What is the relationship between the international rules on the protection of foreigners and those on human rights? (Sect. 1.2)
3. What is the position of the ICJ in the *LaGrand*, *Avena* and *Jadhav* cases in relation to who enjoys rights under Article 36 of the Convention on Consular Relations? (Sect. 1.3)

References

ICJ (2001) ICJ Reports
ICJ (2019) ICJ Reports
PCIJ (1923) Advisory opinion of 7 February 1923 on Nationality Decrees Issued in Tunis and Morocco. PCIJ Publications, Series B, No. 4
PCIJ (1924) Judgment of 30 August 1924 in the *Mavrommatis Palestine Concessions* case. PCIJ Publications, Series A, No. 2

Chapter 2
Theoretical Foundations and General Characteristics of Human Rights

Contents

Abstract The chapter examines the main theoretical foundations of human rights, namely the natural law theories, the theory of social consent, the positivist theories and the Marxist-inspired theories. Particular attention is then paid to the general characteristics of human rights and thus to the universality, indivisibility and inalienability of human rights, whose practical importance is ultimately greater than the theoretical underpinnings of human rights. On the one hand, the discussion centres on cases of judicial dialogue—both between national courts and between national and international courts—aimed at ensuring a uniform application of human rights. On the other, it focuses on instances of conflicting case law and lack of coordination arising from multiculturalism, relativism and opposing cultural views, highlighting possible solutions flowing from national and international jurisprudence.

2.1 Natural Law Theories

There are numerous theories on the legal basis of international human rights protection, some of which are also used to determine the basis of international law. In this regard, the prevailing scholarly theories are those that rely on the natural right of

P. Pustorino, *Introduction to International Human Rights Law*,
https://doi.org/10.1007/978-94-6265-563-8_2

the individual to the protection of his or her rights, on the consent of the entitled persons and on positivist conceptions of human rights. These are subdivided into further scholarly positions, which, while exhibiting some unique elements, can be brought within the framework of those mentioned just now. To provide a complete picture, also worthy of separate mention, within the framework of the examination of the universal character of human rights, are Marxist-inspired theories since they have, in the final analysis, as their main objective the challenging of the general characteristic of the universality of human rights.

Starting from the analysis of the theory that refers to the natural right of the individual to the protection of his or her rights, at the outset it should be said that it is invoked in very different ways respectively by natural law lawyers, for whom natural law originates from the human being, and by theologians, who by contrast maintain its divine origin, rooted in particular in Christian doctrines. The latter have contributed significantly to the affirmation of the importance of the human being, especially in his or her "individuality" and personal dignity, as well as of the need to eliminate all forms of discrimination.

The natural law approach is also informed by the so-called self-evidence theory, according to which human rights, insofar as they are inherent to the human being, are self-evident and do not require a theoretical and normative justification. The legal sources on human rights, whether of a domestic or international nature, are thus considered solely as reproducing what is already inherent in human beings. Those sources merely bring out, on a normative level, the characteristics and particularities of human beings and the rights associated with them.

Whatever the "variant" of the different theories that identify the legal foundation of human rights in natural law may actually be, the fact remains that these views are united by the idea that the matter in question is removed from the margin of appreciation of the State, which can only confirm the existence of human rights and facilitate their affirmation on a normative level. Consequently, the national and international legal regime of human rights is declaratory and not constitutive of the rights themselves.

A famous reference to human rights as natural rights, which States can only confirm in their existence, is found in the dissenting opinion of Judge Tanaka in the ICJ Judgment of 18 July 1966 in the *South West Africa* cases,[1] according to which the principle of protection of human rights "is derived from the concept of man as a *person*". States, according to this approach, cannot create human rights but only confirm their existence and ensure their adequate legal protection. It follows that the role of the State is "no more than declaratory", as human rights exist "with the human being" and "independently of, and before, the State".[2]

In international case law, some explicit or implicit references to natural law are to be found, although these are often additional considerations to arguments based on positive law. Thus, in the Inter-American Court of Human Rights ("IACtHR") judgment of 20 January 1989 in the *Godínez Cruz* v. *Honduras* case on forced

[1] ICJ 1966.

[2] *Id.*, p. 297.

disappearances and murders committed by State organs, the Court stated that the State has the right to use force to counteract the commission of particularly serious crimes, while noting however that State power "is not unlimited, nor may the State resort to any means to attain its ends", since it 'is subject to law and morality".[3]

Natural law theories have the merit of linking the legal aspects of the matter to moral ones and of making it clear that human rights are an integral and indispensable part of the human being.

That said, these theories have several theoretical and practical weaknesses. From a theoretical perspective, the theories referred to here are, first of all, a weak legal ground, which is negatively reflected in the establishment and application of the relevant rights, especially at the legal level. In this regard, reference is often made to vague notions and concepts, such as the sense of humanity, which should entail respect for one's own rights and those of others, but which in reality, when referred to in a generic way, can hardly constitute a barrier to the violation of human rights.

Again from a theoretical standpoint, the view that human rights are immanent and inherent in human beings seems contradictory because in reality they can be limited, sometimes significantly, and even ignored altogether, when, for example, derogation clauses in human rights treaties apply to many individual or collective rights for serious emergency situations.[4]

The theories that identify the basis of human rights in natural law also appear rather general and imprecise as regards the content of the rights protected, which, on the contrary, varies considerably depending on the nature of the rights concerned, the normative sources that cover them and the corresponding obligations of States.

Moreover, precisely because of the limited protection afforded by human rights theories rooted in natural law, they risk having the undesirable effect of standardising the protection of human rights downwards, with the consequence of weakening the overall level of protection of individual and collective rights.

Finally, the reference to natural law as the legal ground for human rights seems inadequate to resolve some particularly complex current issues concerning the application of human rights law. In fact, as will be seen later when assessing the characteristics of universalism and relativism in the field of human rights,[5] more and more often, at the national and international level, conflicts exist, on the one hand, between the rights of the individual or of a plurality of individuals and State rights or interests, for example with reference to the protection of public order or internal security. On the other hand, a conflict between individual or collective rights may arise where, for example, the right of an individual to profess his or her religion clashes with the similar right of another individual to profess a different religion or to safeguard his or her position of secularism or agnosticism. These conflicting situations show that, more than in the past, the right of each individual is limited by the holding of the same right or other rights by different persons such as States, individuals, minorities, indigenous peoples, etc. This makes it necessary to engage

[3] See para 162 of the judgment.

[4] On the derogation clauses regarding the human rights treaties, see Chap. 3, Sect. 3.9.

[5] See *infra*, Sects. 2.4–2.5.

in a complex work of preventive balancing of these opposing rights at the time of formulating the legal rules, and of subsequent and coordinated interpretation of the various rights and interests that come into play in actual cases. In such instances, recourse to natural law can hardly support the interpreter in identifying the concrete solution to be adopted.

2.2 The Theory of Social Consent

A further scholarly theory is based on the idea that the legal basis of human rights lies in the consent of the populace. According to this position, human rights are those rights that are recognised as such by a specific community of persons that, at a certain moment in history, forms a social unit. The community of persons, which is not necessarily limited to natural persons acting individually or collectively, but may include some legal persons, can be identified in a national community, or, more broadly, in the international community understood as a "universal community of persons".

The problematic issues concerning the theory under consideration relate, on the one hand, to the identification of the members and thus of the communities of individuals relevant for the purpose of formulating consent and, on the other hand, to the nature and manner of manifestation of consent to be taken into account. In principle, consent can be manifested either expressly or implicitly. In the former case, the natural manifestation of consent is expressed in the rules adopted by the representatives of the population through legislative bodies, and so the theory of consent tends to be strictly linked with positivist theories. In the latter case, the theory runs the risk of being based on subjective, if not entirely discretionary, interpretations, which tend to ascertain in an approximate way the existence of consensus on certain rules or conduct considered accepted or tolerated by the members of society gathered in a plurality of social bodies.

The theory in question seems to display some kinship with the "European consensus" doctrine used by the European Court of Human Rights ("ECtHR") as a relevant legal parameter for interpreting the rules of the European Convention for the Protection of Human Rights and Fundamental Freedoms of 4 November 1950 ("ECHR") in an evolutionary sense, with particular reference, for example, to questions concerning the birth or end of life (medically assisted reproduction, surrogacy, euthanasia, etc.), or the application of the notion of family to unions between individuals of the same sex.[6] However, in these cases, the European consensus is inferred from a series of precise factors and elements, including not only the statements and conduct of individuals and communities operating at the national level but also the rules followed by State institutions, through the adoption of national laws and their implementation in case law. That confirms the fact that the theory of consensus is substantially absorbed into positivist theories.

---

[6] See Chap. 6, Sects. 6.3–6.4 and Chap. 9, Sect. 9.1.5.

2.3 The Positivist Approach

Other scholarly theories relevant to human rights are those of a positivist nature, which are based on the transformation of human rights into positive law, written or unwritten, national or international. These theories therefore imply that human rights stem from their original natural and/or moral dimension and are expressly regulated at the legal level.

Positivist theories necessarily focus on the essential role played, above all, by the State. But also by other actors operating within the human rights framework, for example international organisations, with reference especially to the functions of producing and implementing norms containing individual or collective rights. Moreover, advocates of these theories tend to distinguish between different human rights according to their importance and thus the different degree and effectiveness of normative protection.

Positivist theories, as mentioned in the previous section, are closely related to the view that identifies the consensus of the populace as the legal ground for human rights. In fact, it is easy to see how social consensus is often translated, in the various forms provided for by the international legal order and national legal systems, into rules of positive law. At the same time, however, the theory of social consensus can play an important role in testing positive law in order to eliminate or at least reduce the "hiatus" between the convictions of citizens and certain legal rules, thus making it necessary to interpret them in an evolutionary way and possibly to make adjustments so as to bring them into line with common social feeling.

What has just been said shows how the various scholarly theories on the legal foundation of human rights do not necessarily have to be analysed in terms of opposition to each other, but can well be reconciled. From this point of view, if one considers, as we do, that legal rules are indispensable for an adequate and effective protection of human rights, this does not detract from the fact that the addressees of the rules can comply with them not only because the rules contain legal obligations but also because it is "right" to do so in as much as those rules correspond to duties of a moral nature, commonly held by national societies and the international community. Understood in this way, the reference to natural law and social consensus can, in our view, contribute both to a broad interpretation of the human rights protected by legal rules and to stimulating national and international legislators to expand and improve the catalogue of rights existing at the normative level and also to eliminate any 'distortions' established by positive law.[7]

[7] One example is the serious forms of racial or sexual discrimination that have found their way into national law in the past and to a lesser extent even recently.

2.4 Universality, Indivisibility and Inalienability of Human Rights and Its Practical Implications

The assertion, commonly expressed in both scholarly opinion and practice, that human rights are universal, indivisible and inalienable, is to be accepted.

This result, in terms of defining the nature of human rights, which today appears to be well settled, has not been achieved smoothly. Apart from what will be mentioned in the following subsection about the limits placed on the universal character of human rights due to forms of relativism, it must first be said that, since the foundation of the current international human rights setup, there have been currents of thought, for example those of Marxist inspiration, which have radically challenged that setup. The Marxist approach considered the universal human rights regime to be the expression of Western values and principles and aimed at protecting only certain social categories of individuals—belonging to the "bourgeoisie"—ignoring the needs and requirements of the majority of the population, especially the economically and culturally weaker. According to those latter theories, there was a need to abandon any form of isolation and individualism of the human being, viewed as an expression of the capitalist vision opposed by Marx, in favour of an approach that would value the "community" aspect and could be fully realised through the communist revolution, so as to limit the selfish and utilitarian expressions of individuals and focus on the aspects of protection and realisation of the entire national community. This implied that the individual not only had rights vis-à-vis the State but also duties vis-à-vis the community as a whole.

More recently, there has been no shortage of fundamental objections from significant groups of States, such as the socialist countries themselves and, following the extensive decolonisation process that took place in the 1960s and 1970s, newly independent states. The latter, in the context of the broader phenomenon of contestation of some international norms created before their formation, have also criticised the rules regarding specific human rights, especially those of an economic nature like the right to property. They advocate greater discretion for the territorial State to nationalise or expropriate property belonging to foreigners, including the obligation of the territorial State to pay compensation commensurate with the economic value of the expropriated property.

These forms of objections to the nature of human rights are not confined to "history". Proof of this lies in the fact that a more limited contestation, above all of the universal nature of human rights, is currently raised by some Islamic states, whose extreme positions in terms of the compression of certain individual rights—especially in relation to the persons who enjoy those rights, for example women—go well beyond the legitimate appreciation of relativism in the field of human rights, more about which later.

It is our opinion that if the aforementioned theories aimed at challenging the concept of the universality of human rights in the sense referred to above—thus without referring to specific and, in principle, acceptable claims of cultural relativism or regionalism—were to be accepted, the very character of the universality of human rights would be undermined. That in turn would have disastrous effects in terms of the generalised and effective protection of individual and collective human rights.

Having said that, let us look in detail at what is meant by universal, indivisible and inalienable rights.

2.4.1 Universality

The expression universality seeks to affirm that human rights are due to every human being, without any distinction. This essential feature of human rights harks back to the previously mentioned conception of the rights inherent to the human person, including theories of Christian origin.

The universality of human rights has influenced, albeit to a limited extent, the law on human rights, excluding for instance the operation of the reciprocity mechanism with regard to the application of certain international human rights rules. From this point of view, treaties on human rights and on international humanitarian law are an exception within the framework of treaty law, as already stated by the ICJ in the advisory opinion of 21 June 1971 on the *Legal Consequences for States of the Continued Presence of South Africa in Namibia (South West Africa) Notwithstanding Security Council Resolution 276 (1970)*[8] and, at the normative level, in Article 60, paragraph 5, of the Vienna Convention on the Law of Treaties of 23 May 1969 ("VCLT"). The above-mentioned provision in fact excludes the said treaties from the application of the rule *inadimplenti non est adimplendum* on the extinction or suspension of treaties for breach by a contracting State. Consequently, the application of these agreements must be ensured in an absolute and objective manner, their observance not being conditional on observance by the other contracting States.

However, some clarifications must be made regarding the universality of human rights. First of all, it does not imply that all individuals are addressees of the same rights and that they have the same content in the various geographical areas that make up the international community. This is moreover evident with regard to the analysis of human rights treaties. One should consider, on the one hand, that in some geographical areas (Europe) there are many regional human rights conventions, while in others (Asia) there is a greater reluctance on the part of States to conclude this type of convention. On the other hand, that States are free not only to ratify such treaties but also to make reservations to them within the limits of the regime applicable in this regard, and also to derogate from them, or to restrict their scope of application, in accordance with the derogation and restriction clauses sometimes provided for in such treaties.[9]

---

[8] In the opinion, having stressed that "member States are under obligation to abstain from entering into treaty relations with South Africa in all cases in which the Government of South Africa purports to act on behalf of or concerning Namibia", the Court added that "the same rule cannot be applied to certain general conventions such as those of a humanitarian character, the non-performance of which may adversely affect the people of Namibia": in ICJ 1971, p. 55, para 122.

[9] On this issue, see Chap. 3, Sect. 3.9.

Moreover, universality, like the other characteristics of human rights, cannot be understood in absolute terms. In particular, it does not mean a uniform and global sharing of the values underlying each specific human right. This natural limitation of human rights is plain to see from an examination of some regional legal instruments. For example, in the Bangkok Declaration of 2 April 1993, adopted by some Asian countries and not of a binding nature, it is stated that although human rights "are universal in nature", they must be considered "in the context of a dynamic and evolving process of international norm-setting", bearing in mind the significance of national and regional particularities and various historical, cultural and religious backgrounds.[10]

This trend is strengthened from a general point of view through reference to the notion of legal and cultural multiculturalism, which would include the various regional forms of human rights protection and which, to some extent, would even flank the objective of universalism, without thus opposing it. In practice, however, it is not always easy to bring values and principles concerning individual or collective rights applied in different regional and cultural contexts within a "common denominator".

It should be made clear that the situation of potential conflict between various interpretations of the same right applied in different geographic and cultural contexts does not exist only, as it might be thought at first sight, for human rights that receive less protection at the international level, but also for "strong" rights. For example, while there is a consensus on the need to protect the right to life, there is no agreement between States on the moment from which life begins (whether at conception, or more likely at birth),[11] whether birth control policies practised by some States are lawful and what the correct balance between the right of the unborn child and the rights of the parents, especially the mother, is in case of conflict.

It should further be noted that the above-mentioned potential contrast between different interpretations of the same right may arise both, of course, in relation to countries that are culturally and legally different, and in relation to countries that are culturally and legally similar, but which have different internal sensitivities, for example because of the conflicting religious convictions of their citizens or because of the presence of numerous ethnic, linguistic or religious minorities.

However, the question of conflict between different interpretations of a specific universal right should not be overemphasised. In fact, it is not uncommon in practice to find cases of significant dialogue both between national courts and between the latter and courts or bodies of an international nature with a view to applying certain human rights in a basically uniform manner. Particularly noteworthy are cases of coordination by courts of countries with strong local traditions and belonging to geographic areas where there are no effective international systems to oversee observance of human rights.

---

[10] See para 8 of the Declaration.

[11] On this issue, see Chap. 6, Sect. 6.2.4.

A significant example is given by the judgment of the Japanese Supreme Court of 4 September 2013, in which it was declared that a provision of the Civil Code—reflecting a longstanding and consolidated national tradition—that discriminated against children born out of wedlock in matters of succession was unconstitutional. This was done by taking into account both the binding effect in domestic law of certain universal conventions on human rights ratified by Japan—the International Covenant on Civil and Political Rights of 16 December 1966 ("ICCPR") and the Convention on the Rights of the Child of 1989—and the recommendations adopted by the supervisory bodies of these conventions, which had pointed out that the aforementioned national provision was contrary to international law.[12]

Another significant example of coordination between international courts and supreme courts of States with strong local traditions is given by the judgment of the Indian Supreme Court of 6 September 2018. That ruling declared that laws that criminalised homosexual relations occurring in private and between consenting individuals were unconstitutional also in light of the reference to universal and regional legal instruments on human rights and the case law of the ECtHR.[13]

Even more recently can be cited the judgment of the Canadian Supreme Court of 27 May 2022 which, extensively referring to the jurisprudence of the ECtHR on the so-called right to hope and therefore on the need to foresee at the national level the possibility for every prisoner of being released on the basis of an effective review process, declared unconstitutional the provision of the Canadian criminal code which established the automatic application of the 25-year prison punishment for each murder committed by the individual in the same case (for a total of 150 years in the case at stake), de facto excluding any possibility of release of the person in question.[14]

Still on the subject of the universality of human rights, it should finally be borne in mind that another significant limitation to the uniform application of human rights is the fact that, especially in relation to countries situated in geographical and cultural areas where the protection of human rights is still less advanced, the level of protection of certain individual or collective rights may originally be particularly low. There comes to mind the serious discrimination suffered in the past, and to some extent today, by large categories of individuals on the basis of race, ethnicity, religion or gender. In such cases, strong corrective measures are needed to remedy a wholly unsatisfactory original situation, thus requiring the States concerned to take further and more incisive action to bring themselves into line with the universally accepted level of protection.

---

[12] See *Special appeal against the ruling that dismissed the appeal filed against the ruling on the division of estate*, paragraph 3(3)(C) of the English translation of the judgment available online at www.courts.go.jp/app/hanrei_en/detail?id=1203.

[13] See *Navtej Singh Johar & Ors. v. Union of India, Thr. Secretary, Ministry of Law and Justice*, paras 150–153, in which reference is made to the Universal Declaration of Human Rights of 10 December 1948 ("UDHR"), the ICCPR and the ECHR.

[14] See the case *Her Majesty The Queen and Attorney General of Quebec v. Alexandre Bissonnette*, in particular para 104.

2.4.2 Indivisibility and Interdependency

The term indivisibility refers to the close dependence between the various human rights, which complement and reinforce each other. This characteristic of human rights, in addition to having a theoretical justification based on the connection between rights of a similar nature belonging to the same holder (the individual, in an isolated or collective form) and pursuing common objectives (such as strengthening the protection of the human person), is confirmed in practice by the fact that some recent rights are derived from other human rights, especially those of a fundamental nature. Thus, for example, the right to food, the right to water, the right to decent living conditions, as well as the right to housing and the right of access to essential public services derive from the right to life and the right to dignity of the human person.[15] Therefore, the statement of principle made by the IACtHR in its judgment of 19 November 1999 in the *'Street Children' (Villagran-Morales et al.) v. Guatemala* case, according to which the right to life is a fundamental right and its exercise "is essential for the exercise of all other human rights", is commendable. Consequently, for the Court where the right to life is not respected, "all rights lack meaning".[16]

The feature of the indivisibility of human rights operates in practice in a very articulated way. In fact, a particular human right, especially if a recently recognised one, can be "intertwined" with a plurality of other individual or collective rights. For example, if it is true, as noted above, that the right to food and the right to housing derive principally from the right to life and the right to human dignity, it is equally true that the same rights, in turn, complete and give effect to other rights, such as the right to health and the right to private and family life.

The IACtHR itself has made even more specific use of the character of the interdependence and indivisibility of human rights, in particular in order to extend its jurisdiction to ascertain violations of rights that do not have an adequate basis in the American Convention, in particular economic and social rights. This relying on the very general wording of Article 26 of the Convention, which obliges States Parties to adopt measures aimed at progressively achieving the full realisation of rights in the economic, social, educational, scientific and cultural spheres. In the judgment of 31 August 2017 in the *Lagos del Campo v. Peru* case, the Court thus highlighted "the interdependence and indivisibility of civil and political rights and economic, social and cultural rights", which should all be understood "as human rights, without any specific hierarchy, and be enforceable in all cases before the competent authorities".[17]

The view that the characteristic of indivisibility and interdependence can be used in practice to broaden the scope of protection of human rights, without therefore being limited to the theoretical aspects of the matter, is further bolstered by treaty law, in particular, the rules on reservations deemed incompatible with the object and purpose of treaties. In this regard, reference should be made to the *Guide to Practice*

---

[15] On these rights, see Chap. 6, Sects. 6.5–6.5.2.

[16] See para 144 of the judgment.

[17] See para 141 of the judgment.

on Reservations to Treaties, approved in 2011 by the ILC to support the interpretation and application of the provisions contained in the VCLT. The document, which is not mandatory, points out that the examination of compatibility with the object and purpose of a treaty may also be based on the interdependence of the rights provided for in that treaty.[18] In our view, it follows that the interdependent nature of the rights enshrined in human rights conventions may constitute a significant and general limitation on the making of reservations to such treaties.

However, as with the other general characteristics of human rights—universality and inalienability—the aspect of indivisibility must be recognised in relative and not absolute terms. In this sense, indivisibility is evident in the relationship between fundamental human rights, thus protecting the essential values of the human person. It is likewise evident in the relationship between a specific human right and its "derivatives", i.e. rights that are directly derived from another human right, as in the abovementioned case of the right to life from which numerous other related substantive rights flow. The relationship between substantive human rights and related procedural rights deriving from the same international norm is equally evident, as in the case of the State obligation to carry out adequate investigations and judicial proceedings following the violation of the right to life or the right not to be tortured. In other cases, however, establishing the element of indivisibility may not be as easy.

Linked to the aspect of the indivisibility of human rights is the view that the protection of individual and collective rights is "pervasive", protecting the human being in his or her entirety, as a body and as a spiritual and cultural entity, thus extending to the protection of opinions, beliefs and manifestations of an artistic, literary, religious nature, etc.

It should be finally noted, however, that in the light of the formidable developments that have taken place in the field of international human rights protection, indivisibility no longer seems, in our opinion, sufficient to describe the complexity of the phenomenon of human rights as well as the close connection existing between numerous individual or collective rights. More appropriate in this regard would appear to be the constant and necessary *coordination* that must be ensured between the various human rights, as well as the *integration* of the various legal regimes, found at the universal and regional level, which operate in the field of human rights and often overlap when dealing with specific cases.

2.4.3 *Inalienability*

Finally, human rights cannot be waived by their holders. The fact that human rights cannot be renounced implies, for example, the unlawfulness of practices detrimental to women's or children's rights, a pretext for which is often the presumed consent of the persons concerned or their legal representatives, as in the case of forced marriages

[18] See Recommendation No. 3.1.5.6.

of minors, considered valid or at least tolerated in some African or Asian countries, or female genital mutilations.

The fact that human rights are inalienable is called into question by the voluntary practices of ceding certain rights for economic purposes, such as the right to the image and privacy, which will be discussed when analysing the right to private and family life.[19] Again, the truth is that the inalienability of human rights as general characteristic is not absolute. Consequently, only human rights of a fundamental nature are truly inalienable, while others may be subject to total or partial waiver, including for economic purposes.

Renunciation, however, not only must come from the holder of the right but must also be "free", i.e. not dictated by third parties or by conditions of an economic necessity. Moreover, it should be pointed out that the renunciation in question does not at all mean giving up formal ownership of the right under consideration and its possible exercise in other circumstances, but only waiver of that right in certain specific situations, delimited in terms of substance and time.

What has been said in terms of waiving the exercise of certain rights is also in line with the possibility for the State to derogate from or restrict certain human rights for reasons of national emergency or to balance these rights against other State and individual rights or interests.[20]

2.5 Universality Versus Relativism: The Necessity to Balance Universality and Multiculturalism on Human Rights

The issue of the possible conflict between the demands of universalism and multiculturalism, which has the potential to include the most radical forms of relativism in the field of human rights, has already been touched upon in the previous sections. The issue has been problematic as regards the conflict between certain human rights, including those of a fundamental nature, and the right to cultural diversity, which is regulated, at the regional level, in Article 22 of the Charter of Fundamental Rights of the European Union ("CFREU"), which respects cultural, religious and linguistic diversity, and in the preamble to that same legal instrument.

At the universal level, reference should be made, in the first place, to the United Nations Educational, Scientific and Cultural Organization ("UNESCO") Universal Declaration on Cultural Diversity of 2 November 2001, according to which cultural diversity "is as necessary for humankind as biodiversity is for nature",[21] and again in the UNESCO context, to the Convention on the Protection and Promotion of the Diversity of Cultural Expressions of 20 October 2005. The Convention establishes a general limit to reliance on the right to cultural diversity, providing in Article 2

---

[19] See Chap. 9, Sect. 9.1.3.

[20] On these issues, see Chap. 3, Sect. 3.9.

[21] See Article 1.

(Guiding Principles) that the provisions of the Convention may not be invoked in order to infringe the human rights set forth "in the Universal Declaration of Human Rights or guaranteed by international law", or to limit their scope. In our view, however, the rule must be interpreted restrictively, so as to exclude the lawfulness of conduct engaged in on the pretext of cultural diversity that involves the violation of rights protected by principles or norms of particular importance, such as the norms of *jus cogens* or certain norms of general international law, with particular reference, for example, to serious violations of the rights of women or children.

It is therefore to be welcomed that there is a tendency in practice to prohibit conduct detrimental to fundamental human rights carried out on the pretext of cultural diversity. In this regard, Article 5 of the Convention on the Elimination of All Forms of Discrimination against Women of 18 December 1979 imposes an obligation on States Parties to take all appropriate measures "to modify the social and cultural patterns of conduct of men and women, with a view to achieving the elimination of prejudices and customary and all other practices which are based on the idea of the inferiority or the superiority of either of the sexes". Similarly, Article 24(3) of the Convention on the Rights of the Child of 20 November 1989 provides for the obligation of States Parties to take all effective and appropriate measures with a view to abolishing traditional practices prejudicial to the health of children.

Among the customary practices that should be considered prohibited, but are still followed in some African countries—especially in the so-called Horn of Africa—and, in a more limited form, in some Western countries where communities from those same African countries live, is that of female genital mutilations. The prohibition of such practices has been formally provided for in Article V, subparagraph b), of the Protocol to the African Charter on Human and Peoples' Rights on the Rights of Women in Africa of 11 July 2003, on the basis of which States are required to prohibit, also through legislative measures backed by sanctions, all forms of female genital mutilations.

Some international bodies, although lacking binding powers, have strongly condemned such intolerable practices. As far back as 2000 the Human Rights Committee ("HRC"), set up by the ICCPR of 1966, had noted, in its *General Comment No. 28* of 29 March 2000 on Article 3 (The Equality of Rights Between Men and Women), that States Parties are required to eliminate, through legislation or other appropriate measures, "all cultural or religious practices which jeopardize the freedom and well-being of female children".[22] In a similar vein, the Committee on Economic, Social and Cultural Rights ("CESCR"),[23] in its *General Comment No. 21* of 21 December 2009 on the "Right of Everyone to Take Part in Cultural Life", pursuant to Article 15 of the International Covenant on Economic, Social and Cultural Rights of 16 December 1966 ("ICESCR"), underlined that practices such as genital mutilations and allegations of the practice of witchcraft[24] constitute violations of the right in question.

---

[22] See para 28.

[23] On the establishment and powers of this Committee, see Chap. 5, Sect. 5.2.2.

[24] See para 64.

The United Nations General Assembly ("UNGA"), with Resolution of 20 December 2012,[25] also addressed the issue of female genital mutilations. From the perspective of prevention of such conduct, the GA recommended that member states enhance awareness-raising and education regarding the prohibition of these practices, which seriously violate various human rights—for example, the right to life, the right to the protection of human dignity and the right not to be subjected to inhuman or degrading treatments—while, from the perspective of their repression, it urged states to enact laws prohibiting female genital mutilations. Finally, the resolution calls for the protection and assistance of women who have been subjected to such treatment or are at risk of undergoing it so as to provide them with physical and psychological support services.

Finally, let us consider the possibility for States to provide for limitations to lesser rights on the basis of the principle of cultural diversity or relativism. In our view, limitations appear to be lawful provided, first, that the requirements in question are objectively based on values, principles and traditions inspired by historical, religious or cultural reasons; second, that an adequate balance is ensured between the various rights and interests that may conflict in the particular case; and, third, that the measures actually adopted comply with the principle of proportionality.

As a clear example of the absence of any will to find balanced solutions on the relationship between universality and cultural diversity in the framework of human rights, one can cite the Arab Charter on Human Rights of 22 May 2004 ("ArCHR"), which amends the previous version of 1994, both concluded within the framework of the Arab League. In the most recent legal instrument, Article 3(1) refers to the principle of non-discrimination on the basis of sex, language, race, religion, etc., specifying that men and women "are equal in human dignity, in rights and in duties", only to then proceed to lay down in a contradictory manner that formal equality between men and women operates "within the framework of the positive discrimination established in favour of women by Islamic Shari'a and other divine laws, legislation and international instruments".[26]

2.5.1 Relativism and Opposing Conceptions of Cultures

Finally, it should be borne in mind that in a given case, different conceptions of cultures could well conflict and may need to be properly balanced. This may be the case, for instance, in situations of socio-cultural integration of individuals or communities coming from very different legal and cultural backgrounds. In this case, conflicting values and rights must be balanced on the basis of their general relevance, their cultural importance for the specific communities invoking them and, finally, assessing the proportionality of the measures adopted by the State.

---

[25] A/RES/67/146.

[26] See Article 3(3) of the Charter.

It is therefore not uncommon for domestic supreme courts to give different answers to similar cases. For example, in its judgment of 2 March 2006 in *Balvir Singh Multani, et al. v. Commission scolaire Marguerite-Bourgeoys, et al.*, the Canadian Supreme Court granted an appeal concerning a minor belonging to the Sikh religious community who, contrary to the decision of the governing board of his school, wished to wear a kirpan at school, i.e. a knife that is an essential religious symbol for Sikhs. According to the Supreme Court, although the council's decision to prohibit the wearing of a kirpan "was motivated by a pressing and substantial objective",[27] namely to ensure an adequate level of safety at the school, the interference by the school authorities was excessive. Indeed, the decision to establish an absolute prohibition against wearing a kirpan did not fall within a range of reasonable alternatives[28] and meant that it would have been impossible for the child to attend school because he would not have been able to do so without respecting his religious convictions. The Supreme Court therefore recognised the child's right to bring the kirpan to school, while at the same time laying down certain precautions for safety reasons, such as "hiding" the kirpan in a special case.

By contrast, in its judgment no. 2484 of 15 May 2017, the Italian Court of Cassation dismissed an appeal of an Indian citizen of Sikh religion, who had been sentenced by a trial court to pay a fine because he had refused to hand over his kirpan to the Italian authorities. The Court stated that although a multi-ethnic society must promote the integration and preservation of the culture of origin of foreigners, thus ensuring social and cultural pluralism, this objective cannot exceed the limit "constituted by respect for human rights and the legal civilization of the host society". In particular, the Court was of the view that there exists an obligation "for immigrants to conform their own values to those of the western world in which they have freely chosen to insert themselves", since in a multi-ethnic society "conflicting cultural archipelagos cannot be formed according to the ethnic groups which compose it ... hindering the unitary cultural and legal fabric of our country which identifies public security as an interest to be protected".[29]

In our opinion, there are a number of reasons for the divergent decisions of the supreme courts in question. Firstly, the different legislative and social contexts existing in the two countries, leading to dissimilar degrees of acceptance of cultural and religious demands other than local ones. Secondly, the difference in age of the two individuals involved, a minor in the first case, an adult in the second one, and the fact that, in the Canadian case, the right to education of the minor was also at stake, which would have been prejudiced by the ban on wearing the kirpan. At any rate, it seems that the Canadian decision was able to struck a more correct and "courageous" balancing of the different cultural values at stake. In Italy, by contrast, the local conception of the relevant cultural values took precedence without adequately assessing the cultural needs of the appellant and hence without exploring the possibility of adopting a more nuanced solution.

---

[27] See para 44 of the judgment.

[28] *Id.*, paras 50 ff.

[29] See para 2.3 of the conclusions on points of law of the judgment.

2.6 The New Perspective Based on Individual and Collective Human Rights

A further characteristic of a general nature which is worth mentioning in this part of the book, although strictly speaking concerning questions relating to the classification of human rights,[30] is the individual and collective nature of human rights.

In the past, it was common ground that human rights had a predominantly individual dimension, with some exceptions, for example with reference to the principle of self-determination of peoples and, more recently, to the right to development.[31] The individual character of the protection of the human person at the international level was also motivated by the objections of Western countries to the acceptance of the collective dimension advocated by socialist countries and mentioned above.[32] This approach is now to be considered completely outdated as the current legal framework, and especially the practice of applying it, appear to be unquestionably based on a "dualistic" approach, on the basis of which most human rights can take on both an individual and a collective dimension, even in relation to the same case.

This particular connotation of human rights is evident in relation to certain rights, such as religious freedom, freedom of opinion and expression, and the right to education, which can be exercised both by individuals and by a plurality of persons, sometimes availing themselves of institutional forms through which they can express their beliefs and opinions as well as receive those of others. Consider, on the one hand, the enjoyment of the aforementioned rights by religious or political groups, or within places of worship or educational institutions; on the other hand, the various persons operating in the information and education system, which continuously convey an enormous mass of news and opinions coming from individuals or communities.

The same holds true with regard to other rights that are mainly invoked in practice at the individual level, for example the right to private and family life, which may well be exercised also in collective form, where violations of rights enjoyed by a private household or family as a legal entity independent of its individual members are at issue.

Finally, it should be noted, as discussed in Chap. 13, that the ownership of certain human rights, as well as of certain obligations under international law, by collective entities, such as minorities, indigenous peoples, insurrectionary movements and multinational corporations themselves, is entirely undisputed. This further demonstrates that the purely individual approach to human rights has been superseded, both in relation to the holding of the right, which can be granted to an individual, a plurality of individuals or a collective entity, and to the very manner of the actual exercise of the right in question.

Another issue is the "practical" difficulty of invoking certain collective rights, for example certain rights held by minorities, before courts or bodies competent

---

[30] See Chap. 6, Sect. 6.1.

[31] See Chap. 12, Sects. 12.1–12.2.

[32] See *supra*, Sect. 2.4.

to enforce human rights conventions.[33] In this case, however, it is not the question of the *ownership* of the rights concerned by the collective entity, which cannot be contested, but only the question of the effective *exercise* of these rights before international courts or bodies. From this point of view, we consider that, at the moment of the "individual" exercise of certain human rights, which in reality assume a dual dimension that is both individual and collective, the interested parties act both in their own specific interest and in the interest of the group whose rights are also violated, de facto acting as a "representative" when it comes to pleading rights of a collective nature before the courts.

Comprehension Check and Tasks

1. Natural law is one of the generally recognised legal foundations of human rights. What does it mean to link human rights to natural law and what are the consequences in terms of the protection of human rights? (Sect. 2.1)
2. Human rights are universal in nature. What is meant by the universality of human rights and what is the relationship between universality and relativism, with particular regard to the Bangkok Declaration of 1993? (Sect. 2.4.1)
3. On the subject of universality and relativism, of particular importance is the effort of some national supreme courts to coordinate the application of domestic rules and traditions with international rules. What have the Japanese Supreme Court (2013) and the Indian Supreme Court (2018) stated in this respect? (Sect. 2.4.1)
4. What is meant by the inalienability of human rights? (Sect. 2.4.3)
5. Cultural diversity is a fundamental aspect of human rights. What is the correct balance between, on the one hand, the demands of cultural diversity and multiculturalism and, on the other hand, the demands of universality of human rights? (Sect. 2.5)
6. On the issue of relativism and opposing conceptions of cultures, national supreme courts have sometimes adopted different positions. What were the legal issues addressed by the Canadian Supreme Court (2006) and the Italian Supreme Court (2017) and which position would you maintain is the most correct and why? (Sect. 2.5.1)

[33] On this issue, see Chap. 13, Sect. 13.4.1.

References

ICJ (1966) ICJ Reports (Second Phase), Ethiopia v. South Africa, Liberia v. South Africa
ICJ (1971) Advisory opinion of 21 June 1971 on the Legal Consequences for States of the Continued Presence of South Africa in Namibia (South West Africa) Notwithstanding Security Council Resolution 276 (1970). ICJ Reports

Chapter 3
International Legal Sources on Human Rights: The Universal Level

Contents

Abstract The chapter focuses on the international legal sources on human rights at the universal level. Both the application of the sources of international law to the field of human rights and their implementation in national legal orders are characterized by peculiarities, challenges and limitations, which this chapter discusses with reference to the nature and content of each specific legal source. Of particular importance are the notion of jurisdiction enshrined in various human rights treaties, as interpreted in international jurisprudence, and the horizontal application of some human rights norms and the related due diligence obligations of the State. Finally, the chapter also discusses the relationship between the human rights regime and international humanitarian law.

P. Pustorino, *Introduction to International Human Rights Law*,
https://doi.org/10.1007/978-94-6265-563-8_3

3.1 *Jus Cogens* and Customary International Law: Connections and Overlapping between the Two Legal Sources

The normative sources of human rights coincide with those existing for the other sectors of international law. Therefore, the differences do not concern the identification of the sources but rather their application to the specific field of human rights. This makes it possible to highlight some particular characteristics of these sources when they are used for the protection of the rights of the human being. What has just been stated is in line with the scholarly view that the field of human rights is not a separate and independent area that is "impermeable" to the developments found in other sectors of international law. Instead, this field constitutes an integral and essential part of international law that has a significant and constant impact on the structure and functioning of international law and the international community, without however modifying its traditional features in a radical or revolutionary way, as some other authors claim.

Starting by analysing *jus cogens*, it should be noted at the outset that, in relatively recent times, it has undergone significant changes as regards its content and objectives in at least two respects.

Firstly, it is now accepted that the peremptory norms of international law prohibit not only gross violations of human rights committed against a plurality of individuals, as in the case of genocide, but also extend to serious violations committed against single individuals, as in the case of torture.

In addition, thanks to the formidable contribution made by the UN to the development of human rights, a significant expansion of *jus cogens* has already taken place as regards the protection of human rights previously already governed by general international law or treaties, such as the right not to be subjected to slavery or apartheid. This extension of the scope of *jus cogens* has given rise to a symmetrical extension of the application of customary international law in the field of human rights. As a result, general law is progressively tending to protect rights previously excluded from the scope of protection afforded by this source of law, such as the right not to be discriminated against, the right to property, the right of access to justice and to a fair trial, etc.

However, a caveat is necessary with regard to what actually constitutes human rights rules that have acquired the rank of *jus cogens* and customary law respectively. Similarly to what can be seen with reference to international humanitarian law ("IHL"), there is in fact a tendency—at times followed by international courts and even more by non-judicial bodies operating at the international level—to liberally consider certain conventional legal rules as falling within the realm of *jus cogens* or general international law. This is due to the fact that the protection of human rights is informed not only by legal principles and rules but also by moral demands and needs,[1] which at times can prevail and "force the hand" of the interpreter when establishing international norms.

In addition, it is not infrequent for international bodies competent in the field of human rights, even more so if they are not well-known at the international level, "to seek publicity" by endorsing risky interpretations regarding the legal nature of certain norms on human rights. This tendency can be tolerated if it contributes to the normal dialectic between international and domestic courts and bodies. If, however, it goes beyond the limits of such a dialectical relationship, it risks creating conflict between national or international courts and compromising the principle of legal certainty, with negative repercussions also in terms of the credibility of the bodies in charge of scrutinising compliance with human rights.

Finally, worth mentioning is the fact that the undeniable developments in the field of the protection of human rights have also affected how customary law is ascertained. Firstly, as regards attaching more weight to the element of *opinio juris ac necessitatis* compared to the element of *diuturnitas*. Secondly, albeit in a lesser form, as regards what practice is relevant for the formation of customary norms, which no longer seems to be limited to State practice but includes the practice of international organisations and also some non-State actors, who increasingly contribute, directly or indirectly, to the formation of rules of general international law.

3.2 Specific Features of the Peremptory Norms Regarding Human Rights

We now turn to examine some specific aspects of *jus cogens* that come to the fore when applying peremptory norms to the field of human rights.

It is well-known that in the VCLT, contravention of the peremptory norms of international law is sanctioned by the nullity of the conflicting treaties[2] or, if the peremptory norm emerges after the entry into force of the treaty in question, by their termination.[3] The regime in question is also strengthened by the provision of a jurisdiction clause which allows the parties to the dispute on the matter of contravention of the peremptory norm to submit it "to the International Court of Justice for a decision unless the parties by common consent agree to submit the dispute to arbitration".[4]

---

[1] See Chap. 2, Sect. 2.1.

[2] "A treaty is void if, at the time of its conclusion, it conflicts with a peremptory norm of general international law": Article 53.

[3] "If a new peremptory norm of general international law emerges, any existing treaty which is in conflict with that norm becomes void and terminates": Article 64.

[4] *Id.*, Article 66, para 1, subpara a.

That said, some legal scholars and courts[5] are in favour of applying the above principle also to customary norms, thus asserting that rules of general international law that conflict with *jus cogens* are void. That view, though valid from a theoretical point of view—in view of the same normative rank attributed in the international legal order to treaties and custom—entrusts the interpreter with excessive discretion. This is because, unlike provisions of treaties, customary norms are not *written rules* apart from the complex question of agreements codifying general law.[6] It is therefore not easy for the interpreter to identify both the content of the customary norms relevant to the specific case and the aspects of incompatibility with peremptory norms. Moreover, in the absence of a mechanism similar to the one mentioned above, which allows the submission to the ICJ in case of conflict between peremptory norms and treaty provisions, international courts and, even more so, domestic courts could adopt questionable decisions on the matter of conflict between customary and peremptory norms, thereby undermining the principle of legal certainty.

Another particular feature of peremptory norms in the field of human rights concerns the content of State obligations to comply with them. In fact, according to the praiseworthy position adopted in international case law, the peremptory norm on the prohibition of torture—but this is also true for other prohibitions established by *jus cogens* such as the prohibition of slavery—also includes the obligation for States to enact legislation for cases covered by the international norm. In other words, the peremptory norms in question contain a positive obligation for States to legislate, establishing specific offences corresponding to those established at the international level and also commensurate with the gravity of the violations in question.[7]

Equally worthy of support is the view, also deriving from an examination of international case law and practice, according to which infringement of peremptory norms has the effect of invalidating domestic legislation envisaging amnesties or equivalent measures adopted in favour of individuals responsible for acts of torture.[8] Although in such cases a ruling by a domestic supreme court is generally necessary in order to formalise in the national legal systems the invalidity of the legislative acts contrary to peremptory norms.

This specific effect of peremptory norms in relation to human rights has been explored in particular by the IACtHR, which has held as incompatible with the American Convention of Human Rights of 22 November 1969 ("ACHR") the amnesties adopted by some South American countries applicable also to international crimes committed by civil and military officials of pre-existing dictatorial regimes. The principle in question was affirmed in the judgments of 14 March 2001 in the case of *Barrios Altos v. Peru* and of 26 September 2006 in the case of *Almonacid-Arellano*

[5] See, for example, the judgment of 10 December 1998 adopted by the Trial Chamber of the International Criminal Tribunal for the former Yugoslavia ("ICTY") in *Prosecutor v. Anto Furundžija*, IT-95-17/1-T, para 153.

[6] In fact, the codification treaties do not always correspond to customary law, given that some norms may be based on the progressive development of international law, as indicated in Article 13 of the UN Charter with reference to the competence vested in the UNGA in this matter.

[7] See ICTY judgment in *Furundžija*, cit., para 149.

[8] ICTY, *Furundžija*, cit., para 155.

et al. v. Chile. In the 2001 judgment, the IACtHR stated that "all amnesty provisions, provisions on prescription and the establishment of measures designed to eliminate responsibility are inadmissible", since such provisions aim to prevent "the investigation and punishment of those responsible for serious human rights violations such as torture, extrajudicial, summary or arbitrary execution and forced disappearance", which constitute violations of "non-derogable rights recognized by international human rights law".[9] Therefore, according to the Court, infringement of peremptory norms had as a consequence the invalidity of the domestic measures in question because they "may not continue to obstruct the investigation of the grounds on which this case is based or the identification and punishment of those responsible".[10]

In the subsequent *Almonacid-Arellano* case, the IACtHR confirmed its stance, observing that national laws granting amnesty to perpetrators of international crimes "leave victims defenseless and perpetuate impunity for crimes against humanity". For that reason, these measures are clearly at odds with the object and purpose of the ACHR and cannot have "any legal effects" because they constitute an obstacle to the identification of those responsible for international crimes and their punishment.[11]

In both of the above cases, the amnesty measures were subsequently declared unconstitutional at the national level.

The above approach adopted by the IACtHR is reflected in the similar position taken by the ECtHR in the judgment delivered by the Grand Chamber on 17 September 2014 in *Mocanu and Others v. Romania*. In that case, citing its previous case law on the point and with reference to conduct of State bodies that may constitute acts of torture or inhuman or degrading treatment, the Court held that criminal proceedings cannot be interrupted because of the operation of the rules on the statute of limitations and that an amnesty or pardon "should not be tolerated in such cases".[12]

This well-established trend in international human rights case law has also been endorsed by the International Criminal Court ("ICC") in its decision of 5 April 2019 concerning the proceedings initiated against one of Gaddafi's sons. The Court stated that the application of national laws providing for an amnesty for individuals accused of international crimes, as occurred in the present case with Libyan Law 6/2015, "is incompatible with internationally recognized human rights".[13]

Finally, it should be noted that a violation of *jus cogens* in the field of human rights also has effects at the level of the international responsibility of the State envisaging

[9] See para 41 of the judgment.

[10] *Id.*, para 44.

[11] See para 119 of the judgment.

[12] See applications nos. 10865/09, 45886/07 and 32431/08, para 326 of the judgment. That same incompatibility with peremptory norms on the prohibition of torture is also highlighted by the UN Committee Against Torture ("CAT"), set up by the Convention against Torture and Other Cruel, Inhuman or Degrading Treatment or Punishment of 10 December 1984 (see Chap. 5, Sect. 5.2.5), in *General Comment No. 2* of 24 January 2008, on the "Implementation of article 2 by States parties", para 5.

[13] See the decision of the Pre-Trial Chamber *on the Admissibility Challenge by Dr. Saif Al-Islam Gadaffi pursuant to Articles 17(1)(c), 19 and 20(3) of the Rome Statute, The Prosecutor v. Saif Al-Islam Gaddafi*, CC-01/11-01/11, paras 77–78.

"aggravated" liability in the case of violation of peremptory norms. Peremptory norms, as will be seen more clearly later on in this book,[14] entail obligations *erga omnes* owed to the entire international community, which is consequently involved in the phase of "reaction" to the violation of such obligations.

3.3 The General Principles of Law

The general principles of domestic law are a further important normative source of human rights. Already contemplated as sources of international law in Article 38 of the Statute of the ICJ, in the past these principles have played a significant role in order to fill the many gaps in relation to the protection of human rights. This has occurred both in the international legal order and within the framework of special regulatory systems, such as the European Union ("EU"), which for some time has made almost exclusive reference to the common constitutional traditions of the Member States, in addition to the ECHR, to ensure the protection of human rights in the EU.

At present, the general principles of domestic law would seem to be of less importance in the system of international sources in view of the vast number of customary rules and especially treaties designed to protect human rights. However, the significance of general principles of domestic law should not be underestimated. On the one hand, with reference to specific individual or collective rights of more recent formation, such as social rights, underpinned by broad and advanced regulation at the national level, or the rights in the field of bioethics, regulated in detail in some national systems to an extent that appears to be lacking at the international level. On the other hand, the general principles of domestic law continue to play an incisive role in normative areas contiguous to the field of human rights, for example, in international criminal law, where reference to domestic substantive and procedural law is still very useful in addressing the shortcomings of the international legal framework applicable to trials before international criminal tribunals. In this regard, the principle of legality (embodied in the principle of *nullum crimen* and *nulla poena sine lege* and in the principle of non-retroactivity of the criminal law), the principle of equality between the prosecution and the defence, etc.,[15] may be very relevant.

It must also be pointed out that the repeated recourse in practice to the aforementioned principles of domestic law has meant that a large part of those principles has been progressively absorbed into customary law and treaties on the subject of human rights. This highlights the existence of a virtuous process of constant coordination between national systems and international law in the field of human rights, whose roots, as aforesaid,[16] go back to the original formation at the national level of the rules to protect the rights of the human being.

---

[14] See Chap. 14, Sects. 14.1–14.2.

[15] On these rights, see Chap. 8, Sects. 8.2–8.3.

[16] See Chap. 1, Sect. 1.1.

Finally, likewise in the field of human rights protection there may be general principles of law that are not drawn from national legal systems but from the international legal system itself, in particular, from an examination of some norms of general international law and of conventional rules. These principles can operate *transversally* in relation to different issues in the field of human rights. For example, one of the general principles of international law that takes on particular importance in the field of human rights is the principle of proportionality, which is widely used in international case law to assess the lawfulness of national measures either derogating from certain international treaties or limiting certain human rights protected at treaty level.[17]

3.4 International Treaties: An Overview

Among the most important normative sources of international human rights law are the existing international treaties on the subject, which are now very numerous and can be subdivided depending on their universal or regional character, the individual or collective rights they protect, and also the level of protection afforded, focusing in particular on the greater or lesser effectiveness of the norms and of the system of scrutiny of observance of the treaty rules.

It should also be added that some treaties drafted within the framework of the UN are considered of particular importance in that they have played—and in part still play—a "guiding function", even outside the UN system, for the conclusion of further international treaties of a general or specific nature (i.e. regarding the protection of specific human rights), and for supporting the activities carried out by numerous principal and subsidiary bodies of the UN and other international organisations.

These are the so-called *core treaties*, generally understood, not without a certain amount of discretion, as encompassing the two Covenants of 16 December 1966 (respectively the ICCPR and ICESCR), the Convention on the Elimination of All Forms of Racial Discrimination of 21 December 1965, the Convention on the Elimination of All Forms of Discrimination against Women of 18 December 1979, the Convention against Torture and Other Degrading, Inhuman or Cruel Treatment or Punishment of 10 December 1984 and the Convention on the Rights of the Child of 20 November 1989. To these treaties must be added at least the Convention on the Prevention and Punishment of the Crime of Genocide of 9 December 1948 and the Geneva Convention Relating to the Status of Refugees of 28 July 1951. As proof of the general importance now acquired by these agreements, it should be pointed out that several of the rules contained in the treaties in question today correspond to customary norms and, to a lesser extent, *jus cogens*.

[17] See *infra*, Sect. 3.9.

3.5 Particular Nature of Human Rights Treaties Obligations—Limits to the Application of the General Regime on the Law of Treaties

Some special features of human rights treaties need to be addressed.

The first well-known general characteristic of human rights treaties is that they do not aim at the protection of State rights and interests, but rights and freedoms owed to individuals or groups of them, regardless of their citizenship, with the consequence that protection is extended both to stateless persons and to nationals of the State whose conduct is under consideration. The actual beneficiaries of human rights treaties are in fact individuals as such. This indisputable element has led some scholars to surmise that individuals are full or limited subjects of international law.[18]

As already noted in the analysis of the notion of universality of human rights,[19] the treaties regarding this specific sector also have an objective and absolute character, as opposed to the synallagmatic character of other treaties, which is based on the principle of reciprocity in terms of compliance with their provisions. From this characteristic, which has long been pointed out in the case law and practice of the bodies charged with scrutinising observance of human rights treaties,[20] it follows that the violation by a State of such treaties does not enable the other States parties to invoke their extinction or suspension, in application of the rule *inadimplenti non est adimplendum* provided for in the VCLT.[21]

Provisions in human rights treaties often envisage substantive and procedural obligations *erga omnes partes*. Thus, the obligations of the State party are assumed vis-à-vis all other States parties, which may react to treaty violations in the manner provided for in the treaty in question and also in general international law (unless customary norms on State responsibility are derogated from in the treaty). Among the possible consequences of violations of *erga omnes partes* obligations laid down in some human rights treaties, worth mentioning is the system of inter-State applications that can be brought by States parties not having a direct interest in the violation of treaty obligations by another State party.

The particular nature and purpose of inter-State applications provided for in the framework of some human rights treaty systems are highlighted by the ECtHR (Grand Chamber) in its judgment of 12 May 2014 in *Cyprus v. Turkey*. This case concerned serious violations of the ECHR committed by Turkey against Cypriot citizens residing in the Turkish Republic of Northern Cyprus, an entity created after the Turkish military occupation of 1974 and not internationally recognised. In that judgment it is clarified that a State application to the ECtHR may have a twofold purpose. First of all, the aim of the application may be "[to] complain about

---

[18] On this issue, see Chap. 13, Sect. 13.3.

[19] See Chap. 2, Sect. 2.4.1.

[20] See, for example, the decision of 11 January 1961 by the European Commission of Human Rights ("ECommHR") in the case of *Austria v. Italy*, appl. 788/60.

[21] See Article 60(5) of the Convention.

general issues (systemic problems and shortcomings, administrative practices, etc.) in another Contracting Party" from which violations against a plurality of individuals have resulted. In this case, the applicant State's objective "is that of vindicating the public order of Europe within the framework of collective responsibility under the Convention".

In other cases, the application brought by a State party serves a different purpose, that is, to denounce violations of the ECHR committed against its own nationals, with the effect that in this situation the complaint is akin to a claim filed in the context of diplomatic protection.[22] In relation to this second type of action brought by States, the Court has specified that, if a "just satisfaction" under Article 41 ECHR were to be recognised, it would be granted "for the benefit of individual victims".[23]

It should be clarified that in both cases just referred to, the State party to the human rights treaties does not act on the basis of the existence of damage occasioned to the State but rather to complain about violations committed against private natural and legal persons and to support the related claims for reparation. This particular aspect of the mechanism based on inter-State applications is clarified again by the ECtHR (Grand Chamber) in its inadmissibility decision of 18 November 2020 in *Slovenia v. Croatia*. For the Court, in fact, applications brought by States aimed at asserting human rights violations committed against governmental entities are not admissible since, "according to the very nature of the Convention", also in the framework of inter-State applications, "it is always the individual, and not the State" that is directly or indirectly affected, including from an economic point of view, by the violation of one of the rights protected by the ECHR.[24]

This highlights the difficulty of applying the general rules on treaty law to human rights conventions. This difficulty concerns the entire legal framework on treaty law as it includes problematic issues related to the interpretation of treaty provisions, reservations to such conventions, mechanisms for termination and suspension of treaties as well as questions concerning the succession of States to human rights treaties.

By way of example, it may be useful to refer to the well-known problem of reservations to conventions on human rights. In this regard, there appears to be a well-established tendency in the case law and practice of the bodies in charge of scrutinising compliance with some human rights treaties—ECtHR, IACtHR, HRC and the African Commission on Human and Peoples' Rights ("ACommHPR")[25]—to consider invalid, and therefore null and void, any reservations deemed contrary to

---

[22] See appl. no. 25781/94, paras 44-45 of the judgment. The legal action can of course also be initiated by the State party in the interest of nationals of other States.

[23] *Id.*, para 46.

[24] Appl. no. 54155/16, para 66 of the decision.

[25] See the ACommHPR report of 17 February 2016, made public on 28 April 2018, in the case of *Hossam Ezzat and Rania Enayet (represented by the Egyptian Initiative for Personal Rights and INTERIGHTS) v. Arab Republic of Egypt*, communication no. 355/07, concerning the reservations made by Egypt to certain provisions of the 1981 African Charter (including Article 8 on religious freedom), compliance with which was made conditional by Egypt on the compatibility of the provisions "with the Islamic Law".

the object and purpose of the treaty or not in accordance with the rules on reservations in the human rights treaties in question. For example, in its judgment of 4 March 2014 in *Grande Stevens v. Italy*, the ECtHR declared that the reservation made by Italy to Articles 2–4 of Protocol No. 7 to the ECHR was null and void[26] because devoid of the requirements as to precision and clarity concerning details of national rules allegedly incompatible with the provisions in question when making the reservation.[27] Although the case concerned only the application of the reservation in relation to Article 4 of the Protocol, on the right not to be tried twice for the same offence (principle of *ne bis in idem*),[28] the decision on the nullity of the reservation also has effects in relation to Articles 2–3 of the Protocol.

The aforementioned position adopted by bodies charged with scrutinising observance of human rights is a departure from the complex and questionable system of acceptance and objection with regard to reservations, including those potentially incompatible with the object and purpose of the treaty, established by the VCLT.

In our view, this trend in human rights treaty practice constitutes a development to be welcomed, enhancing the particular nature of these treaties and aimed at ensuring effective and uniform application of these conventions and thus ultimately increasing the general level of human rights protection. However, we believe that this trend can only be restricted to cases in which there is a body, endowed with binding powers, scrutinising compliance with the agreement in question. If this is not the case, and without prejudice to the willingness of States to accept the non-binding decisions of such bodies, there is no alternative but to rely on the cumbersome system established by the VCLT, which consists of a plurality of bilateral relationships between the State making the reservation and the States that accept, including implicitly, or object to the content of the reservation.

3.6 The Notion of Jurisdiction in Human Rights Treaties and Their Extraterritorial Application

The application of treaties on human rights must be ensured by States parties not only in their own territory and in the sea and air spaces over which the State exercises its sovereignty[29] but also in the areas in which the State has "jurisdiction", understood as the power of government or control over areas and communities of people over which the State does not wield sovereign power. The notion of jurisdiction is therefore

[26] The reservation stated that the above-mentioned rules of the Protocol could apply only to offences classified as criminal by Italian law.

[27] See appl. nos. 18640/10, 18647/10, 18663/10, 18668/10 and 18698/10, paras 204–211 of the judgment.

[28] On this right, see Chap. 8, Sect. 8.2.

[29] See Article 2 of the Chicago Convention on International Civil Aviation of 7 December 1944: "For the purposes of this Convention the territory of a State shall be deemed to be the land areas and territorial waters adjacent thereto under the sovereignty... of such State".

much broader than that of sovereignty and has been clarified in international case law, albeit with some interpretative uncertainties.

It is common ground that the jurisdiction of States parties in regard to human rights treaties exists in situations in which the power of government of the State is traditionally exercised on foreign territory, in particular with reference to acts or omissions committed by the State organ that carries out diplomatic and consular functions abroad, exercising "authority and control" both with regard to citizens of the national State and citizens of other States. Equally well-established, from the point of view of the operation of State jurisdiction abroad, is the case in which the organs of a State carry out "executive or judicial functions on the territory of another State" with the consent of the territorial State.[30]

It is similarly accepted that the notion of jurisdiction applies in relation to human rights violations committed on military aircraft and vessels of the State operating outside the territory of the State, for example, in relation to activities following the transfer of migrants to naval vessels.[31]

3.6.1 *The Territorial or Spatial Control Criterion*

There appears to be a well-established tendency in practice to recognise the extraterritorial application of human rights treaties where the State has effective control over foreign territory, exercised for example through stable forms of military occupation, as affirmed by the HRC in its *General Comment No. 36* of 30 October 2018 on Article 6 (Right to Life).[32] This control may be the effect of conduct in violation of the principle prohibiting the use of force, with regard to international armed conflicts,[33] and the principle of self-determination of peoples, as in the case of the Palestinian territories occupied by Israel since 1967, the Turkish military occupation of the northern part of Cyprus in 1974, the military occupation of Nagorno-Karabakh by Armenia in the 1990s, the unlawful annexation of Crimea by Russia in 2014 and the control by Russia of some other parts of Ukraine after the armed attack carried out in February 2022. With regard to the Crimea case, the ECtHR (Grand Chamber), in its decision of admissibility of 16 December 2020 in *Ukraine v. Russia (Re Crimea)*, held that, in view of the illegality of Russia's takeover of the territory of Crimea, Russian

---

[30] For both of the above scenarios, see the statements of the ECtHR (Grand Chamber), respectively, in its decision of inadmissibility of 12 December 2001 in *Banković and Others v. Belgium and 16 Other States*, appl. no 52207/99, paras 134–135, and in its judgment of 16 September 2014 in *Hassan v.* the *United Kingdom*, appl. no. 29750/09, para 74.

[31] This issue is explored further in Chap. 10, Sect. 10.1.

[32] See para 63.

[33] According to the ECtHR (Grand Chamber), in cases of international armed conflict, effective control over foreign territory can only be established in the phase of stabilisation of territorial control and not in the preceding period characterised by armed confrontations between States "seeking to establish control over an area in a context of chaos", which are moreover governed by IHL: judgment of 21 January 2021, *Georgia v. Russia (II)*, appl. no. 38263/08, paras 126 and 137.

jurisdiction still operates under the ECHR by way of effective control over foreign territory and not in light of the principle of sovereignty over national territory.[34]

It should be pointed out that, in some of the cases referred to above, in particular those of Northern Cyprus, Nagorno-Karabakh and Donbass in Ukraine, autonomous State entities have been established, not internationally recognised and supported at a political-military level by Turkey, Armenia and Russia respectively. With reference to the Republic of Nagorno-Karabakh, the ECtHR (Grand Chamber), in its judgment of 16 June 2015 in *Chiragov and Others v. Armenia*, ruled that the said entity "and its administration survive by virtue of the military, political, financial and other support given to it by Armenia",[35] consequently holding that the respondent State had jurisdiction in relation to the serious human rights violations committed on the territory of Nagorno-Karabakh.

Effective control of foreign territory may also derive from lawful conduct of foreign States, for example, under authorisation of the UN Security Council ("UNSC"), as in the case for the Anglo-American military occupation on the basis of Resolution 1483 of 22 May 2003,[36] adopted at the end of the international armed conflict on Iraqi territory concerning Anglo-American military aggression against Iraq. Here again, reference may be made to ECtHR case law developed in relation to violations of the ECHR committed in Iraq by the UK during the military occupation.[37]

Precisely with reference to that case law, it is however doubtful whether, during a lawful occupation, all the activities carried out on foreign territory are capable of activating the jurisdiction of the occupying State and thus leading to the application of the ECHR. In its decision of inadmissibility in *Miller v. United Kingdom*, the ECtHR seems to rule out that hypothesis, stating that, whereas in the cases previously submitted for its examination it was a matter of establishing violations of the ECHR committed in Iraq by the UK military "in the course of security operations", in this instance the case concerned operations carried out by British military forces aimed "to restore and maintain law and order" and that therefore in the circumstances the question of jurisdiction under Article 1 ECHR "is potentially complex".[38]

On this issue, the lack of further clarification by the Court, due to the fact that the application was considered manifestly unfounded, does not clarify the criterion for distinguishing the activities carried out by the occupying State for the purposes of the extraterritorial application of the ECHR. In our view, in order to establish the jurisdiction of the Contracting Party to the ECHR, the nature and purpose of the activities carried out by the occupying State are relevant only as factors for verifying

---

[34] Appl. nos. 20958/14 and 38334/18, paras 338 ff. and in particular paras 348–349 of the decision.

[35] Appl. no. 13216/05, para 186 of the judgment. In relation to the occupation of part of Cyprus by Turkey and the subsequent establishment of the Turkish Republic of Northern Cyprus, there is a large body of ECtHR case law stemming from individual applications by Cypriot citizens alleging violations of various ECHR provisions and, to a much lesser extent, from inter-State applications.

[36] See the preamble to the resolution.

[37] See, for example, the Grand Chamber judgment of 7 July 2011 in *Al-Jedda v. United Kingdom*, appl. no. 27021/08.

[38] See the decision published on 25 July 2019, appl. no. 32001/18, para 78.

the intensity and duration of the effective control exercised over foreign territory, which may also be inferred from other factors.

The broadening, in the sense just described, of the notion of jurisdiction included in some human rights treaties, and the consequent responsibility of the State party occupying in a stable and effective manner the territory of another State, should also imply the corresponding exclusion of the responsibility of the occupied State also in relation to human rights norms, provided of course that the occupied State is effectively deprived of its sovereign powers.

However, ECtHR case law does not rule out that respect for the rules contained in the ECHR is incumbent both on the occupied State—requiring it in particular to take all possible measures to ensure respect for the rights guaranteed by the ECHR[39]—and on the occupying State, including where the latter operates through the creation of a local government of a secessionist nature, as happened in Transnistria, formally part of Moldova, but in fact under Russian control.

With regard to the concurrent responsibility of the occupied State, the conclusions of the ECtHR seem to depart, in our opinion, from what is provided for by general international law and raise particular doubts precisely in relation to the fact that compliance with most human rights obligations, unlike other international obligations, requires that the State under consideration have effective control of the territory, which appears to be absent in the case referred to above.

Some bodies charged with scrutinising observance of human rights treaties have further expanded the notion of jurisdiction under review to include cases where the control exercised by the State over foreign territory is very limited in time and space. In this way, the responsibility of the State party to human rights treaties has sometimes been established in situations of short-term territorial control, resulting mainly from incursions of security forces into foreign territory.[40] This hypothesis seems to straddle the line between territorial control exercised by the State and personal control, which will be discussed below.

3.6.2 The "Personal" Control Criterion

In relation to situations in which control of a territorial nature is absent or very limited, it is worth noting the tendency followed by some human rights courts and treaty bodies to apply the criterion of "personal" control exercised by the foreign State over certain individuals operating abroad. This tenuous form of control is

---

[39] See ECtHR (Grand Chamber) judgment of 8 July 2004 in *Ilaşcu and Others v. Moldova and Russia*, appl. no. 48787/99, para 331, the statements contained therein have been repeatedly cited, for example in the judgment of 15 October 2019 in *Grama and Dîrul v. Republic of Moldova and Russia*, applications nos. 28432/06 and 5665/07, para 17.

[40] See Inter-American Commission on Human Rights ("IACommHR") report no. 112/10 of 21 October 2010 in *Ecuador v. Colombia*, concerning the incursion of Colombian military into Ecuador for the purpose of killing or capturing members of the *Fuerzas Armadas Revolucionarias de Colombia* (FARC).

invoked, for example, in cases of the deployment of national army contingents in international operations authorised or instituted by the UNSC, where the national State of the contingent does not exercise effective control over the foreign territory but only control over single individuals and in relation to isolated events,[41] or in the cases of coercive activities carried out abroad by national authorities against individuals with the complicity of local authorities.[42]

Recently, the personal concept of jurisdiction was even applied, for the very first time in ECtHR case law, in relation to the assassination of Mr Alexander Litvinenko, a former Russian spy who was poisoned with radioactive polonium in London in 2006 by Russian agents. In this regard, the Court stated that "the principle that a State exercises extraterritorial jurisdiction in cases concerning specific acts involving an element of proximity should apply with equal force in cases of extrajudicial targeted killings by State agents acting in the territory of another Contracting State", concluding that, in the present case, "the administration of poison to Mr Litvinenko... amounted to the exercise of physical power and control over his life" by Russia.[43]

An examination of international case law on the application of the criterion of personal control shows, firstly, that this criterion is of a subsidiary nature vis-à-vis the more convincing one of territorial control and, secondly, that recourse to the criterion in question is made on the basis of a teleological interpretation of the treaty provisions, thus enhancing the specific aims of human rights treaties. According to the ECtHR, indeed, "accountability in such situations stems from the fact that Article 1 of the Convention cannot be interpreted so as to allow a State party to perpetrate violations of the Convention on the territory of another State, which it could not perpetrate on its own territory".[44]

However, this trend implies a great extension of the notion of jurisdiction contained in human rights treaties and can lead to subjective interpretations of the level of personal control required for extraterritorial application of treaty provisions, as in the case of the non-binding decision made on 4 November 2020 by the HRC and concerning Italy's failure to rescue migrants whose vessel sank in the Maltese search and rescue zone in 2013. According to the HRC, some factual elements established "a special relationship of dependency" between the individuals on the vessel in distress and Italy—namely, the initial contact made by the vessel in distress with the Italian authorities, the close proximity of an Italian navy ship to the vessel in distress and the involvement of Italy in the rescue operation as well as the relevant legal obligations incurred by Italy under the international law of the sea.[45]

---

[41] See the judgment of 20 November 2014 adopted by the ECtHR (Grand Chamber) in the case of *Jaloud v. Netherlands*, appl. no. 47708/08, concerning the responsibility of the troop-contributing State for the wrongdoing committed by its soldiers in Iraq in 2004 during operations carried out following the establishment of a checkpoint.

[42] See ECtHR (Grand Chamber) judgment of 12 May 2005 in *Öcalan v. Turkey*, appl. no. 46221/99, para 91.

[43] Judgment of 21 September 2021, *Carter v. Russia*, appl. no. 20914/07, paras 130 and 161.

[44] Judgment of 24 June 2008, *Solomou and Others v. Turkey*, appl. no. 36832/97, para 45.

[45] See *A.S., D.I., O.I. and G.D. v. Italy*, CCPR/C/130/D/3042/2017, para 7.8.

The notion of control exercised by the State over a person, for the purposes of extraterritorial application of human rights treaties, finds further support in the IACtHR's advisory opinion of 15 November 2017 on the Environment and Human Rights in relation to a case concerning environmental damage of a transboundary nature.[46] In the opinion, in which the ECtHR case law cited above is extensively referred to, the IACtHR stressed that "a person is subject to the "jurisdiction" of a State in relation to an act committed outside the territory of that State (extraterritorial action) or with effects beyond this territory, when the said State is exercising authority over that person or when that person is under its effective control, either within or outside its territory".[47] On the basis of this assumption, the Court held the State of origin responsible for environmental damage for the harmful events caused to individuals residing in other States and deemed to be under the jurisdiction of the State of origin. This was because, according to the Court, there was "a causal link between the act that originated in its territory and the infringement of the human rights of persons outside its territory".[48]

The same approach has been followed, more recently, by the UN Committee on the Rights of the Child ("CRC") in its non-binding decision of 22 September 2021 in *Sacchi and Others v. Argentina.* In that case the Committee, although declaring the communication to be inadmissible for failure to exhaust domestic remedies, applied the principle of the "individual" extraterritorial responsibility of the State party to the Convention on the Rights of the Child for the serious consequences of climate change due to carbon emissions. Highlighting that "the appropriate test for jurisdiction in the present case" is that adopted by the IACtHR in its advisory opinion OC-23/17, the Committee found that "when transboundary harm occurs, children are under the jurisdiction of the State on whose territory the emissions originated ... if there is a causal link between the acts or omissions of the State in question and the negative impact on the rights of children located outside its territory, when the State of origin exercises effective control over the sources of the emissions in question".[49]

Consequently, the CRC found that "through its ability to regulate activities that are the source of these emissions and to enforce such regulations, the State party has effective control over the emissions" that harmed the children outside its territory, and that there was "a sufficient causal link" between the harm alleged by the authors and the State party's conduct for the purposes of establishing jurisdiction. In terms of assessing the victims' status, the Committee stated that "as children, the authors are particularly impacted by the effects of climate change, both in terms of the manner in which they experience such effects as well as the potential of climate change to affect them throughout their lifetime, in particular if immediate action is not taken".[50]

The interpretation of the CRC appears even more extensive than that of the IACtHR. Whereas the case addressed in the IACtHR advisory opinion both the

---

[46] See OC-23/17.

[47] *Id.*, para 81.

[48] *Id.*, para 101.

[49] See CRC/C/88/D/104/2019, para 10.7.

[50] *Id.*, para 10.13.

transboundary environmental damage and the specific responsibility of the State of origin were easily identifiable, in the *Sacchi* case the climate change and the subsequent environmental damage constitute, as noted by the CRC, "a global collective issue that requires a global response"[51] and therefore it is much more complex to ascertain the existence of the "pro-quota" jurisdiction of individual States.[52]

3.6.3 Extraterritorial or Indirect Application of Human Rights Norms and the Expulsion of Individuals

Extraterritorial application, even though sometimes referred to in case law and literature by different names (e.g. indirect application), has also been largely discussed by the bodies charged with scrutinising observance of human rights treaties according to which it is prohibited, for the State party to such treaties, to extradite, expel or hand over individuals who risk being subjected to torture or inhuman or degrading treatment in the country of final destination. According to a further broad interpretation, the removal of persons with serious health problems that cannot be adequately treated in the country of origin is likewise prohibited.[53]

3.7 Human Rights Treaties and Their Horizontal Application (*Drittwirkung*)

A further element of development in the field of the application of human rights treaties is the tendency—observable in the practice of various bodies charged with scrutinising observance of the treaties—to derive from the provisions of those treaties positive obligations for States parties concerning the prevention and repression of violations of human rights committed at the level of inter-individual relations (so-called *Drittwirkung* or horizontal application of human rights treaties).

This trend, which—it should be pointed out—is not to be considered "generalised" in the sense that it is not entirely established in the practice of all such bodies, was in the past limited to the interpretation of treaty provisions protecting fundamental rights, such as the right to life and the right not to be subjected to torture and inhuman or degrading treatment. The link between the fundamental nature of a particular human right and the horizontal application of the treaty provision protecting it is amply highlighted in ECtHR case law.[54] However, that case law and also the practice

[51] Paragraph 10.8.

[52] On national climate change case law, see Chap. 12, Sect. 12.4.

[53] On these issues, see Chap. 6, Sect. 6.2.2.

[54] See, for example, the judgment of 9 June 2009 in *Opuz v. Turkey*, appl. no. 33401/02, para 120.

of the HRC[55] contain numerous decisions extending the application of the principle of State responsibility for violations of an inter-individual character to cases concerning rights that are not of a fundamental nature.[56]

In cases of inter-individual violations of human rights treaty provisions, the responsibility of the State party is based on the failure to comply with the principle of due diligence. Therefore, liability is established when the State has not adopted all the necessary measures to prevent and repress violations committed between private individuals. The criteria used for verifying compliance with the principle of due diligence include the effective ability of the State to deal with such harmful conduct, which must be modulated according to the characteristics of the specific case. In other words, consideration should be given to the perpetrators and victims of the violation, also from the point of view of their particular vulnerability; the *locus commissi delicti*; or a situation of difficulty in which the State may find itself, for example due to serious disturbances, armed conflicts or serious health emergencies, as in the case of the COVID-19 pandemic.

Another criterion is the State's effective knowledge of the risk of violations against certain individuals, as affirmed by the IACtHR in its judgment of 26 September 2018 in *López Soto et al. v. Venezuela*, concerning the responsibility of the State for acts of torture and sexual slavery committed between private individuals.[57] In addition, the measures adopted by the State to prevent and repress the aforementioned violations must be assessed on the basis of the principle of proportionality.

3.7.1 State's Due Diligence and Domestic Violence

Some cases concerning the tendency to apply certain international human rights norms to violations of an inter-individual nature concern domestic violence.

In the well-known *Osman v. United Kingdom* case, the ECtHR held that the Contracting Parties had a positive obligation to adopt effective criminal law provisions and to take appropriate preventive and suppressive measures to protect individuals whose lives are at risk from the criminal conduct of other individuals. For the Court, it is necessary to assess whether the national authorities "knew or ought to have known at the time of the existence of a real and immediate risk to the life of an identified individual or individuals from the criminal acts of a third party and that they failed to take measures within the scope of their powers which, judged reasonably, might have been expected to avoid that risk".[58]

[55] See *General Comment No. 16* of 8 April 1988 on Article 17 (Right to Privacy), according to which States Parties are required to prevent interference with the right to private and family life "whether they emanate from State authorities or from natural or legal persons": para 1.

[56] On the application of this tendency with regard to the right to private and family life, freedom of opinion, expression and information as well as the right to property, see Chap. 9, Sects. 9.1–9.3, and Chap. 11, Sect. 11.1.

[57] See paras 137 ff. of the judgment.

[58] See judgment of 28 October 1998, appl. no. 87/1997/871/1083, para 116.

In its subsequent judgment of 2 March 2017 in *Talpis v. Italy*, the ECtHR stressed the particular character that State due diligence takes on in this specific area of law, given that the violations in question are often repeated over time and committed within the same family unit.[59] The case concerned the inertia shown by the Italian judicial and police authorities in the face of death threats—unfortunately put into practice—made by a husband against his wife and children. For that reason, the Court found that Italy had breached its positive obligations to protect the right to life and the right not to be subjected to inhuman or degrading treatment, in view—as regards the latter breach—of the state of fear and distress produced in the victim by the failure of the State bodies to act.

In more recent case law, the ECtHR has further clarified the criteria applicable to State responsibility under the ECHR for violations of the right to life in cases of domestic violence. In its judgment of 15 June 2021 in *Kurt v. Austria*,[60] the Grand Chamber, recalling the need to protect the children victims of domestic violence as particularly vulnerable individuals, stated that the State has a positive obligation under Article 2 of the Convention to provide an immediate and adequate response to allegations of domestic violence and that special diligence is required to know whether there is a real and immediate risk to the life of the members of the family. More specifically, the authorities have the duty to carry out a "lethality risk assessment", which has to be "autonomous, proactive and comprehensive", taking into account, inter alia, the recurrence of successive episodes of violence within the family unit so as to adopt preventive operational measures which must be "adequate and proportionate to the level of the risk assessed".[61]

In the context of case law on domestic violence, the ECtHR has also clarified that the Contracting Parties to the ECHR have the positive obligations to set up and apply a legal system for punishing all forms of domestic violence, whether occurring offline or online, and to provide sufficient safeguards for the victims. For this reason, in the case of *Volodina v. Russia (No. 2)*,[62] the Court held that Russia had violated the right to private and family life (Article 8 ECHR) in that it had failed to protect the applicant against repeated cases of cyberviolence by her partner who had created fake profiles in her name, published her intimate photos, tracked her movements and even sent her death threats via social media.

3.8 Human Rights Treaties and International Humanitarian Law

According to well-established international case law, the customary and treaty rules on human rights are applied also during international and non-international armed

[59] See appl. no. 41237/14, para 122 of the judgment.

[60] Appl. no. 62903/15.

[61] See para 190 of the judgment.

[62] Judgment of 14 September 2021, appl. no. 40419/19.

conflicts. It follows that the same State conduct in the context of an armed conflict may constitute a violation of both *jus in bello* and rules on human rights.

Limiting ourselves to an examination of the case law of the ICJ, which has repeatedly affirmed the joint application, in armed conflicts, of the rules on human rights (especially with reference to treaty provisions of particular importance) and those of international humanitarian law ("IHL"), worth mentioning are, first of all, some well-known advisory opinions in which the Court has clarified its position on the point.

In its advisory opinion of 8 July 1996 on the *Legality of the Threat or Use of Nuclear Weapons*, the ICJ noted that human rights law, and in particular the regime provided by the ICCPR, continues to apply during armed conflicts, subject to the clause in Article 4 of the Covenant enabling a State party to derogate from some of the provisions therein.[63]

In its subsequent advisory opinion of 9 July 2004 on the *Legal Consequences of the Construction of a Wall in the Occupied Palestinian Territory*, the Court confirmed its position, rejecting the Israeli argument that the human rights conventions ratified by Israel are not applicable to territories occupied by force. The ICJ also outlined the different relationships between human rights and IHL, stressing that three situations may arise: "some rights may be exclusively matters of international humanitarian law; others may be exclusively matters of human rights law; yet others may be matters of both these branches of international law".[64]

The position of the Court has been further consolidated in cases of disputes between States. In its judgment of 19 December 2005 on the *Armed Activities on the Territory of Congo*, the ICJ referred to the three situations described above regarding the relationship between human rights and IHL, citing some treaties both on IHL and on human rights, at the universal and regional level, as applicable to the case.[65] Again, in its order of 15 October 2008 in the *Application of the International Convention on the Elimination of All Forms of Racial Discrimination*, the Court stated that the convention in question also applies in cases of armed conflict.[66]

In international armed conflicts, the application of the human rights regime also depends on the level of the territorial or personal control obtained by the State. As correctly indicated in 2011 by the Office of the UN High Commissioner for Human Rights ("OHCHR") and reiterated in 2022 in the Organization for Security and Co-operation in Europe ("OSCE") *Report of Violations of International Humanitarian and Human Rights Law, War Crimes, and Crimes against Humanity Committed in Ukraine since 24 February*, "the more effective the control over persons or territory, the more human rights law would constitute the appropriate reference framework".[67]

[63] In ICJ 1996, p. 240, para 25.

[64] In ICJ 2004, p. 46, para 106.

[65] See ICJ 2005, pp. 243–244, para 217.

[66] See ICJ 2008, p. 387, para 112.

[67] See respectively OHCHR, *International Legal Protection of Human Rights in Armed Conflict*, November 2011, Doc. HR/PUB/11/01, p. 63, and the Report submitted by the Mission of Experts

The natural overlaps between the rules of IHL and those on human rights can be resolved by interpretation on the basis of various legal principles, such as the principle of *lex specialis*, which often gives priority to IHL, and the principle of complementarity or coordination between normative sources. In our view, however, these principles should not be applied *a priori*, i.e. on the basis of an *ex ante* assessment of the principle which is considered in the abstract the most appropriate to solve the incompatibilities between the legal rules belonging to the two legal fields in question, but rather in the light of a specific examination of the actual case, of the potentially applicable rules and of their concrete effects in terms of protection of the rights of the various persons involved. Indeed, a prejudicial application of one or the other sets of rules may lead to the reduction of the level of protection of human rights assured in the case in question and therefore be contrary to the purposes of both human rights law and *jus in bello*.

Finally, it should be recalled that the application of human rights treaties to situations of international or non-international armed conflict is subject to the jurisdiction of the State Party involved in the conflict. This constitutes an obstacle to the possibility of having recourse to the aforementioned treaties, where it is not possible, on the basis of the criteria examined above,[68] to ascertain the existence of a jurisdictional link based on the effective control of the territory that is the object of the armed clashes, or on the exercise of "State agent authority and control" over the individuals who invoke the violation of human rights.

3.9 Derogation and Limitation Clauses in Human Rights Treaties

Some human rights treaties contain derogation clauses in the event of armed conflict, whether international or non-international, or for other emergency situations, for example to protect national security. These clauses provide for a number of substantive limits, such as the non-derogation of certain treaty provisions protecting fundamental rights, which vary according to the legal instrument under consideration and are sometimes interpreted extensively in the case law of bodies charged with scrutinising observance of human rights treaties. The IACtHR has thus broadly interpreted the limit set by the non-derogable nature of the judicial guarantees essential for the protection of fundamental rights in the ACHR,[69] including the right to apply to a court to verify the lawfulness of the arrest or detention of an individual and the right to an effective remedy for a violation of one's substantive rights.[70]

established under the Moscow Mechanism, 13 April 2022, ODIHR.GAL/26/22/Rev.1, p. 53, para 4.

[68] See *supra*, Sects. 3.6.1–3.6.2.

[69] See Article 27(2) of the Convention.

[70] See the advisory opinion of 6 October 1987 on *Judicial Guarantees in States of Emergency*, No. OC-9/87, para 41.

Moreover, the treaty rules that allow derogations from certain provisions often contain procedural obligations for the State party wishing to invoke them, such as obligations to formally notify derogation measures, which must be complied with by States parties when using the mechanism in question.

In addition to the above-mentioned provisions of a substantive and procedural nature, in the practice of the bodies charged with scrutinising observance of human rights treaties reference has been made to the principles of necessity and proportionality for the purposes of assessing the merits of the measures adopted by the State in emergency situations. In this way, consideration is given, on the one hand, to the nature of the national measures adopted and the actual effects produced on human rights, and, on the other hand, to the aspects of the duration of such measures and the identification of the persons targeted by the restrictive measures. Finally, a rigorous assessment is made of the aims pursued by the State in adopting the acts in question, in particular, by analysing whether the measures applied are in fact intended to protect the State institutions and the national population or, as has often been the case in practice, whether they lack that aim and are instead intended to restrict without adequate justifications the rights of the entire national community or a part of it.

In a recent judgment and in accordance with its well-settled case law, the ECtHR stated that in the context of Article 15 the words "other public emergency threatening the life of the nation" refer to "an exceptional situation of crisis or emergency which affects the whole population and constitutes a threat to the organised life of the community of which the State is composed". The Court added that in order to justify a derogation "the emergency should be actual or imminent; that it should affect the whole nation to the extent that the continuance of the organised life of the community was threatened; and that the crisis or danger should be exceptional, in that the normal measures or restrictions, permitted by the Convention for the maintenance of public safety, health and order, are plainly inadequate".[71]

Of a different nature are the clauses restricting certain human rights—the right to private and family life, the right to religious freedom, freedom of opinion and expression, the right to property, etc.—generally laid down in the relevant treaties. As in the case of derogations, the mechanism for restricting certain human rights vary depending on the legal instrument under consideration. If some—like the UDHR[72]—establish general restriction clauses applicable to a series of human rights, in most legal instruments recourse to *ad hoc* restrictions is preferred, i.e. contained in the same provision that enshrines the individual or collective right.

The topic of restrictions on certain human rights will be examined in greater depth later on in this book when the individual and collective human rights in question are examined. At this point suffice it to say that these limitations—which must be interpreted restrictively because they constitute exceptions to the respect for the rights of the human person—serve to balance the exercise of the rights subject to limitation with other individual or collective rights or having regard to general interests of the State considered to be of particular importance. Consequently, in order to ascertain

[71] See judgment of 21 September 2021, *Dareskizb Ltd v. Armenia*, appl. no. 61737/08, para 59.

[72] See Article 29, para 2.

the legality of the restrictions imposed by the State, bodies charged with scrutinising observance of human rights treaties subject the measures adopted by the State to a series of progressive tests: first, the legality test is applied, ascertaining the existence of an adequate and clear legal basis for the adoption of the national measures; second, the necessity of the State's interference is verified, which must be warranted in light of the protection of specific general or individual interests; third, the measures adopted are tested for proportionality, analysing the scope, concrete effects and duration of the State's actions.

As we have said, the purposes of the restrictions to the human rights provided for in the relevant treaties are expressly indicated in the same treaties. This implies that restrictions for other purposes are not allowed. This is the reason why some treaties, as the ECHR, include a clause according to which "The restrictions permitted under this Convention to the said rights and freedoms shall not be applied for any purpose other than those for which they have been prescribed".[73] Obviously, the mere fact that a restriction of a Convention right does not meet the requirements of a clause permitting some restrictions does not automatically raise an issue under Article 18. A specific examination of a complaint under Article 18 is only warranted if the claim that a restriction had been applied for a purpose not prescribed by the Convention was a fundamental aspect of the case. In situations where a right was restricted for a plurality of purposes—both within and outside of those prescribed by the Convention—the ECtHR took the view that the presence of an ulterior purpose could give rise to a breach of Article 18 if the said purpose is "predominant".[74]

In practice, there is no shortage of State measures that seem to straddle the line between those that can be adopted on foot of derogations from human rights treaties and those rooted in restrictions to many individual or collective rights. For example, particularly restrictive measures affecting several human rights—freedom of movement and assembly, personal freedom and security (especially for individuals subject to mandatory quarantine), right to property (in relation to privately owned real estate requisitioned for public use), surveillance that interferes with private and family life etc.—have been adopted in 2020-2022 by many States to counter the global health emergency caused by the spread of COVID-19.

This very serious health situation, classified by the WHO as a pandemic, would seem to fall within cases in which it would be possible to rely on the derogation clauses—invoked by several States in relation to the ECHR, the ACHR and the ICCPR[75]—rather than resorting to simple restrictions of certain human rights. That said, we consider that provided that they comply with the aforementioned principles of legality, necessity and proportionality, the restrictive measures not based on the derogation mechanism are to be considered compatible with the respective human rights treaties in so far as they are aimed at protecting the life and health of the national

[73] Article 18.

[74] ECtHR (Grand Chamber), judgment of 28 November 2017, *Merabishvili v. Georgia*, appl. no. 72508/13.

[75] The derogation measures were adopted respectively pursuant to Article 15 ECHR, Article 27 ACHR and Article 4 ICCPR.

populations in the face of a very serious health emergency. In this regard, however, the legal basis, the ambiguous and at times contradictory nature, as well as the particular duration of the restrictive measures adopted by some countries, raise various doubts as to their compatibility with the principles of legality and proportionality.[76]

Finally, particularly significant restrictions on the enjoyment of certain human rights are also envisaged for individuals who are subject to specific and legitimate measures of deprivation of their liberty. In this regard, it should be noted that even in respect of such individuals, for example, prisoners, the State enforcing the restrictive measures is obliged to respect fundamental rights like the right to life or the right not to be subjected to torture or inhuman or degrading treatment.[77] Moreover, limitations on other human rights like the right to privacy, religious freedom and freedom of expression, can be considered lawful only if they are necessary and proportionate to the ends to be achieved.

From this point of view, it is logical that, in relation to these cases, the States enjoy a wide margin of appreciation with reference to the question of the balance between the interest of the individual deprived of personal liberty to the enjoyment of certain human rights and the general interest of the State to guarantee the security of the national population. But it is equally logical that evidently disproportionate measures, for example a blanket ban without valid justification on the exercise of certain human rights like right of detainees to vote,[78] are to be considered contrary to international human rights law.

3.10 Human Rights Treaties and National Implementation: Domestic Rank, Direct Applicability and Direct Effect—The Difference between Immediate and Progressive Obligations

It is commonly recognised that one of the main conditions for ensuring effective respect for international rules, in particular in the field of human rights, is their prompt and complete transposition into domestic law. This implementation varies according to how open national legal systems are to the international order and is thus influenced by the monistic or dualistic approach adopted at the domestic level in relations between national and international law.

The other fundamental element affecting compliance with international law at the domestic level is how national law is adapted to that end and the corresponding rank

[76] The conditions that the power to derogate from certain provisions of the ICCPR is subject to have been highlighted, precisely in connection with the COVID-19 pandemic, by the HRC in its unusual *Statement* of 24 April 2020, CCPR/C/128/2.

[77] On the case law concerning the application to prisoners of the right not to be subjected to inhuman or degrading treatment, see Chap. 7, Sect. 7.2.2.

[78] In this regard, see the statements of the ECtHR (Grand Chamber) in its judgment of 6 October 2005, *Hirst v. the United Kingdom* (no. 2), appl. no. 74025/01, paras 56 ff.

afforded to international rules at the domestic level, often recognised on the basis of constitutional provisions.

It used to be argued in the past (often in a specious manner) that obligations contained in human rights treaties were merely programmatic in nature, with the effect that States parties were not obliged to adopt corresponding and immediate measures at the domestic level. That view, which shaped how treaty provisions were considered at the domestic level, has long since been superseded. There is no doubt that international obligations on human rights, whether based on custom or treaty, mainly take the form of self-executing norms in national legal systems. Consequently, there is no need, at least in principle, for any additional domestic legislation (direct applicability) and the norms are such as to provide for individual or collective rights that are directly enforceable before national courts (direct effect).

With regard to the general content of the obligations established in human rights treaties, in earlier times most of such obligations required to refrain from doing something (negative obligations), for example, an obligation to refrain from engaging in conduct detrimental to human rights. However, nowadays, treaties and case law have reached a stage that envisages a series of obligations to do something (positive obligations), which imply a series of measures by States, including of a legislative nature, so as to ensure effective compliance with international standards. This development has ensured the achievement of a much higher overall level of human rights protection.

It should be pointed out that the positive obligations of the State are not only *specific*—that is, regarding respect for individual human rights and specific State conduct—but sometimes are much broader to the extent of entailing *general* positive obligations, inferable from one or more treaty provisions or even from the entire framework of the treaty concerned. This second type of positive obligations requires the State to set up a broad and adequate legislative, administrative, judicial and police apparatus so as to prevent and repress violations of a plurality of human rights committed by State bodies or private individuals. In this regard, as highlighted by the pandemic caused by the spread of COVID-19, the State also has a positive obligation of a general nature to establish an adequate system of protection of the health of individuals under its jurisdiction. Fulfilment of these positive obligations often becomes indispensable in order to avoid the ascertainment of systemic problems and shortcomings, which derive precisely from dysfunctions and gaps in the system of the State in question and which, if not eliminated, imply "serial" violations by the same State of the relevant international norm.

On the other hand, the nature and content of certain obligations contained in treaties mainly to protect economic and social rights, such as the ICESCR, are different. These rights are in fact protected not only by providing for obligations that must be fully and immediately fulfilled but also on the basis of obligations which are considered binding but which are to be implemented progressively, according to the formula used by the CESCR itself in its *General Comment No. 3* of 14 December 1990 on "The Nature of States Parties' Obligations".[79]

---

[79] See para 1.

With reference to the above-mentioned progressive obligations provided for in the treaties on the protection of economic, social and cultural rights, it should be noted that the rationale for the granting of a wide margin of discretion, in terms of national measures to be adopted and the time frame within which to adopt them, is mainly due to the serious difficulties encountered by States in guaranteeing effective respect for these rights. This is so both because of the economic resources to be employed and because of the complexity of the reforms necessary to adapt the national structures and institutions to what is required by the treaty provisions. Nonetheless, on the basis of those treaty obligations, States parties are obliged to take a series of gradual steps to ensure progressive and complete respect for human rights—steps that must be in accordance with the principles of reasonableness and proportionality of the measures actually adopted—thus excluding regressive measures in the level of protection already existing at the national level.

It should also be stressed, as noted by the IACtHR in its judgment of 8 March 2018 in *Poblete Vilches et al. v. Chile,* that the same treaty provision may contain both obligations to be progressively achieved and obligations that must be complied with immediately by States parties. For the Court "the progressive realization means that the States Parties have the specific and constant obligation to make the most expeditious and effective progress possible towards the full effectiveness" of the rights "and this should not be interpreted in the sense that, while implementation is underway, these obligations are deprived of specific content; moreover, this does not mean that the States may postpone indefinitely the adoption of measures to give effect to the rights in question ... Therefore, there is also an obligation of non-retrogressivity in relation to rights that have been realized. Regarding the obligations of an immediate nature, these consist in adopting effective measures in order to guarantee access, without discrimination, to the benefits recognized for each right. Such measures must be adequate, deliberate and specific in order to achieve the full realization of such rights".[80]

The above point on the nature of conventional obligations in the field of human rights makes it clear that, when transposing internally agreements containing above all positive obligations, States parties cannot confine themselves to adapting their national legal systems at the time of the implementation of the specific treaty under consideration within their national systems. They must also intervene at a later stage—in particular, following decisions by the bodies charged with scrutinising observance of the aforementioned treaties, which sometimes interpret the conventional obligations in a particularly extensive manner. And the same is true in relation to additional protocols that reinforce and supplement the protection of human rights established by the original treaty. It is thus a matter of constant monitoring to ensure that a national legal system remains in line with international conventions and related agreements, as interpreted by the bodies charged with scrutinising observance of the relevant treaty provisions. The case of the ECHR and the additional protocols subsequently adopted is emblematic in this sense.[81]

---

[80] See para 104.

[81] See Chap. 4, Sects. 4.1–4.3.

3.11 Soft Law

Non-mandatory international rules, or soft law, are generally relevant in international law both as an exhortation and a stimulus to States—and other subjects of international law—to respect the legal rules. Soft law rules are also specifically relevant for the development of general international law, since, according to established domestic and international case law, they are part of the *opinio juris ac necessitatis* of States and international organisations. Moreover, soft law is sometimes referred to in the interpretation of the already created rules of general international law and treaties, often underpinning an extensive interpretation.

The most incisive example of soft law in the framework of human rights is undoubtedly the UDHR, approved by the UNGA on 10 December 1948. A forerunner of that legal instrument at the regional level is the American Declaration of the Rights and Duties of Man, approved by the Organization of American States ("OAS") on 2 May 1948.

Although not binding, the UDHR is of particular importance at the general level in that it constitutes the first legal instrument of a universal nature in the field of human rights, thus marking the passage, as has been noted,[82] from the period in which the protection of human rights was mainly based on principles and rules of domestic law to a new phase of formation of international rules for the protection of every human being.

The observation that the Declaration is an expression of the legal and cultural values of Western states is certainly true, but frankly it is not clear what the alternative was at the time; except, of course, not adopting any legal instrument at all, a choice that would have had considerable negative effects on the evolution of the international protection of human rights.

The UDHR deals mainly with civil and political rights, but there are also references to economic, social and cultural rights. On the basis of practice following the Declaration, it is arguable that it is now an essential legal parameter of reference in the UN system, as evidenced by the fact that it has been included among the legal instruments whose observance must be ascertained by the Human Rights Council ("HRCoun") in the performance of its Universal Periodic Review ("UPR").[83]

It is indeed indisputable that the UDHR has been used as a legal model both within the UN—for example for the preparation of the ICCPR and ICESCR—and also outside of it, in particular, for the drafting of international conventions of a regional nature. From this last point of view, it should be pointed out that, for example, in the preamble of the ECHR, the main purposes of the UDHR are recalled, stating that the Declaration "aims at securing the universal and effective recognition and observance of the Rights therein declared", and adding that European States intend "to take the first steps for the collective enforcement of certain of the rights stated in the Universal Declaration". Finally, both in international and domestic case law,

[82] See Chap. 1, Sect. 1.1.

[83] See Chap. 5, Sect. 5.3.2.

there is ample reference to the UDHR in order to ascertain the existence of rules of general international law on human rights.

Comprehension Check and Tasks

1. What are the specific features of *jus cogens* as applied to the field of human rights? (Sect. 3.2)
2. What are the reasons that make recourse to the general principles of law still important in the context of human rights? (Sect. 3.3)
3. Why is it difficult to apply the regime of the Vienna Convention on the Law of Treaties to human rights treaties? (Sect. 3.5)
4. What is the meaning of the criterion of "personal control" in the context of jurisdiction and what is new about *Carter v. Russia* (2021)? (Sect. 3.6.2)
5. In the context of the inter-individual application of human rights norms, when is it possible to hold the State responsible? (Sect. 3.7)
6. What did the ECtHR hold in the *Osman* case (1998) and how did it differ from the *Volodina v. Russia (No. 2)* case (2021)? (Sect. 3.7.1)
7. Is the position of some States that only IHL applies in armed conflicts correct? (Sect. 3.8)
8. In *Dareskizb Ltd v. Armenia* (2021) the ECtHR reiterated its position on the limits of the power of derogation under Article 15 ECHR. Focus on these limits (Sect. 3.9)
9. Does soft law continue to play an important role in the development of human rights? (Sect. 3.11)

References

ICJ (1996) Advisory opinion of 8 July 1996 on the Legality of the Threat or Use of Nuclear Weapons. ICJ Reports

ICJ (2004) Advisory opinion of 9 July 2004 on the Legal Consequences of the Construction of a Wall in the Occupied Palestinian Territory. ICJ Reports

ICJ (2005) Judgment of 19 December 2005 on the Armed Activities on the Territory of Congo (Democratic Republic of Congo. v. Uganda). ICJ Reports

ICJ (2008) Order of 15 October 2008 in the Application of the International Convention on the Elimination of All Forms of Racial Discrimination (Georgia v. Russian Federation). ICJ Reports

Chapter 4
International Legal Sources on Human Rights: The Regional Level

Contents

Abstract This chapter examines the regional international legal regimes in the field of human rights, with particular attention to the ECHR, the general functioning of the ECtHR and the mechanisms of individual and inter-State applications to the Strasbourg Court. It further analyses the means to ensure compliance with the general and individual measures adopted by the ECtHR towards States parties that have violated the ECHR. Finally, it examines the human rights conventions and control mechanisms established within the framework of the American, African, Arab and Asian systems, highlighting their strengths, shortcomings and prospects for development.

4.1 The European Convention on Human Rights and the European Court of Human Rights

It is now necessary to analyse some regional systems of human rights protection, paying particular attention to the system of the ECHR, as it is the most advanced

P. Pustorino, *Introduction to International Human Rights Law*,
https://doi.org/10.1007/978-94-6265-563-8_4

and effective mechanism of human rights protection and has largely influenced other treaty-based systems of a regional nature.

The system of the ECHR—so called because it includes the Convention adopted on 4 November 1950 and the subsequent additional protocols—today avails itself of a single body in charge of scrutinising observance thereof, the ECtHR.[1] That has replaced the more articulated but less effective system of dual scrutiny, which was centred on the role played, on the one hand, by the European Commission of Human Rights ("ECommHR") and, on the other hand, by the Committee of Ministers of the Council of Europe ("CMCoE") and the Court itself.

The ECommHR had both administrative and quasi-judicial functions, issuing decisions on the admissibility of the applications submitted to it and adopting, in case of admissibility of the application, a report on the merits of the dispute. For its part, the CMCoE was entrusted with the adoption of a binding decision on the merits of the applications. And then there was the Court itself, cases to which could be submitted at the request of the Contracting Parties, the ECommHR and, after the entry into force of Protocol No. 9, natural and legal persons.

Currently, the ECtHR "shall sit in a single-judge formation, in Committees of three judges, in Chambers of seven judges and in a Grand Chamber of seventeen judges".[2] A single judge has limited jurisdiction, being able solely to declare "inadmissible or strike out of the Court's list of cases an application … where such a decision can be taken without further examination". In the Court's case law, the applications that fall within the jurisdiction of the single judge, the grounds for whose decisions are very limited in the practice, are those which are unfounded and therefore bound to be dismissed. If "the single judge does not declare an application inadmissible or strike it out", including in relation to some of the complaints submitted by the applicant, "that judge shall forward it to a committee or to a Chamber for further examination".[3]

The Committees also have specific competence in assessing an individual application and, in particular, may declare it inadmissible or strike it out, with a final decision adopted unanimously. Or "declare it admissible and render at the same time a judgment on the merits", but only unanimously,[4] "if the underlying question in the case, concerning the interpretation or the application of the Convention or the Protocols thereto, is already the subject of well-established case-law of the Court".[5] This happens, for example, in cases of so-called repetitive applications where the State's responsibility is "unquestionable" in that it is based on pre-existing case law.

In the event that no decision or judgement has been adopted pursuant to Articles 27 and 28 ECHR and the matter has been referred to one of the Chambers of the

[1] The Court's functions in this regard are flanked, as will be seen, by the role still played by the CMCoE.

[2] See Article 26(1) ECHR. To which must be added those of the Sections of 9 to 10 judges, from which the actual members of the Committees and of the Chambers are chosen.

[3] See Article 27 ECHR.

[4] In the event that unanimity is not achieved, the case must be referred to the Chamber.

[5] See Article 28 ECHR.

Court, the Court will rule, exceptionally and also on the basis of separate decisions, on the admissibility and merits of individual and inter-State applications.[6]

Finally, "where a case pending before a Chamber raises a serious question affecting the interpretation of the Convention or the Protocols thereto, or where the resolution of a question before the Chamber might have a result inconsistent with a judgment previously delivered by the Court, the Chamber may, at any time before it has rendered its judgment, relinquish jurisdiction in favour of the Grand Chamber". Until the entry into force of Protocol No. 15 to the ECHR on 1 August 2021,[7] the relinquishment of jurisdiction in favour of the Grand Chamber could be blocked by one of the parties to the dispute, although the ECtHR had already interpreted the clause allowing opposition by the parties restrictively.[8]

A further competence of the Grand Chamber relates to referrals, i.e. a request for review of a judgment rendered by a Chamber, which can be presented by any of the parties to the dispute within a period of three months after the date of the judgment of the Chamber. In this case, the request is screened by a panel of five judges of the Grand Chamber, which assesses "if the case raises a serious question affecting the interpretation or application of the Convention or the Protocols thereto, or a serious issue of general importance".[9] In both cases, the Grand Chamber rules on the admissibility and on the merits with a final judgment.

The modifications made to the original structure of the ECHR are considerable. They have concerned both the widening of the catalogue of human rights, sometimes with repeated interventions concerning the same right (for example, the death penalty, originally allowed in some cases by Article 2 ECHR, was first abolished in time of peace by Protocol No. 6, and then abolished also in time of war by Protocol No. 13),[10] and the way in which observance of the ECHR is scrutinised. In this respect, under Protocol No. 11, a single permanent court was set up and the principle of automatic acceptance of its jurisdiction to receive individual or State applications was established.

In addition, Protocol No. 16, in force since 1 August 2018, provides for the option, for the "highest courts and tribunals of a High Contracting Party" to request the ECtHR for an advisory opinion—similar in many respects to the provisions of EU law on the request for preliminary rulings from the Court of Justice of the

---

[6] See Article 29 ECHR. In the event of a decision on admissibility by the Committee or the Chamber, the application—before the adoption of the judgment on the merits—is communicated to the government of the respondent State, which is required to respond to the questions posed by the Court with observations that are also sent to the applicant for possible clarifications.

[7] See Article 3 of the Protocol.

[8] See the decision of 18 February 2021, *Grzęda v. Poland*, appl. no. 43572/18, in which the Court relied on both the Brighton Declaration of 2012, in which the Contracting Parties to the ECHR unreservedly agreed to a collective policy of refraining from objecting to relinquishment pending the entry into force of Protocol No. 15, and the ratification by Poland and all other Contracting Parties of that same protocol.

[9] See Article 43 ECHR.

[10] For more on the issue of the abolition of the death penalty among the Contracting Parties to the ECHR, see Chap. 6, Sect. 6.2.5.

European Union (ECJ)[11]—"on questions of principle relating to the interpretation or application of the rights and freedoms defined in the Convention or the protocols thereto".[12] The above-mentioned ECtHR advisory opinion is not binding, but it is to be presumed that it will be taken into the utmost consideration by the national court requesting the opinion and also by the courts of other countries (at least of the Contracting Parties to Protocol No. 16), in order to prevent the presentation of individual applications that could be based precisely on the solutions indicated by the ECtHR and possibly not followed at the national level. Furthermore, we believe that, even when a national supreme court decides not to request an opinion from the Strasbourg Court, the mere fact that such an eventuality is taken into consideration may induce the domestic court to evaluate with greater attention the case law of the ECtHR, as can be deduced from the statements of the Supreme Court of the Netherlands in the *Urgenda case.*[13]

The mechanism referred to in Protocol No. 16 was used for the first time by the French Supreme Court, which, in its judgment No. 638 of 5 October 2018, decided to stay the national proceedings and make a request to the ECtHR for an advisory opinion. In particular, the French court asked, *inter alia,* whether Article 8 ECHR, on the subject of the right to private and family life, was breached by the conduct of a Contracting Party that accepts a request for entry in the civil registers of the birth certificate of a child born abroad following recourse to surrogacy with regard to the biological father while refusing the same entry with regard to the "intended mother", who has no biological link with the child.[14]

A second advisory opinion based on the mechanism of the said Protocol No. 16 was adopted by the ECtHR on 29 May 2020 at the request of the Armenian Constitutional Court and concerns the interpretation of Article 7 ECHR, with particular reference to the principle of legality in criminal matters and the related principle of non-retroactivity of criminal laws.[15] Since then, further requests for advisory opinions have made to the ECtHR.

Finally, for the sake of completeness, it should be noted that the ECtHR, pursuant to Article 47 ECHR, also has a wider but little-used-in-practice power to give advisory opinions, at the request of the CMCoE, "on legal questions concerning the interpretation of the Convention and the Protocols thereto".

[11] See Article 267 of the Treaty on the Functioning of the European Union ("TFEU").

[12] See Article 1(1) of the Protocol.

[13] See the judgment of 20 December 2019, para 5.6.4, which ruled out requiring an advisory opinion because of the clarity of ECtHR's case law and the specific request of the parties to the dispute to issue a decision "before the end of 2019". On the *Urgenda* case, see Chap. 12, Sect. 12.4.

[14] For the content of the opinion issued by the ECtHR on 10 April 2019, see Chap. 6, Sect. 6.3.2.

[15] For the content of that opinion, see Chap. 8, Sect. 8.3.

4.2 Individual and Inter-State Applications to the ECtHR: The Admissibility Conditions

Both individual and inter-State applications may be submitted to the ECtHR.[16]

As for individual applications, they can be filed by single individuals, groups of them or NGOs (a broad expression which also includes legal persons) on condition that they can prove to be a "victim" of a violation of one of the rights provided for in the ECHR or in the additional protocols. As regards the status of victim of NGOs, the trend that can be inferred from the examination of the case law of the Court was, until recently, rather restrictive, excluding the admissibility of applications originating from associations representing collective interests but not specifically harmed by violations committed by the State. In this regard, it is worth mentioning, for example, the inadmissibility decision of 16 December 2008 in *Ada Rossi and Others v. Italy*, concerning the application lodged by several individuals and NGOs, operating in the field of protection of severely disabled persons or persons in a vegetative state. The applicants challenged the lawfulness, under the ECHR, of the decisions of the Italian courts on the interruption of artificial nutrition and hydration practices in respect of a person in an irreversible vegetative state. Citing its previous case law, the Court stated that it is not sufficient for the individual applicant to claim that "the mere existence of a law violates his rights under the Convention", it is also necessary that "the law should have been applied to his detriment".[17]

In its most recent case law, exhibiting a greater openness towards NGOs acting on behalf of particularly important collective interests, the ECtHR has held that actions brought by such entities are admissible where the victim lacks legal capacity to act, where there are no relatives who can represent him or her and where the NGO in question has been specifically and actively involved in the case at the domestic level, for example, by bringing actions on behalf of the individual before national bodies or courts for violation of fundamental human rights.[18] In such cases, the Court recognises to NGOs the role of de facto representatives of the actual victim. From this point of view, it would seem that the ECtHR's case law values the *substitutive* role played by NGOs, in the absence of other persons with standing to bring legal action or capable of bringing legal action, not only in the interest of the individual involved in the actual case but also of the community as a whole, in order for a violation of human rights of great importance to be ascertained.

As regards the concept of victim of the violation of one of the rights covered by the ECHR or the additional protocols, it should be pointed out that the Court, particularly in the case of violation of rights of a fundamental nature, generally regards as admissible both applications brought by *indirect* victims, for example

[16] See Articles 33–34 ECHR.

[17] Appl. nos. 55185/08 and others.

[18] In this regard, see the judgment of 10 July 2014 in *Centre for Legal Resources on behalf of Valentin Câmpeanu v. Romania*, appl. no. 47848/08, paras 104 ff., in relation to the violation of the right to life.

by the close relatives (children, parents, brothers and sisters) of the direct victim,[19] and those brought by *potential* victims. This second category of victims arises, for example, in the case of the adoption of a national legislative measure which, although not yet applied to the applicant, is of direct concern to him or her in view of the application *ratione personae* of the legislation in question. This has occurred both with regard to domestic measures of deportation or extradition of individuals in contrast with the provisions of the ECHR (for instance in cases in which the individual risks being subject to torture in the country of final destination), and with regard to national laws providing for criminal sanctions against homosexuals. More recently, the same trend can be seen with regard to domestic provisions prohibiting the wearing of the Islamic veil in public places or potentially affecting a large number of people, for example mass wire-tapping.

With regard to potential victims of ECHR violations, the Strasbourg Court, in the recent inadmissibility decision of 18 November 2021 in *Róisín Shortall and Others* v. *Ireland*, clarified again that "in order for an applicant to be able to claim to be a victim in such circumstances, he or she must produce reasonable and convincing evidence of the likelihood that a violation affecting them personally would occur", stressing expressly that "mere suspicion or conjecture is insufficient in this respect".[20]

The other main conditions laid down in Article 35 ECHR for the admissibility of individual applications are the exhaustion of all domestic remedies, limited to those that are accessible and effective,[21] and observance of the limit of four months from the date on which the final domestic decision was taken (the time limit was six months before the entry into force of Protocol No. 15 on 1 August 2021).

Moreover, the Court will not deal with any application that is substantially the same as a matter that has already been examined by the Court or has already been submitted to another procedure of international investigation or settlement and contains no relevant new information.

And neither will the Court hear applications that are manifestly ill-founded or constitute an abuse of the right to file an individual application.[22] With reference to this latter scenario, reference can be made to the ECtHR's recent decision of 7 October 2021 in *Zambrano v. France* concerning an application lodged by an individual against national regulations on the COVID-19 health pass system following vaccination.[23] The applicant had even set up a website inviting the public to submit similar applications to the Strasbourg Court, which were indeed submitted. In the decision of inadmissibility, the ECtHR noted that the applicant's real objective, part

[19] On the link between the extension of the notion of *indirect* victim and the violation of one of the norms "les plus fondamentales du système de la Convention", see the ECtHR's judgment of 19 March 2020 in *Fabris and Parziale v. Italy*, appl. no. 41603/13, para 37.

[20] See appl. no. 50272/18, para 48.

[21] In the case of applications notified to the government of the respondent State, the lack of prior exhaustion of domestic remedies must be specifically raised by the State, whereas, in the earlier stages of judicial proceedings, the Court may proceed of its own motion, declaring the actions inadmissible on the ground that this condition of admissibility has not been met.

[22] These additional conditions of admissibility can be raised by the Court of its own motion.

[23] See appl. no. 41994/21.

of a veritable legal strategy, was to bring about "congestion, excessive workload and a backlog" at the Court, in order to "paralyse its operations", thus abusing the right to file an individual application.

Lastly, following the entry into force of Protocol No. 14, a so-called *de minimis* criterion of admissibility for individual applications was introduced, which requires that the victim must have suffered a "significant disadvantage", above all in economic terms. In other words, the individual harm must exceed a minimum threshold of gravity, which varies according to the right infringed and the personal conditions of the victim, unless the issue is considered particularly important within the framework of the ECHR and therefore requires an examination of the application on the merits.[24] The *de minimis* criterion, which is used by the Court in a rather discretionary way, is clearly inspired by the need to reduce its enormous workload but does not seem to be in line with the need to ensure a uniform and effective protection of human rights protected in the system of the ECHR.

With reference to applications filed by States, the ECHR does not expressly lay down any grounds of inadmissibility. However, the ECtHR has focused on this issue, pointing out that some of the conditions of inadmissibility for individual applications are also applicable to inter-State applications, in particular, the failure to comply with the rule of prior exhaustion of domestic remedies, which does not apply in cases where the applicant State invokes the alleged existence of an administrative practice of violations of the Convention and not of individual and specific violations,[25] and the deadline of six months (now four months) within which to lodge the application.

On the basis of an interpretation in line with the rules governing international jurisdiction, the Court has also specified that, similarly to an individual application, an application filed by a State can be declared inadmissible if totally unfounded or lacking the minimum requirements to constitute "a genuine allegation in the sense of Article 33 of the Convention".[26]

4.3 Scrutiny by the ECtHR—Nature and Scope of ECtHR Judgments and the Role of the Committee of Ministers

As stated in Article 19 ECHR, compliance with the obligations contained in the Convention is ensured through the establishment of the ECtHR. In addition, it is provided that final judgments of the Court are binding on the Contracting Parties.[27]

[24] With the entry into force of Protocol No. 15, the fact that the case in question was not adequately examined at the national level was eliminated as a further exception to the application of the *de minimis* criterion.

[25] On this issue, see the statements of the ECtHR (Grand Chamber) in its decision of partial admissibility of 16 December 2020, *Ukraine v. Russia (Re Crimea)*, appl. nos. 20958/14 and 38334/18, paras 363 ff.

[26] See the inadmissibility decision of the Grand Chamber of 18 November 2020, *Slovenia v. Croatia*, appl. no. 54155/16, paras 40–41.

[27] See Article 46(1) ECHR.

From a general point of view concerning its judicial function, the ECtHR adopts decisions and judgments of a very different nature and content, both on the basis of what is established by the ECHR and the Rules of Procedure of the Court, and in the light of the developments in case law followed by the Court itself. It should be noted that some of the types of decisions that will be analysed below are also adopted, albeit under different names, by other courts whose function is to ensure compliance with human rights conventions.[28]

The Court may first of all make decisions relating to provisional measures, which, since the judgment delivered by the Grand Chamber on 4 February 2005 in *Mamatkulov and Askarov v. Turkey*,[29] have been regarded as binding for the Contracting Parties and concern almost exclusively urgent measures intended to avoid a real risk of fundamental rights being infringed: for example, where there is a risk that a State will execute measures entailing the extradition or deportation of foreigners to countries where the individuals in question may be subjected to the death penalty, torture or inhuman or degrading treatment.

The ECtHR's decisions on provisional measures are generally enforced at the national level. As stated by the Italian Court of Cassation, in its judgment No. 20514 of 28 May 2010 concerning the quashing of the decision issued by the trial court regarding the deportation of certain foreigners who risked inhuman or degrading treatment in the State of final destination, "all the institutions of the Republic are required to comply with the obligations arising from the rulings, including provisional ones, of the Strasbourg Court".[30]

The ECtHR also adopts, on the basis of well-settled case law, several other types of judgments, which can be grouped as follows.

The most frequent type of judgment of the Court, which can be defined as "ordinary", is one whereby the Court ascertains the violation of the rules of the ECHR and the additional protocols, granting, if necessary, "just satisfaction" to the injured party under Article 41 ECHR. In the case law applying the above mentioned provision, the right to just satisfaction—a rather ambiguous term—has been interpreted as the right to receive compensation for the pecuniary and non-pecuniary damage suffered by the applicant, which, in some cases, has been assessed by the Court to be enormous in economic terms.

Since its judgment of 13 July 2000 in *Scozzari and Giunta v. Italy*,[31] the ECtHR (Grand Chamber) has widened the types of judgments it can adopt, granting itself the right to indicate, to the Contracting Party whose legal system is deemed not to be in line with the provisions of the ECHR or its additional protocols, general or individual measures, which may also coexist in the specific case.

---

[28] For example, judgments concerning general and individual measures against the State held responsible for the violation of human rights have been adopted by the IACtHR.

[29] See appl. nos. 46827/99 and 46951/99.

[30] See para 11 of the judgment.

[31] See appl. nos. 39221/98 and 41963/98.

It should be noted that, reacting to positions of domestic case law aimed at attributing a different weight to the decisions of the ECtHR,[32] as for example asserted by the Italian Constitutional Court,[33] the Strasbourg Court (Grand Chamber) specified, in its judgment of 28 June 2018 in *G.I.E.M. S.r.l. and Others v. Italy*, that its judgments "all have the same legal value" and that the binding character and interpretative value of the aforementioned decisions "cannot therefore depend on the formation by which they were rendered".[34]

4.3.1 ECtHR General Measures

The general measures may be of various kinds and thus imply recourse, by the State, to concrete actions or measures of a legislative or administrative nature and also have as their object a modification with respect to stances adopted in domestic case law considered incompatible with the system of the ECHR. These general measures are justified by the Court on the basis of the existence of systemic and structural problems in the national legal systems of the Contracting Parties, which lead to repetitive violations of the same Convention provisions. Some of these judgments are called "pilot judgments", as they set out for the State a set of measures to be applied in order to solve the structural problems found and consequently have an effect on all applications of similar content brought before the Court against the State in question. The ECtHR judgments may be stayed pending the adoption of implementing measures by the State.[35] For these reasons, it is particularly important that the pilot judgment be complied with fully and promptly, which is not always the case in practice.[36]

In general, the State is afforded wide discretion as to the instruments to be adopted and the time limits within which to comply with those general measures. However, on rare occasions which it considers to be particularly serious, the Court does not hesitate to determine the content (including in terms of the legal form of the measures

[32] Positions similar to those in the case law of Contracting Parties to the ECHR have been adopted with respect to the ACHR by the Colombian Constitutional Court. In its judgment of 16 July 2004 (C-500/14), para 8.3.2, that Court ruled that whether the IACtHR's case law was uniform and well-settled ("uniforme y reiterada") should be a criterion used in assessing the weight of IACtHR decisions in the context of judgments on constitutionality, a stance reiterated in its judgment of 22 June 2016 (327/16), Part VI.

[33] See judgment No. 49 of 26 March 2015 stating that the Italian courts are obliged to comply with ECtHR judgments solely if they constitute a well-settled interpretation or are "pilot judgments": para 7 of the conclusions on points of law.

[34] Appl. nos. 1828/06 and 2 others, para 252 of the judgment.

[35] The importance of pilot judgments is confirmed by the fact that the procedure necessary for the adoption of these decisions is now contained in Article 61 of the Rules of Procedure of the Court.

[36] For a well-known case on the failure to implement general measures indicated to the State in a pilot judgment, see the Grand Chamber's judgment of 12 October 2017 in *Burmych and Others v. Ukraine*, appl. no. 46852/13.

to be adopted, often consisting of legislative acts), the purposes and the deadlines for eliminating dysfunctions in the national regulatory system.

4.3.2 ECtHR Individual Measures

The individual measures specified by the ECtHR are generally motivated by specific situations of non-compliance with the provisions of the ECHR and the additional protocols, which, in the view of the Court, can be overcome through recourse to *ad hoc* solutions, thus leaving a reduced margin of appreciation for the States when it comes to implementing the measures. In this regard the Court's decisions would seem to draw inspiration from the form of reparation applicable to the international responsibility of States, consisting of *restitutio in integrum*. In fact, the individual measures indicated by the Court may, for example, take the form of the review of criminal proceedings unfairly conducted at the national level, the return of wrongfully confiscated property, the release of prisoners unlawfully convicted at the domestic level, etc.

4.3.3 ECtHR "Warning" Judgments

Another type of decision adopted by the ECtHR that is worthy of mention is a so-called "warning" judgment. On these occasions the Court, while ruling out a violation in the case before it, issues a warning to the relevant State, cautioning that in the future the Court could well change its position on the legal issue submitted for its examination and therefore consider the State's conduct as no longer compliant with the ECHR and the additional protocols. The legal questions under consideration often concern modern and controversial applications of certain human rights, where a literal and systemic interpretation of the provisions of the Convention and its protocols does not offer any appreciable solution. It is therefore necessary for the Court to look outside the system of the ECHR, analysing both other international legal instruments and the legislation and case law of the Contracting Parties in order to determine the existence of a "European consensus" on the legal question under consideration, which is thus used as a legal parameter of reference for resolving the specific case.

Warnings are not limited solely to borderline cases of lawful conduct vis-à-vis the ECHR but may also relate to the dividing line between various degrees of gravity of a violation. For example, the Court has held that State conduct which, at the time of the Court's assessment, constituted inhuman or degrading treatment may in the future be considered an act of torture, because of the greater gravity attributed to that conduct in the light of the examination of legislative developments and scientific advances concerning such harmful practices.[37]

Some actual examples may be useful to understand the Court's reasoning in the matter of warning judgments. For instance, a warning judgment was issued in connection with the protection of transsexuals in the context of the right to private and family life under Article 8 ECHR, where the Court first warned the United Kingdom about the inadequacy of its legislation that did not allow the rectification of civil registers in order to record changes of sex and therefore of name of transsexuals. The Court then found the State liable in its judgment of 11 July 2002 in *Christine Goodwin v. United Kingdom*.[38] More recently, the Court affirmed that an individual's right to have his or her personal data amended in the relevant civil register can be invoked as soon as the person in question has been judicially authorised to change sex, but before undergoing surgery.[39] This recent development in the case law of the Court raises, in our opinion, some doubts in relation to the principle of legal certainty, particularly with regard to the eventuality that, once authorisation to change sex has been obtained, the person concerned is unwilling or unable to undergo surgery.

The ECtHR also issued a warning judgment in relation to the legislative measure adopted by France—Law No. 2010-1192 of 11 October 2000—prohibiting the covering of one's face and hence outlawing the wearing of the Islamic veil in public places. More specifically, in its judgment of 1 July 2014 in *S.A.S. v. France* concerning a case of full headscarf ("niqab"), which therefore covered the applicant's entire face, the Court held that the above-mentioned legislation was not contrary to Articles 8 and 9 ECHR on, respectively, the right to private and family life and religious freedom. That outcome was due both to the wide margin of appreciation to be granted to the Contracting Parties in such situations and to the absence of a European consensus on the wearing of the Islamic headscarf in public places. However, the Court warned the respondent State about the possibility of the formation of a future European consensus against legislation of the type at issue in the case.[40]

It is by no means certain that the warning given by the Court will result in a subsequent finding of a violation in later case law. The warning could remain in place for a long time in light of a continuing situation of uncertainty at the European level. Or it could well happen that the warning is no longer warranted because the European consensus converges on the position taken by the Contracting Party initially considered by the Court as potentially damaging to one of the rights protected by the ECHR system. This second eventuality would seem to be possible precisely as a result of the growing conviction of the legitimacy, in the light of the ECHR, of legislative measures banning the wearing of the full Islamic veil in public places.[41] On condition that such measures are the expression of a well-considered balancing

[37] On this point, see Chap. 6, Sect. 6.2.

[38] Appl. no. 28957/95.

[39] In this regard, see judgment of 11 October 2018 in *S.V. v. Italy*, appl. no. 55216/08.

[40] See appl. no. 43835/11.

[41] On recent developments in ECtHR case law on the subject of the Islamic headscarf, see Chap. 9, Sect. 9.2.1.

of the rights and interests at stake (freedom to manifest one's own religious belief, needs of national security etc.) and are also in accordance with the principle of proportionality.

In the Court's view those conditions were met in the above-mentioned French case, as further shown by the judgment of 26 November 2015 in *Ebrahimian v. France*[42] concerning a ban on wearing the Islamic headscarf in a public hospital, resulting in the non-renewal of the employment contract of a woman of Islamic religion who insisted on wearing the headscarf.

The conditions were also met in a case concerning Belgian legislation from 2011 mirroring the French law banning the wearing of the Islamic headscarf in public places. According to the Court,[43] the legislation in question had been adopted at the end of a complex legislative process that made it possible to strike a proper balance between the various conflicting general and individual interests and also provided for proportionate penalties in the event of violation of the ban.

It is therefore not surprising that the Belgian case, following a reference for a preliminary ruling by a national court, also ended up before the ECJ, which adopted the same solution described above. Particularly striking is the fact that the Luxembourg Court,[44] while obviously basing its decision on EU law (although citing Article 9 ECHR and the constitutional traditions common to the Member States) referred to principles and values relied on by the Strasbourg Court, such as the neutral stance that can be adopted by the State and the use of non-discriminatory practices against certain categories of individuals for religious or other reasons.

4.3.4 Supervision of the Execution of Judgments

Finally, it should be noted that the supervision of compliance with ECtHR judgments is the responsibility of the CMCoE. On the basis of the amendments made to article 46 ECHR by Protocol No. 14, the Committee, on the one hand, if it "considers that the supervision of the execution of a final judgment is hindered by a problem of interpretation of the judgment, may refer the matter to the Court for a ruling on the question of interpretation".[45] On the other hand, the Committee, "after serving formal notice on that Party" to comply with a final judgment of the Court, may "refer to the Court the question whether that Party has failed to fulfil its obligation" to abide by the final judgment of the Court.[46]

---

[42] Appl. no. 64846/11.

[43] See the judgment of 11 July 2017, *Belcacemi and Oussar v. Belgium*, appl. no. 37798/13, concerning, again, an Islamic headscarf.

[44] See the judgment of 14 March 2017 in *Achbita*, C-157/15.

[45] See Article 46(3) ECHR.

[46] See Article 46(4) ECHR.

In the case of *Ilgar Mammadov v. Azerbaijan*,[47] the CMCoE in its resolution of 7 December 2017 served formal notice on Azerbaijan to comply with the judgment of 22 May 2014 concerning violation of Articles 5, 6 and 18 ECHR, respectively on personal freedom and security, fair trial and State restrictions used for purposes other than those established by the ECHR, following the unlawful conviction and detention of an individual responsible solely for having criticised the work of the government. When Azerbaijan did not comply, the Committee initiated infringement proceedings before the Court.

Referring to the principle of good faith in the execution of decisions adopted by it, the Grand Chamber, in its judgment of 29 May 2019,[48] found that Azerbaijan had breached its obligation to comply with the final judgments of the Court. Pursuant to Article 46(5) ECHR, the matter was therefore again referred to the CMCoE "for consideration of the measures to be taken", with the effect that the Committee once again dealt with the case, which concluded after much delay with a judgment of acquittal of 23 April 2020 issued by the Azerbaijani Supreme Court, the awarding of compensation to Mammadov and his subsequent release.

4.4 The Other Regional Human Rights Courts

Finally, it is necessary to look at some other regional systems for the protection of human rights and the bodies in charge of scrutinising compliance with the conventions involved.

4.4.1 The Inter-American Court of Human Rights

An advanced system of human rights protection was established among American countries through the conclusion of the ACHR of 22 November 1969.

It provides that "any person or group of persons, or any non-governmental entity legally recognized in one or more member states of the Organization" may lodge petitions with the Commission "containing denunciations or complaints of violation of this Convention by a State Party"[49] after the exhaustion of domestic remedies. Provision is also made for inter-State communications between Organisation of American States (OAS) Members. For this latter mechanism and unlike petitions of an individual nature, it is necessary to ascertain that both States involved in the proceedings have recognised the competence of the IACommHR to receive and examine this type of communication.[50]

---

[47] Appl. no. 15172/13.

[48] Appl. no. 15172/13.

[49] See Article 44 ACHR.

[50] *Id.*, Article 45.

For all types of complaints submitted to the IACommHR, the aim of the Commission is to achieve a friendly settlement of the dispute. It follows that the Commission is not judicial in nature. If the Commission determines that a State party is in breach of the Convention, it is obliged to draw up a non-binding report, including proposals and recommendations for the offending State, and to forward it to the States concerned. Within three months after the sending of the report, the Commission, or the State party to the dispute, may bring an action before the Court, but only against States that have accepted the jurisdiction of the Court to examine such disputes.[51]

The American system of human rights exhibits different characteristics from that of the ECHR with reference to the supervision of the execution of IACtHR judgments, which is not carried out by a political body—as is the case under the ECHR through the CMCoE (although with the important changes mentioned above)[52]—but directly by the Court. On the one hand, the Court monitors the implementation of its judgments on the basis of a detailed report that the respondent State is required to submit to it in relation to the specific case and "observations to those reports by the victims or their legal representatives". The Commission shall present observations both to the State's reports and the observations of the victims or their representatives. If the Court deems it to be appropriate, it "may convene the State and the victims' representatives to a hearing in order to monitor compliance with its decisions; the Court shall hear the opinion of the Commission at that hearing".[53] On the other hand, the Court reports annually to the General Assembly of the OAS on the implementation of its judgments, pointing out, if necessary, critical points regarding the implementation of certain decisions by the States held responsible and formulating "pertinent recommendations" in that regard.[54] This has allowed the Court, through an extensive interpretation of the rules of the ACHR and its own Rules of Procedure, to proceed to a rather precise examination of compliance with its judgments.

At the request of OAS Member States, the IACtHR may also give advisory opinions on the interpretation of the ACHR or other treaties concerning the protection of human rights in the Americas. This IACtHR competence, which the Court considers to be an expression of its broad and unrestricted ("*amplio y no restrictivo*") power of interpretation,[55] has been repeatedly invoked by the Member States and has enabled the Court to clarify the scope of many obligations, both substantive and procedural, contained in the ACHR and other human rights treaties. Again at the request of an OAS Member State, the Court can provide it with an opinion on the compatibility of any of its domestic laws with the ACHR.[56]

---

[51] *Id.*, Articles 61–62.

[52] See Sect. 4.3.4.

[53] See Article 69 of the Rules of Procedure of the Court.

[54] See Article 65 ACHR.

[55] Recently, see the opinion of 9 November 2020, OC-26/20, on *The Obligations in Matters of Human Rights of a State that has Denounced the American Convention on Human Rights and the Charter of the Organization of American States*, para 14.

[56] Finally, at the request of certain OAS organs, the Court may also give advisory opinions concerning their activities; see Article 64, paras 1–2, ACHR.

4.4.2 *The African Court on Human and Peoples' Rights and the New African Court of Justice and Human Rights*

The most significant aspect of the African system for the protection of human rights consists in the adoption, on 27 June 1981 and within the framework of the Organization for African Unity (now the African Union, "AU"), of the African Charter on Human and Peoples' Rights ("ACHPR") and the machinery for ensuring compliance therewith. On the basis of the ACHPR, the African Commission on Human and Peoples' Rights ("ACommHPR") was established, which, although lacking binding powers, is tasked with examining both the periodic reports of States parties on compliance with the Charter as well as inter-State communications concerning violations of the Charter itself, and communications submitted by individuals or non-governmental organisations complaining of similar violations.

With the Protocol of 10 June 1998, the African Court on Human and Peoples' Rights ("ACtHPRA") was created. In addition to having an important advisory function, it has broad adjudicatory powers in relation to disputes on the interpretation and application of the African Charter, the 1998 Protocol and any other human rights treaty ratified by the States parties to the dispute.[57] This considerable jurisdiction *ratione materiae* has allowed the Court, after an initial more restrictive approach, to establish the violation by AU Member States of human rights that are grounded in relevant international treaties concluded also at the universal level (in particular the ICCPR and the ICESCR). This was the case in the judgment of 11 May 2018 in *Association Pour le Progrès et la Défense Des Droits Des Femmes Maliennes (APDF) and the Institute for Human Rights and Development in Africa (IHRDA) v. Republic of Mali*,[58] concerning numerous violations committed by Mali following the implementation in the country of legislation, adopted in 2011, which discriminates against women in various matters, in particular as regards the age at which they can marry compared to men, their inheritance rights, etc.

The Court's adjudicatory function comes into play on the basis of cases submitted by the Commission (if the same case has previously been submitted to the Commission itself), by the States parties to the dispute before the Commission, by the State Party whose citizen is a victim of violations committed by other States, or by individuals and particularly qualified non-governmental organisations with observer status before the Commission. In the latter instance, the application is admissible on condition that the respondent State has made a prior declaration of acceptance of the Court's jurisdiction, which in practice may also be withdrawn by the State making the declaration, as unfortunately happened as regards several countries (Benin, Côte d'Ivoire, Rwanda and Tanzania) between 2016 and 2020. Unlike with individual applications to the ECtHR, the African system does not demand the status of victim of a specific violation be demonstrated because the relevant rules "do not require

[57] See Article 3(1) of the Protocol.

[58] Appl. no. 046/2016.

individuals or NGOs to demonstrate a personal interest in an Application in order to access the Court, especially in the case of public interest litigation".[59]

ACtHPRA judgments are binding and are transmitted to the parties to the dispute and to all other AU Member States, to the ACommHPR and to the AU Executive Council, which monitors their proper implementation on the basis of annual reports submitted by the Court—which gives an opinion on States' compliance with the judgments concerning them—to the Conference of Heads of State and Government of the AU.

Finally, it should be noted that the Protocol adopted on 1 July 2008 approved the Statute of the African Court of Justice and Human Rights ("ACtJHR"), which, once in force, will lead to repeal of the aforementioned Protocol of 10 June 1998 and hence the end of the ACtHPRA. The jurisdiction vested in the ACtJHR is even broader than that of the ACtHPRA established in 1998, covering, specifically in the field of human rights, disputes on the interpretation and application of the rules of the ACHPR, the Charter on the Rights and Welfare of the Child, the Protocol to the African Charter on the Rights of Women in Africa and any other human rights treaty ratified by the parties to the dispute submitted to the Court.[60]

4.5 The Arab and Asian Systems of Human Rights Protection

4.5.1 The Arab System

Some doubts have already been raised about the lack of balanced solutions concerning the relationship between universality and cultural diversity in the framework of the ArCHR of 2004, in particular, in the face of the evident discrimination between men and women admissible under Article 3 of the Charter.[61] On a more general level, it should be noted that the Arab Charter protects several human rights belonging to the first and second generation and has established a system, albeit a weak one, for monitoring compliance with the provisions of the Charter, centred on the functioning of the Arab Human Rights Committee, which is tasked with examining periodic State reports (every three years) on compliance with the Charter. State reports are the subject of "recommendations in accordance with the aims of the Charter", to be annexed to the annual report, which is then presented by the Committee to the Arab League Council and subsequently made public.[62]

---

[59] See the judgment of the ACtHPRA of 27 November 2020, *XYZ v. Republic of Benin*, appl. no. 010/2020, para 48.

[60] See Article 28(1)(c) of the Statute of the ACtJHR.

[61] See Chap. 2, Sect. 2.5.

[62] See Article 48 of the Arab Charter.

An important step forward in the protection of human rights by Arab countries was taken with the approval, on 7 September 2014, of the statute, which has not yet entered into force, of the Arab Court of Human Rights, vested with jurisdiction to adjudicate on disputes relating to the interpretation and application of the ArCHR or "any other Arab convention in the field of human rights involving a member State".[63]

A right of access to the Court is granted to States claiming violation of the human rights of their nationals—hence in accordance with the concept of diplomatic protection—on condition that both the applicant State and the respondent State are parties to the Statute of the Court, or have accepted its jurisdiction "whether in a specific case or in general". A further and optional *locus standi in judicio* is provided for in favour of non-governmental organisations accredited as human rights bodies in the respondent State and expressly authorised by the latter to bring actions against it.[64]

4.5.2 The Asian System

More elementary in nature is the system of protection of human rights established among the countries of South East Asia, which was touched upon in the analysis of the Bangkok Declaration of 1993 in the context of the topic of the universality of human rights.[65]

Among the other non-mandatory instruments adopted by the Association of Southeast Asian Nations (ASEAN), worth mentioning is the Declaration on Human Rights of 18 November 2012, which contains not only a list of several traditional rights—civil, political, economic, social and cultural rights—but also a detailed reference to the right to development, classified as "an inalienable human right", and to the right to peace, the latter accompanied by the commitment of ASEAN member countries "to enhance friendship and cooperation in the furtherance of peace, harmony and stability in the region".[66]

Another important and specific feature of the aforementioned Declaration is the provision therein to the effect that the enjoyment of human rights must be balanced by "corresponding duties", since every human being "has responsibilities to all other individuals, the community and the society where one lives". That provision is completed by the further one that human rights must be exercised "with due regard to the human rights and fundamental freedoms of others".[67]

In our opinion, the content of these clauses reflects the influence, in some of the most important countries of South East Asia, of the previously mentioned Marxist doctrines concerning the value of the "community" dimension of human rights, aimed both at protecting the interests of the national community as a whole, and at affirming

---

[63] See Article 16 of the Statute.

[64] *Id.*, Articles 19–20.

[65] See Chap. 2, Sect. 2.4.1.

[66] See points 35–38 of the Declaration.

[67] *Id.*, paras 6 and 8.

the existence of the individual's duties towards the national community.[68] From a practical point of view, both the reference to the duties that the single individual possesses towards other individuals and the national community, and the clarification of the necessary balance between the various individual rights, allow a greater and at times excessive limitation of individual rights.

Comprehension Check and Tasks

1. What are the bodies established by the ECHR to ensure observance thereof and what is the specific role of the CMCoE, also in the light of the changes introduced by Protocol 14? (Sects. 4.1–4.3)
2. What is new since the entry into force of Protocol 16? (Sect. 4.1)
3. What are the general measures indicated by the ECtHR and what situations may warrant their adoption? (Sect. 4.3.1)
4. In the event of a warning judgment, is a subsequent finding of violation by the State in question automatic? (Sect. 4.3.3)
5. Which body monitors the enforcement of IACtHR judgments? (Sect. 4.4.1)
6. What is the jurisdiction of the ACtHPRA? (Sect. 4.4.2)

[68] See Chap. 2, Sect. 2.4.

Chapter 5
The United Nations and Human Rights

Contents

Abstract The chapter examines the contribution of the United Nations to the creation and progressive development of international human rights law. It first focuses on the main control bodies established by human rights treaties concluded within the framework of the UN. While these bodies do not adopt binding acts, their decisions are sometimes taken into consideration by national—even supreme—courts. Afterwards, the role played by the main UN organs in the field of human rights is analyzed, paying specific attention to the practice of the Security Council and to the interplay between its functions and those of the International Criminal Court.

P. Pustorino, *Introduction to International Human Rights Law*,
https://doi.org/10.1007/978-94-6265-563-8_5

5.1 The Contribution of the UN to the Development of the International Protection of Human Rights

As mentioned in Chap. 1,[1] the birth and functioning of the UN constituted a fundamental *watershed* in terms of the development of the protection of human rights, contributing decisively to the process of internationalisation of that area of law and ensuring an increased effectiveness of the system of protection of individual and collective rights.

In the UN Charter, respect for rights of human beings is among the aims of the organisation, whose purposes include promoting and encouraging "respect for human rights and for fundamental freedoms for all without distinction as to race, sex, language, or religion".[2] A position that is reaffirmed in similar terms in Article 55, in which, with a view to creating conditions of stability and well-being which are necessary for peaceful and friendly relations among nations, it is declared that the UN is to promote "universal respect for, and observance of, human rights and fundamental freedoms for all without distinction as to race, sex, language, or religion".[3]

The said provisions of the Charter are however informed by an *inter-State logic* and are designed to further the attainment of the UN's main objective: the maintenance of international peace and security. Nevertheless, the application of the Charter has led to the superseding of the above-mentioned restrictive approach to the point that the protection of human rights has been afforded separate dignity and importance in the UN framework, so as to untie human rights from the objective of safeguarding international peace and security. The result is the dismantling of one of the fundamental tenets for the protection of State sovereignty: the principle of domestic jurisdiction, contained in Article 2(7) of the UN Charter and applicable to the activities of any UN organ with the exception of the "enforcement measures" taken by the UNSC on the basis of Chapter VII of the Charter. In fact, it is indisputable that the principle of domestic jurisdiction can no longer be invoked by UN Member States, at least with reference to serious violations of human rights.

That said, the overall work of the UN has been marked by the drafting of numerous international treaties, the text of which was conceived within the framework of that organisation, and by the adoption of a very broad series of acts, which though mainly characterizable as *soft law*,[4] have nevertheless contributed significantly to the formation of customary norms on human rights. Also worth highlighting is the more specific function of ascertaining and condemning violations committed by Member States, consisting especially of measures that are non-binding but nonetheless have a strong political dimension, such as the resolutions adopted by various UN organs in reaction to serious violations of human rights. There has been no shortage of binding

[1] See Chap. 1, Sect. 1.1.

[2] See Article 1(3).

[3] See Article 55(3).

[4] On soft law, see Chap. 3, Sect. 3.11.

measures either, adopted by the UNSC in response to gross violations of human rights committed by States, natural persons or legal entities.

5.2 The Monitoring Bodies Set Up in the UN Human Rights Treaties

There are many bodies monitoring the observance of human rights protected by conventions drawn up within the framework of the UN, and they have various functions and powers even if not binding. It is thus not possible to give a complete account of the work done by those bodies, which is often similar and sometimes overlaps in practice. In any event, some of these systems of controls will be referred to later, when analysing certain individual or collective rights that have their basis in international treaties establishing forms of scrutiny of compliance with treaty provisions, such as the 1973 Convention on the Elimination and Punishment of the Crime of Apartheid.[5] We will therefore concentrate on examining a number of monitoring bodies, chosen both because they are particularly relevant at the international level and because their decisions, while not binding, have sometimes been implemented at the national level.

5.2.1 The Human Rights Committee

Commencing the analysis from the ICCPR, it should be noted that it provides for a detailed system of controls, centred on the functions of the HRC established by the Covenant and based on the obligation of States to submit periodic reports on the overall state of compliance with their conventional obligations as well as the right to submit individual and inter-State communications.

Periodic reports,[6] formally addressed by States to the UN Secretary-General ("UNSG"), are now sent at the request of the Committee whereas in the past they were sent at some predetermined intervals. However, there were and still are serious delays in sending the reports. In this regard, the Committee does not have fact-finding powers, although it can rely on the work of other UN international human rights bodies, UN specialised agencies and non-governmental organisations in order to establish the facts relevant to the assessment of a State's report.

The Committee has no binding powers and can only establish a follow-up procedure on compliance with the "reports" and "general comments" adopted in relation to this specific competence. Comments that can be then transmitted to States Parties, which in turn are entitled to submit "observations on any comments", and to the Economic and Social Council ("ECOSOC"). It should be noted that the Committee

[5] For an examination of that Convention, see Chap. 7, Sect. 7.8.

[6] See Article 40 ICCPR.

may proceed to examine a State situation even if the report is not sent, a problem that is catered for by the appointment of a special rapporteur.

In relation to inter-State communications concerning violations of the provisions of the Covenant, they can be submitted to the HRC on condition that the States concerned have recognised "at any time" the competence of the Committee to receive and consider such communications.[7] The procedure in question is rather cumbersome and consists of a first phase which can be defined as diplomatic and operates exclusively at a bilateral level between the two States concerned. In the event that the matter is not resolved "to the satisfaction of both States Parties", either one may refer the matter to the Committee. Even at this stage, the role of the monitoring body is predominantly diplomatic in nature, as the HRC can offer its "good offices" to resolve the issue, while respecting the human rights protected by the Covenant. If this attempt fails, the Committee can finally decide on the merits within one year after the matter was referred to it, affording the parties in the meantime the opportunity to make submissions.

The final report of the Committee is not binding and is communicated to the parties to the proceedings, which, if they consider that the solution indicated by the Committee is not satisfactory, may request the HRC to establish a non-binding conciliation procedure, the triggering of which is subject to the "prior consent of the States Parties concerned".[8] The conciliation commission so established also lacks binding powers.

Finally, the First Optional Protocol, adopted at the same time as the ICCPR, provides for the possibility of submitting individual communications concerning violations of the provisions of the Covenant, but only against States that have ratified the Protocol in question. The standard conditions for admissibility of communications include the rule of prior exhaustion of all available domestic remedies, except those whose application is "unreasonably prolonged" at the national level. In addition, it is provided that the HRC may not consider any individual communication "unless it has ascertained that the same matter is not being examined under another procedure of international investigation or settlement", thereby meaning that the absence of pending litigation at the time of the submission of the communication to the HRC is another condition of admissibility. No formal time limits are set for the submission of a communication compared to when the violation was committed.

The rules on admissibility of individual communications submitted to the Committee are hence less restrictive than those laid down in other treaty-based human rights systems, but some States Parties have made reservations to the rules under consideration, including an international *lis pendens* clause, in order to avoid duplication of pending applications or conflict with decisions already taken by other international bodies. However, the Committee has recently interpreted such reservations restrictively, ruling out that the inadmissibility decision of a single judge of the ECtHR, which does not entail an examination "however limited on the merits" of the dispute, constitutes an obstacle to the Committee's examination of the same

---

[7] See Article 41 of the Covenant.

[8] See Article 42 of the Covenant.

case.[9] The Committee's position appears to be acceptable in view of the previously mentioned fact that decisions taken by a single judge of the Strasbourg Court do not specify in detail the inadmissibility grounds.[10]

Furthermore, in the practice of the HRC, there has been a clear tendency to treat individual communications submitted after a long period of time has elapsed and without the author of the communication being able to provide adequate justification in this regard as an abuse of the right to make submissions.[11] On the one hand, this stance seeks to standardise the interpretation and application of the procedural rules in the matter of individual complaints or applications submitted to the various bodies charged with scrutinising observance of human rights conventions. On the other hand, it seeks to safeguard the principle of the rule of law, thus avoiding an analysis of the lawfulness of State conduct dating back in time.

Individual communications, which can also be the subject matter of interim measures, are decided by non-binding "views", which are transmitted to the State concerned and to the individual who has triggered the procedure. Those views can include "recommendations" concerning, for example, the modification of laws or administrative acts, compensation for the harm suffered by the individual or the punishment of those responsible for certain conduct in violation of the rights contained in the Covenant. Again in this case, there is a follow-up procedure which may lead to further positions being taken by the Committee.

5.2.2 *The Committee on Economic, Social and Cultural Rights*

The monitoring system established by the ICESCR is similar to that of the ICCPR and hence a short overview suffices here.

At the outset it should be noted that the second Covenant did not initially provide for a specific body to monitor compliance with its provisions. That body was subsequently created, under the name of the Committee on Economic, Social and Cultural Rights (CESCR), by ECOSOC with Resolution No. 17 of 28 May 1985.

Originally, i.e. before the entry into force of the Optional Protocol mentioned below, there was solely a procedure for the submission of periodical reports by the State party to the Covenant[12] to the UNSG and forwarded by the latter to ECOSOC,

---

[9] See views of 13 March 2020, *Elena Genero v. Italy*, CCPR/C/128/D/2979/2017, para 6.2.

[10] See Chap. 4, Sect. 4.2.

[11] The said tendency now finds its legal basis in the Rules of Procedures of the HRC. Pursuant to Article 99(b), applicable to communications received by the Committee as of 1 January 2012, "a communication may constitute an abuse of the right of submission, when it is submitted five years after the exhaustion of domestic remedies by the author of the communication, or, where applicable, three years from the conclusion of another procedure of international investigation or settlement, unless there are reasons justifying the delay, taking into account all the circumstances of the communication".

[12] See Articles 16–17 ICESCR.

which undertook a summary examination and, if it deemed appropriate, forwarded the reports to the former UN Commission on Human Rights ("UNCommHR"), to the UNGA and to other UN organs. That task is now vested in the CESCR.

On the basis of the Optional Protocol approved by the UNGA, further to Resolution No. 63/117 of 10 December 2008, CESCR has been granted new competences in the examination of communications coming from States, individuals or groups of individuals subject to the jurisdiction of States parties claiming to be victims of a violation of one of the rights protected by the Covenant. While the competence of the Committee to receive individual communications is *automatic* following the ratification of the Protocol in question, for State communications it is necessary that both the State sending the communication and the State accused of the violation have made a specific declaration of acceptance of the competence of the CESCR to receive and consider such communications.

The conditions of admissibility for individual communications are similar to those governing communications that can be submitted to the HRC as well as those governing applications to the ECtHR.[13] In relation to the Committee's consideration of the merits of individual communications, the provisions of Article 8(4) of the 2008 Protocol are particularly relevant: in examining that type of applications the CESCR must assess "the reasonableness of the steps taken by the State Party", taking into account the fact that the State Party "may adopt a range of possible policy measures for the implementation of the rights set forth in the Covenant". The content of these *generous* provisions of the Protocol reflects the aforementioned nature of most of the substantive obligations established by the Covenant, consisting of obligations to be progressively achieved, which grant the State a wide margin of appreciation both with regard to the timing and the manner of implementation of the provisions of the Covenant.[14]

Assessments of the merits of individual communications are contained, again in this case, in non-binding "views" with accompanying "recommendations" communicated to the parties to the proceedings. The State is obliged to take them into consideration and, within six months after their receipt, to give a written reply setting out the measures adopted following the indications formulated by the Committee.[15]

Inter-State communications that can be submitted to CESCR are regulated in a very similar way to those that can be submitted to the HRC. Likewise in this case, the procedure is initially diplomatic in nature, through consultation with the parties and through the Committee's good offices, after which it becomes contentious if no solution is found. In all cases, the final report adopted by the Committee is not binding.

[13] See Chap. 4, Sect. 4.2.

[14] See Chap. 3, Sect. 3.10.

[15] See Article 9 ICESCR.

5.2.3 *The Committee on the Elimination of Racial Discrimination*

Turning now to analyse other systems for monitoring observance of certain universal conventions on human rights concluded under the aegis of the UN, it is necessary to focus on the competences respectively of the Committee on the Elimination of Racial Discrimination ("CommERD") set up by the International Convention on the Elimination of All Forms of Racial Discrimination of 21 December 1965, the Committee on the Elimination of Discrimination against Women ("CommEDAW") set up by the Convention on the Elimination of All Forms of Discrimination against Women of 18 December 1979, the Committee against Torture ("CAT") set up by the Convention against Torture and Other Cruel, Inhuman or Degrading Treatment or Punishment of 10 December 1984 and finally the Committee on Enforced Disappearances ("CED") set up by the International Convention for the Protection of All Persons from Enforced Disappearance of 20 December 2006.

In relation to CommERD, it should be noted that it is primarily competent to examine reports submitted by States parties every two years, or at the request of the Committee, concerning legislative, judicial, administrative or other measures taken to comply with the provisions of the 1965 Convention. Assessments and possible recommendations of a general nature, which do not have binding effect and are made by the Committee in relation to the various State reports, may be included in the annual report to be submitted to the UNGA.[16]

The CommERD also oversees a cumbersome and consequently inefficient procedure for evaluating inter-State communications. In brief, if a State party considers that any other State party is not giving effect to the provisions of the Convention, it may bring the matter "to the attention of the Committee", which in turn transmits the communication to the State party concerned, which is obliged, within three months, to send its observations to the Committee and to explain any remedies adopted. The two States involved in the procedure, within six months after the receipt by the receiving State of the initial communication, may resolve the dispute in question bilaterally through negotiations or other traditional means of disputes settlement. If these means of disputes settlement fail, either State may refer the matter back to the CommERD.[17]

When examining a rare inter-State communication, the Committee, in a decision on matters related to jurisdiction, pointed out that the procedure in question establishes "an automatic inter-State complaint mechanism", without any prior or subsequent consent of the States parties concerned[18] and specified that this "unique instrument" for resolving inter-State disputes was set up "for the common good of

[16] See Article 9 of the Convention.

[17] *Id.*, Article 11(1)–(2).

[18] See the decision of 12 December 2019, *State of Palestine v. Israel*, CERD/C/100/5, para 3.38.

all States parties"[19] in view of the *erga omnes* nature of the obligations established by the Convention.

Notwithstanding the particular emphasis placed on the procedure in question by the Committee, it should be noted that when it declares that it has jurisdiction to deal with substantive issues concerning inter-State communications, the CommERD can only appoint an ad hoc conciliation commission with the aim of encouraging the States concerned to reach an amicable solution to the dispute based on respect for the Convention.[20] The complex procedure thus comes to an end with the issuing of a report by the conciliation commission, in which the facts of the dispute are ascertained and the appropriate recommendations are adopted with a view to reaching, once again, an amicable solution to the dispute.

The report in question is transmitted to the parties to the dispute, who have six months in which to inform the CommERD of their willingness to carry out what is indicated therein. Upon the expiration of that period, the report is to be transmitted to all other States parties to the Convention.[21] In the inter-State case cited above, the Committee, in its admissibility decision of 30 April 2021, requested its Chair "to appoint, in accordance with Article 12(1) of the Convention, the members of an ad hoc Conciliation Commission which shall make its good offices available to the States concerned with a view to an amicable solution of the matter on the basis of States parties' compliance with the Convention".[22]

Finally, the CommERD has competence in relation to communications submitted by individuals or groups of individuals under the "jurisdiction" of a State Party who claim to be victims of a violation of the Convention by that State, provided that the State Party has recognised the competence of the Committee to receive such communications. In order to facilitate the observance of the Convention, provision is also made for States parties to establish a national body empowered to receive petitions on violations of the Convention. Communications submitted individually or collectively are then transmitted by the CommERD to the State in question, which, within a period of three months, must communicate to the Committee its observations and any remedies adopted, in a manner similar to that of the preliminary phase of the procedure for the examination of inter-State communications by other bodies analysed above. Having examined the substance of the matter, the CommERD must notify the State concerned and the petitioner of its observations and any recommendations, including in its annual report a summary of the communications received and, where appropriate, a summary of the explanations and statements of the States Parties concerned and of its own suggestions and recommendations.[23]

[19] *Id.*, para 3.41.

[20] See Article 12(1) of the Convention.

[21] *Id.*, Article 13.

[22] See para 66 of the Decision, CERD/C/103/R.6.

[23] *Id.*, Article 14.

5.2.4 The Committee on the Elimination of Discrimination Against Women

With reference to the Committee on the Elimination of Discrimination against Women, it should be noted that under the 1979 Convention it examines periodic reports submitted by States parties "on the legislative, judicial, administrative or other measures which they have adopted to give effect to the provisions of the present Convention and on the progress made in this respect".[24] In addition, on the basis of the Optional Protocol of 6 October 1999 and only in relation to States parties to the Protocol, the CommEDAW may conduct inquiries into serious and systematic violations of women's rights in a State party, adopt recommendations to that State[25] and receive communications from individuals or groups of individuals claiming to be victims of a violation of one of the rights covered by the Convention.[26]

As regards CommEDAW decisions on individual communications, it should be noted that, although such decisions are not binding in nature, they are sometimes given effects in whole or in part by supreme national courts of the country that is a party to proceedings before the Committee. For example, in its judgment of 17 July 2018 No. 1263 the Spanish Supreme Court[27] gave effect to the decision adopted on 16 July 2014 by CommEDAW in the case of *Angela González Carreño v. Spain*,[28] in which it (i) found that Spain was responsible for failing to prevent, on the basis of the principle of due diligence, the killing of the applicant's daughter by her father notwithstanding the father's continuous and concrete threats against both women and (ii) awarded monetary compensation to the applicant.

The Court based its reasoning on a coordinated interpretation of the Spanish Constitution (in relation to the provisions giving special legal force to international treaties in general and, more specifically, to treaties on the international protection of human rights),[29] the 1979 Convention and the Optional Protocol cited above. In particular, the Spanish Supreme Court referred to the obligations imposed on the State party respectively to take all necessary measures at the national level to ensure "the full realization of the rights recognized"[30] in the Convention and to give "due consideration to the views of the Committee".[31] On the basis of these assumptions, the Court concluded that Spain was obliged to make financial reparations to the applicant.

From a general point of view, the decision of the Spanish Supreme Court highlights how the raising of the overall level of protection of human rights within the national

---

[24] See Article 18 of the Convention.

[25] See Article 8 of the Protocol.

[26] *Id.*, Article 2.

[27] *María de los Ángeles González Carreño v. Ministry of Justice.*

[28] See CEDAW/C/58/D/47/2012.

[29] See respectively Articles 96 and 10(2) of the Spanish Constitution.

[30] See Article 24 of the Convention.

[31] See Article 7(4) of the Protocol.

legal systems may result not only from the implementation of real legal obligations of the State, but also from a series of other factors and elements—such as, in this case, the non-binding decision of an international body operating at the universal level—capable of triggering a virtuous process that can lead to very significant results in terms of strengthening the protection of human rights at the domestic level.

5.2.5 The Committee Against Torture

With regard to CAT's competence, first and foremost it examines periodic reports submitted by States parties on compliance with the rules of the Convention and may make recommendations to the State party in the form of concluding observations.[32] In addition, it may conduct inquiries into "well-founded indications that torture is being systematically practised in the territory of a State Party"[33] and adopt "general comments" on the interpretation of specific conventional rules. The Committee's competence also covers both inter-State and individual communications alleging violations of the rules of the Convention by a State Party, provided that the States concerned have accepted the CAT's competence to receive such communications.[34] Finally, under the Optional Protocol of 18 December 2002, the Committee against Torture's Subcommittee on Prevention of Torture and Other Cruel, Inhuman or Degrading Treatment or Punishment was established to conduct visits to prevent acts of torture and inhuman or degrading treatment in States where deprivation of individual liberty has occurred (for example, where people are detained) and to make recommendations to States where such visits have taken place.[35]

5.2.6 The Committee on Enforced Disappearances

Established by the 2006 Convention for the Protection of All Persons from Enforced Disappearance,[36] the CED has similar competences to those of the other committees operating within the framework of the UN conventions already analysed. In particular, each State party must submit a report to the CED on the measures taken to give effect to its obligations under the Convention, within two years after the Convention's entry into force for the State party. The report, made available to all States parties through the UNSG, must be considered by the Committee, which may communicate to the State party "comments, observations or recommendations as it may deem

[32] See Article 19 of the 1984 Convention.

[33] *Id.*, Article 20.

[34] *Id.*, Articles 21–22.

[35] See Parts I to III of the Protocol.

[36] See Article 26.

appropriate". The same State party may respond to the observations received "on its own initiative or at the request of the Committee".[37]

Pursuant to Articles 31–32 of the Convention, the CED is also empowered to receive individual and inter-State communications if the State parties concerned, at the time of ratification or at any time afterwards, have declared that they recognise the competence of the Committee respectively "to receive and consider communications from or on behalf of individuals subject to its jurisdiction claiming to be victims of a violation by this State Party of provisions of this Convention"[38] and "to receive and consider communications in which a State Party claims that another State Party is not fulfilling its obligations under this Convention". The individual communications considered admissible are transmitted to the State party concerned, requesting it to provide observations and comments within a time limit set by the Committee. Furthermore, the CED may transmit to the State party concerned for its "urgent consideration" a request that the latter take "such interim measures as may be necessary to avoid possible irreparable damage to the victims of the alleged violation".[39] The CED must inform the author of a communication of the responses provided by the State party concerned and when the Committee decides "to finalize the procedure", it must communicate its views to the State party and to the aforementioned author.[40]

Pursuant to Article 33 of the Convention, if the CED receives reliable information indicating that a State party is seriously violating the treaty provisions, it may, after consultation with the State party concerned, request one or more of its members to undertake a visit, subject to the State's consent, and report back to it without delay. After the visit, the CED will communicate to the State party its observations and recommendations.[41]

Finally, it is necessary to recall a further and particular competence of the CED, provided for in Article 30 of the 2006 Convention. In fact, a request that a disappeared person should be sought and found may be submitted to the Committee, "as a matter of urgency", by relatives of the disappeared person or their legal representatives, their counsel or any person authorised by them, as well as by any other person having a legitimate interest. If the CED considers that the request for urgent action is not manifestly unfounded, does not constitute an abuse of the right of submission, has already been duly presented to the competent bodies of the State Party

[37] See Article 29.

[38] Individual communications are considered inadmissible if they are anonymous, constitute an abuse of the right of submission or are incompatible with the Convention's provisions, or the same matter is being examined under another procedure of international investigation or settlement of the same nature or when all effective available domestic remedies have not been exhausted: see Article 31(2).

[39] See Articles 31(3) and 31(4).

[40] See Article 31(5).

[41] In case of "well-founded indications that enforced disappearance is being practised on a widespread or systematic basis in the territory under the jurisdiction of a State Party", Article 34 empowers the Committee to urgently bring the matter to the attention of the UNGA through the UNSG, after seeking from the State party concerned all relevant information on the situation.

concerned, is not incompatible with the provisions of the Convention or the same matter is not being examined under another procedure of international investigation or settlement of the same nature, it will request the State party concerned to provide it with information on the situation of the persons sought, within a time limit set by the CED. On the basis of the information provided by the State Party concerned, the Committee may transmit recommendations to the State, including the request to take all the necessary measures, amongst which interim measures, to locate and protect the person concerned and to inform the CED, within a specified period of time, of measures taken, taking into account the urgency of the situation. The CED will inform the person submitting the urgent action request of its recommendations and of the information provided to it by the State. The CED must continue its efforts to work with the State party concerned for as long as the fate of the person sought remains unresolved, briefing the person who initially submitted the request.

Precisely in relation to the said competence of the Committee, the Supreme Court of Justice of Mexico recently stated in its judgment of 16 June 2021[42] that the State is under an obligation to comply with the urgent actions of CED, thus confirming the tendency—already mentioned with reference to the competences of CommEDAW—of some national supreme courts to apply non-binding decisions of certain UN committees in national legal systems. According to the Court, the said urgent actions "*están dirigidas a proteger la esfera jurídica de una persona o personas perfectamente delimitadas frente a una violación de derechos humanos que puede generar los peores efectos si no se interviene con prontitud*". On those grounds, "*Estas acciones suponen, entonces, el acceso a una protección reforzada*".[43] It follows for the Court that "*Suponer que las acciones urgentes no establecen obligaciones a cargo de las autoridades responsables, susceptibles de ser supervisadas constitucional o judicialmente, es restar efecto útil a la Convención Internacional para la protección de todas las personas contra las desapariciones forzadas*" and "*disminuir injustificadamente la esfera de protección de las personas sujetas a la jurisdicción del Estado mexicano*", concluding that "*esta Sala no alberga dudas respecto a la obligatoriedad de las acciones urgentes, emitidas por el Comité contra la Desaparición Forzada*".[44]

5.3 The Role of the UN General Assembly, Economic and Social Council and Human Rights Council

Under the UN Charter, the main responsibility for human rights lies with the UNGA and ECOSOC. While these competences have been exercised by the UNGA in the past and still today for the most part, ECOSOC's competences have been progressively reduced: on the one hand, precisely because of the massive intervention in this field by the UNGA, of which ECOSOC is de facto a subsidiary organ despite

[42] See *Amparo en revisión* no. 1077/2019.

[43] See para 130.

[44] *Id.*, paras 132–133.

the fact that it is formally classified as a "principal organ" of the UN under Article 7 of the Charter; and, on the other hand, because the competences originally vested in ECOSOC by various acts adopted within the framework of the UN or by international conventions, as in the case of the CESCR analysed above, have been allocated to other bodies that have subsequently been established, such as the aforementioned CESCR and the Human Rights Council.

5.3.1 The UNGA and ECOSOC

The UNGA and ECOSOC have adopted series of both non-binding resolutions of a general nature (hence not relating to specific countries or situations) and resolutions condemning violations of human rights (including the principle of representative democracy in the case of non-compliance with the result of free elections)[45] committed by a given State and sometimes by non-State actors, such as insurrectional movements or other armed groups.

Through a very extensive interpretation of the UN Charter and its Rules of Procedure, starting in the 1970s the UNGA also decided to follow the practice of objecting to the credentials of national delegates designated by governments installed through coups d'état, or held responsible for gross violations of human rights, including the crime of *apartheid*, as happened with South Africa commencing in 1974 and for about twenty years. This practice, considered by some to be a kind of temporary expulsion or total suspension with regard to the States to which these measures are addressed (insofar as it does not match what is envisaged by Article 5 of the UN Charter), has prevented these States, and South Africa in particular, from exercising a large part of the rights granted by the UN Charter to UN Member States.[46]

In the same historical period, marked by many serious violations of human rights often committed as part of international and non-international armed conflicts, ECOSOC established a legal instrument that for a long time has been the main form of individual *recourse* before an organ established by the UN. Namely the so-called 1503 procedure envisaged by Resolution 1503-XLVIII of 27 May 1970, which tasked the UNCommHR with examining the individual petitions submitted to it relating to serious violations of human rights and, as appropriate, making subsequent recommendations to ECOSOC.

The 1503 procedure, however, did not give rise to specific findings of gross violations of human rights and related sanctions against the State responsible, and was ultimately aimed at gathering information and, at most, urging the State in question to comply with human rights standards and prevent further violations. Nonetheless, this

---

[45] With regard to the Government of Myanmar's disregard for the result of the 1990 elections, see UNGA resolutions no. 47/144 of 18 December 1992 and no. 48/150 of 20 December 1993.

[46] As was effectively stated by the UNGA in the resolution of 9 November 1976, A/RES/31/6I (Situation in South Africa), "the racist regime of South Africa is illegitimate and has no right to represent the people of South Africa": para 1.

procedure, which has been availed of several times with the adoption of numerous resolutions by UNCommHR, has constituted a valuable instrument of political pressure against the State responsible for serious violations of human rights and, more generally, a useful benchmark to verify the level of protection of human rights in the State under consideration.

5.3.2 The Human Rights Council

By Resolution No. 60/251 adopted by the UNGA on 15 March 2006, the Human Rights Council ("HRCoun") was established. On the one hand, it took over the competences regarding a number of procedures previously entrusted to other UN bodies (including the 1503 procedure). On the other hand, it established new and more incisive procedures for monitoring observance of human rights by UN Member States.

In particular, the Complaints Procedure was established by the HRCoun by Resolution No. 5/1 of 18 June 2007. That procedure, which replaces and expands the 1503 procedure, allows individuals, groups of individuals and NGOs to submit communications concerning consistent patterns of gross violations of human rights by a UN Member State, as long as they comply with the well-established conditions of admissibility repeatedly analysed in this chapter.[47] For the purposes of examining those communications, the HRCoun has created two working groups with different functions: the Working Group on Communications, which acts as a *filter* and is charged with checking whether the communication can be examined on the merits, and the Working Group on Situations, which assesses admissible communications on the merit and presents a final report to HRCoun about the violations found. In any case, the final act of the procedure is not binding.

A further competence vested in the HRCoun relates to functions in connection with "special procedures", which can be triggered at the request of a UN Member State or an NGO. They may concern the violation of human rights committed in a specific State or have a "thematic mandate". In this latter case, the causes and remedies of the aforementioned violations, generally perpetrated at the global level, are assessed. Again in these cases, the concluding acts of the procedures are not binding.

Among the other important activities carried out by the HRCoun, worthy of mention is the Universal Periodic Review ("UPR"), which is carried out by the Council every four to five years for all UN Member States.[48] It consists of a periodic examination of how those States comply with human rights law. The legal parameters on the basis of which the UPR is conducted are the UN Charter, the UDHR (a

[47] However, communications from individuals concerning specific and *isolated* human rights violations are not accepted.

[48] Currently, the third review cycle (2017–2022) is underway.

particularly important parameter given that as mentioned before[49] the Declaration in itself is not binding), the human rights treaties ratified by the State under review and IHL. In view of the relevance and breadth of the legal parameters in question, it is evident that the UPR carried out by the HRCoun is far too ambitious and complex.

It should be pointed out that the UPR procedure is complementary to the numerous monitoring activities carried out by other UN organs (to which reference was made earlier)[50] and does not lead to any specific ascertainment of violations of human rights nor to any sanction against the State. However, it is undeniable that this particular procedure, which constitutes, in terms of its characteristics and legal parameters of reference, an absolute novelty in the landscape of systems for checking observance of human rights, is of significant importance in urging the State to comply with what has been established in the legal instruments indicated above, given that the UN Member State cannot evade the examination in question. Furthermore, the procedure in question may be useful for the examined State itself in order to identify the shortcomings of its legal system from the point of view of the protection of human rights and to adopt *unpopular* measures at the national level which may be explained internally by the need to comply with what has been prescribed by the HRCoun.

5.4 The UN Security Council and Serious Violations of Human Rights—The Sanctions Against States

Finally, special attention should be paid to analysing the Security Council's role in relation to human rights.

From a normative standpoint the UNSC is not endowed under the UN Charter with specific competence in the matter of human rights, although it is worth pointing out that the domestic jurisdiction of UN Member States under Article 2(7) of the Charter cannot be invoked against the Council where it adopts coercive measures pursuant to Chapter VII of the Charter. Nevertheless, since the 1960s the Council has developed a particularly extensive practice, starting from the assumption that the serious and systematic violation of human rights may constitute a threat to international peace and security, even in situations where the violations have no effects outside the State concerned.

What is even more striking about the practice followed by the UNSC in the field of human rights is the variety of measures it adopts, which concern the imposition of sanctions against States and non-State actors, the establishment of international missions (*peace-keeping* and *peace-enforcement* operations), the setting up of authorities of a provisional nature at the end of international or non-international armed conflicts and whose competence also encompasses human rights (as in the

[49] See Chap. 3, Sect. 3.11.

[50] See *supra*, Sects. 5.2.1–5.2.6.

classic case of the *United Nations Transitional Authority in Cambodia*)[51] and even the creation of international criminal tribunals.

This practice was first witnessed in the economic embargoes imposed on States whose government was established by a coup d'état carried out by a white minority in contempt of the rights of the black majority of the population, as was the case in Southern Rhodesia,[52] or on States that engaged in apartheid, as in South Africa.[53]

Subsequently, the UNSC adopted similar economic sanctions against a number of other States, such as Iraq, then ruled by Saddam Hussein, in view of the very serious human rights violations committed against the Shiite and Kurdish minorities living in that country.[54] And later against Libya in view of the violations of human rights and IHL committed by the governmental military forces during the civil war in early 2011. In particular, in its Resolution No. 1970 of 26 February 2011, the Council condemned the aforementioned human rights violations in Libya and called for their immediate cessation, while deciding on an arms embargo and individual sanctions against members of the government regime. The UNSC also decided to refer the situation in Libya to the ICC, an issue which will be discussed below.[55]

The Libyan affair is also important for our purposes because, due to the persistence of serious violations of human rights and IHL perpetrated by the government regime (and in part also by the Libyan insurrectional movement), the UNSC decided through its well-known Resolution No. 1973 of 17 March 2011 to authorise UN Member States, "acting nationally or through regional organizations or arrangements, and acting in cooperation with the Secretary General, to take all necessary measures ... to protect civilians and civilian populated areas under threat of attack in the Libyan Arab Jamahiriya",[56] also recalling the doctrine of responsibility to protect on the part of the territorial government.[57] On the basis of that resolution, the UNSC thus authorised the use of force in response to the serious human rights violations committed in the armed conflict in Libya.

By stretching even more significantly the *letter* of the UN Charter's provisions on the UNSC's competence, in particular Article 41 of the Charter, the Council has gone so far as to establish, in the face of massive and repeated violations of human rights and IHL, international criminal tribunals with jurisdiction to prosecute the individuals responsible for the said violations. This was done by setting up ad hoc tribunals for the Former Yugoslavia[58] and for Rwanda.[59]

---

[51] See Resolution No. 745 of 28 February 1992.

[52] See Council Resolutions No. 232 of 16 December 1966 and No. 253 of 29 May 1968.

[53] See Resolution No. 277 of 18 March 1970.

[54] See Resolution No. 688 of 5 April 1991.

[55] See *infra*, Sect. 5.6.

[56] See para 4 of the resolution.

[57] On that doctrine, see Chap. 14, Sect. 14.5.

[58] See Resolution No. 827 of 25 May 1993.

[59] See Resolution No. 955 of 8 November 1994.

5.5 The UN Security Council and Individual Sanctions—Scrutiny of the Lawfulness of Targeted Sanctions from a Human Rights Perspective

Among the instruments used by the UNSC to respond to serious human rights violations are also individual sanctions imposed on natural or legal persons.

It should be pointed out that while this practice of the Council pursues an entirely legitimate objective, i.e. the repression of conduct seriously violating human rights, it does raise a number of issues. On the one hand, it raises questions of conformity with the UN Charter, which does not envisage the adoption of sanctions against individuals but only against States. On the other hand, it may in turn be in conflict with the need to protect the fundamental rights of the persons affected by the sanctions.

The adoption of individual sanctions, consisting, for example, of measures freezing the assets or restricting the freedom of movement of the natural persons sanctioned, still takes place on foot of a summary procedure that—despite certain amendments thereto at Council level—guarantees neither the individual's right to address the UNSC (or its subsidiary bodies delegated to carry out certain functions in the context of that procedure, the Sanctions Committee) nor the individual's rights of defence in order to challenge the substance of the measures.

In fact, the procedure for the inclusion and deletion of natural and legal persons from the lists drawn up for the purpose of imposing individual sanctions (so-called *listing* and *delisting*) is purely intergovernmental in nature and is based on discussions and decisions taken by the delegates of the Member States of the UNSC. Moreover, the procedure in question lacks transparency as regards the procedural and substantive rules applied. We therefore take the view that, irrespective of the content and effects of the restrictive measures adopted against the sanctioned individuals, the procedure referred to above does not in itself comply at least with the basic rules of *due process* and the principle of legality in criminal matters, where the sanctions adopted are criminal if assessed in the light of their very nature and severity.

It is thus not surprising that under those circumstances the Council's resolutions, or rather the acts transposing the resolutions, have been carefully scrutinised by the judiciary—not without hesitation and uncertainty on the part of national and international courts—to establish whether or not they comply with international, EU or national law on human rights. In some instances, the same case has come before national and international courts.

At EU level, initially a restrictive approach was adopted by the former Court of First Instance in two judgments issued on 21 September 2005[60] envisaging a sort of *immunity* for UNSC resolutions in their implementation in the EU legal system, subject to the frankly rather implausible condition that the acts not conflict with *jus cogens*. Since then, however, the CJEU's case law, including in the appeals stemming from the above cases,[61] has adopted an approach of carefully checking compliance

[60] See respectively cases nos. T-315/01, *Kadi*, and T-306/01, *Al-Barakaat*.

[61] See judgment of 3 September 2008, joined cases nos. C-402/05 P and C-415/05 P.

of EU acts transposing UNSC resolutions with the Union's fundamental principles in the field of human rights protection. This position, now well-established, was confirmed, for example, in the Court's judgment of 18 July 2013,[62] which ruled that it was appropriate to refer to the "parallel" and convergent views of the ECtHR expressed in the *Nada* case, which will be discussed shortly. In essence, the CJEU considered that the changes to the procedure for the imposition of individual sanctions by the UNSC was unsatisfactory in that, according to both courts, they "do not provide to the person whose name is listed on the Sanctions Committee Consolidated List … the guarantee of effective judicial protection".[63]

We now come to the equally valuable monitoring of human rights compliance by national courts, in relation to domestic legislation implementing UNSC resolutions on individual sanctions. It should be noted that, as mentioned before, some of these cases have been subject to dual judicial review, first at the national level and then at the international level by the ECtHR.

Limiting our attention to the cases initially examined by national courts, in accordance with the rule of prior exhaustion of domestic remedies, and subsequently by the Court of Strasbourg, first up for analysis is the *Nada* case concerning the internal implementation by Switzerland of UNSC measures providing for the freezing of the financial resources of an individual suspected of terrorist acts, in breach, according to the applicant, of the international rules on the protection of the right to property and the right to a fair trial. In its judgment of 14 November 2007, the Swiss Federal Supreme Court rejected Nada's application, invoking *inter alia* Article 103 of the UN Charter, which provides that the obligations under the Charter—and on the basis of practice also obligations provided for in binding UNSC resolutions—take precedence over the obligations provided for in any other international agreement.

The *Nada* case subsequently came before the Grand Chamber of the ECtHR, which, in its judgment of 12 September 2012, ruled that Switzerland had breached Articles 8 and 13 ECHR concerning respectively the right to respect for private and family life and the right to an effective remedy before a national court. In particular, the Court considered that the absolute ban imposed by the Swiss authorities on leaving Swiss territory was excessive and disproportionate as judged against Article 8, and was not waived even on account of the applicant's serious state of health. The Court also criticised the inaction of the Swiss authorities, which, despite having closed the investigation into Nada in 2005 without finding him responsible for acts of terrorism, informed the Sanctions Committee only in 2009 with obvious prejudice to the applicant's rights.[64]

Subsequently called upon to rule on a case similar to the one examined above, concerning the implementation by Switzerland of UNSC measures against individuals and entities linked to Saddam Hussein's regime, the ECtHR, in the Grand Chamber judgment of 21 June 2016 in *Al-Dulimi and Montana Management Inc*

---

[62] See the judgment of the Grand Chamber in cases C584/10-P, C593/10-P and C595/10-P.

[63] *Id.*, para 133.

[64] See appl. no. 10593/08.

v. Switzerland,[65] confirmed its earlier position. Even though the Court pointed out that, unlike in the previous *Nada* case, the Council resolution at issue—Resolution No. 1483 of 22 May 2003—left a smaller margin of appreciation to UN Member States when implementing restrictive measures, it equally found that Switzerland was responsible for violation of the right of access to an independent and impartial tribunal under Article 6(1) ECHR.

Finally, in some cases the domestic courts have adopted an approach inspired by a logic of adequate balancing of the needs to combat international terrorism—a necessity expressed in the sanctioning measures adopted by the UNSC—and the protection of human rights. From this point of view, UK case law is especially commendable, as it has at times interpreted the national rules transposing the decisions of the Security Council in a manner consistent with primary domestic law and international rules, in particular the provisions of the ECHR. On that basis, the English courts have not hesitated to set aside domestic measures implementing UNSC resolutions, as in the judgment delivered by the High Court of Justice on 10 July 2009 in the *Hay* case and in the judgment delivered by the Supreme Court on 27 January 2010 in the *Ahmed* case.

5.6 The UN Security Council and the International Criminal Court

Finally, when analysing the UNSC's role concerning human rights, a few brief remarks are called for on the relations between the Council and the ICC, with particular reference to the common goal of prosecuting those responsible for international crimes.

The provisions of the Statute of the ICC, approved on 17 July 1998 and in force since 1 July 2002, that are relevant to the relations between the UNSC and the ICC are Articles 13(b) and 16, which contemplate two scenarios of so-called *referral* and *deferral* of a situation in which the commission of international crimes is suspected. Cases of *deferral* whereby the UNSC can temporarily block the investigations conducted by the Court are not uncommon and are very controversial.[66] Of greater importance for our purposes are instead cases of *referral* whereby the ICC can exercise its jurisdiction also in a situation in which one or more such crimes appear to have been committed and "is referred to the Prosecutor by the Security Council acting under Chapter VII of the Charter of the United Nations".

---

[65] See appl. no. 5809/08.

[66] Acting under Chapter VII of the UN Charter, the UNSC, in the resolution of 12 July 2002, no. 1422, requested "consistent with the provisions of Article 16 of the Rome Statute, that the ICC, if a case arises involving current or former officials or personnel from a contributing State not a Party to the Rome Statute over acts or omissions relating to a United Nations established or authorized operation, shall for a twelve-month period starting 1 July 2002 not commence or proceed with investigation or prosecution of any such case, unless the Security Council decides otherwise" (para 1). The request in question was also made in 2003 but was not subsequently renewed.

The provision, which seemed to have a residual character in the context of the exercise of jurisdiction by the ICC, in the sense of constituting a subsidiary head of jurisdiction with respect to the primary heads of jurisdiction contained in Article 13, has already been applied in two cases, relating to crimes committed in Sudan and Libya, neither of which are parties to the Statute of the Court.

The situation in Libya, as mentioned above, was referred by the UNSC to the ICC with Resolution No. 1970/2011 and is still pending, despite the fact that the prosecutions already initiated and the further developments of the investigations are limited mainly due to the scarce cooperation of the Libyan authorities.

In turn, the situation in Sudan, which was referred by the UNSC to the ICC with Resolution No. 1593 of 31 March 2005, exhibits numerous problematic aspects and has created a significant area of conflict between the Court and various African countries and the African Union itself.[67] The African countries have pointed the finger at a *bias* in the Court's work, which is alleged to have initiated investigations and prosecutions almost exclusively against individuals belonging to African States. Moreover, on the legal issues facing the Court, those same countries insist that the rule of customary international law on personal immunity of Heads of State, Government and Foreign Ministers prevails over the provisions of the Statute, further to which the "official capacity as a Head of State or Government, a member of a Government or parliament, an elected representative or a government official shall in no case exempt a person from criminal responsibility under this Statute".[68]

It must be admitted that the decisions progressively taken by the Court to prose cute, in particular, the now former Head of State of Sudan, Al-Bashir, on the basis of a series of very serious charges relating to war crimes, crimes against humanity and the crime of genocide, are not a model of consistency as regards the solutions adopted in order to resolve the contrast between the provisions of the ICC Statute and the above-mentioned international rule that grants personal immunity to the supreme organs of the State. This inconsistency has certainly not lent *credibility* to the arguments put forward by the Court.

On the one hand, the relevant case law of the ICC is based on decisions in which an exception was invoked—on the basis of a supposed rule of general international law considered to correspond to the provisions of Article 27 of the Statute of the Court—to the rule of personal immunity in the case of the commission of international crimes by individuals held responsible and tried before international courts.[69] This view was more recently confirmed in the judgment of 6 May 2019 issued by the Appeals Chamber and concerning Jordan's failure to comply with the request made by the Court regarding the arrest and transfer of Al-Bashir, in which the Court justifies

[67] See Decision on Africa's Relationship with the ICC, Extraordinary Session of the Assembly of the AU, 12 October 2013, para 10(i).

[68] See Article 27(1) of the Statute.

[69] See the decisions of 13 December 2011 made by the Pre-Trial Chamber concerning non-cooperation with the ICC by Chad (ICC-02/05-01/09) and Malawi (ICC-02/05-01/09).

its position by stating that international courts adjudicating on the commission of international crimes "act on behalf of the international community as a whole".[70]

On the other hand, there have been decisions in which it has been affirmed that it was "originally" the UNSC that waived, albeit implicitly, immunity on the basis of the aforementioned Resolution No. 1593/2005 through which, as stated before, the *referral* to the Court was made.[71]

And a different solution again was reached in the decision of the Pre-Trial Chamber of 6 July 2017 concerning the violation by South Africa of its obligations to arrest and transfer Al-Bashir to the Court. Therein it was stated that the *referral* made by the UNSC placed Sudan, a country not party to the ICC Statute, in a position similar to that of States parties to the Statute, for which, as stated above, the principle of irrelevance of immunities for those responsible for international crimes under Article 27 applies.[72]

Even with the hesitations mentioned above, it is undeniable that the ICC has used all the tools at its disposal to prosecute those responsible for international crimes committed in Sudan. While the response of several African States parties to the ICC Statute to allow Al-Bashir to enter and stay temporarily in their respective territories, in clear contrast with their obligations to cooperate with the Court under the Statute, has been one of substantial *indifference* and in some cases of open conflict with the ICC. The UNSC itself has displayed a similar attitude of indifference.

An analogous and open contrast had recently been created between the ICC and the US government in relation to the initiation by the Court of an investigation into international crimes committed in Afghanistan—a country which is a party to the ICC Statute—also by soldiers from countries that are not parties to the Statute, such as the United States.[73] In this regard, it should be noted that, although the United States, as a third country with respect to the ICC Statute, is not obliged to cooperate with the Court, it cannot hinder and even subject to sanctions the members of the Court and its administrative staff who are lawfully exercising their functions. Nonetheless, such sanctions were first threatened by various Trump administration figures and subsequently adopted under the Executive Order of the former President of the United States of 11 June 2020, in which the opening of the investigation by the Court was even characterised as "an unusual and extraordinary threat to the national security and foreign policy of the United States". Accordingly, measures were ordered to freeze movable and immovable property belonging to individuals "directly engaged in any effort by the ICC to investigate, arrest, detain, or prosecute any United States personnel" or "any personnel of a country that is an ally of the United States", as well as measures to suspend visas for access to US territory of those

[70] See ICC-02/05-01/09 OA2, para 115 of the judgment.

[71] See the decision of 9 April 2014 made by the Pre-Trial Chamber concerning non-cooperation with the ICC by the Democratic Republic of the Congo, ICC-02/05-01/09-195.

[72] See ICC-02/05-01/09.

[73] In its judgment of 5 March 2020 (ICC-02/17 OA4), the Appeals Chamber of the ICC, reversing the conclusions reached by the Pre-Trial Chamber in its decision of 12 April 2019 (ICC-02/17), authorised the Prosecutor of the Court to initiate the aforementioned investigation.

individuals and their family members.[74] These measures have been duly cancelled by the Biden administration.

Comprehension Check and Tasks

1. Why has the UN played a key role in the evolution of human rights law? (Sect. 5.1)
2. What are the functions of the Committee on the Elimination of Racial Discrimination? (Sect. 5.2.3)
3. Why is the decision of the Committee on the Elimination of Discrimination against Women in the case of *Angela González Carreño v. Spain* relevant to the development of human rights? (Sect. 5.2.4)
4. The Supreme Court of Justice of Mexico (2021) ruled that the State is under an obligation to comply with the non-binding urgent actions of the Committee on Enforced Disappearances. What is the reasoning behind this position of the Court? (Sect. 5.2.6)
5. What is the Universal Periodic Review and which body carries it out under the UN? (Sect. 5.3.2)
6. Why is it important that some international and domestic courts have carried out a review of the human rights compliance of UN Security Council resolutions on targeted sanctions? (Sect. 5.5)
7. What is the difference between referral and deferral under the ICC Statute? (Sect. 5.6)

[74] See Sections 1 and 4 of the Executive Order.

Chapter 6
Individual and Collective Human Rights: Right to Life

Contents

Abstract After some preliminary remarks on the issue of the classification of human rights, the chapter focuses on the right to life, analyzing the negative and positive obligations of States as well as the horizontal and extraterritorial application of international norms on the right to life. The chapter devotes great attention to the examination of the legal regime applicable to the death penalty and to the most recent and problematic aspects of the right to life—namely the beginning of life and the protection of the unborn; the medically assisted reproduction and surrogacy; the end of life, including euthanasia and the interruption of artificial hydration and nutrition for individuals in a permanent and irreversible vegetative state.

6.1 Classification of Human Rights

The subdivision proposed in the literature between human rights of the first, second, third and fourth generation can be considered as well established by now, even if of limited practical use. This classification relates to the moment in history when the

P. Pustorino, *Introduction to International Human Rights Law*,
https://doi.org/10.1007/978-94-6265-563-8_6

various human rights arose internationally. However, within each category there are important exceptions regarding exactly when individual rights gained official recognition in international law. For example, the right to property, although belonging to the second generation of rights, goes much further back in time than the other rights of that same generation.

Also worth clarifying is that the formation of new generations of rights does not in any way imply that previous generations are complete in terms of effective observance of the rights that they encompass. It should also be pointed out that if, in principle, the rights belonging to older generations enjoy greater protection at the international level, this is not always true. Just think of the limited protection afforded to political rights, belonging to the first generation of human rights, and, conversely, of the broad protection afforded to the principle of self-determination of peoples, a third generation right.

Another method of classifying human rights is based on the different levels of protection enjoyed at the international level. There are rights that are more important and better protected than others (sometimes referred to as *core rights*), the violation of which can imply "aggravated" State responsibility for serious breaches of peremptory norms of general international law[1] and, where that conduct amounts to the commission of an international crime, also criminal responsibility of the individual who has materially committed the violation.

First generation rights are civil and political rights. Second generation rights are economic, social and cultural rights. Third generation rights are the right to self-determination of peoples and the right to development, to which are generally added the right to a clean and healthy environment and the individual right to peace (which, although sometimes provided for at the international level as a collective right pertaining to national peoples,[2] does not seem to have achieved an adequate level of protection at the international level as a human right). Finally, there are fourth generation rights, which have arisen as a result of scientific advances in the field of biomedicine and biotechnology and which are often linked to the rights of previous generations, such as the right to life, in line with the previously mentioned indivisibility of human rights.[3]

Finally, it should be emphasised that human rights obviously have as their holders *real* persons, that is, persons actually existing at the time when the question of the ownership and possible violation of such rights arises. However, in light of certain elements of domestic and international practice, the literature has not shied away from viewing also the rights of future generations as collective rights. This is so, for example, in the matter of the preservation of the environment and the protection of goods of particular importance from an artistic, cultural or historical point of view, which must be safeguarded for the benefit of future populations.

[1] See Chap. 14, Sect. 14.2.

[2] See Article 23(1) of the ACHPR and General Principle No. 38 of the Declaration on Human Rights of 18 November 2012 adopted by ASEAN, which instead recognises this right in individual and collective form.

[3] See Chap. 2, Sect. 2.4.2.

6.2 Right to Life: General Scope and State Obligations

The human right *par excellence* is the right to the protection of life, which protects not only the physical but also the moral and psychological integrity of every human being.

This right is protected in the UDHR, which addresses it in the same provision as the right to personal freedom and security,[4] as well as in a number of universal and regional conventions like Article 6 ICCPR and Article 2 ECHR. It is also protected by a general rule of international law.

The right to life is an absolute right, but the rules providing for it may be derogated from for reasons and in situations expressly provided for in international law. Derogations or restrictions other than those specifically indicated are to be considered contrary to the international law rules on the protection of the right to life. Apart from the question of the death penalty, which will be discussed below, it is possible for individuals to be deprived of their life only by a lawful act of war or, in time of peace, by the police or by private persons in the case of self-defence. Furthermore, the lethal measures must be such as to be considered strictly necessary and proportional since taking the life of another ought to be a last resort for protecting the life of the individual attacked or of other persons in the face of a serious and an actual threat to them. The main purpose of the rules on the right to life, including the exceptions to that right, is thus to prevent arbitrary acts of deprivation of life on the part of national authorities or private persons.

It should be noted that the violation of the right to life by the State can occur not only when individuals are deprived of their life but also when serious damage is caused to the life and physical integrity of individuals without causing death.

It is important to underline that the protection of the right to life, in cases of actions that are potentially detrimental to that right, must be ensured at every stage of the activities that may affect people's lives. In this regard, in its judgment of 27 September 1995 in *McCann and Others v. The United Kingdom*, the ECtHR (Grand Chamber) stated that the protection of the right to life must be ensured not only during the material execution of the harmful conduct but also in the intelligence gathering and preparatory stages of the action in question. According to the reasoning of the Court, a State that intends to resort to lethal measures against an individual, in this case for reasons of combating international terrorism, must firstly assess whether the actual use of force by the national authorities is "strictly proportionate to the aim of protecting persons against unlawful violence". But the State must also verify in advance the necessity of the lethal action, so as to ascertain whether the operation in question is "planned and controlled by the authorities so as to minimise, to the greatest extent possible recourse to lethal force".[5]

As noted, the right to life must be safeguarded both in time of war, hence during international or non-international armed conflicts, and in time of peace, where it operates in relation to actions taken against individuals who are not under the direct

[4] See Article 3 UDHR.

[5] See appl. no. 18984/91, para 194.

control of the police and *a fortiori* in relation to conduct taken when the individual is under the authority and control of the organs of the State (for example, in detention or under arrest). In time of war the sphere of application pertains more properly to IHL. In this regard, it is worth noting that an examination of the international practice and case law of the bodies in charge of scrutinising the observance of some human rights treaties reveals a tendency towards the coordinated application of human rights norms and fundamental principles of IHL: the principle of distinction between civilian and military objectives, the precautionary principle, the principle of proportionality, etc.[6] For example, the IACtHR, in its judgment of 30 November 2012 in *Santo Domingo Massacre v. Colombia*, examined the lawfulness of the vast and brutal military operation conducted by the Colombian military forces against the insurrectionary movement of the Fuerzas Armadas Revolucionarias de Colombia, stating on a general level that it wished to interpret the American Convention "in light of the pertinent norms and principles of international humanitarian law".[7]

6.2.1 Right to Life: Negative and Positive Obligations of the State

The international courts and bodies competent in the field of human rights have dwelt extensively on the content of the right to life. In the light of a particularly extensive interpretation of the legal rules analysed, the courts have deduced specific negative and positive obligations of a substantial and procedural nature incumbent on the State in order to effectively protect the right in question.

More specifically, the State is obliged to comply not only with negative obligations to refrain from jeopardising the life and safety of persons but also with positive obligations to prevent possible injury by the State or private parties, while at the same time ensuring enhanced protection for particularly vulnerable individuals or those who have received specific threats.[8] In this regard, it is the previously mentioned doctrine of the horizontal application (*Drittwirkung*) of human rights norms (on the basis of the general principle of due diligence)[9] which operates in relation to the right to life, as noted by the HRC in its *General Comment No. 36* of 30 October 2018 on Article 6 (Right to Life).[10] The nature and content of the preventive measures to be put in place by the State thus vary according to the severity and imminence of threats against private persons, including threats of a terrorist nature.[11]

[6] On the relationship between these specific issues, see Chap. 3, Sect. 3.8.

[7] See para 211 of the judgment.

[8] In this regard see HRC, *General Comment No. 36* of 30 October 2018, paras 23–24.

[9] See Chap. 3, Sect. 3.7.

[10] See paras 7 and 21 thereof.

[11] In this regard see ECtHR judgment of 13 April 2017 in *Tagayeva and Others v. Russia*, appl. no. 26562/07 and six other applications, para 565.

The positive obligations of prevention also apply in the case where the State, on the basis of national legislation, delegates certain functions of enforcement of public order and national security to private entities. In these cases, those private entities could be considered de facto organs of the State, if acting under State "instructions" or "direction or control", as provided for by Article 8 of the Draft on the Responsibility of States for Internationally Wrongful Acts ("ARSIWA") adopted by the ILC in 2001.

The State must also comply with positive obligations to repress conduct detrimental to the right to life, in particular, adopt effective and rapid measures, including on a judicial level, to determine the reasons for the deprivation of the right to life and to identify and punish those responsible.

It must be emphasised that the various negative and positive obligations on the State operate independently of each other, with the result that even where the State is not held responsible for the breach of the substantive obligation to protect the right to life, since it has not directly caused the injury to the right in question, it may well be found liable for a breach of procedural obligations in the event of the absence or inadequacy of the investigations and procedures necessary to identify and convict those materially responsible for the violations.

The positive obligations incumbent upon the State imply the need to go beyond merely operational measures to safeguard the right to life, such as regulating recourse to lethal force in light of the different weapons' capacity to injure and in accordance with the principles of necessity and proportionality of the harmful conduct. In fact, the State must also adopt measures of a general nature such as laying down a clear and comprehensive legislative framework for the protection of the right to life and for the determination of the limits within which it is possible for public authorities or private individuals to infringe that right. As highlighted by the IACtHR in its judgment of 15 July 2020 in *Workers of the Fireworks Factory in Santo Antônio de Jesus and their Families v. Brazil*, an adequate legislative framework in the terms referred to above also appears necessary to serve a *deterrent* function in order "to dissuade any threat to the right to life".[12] It follows that both the provisions establishing the crimes in question and the criminal sanctions attached to them must be commensurate with the gravity of the harmful conduct that violates the right to life.[13]

A well-known case may help to shed light on the content of the above-mentioned State obligations. In its judgment of 24 March 2011 in *Giuliani and Gaggio v. Italy*, the ECtHR (Grand Chamber) ruled out the responsibility of the State for the conduct of some police forces at the time of a G8 summit in Genoa in 2001, which had caused the death of a young man. According to the Court, the police officer responsible for the death, before shooting, had warned the violent demonstrators belonging to the Black Bloc group. Moreover, according to the Court, the police officer had used the lethal weapons to protect his own life and that of his colleagues in the face of a serious and imminent danger. Consequently, the use of force was to be considered necessary and proportionate to the danger faced by the perpetrator. Finally, in the Court's opinion, the positive obligations of repression were also respected by the

---

12 See para 116.

13 HRC, *General Comment No. 36*, para 20.

State because the investigative and judicial activity following the harmful event was adequate.[14]

Given that the State is obliged to comply with a series of positive obligations concerning the protection of the right to life, it follows that the violation of that right may occur—in line with the general rules on State responsibility—also as a result of acts of omission, where they cause the death of an individual or facilitate the irreversible worsening of his or her state of health. Such a situation occurred, according to the ECtHR, in the case of *Panaitescu* v. *Romania*.[15] In its judgment of 10 April 2012, the Court found that the State was liable for the unjustified delay in providing free treatment and medical services to a cancer patient. The Court also rebuked the contradictory conduct of the State organs: although the domestic courts had established the individual's right to receive the necessary treatment, the administrative authorities had created a series of bureaucratic obstacles to the effective granting of the treatment, with the result that the patient was treated with serious delay and therefore died. Finally, it should be noted that, in this decision, the Court rejected the arguments put forward by the State to justify its omission, consisting in the lack of economic resources to deal with all cases of serious illness. That stance appears to be in line with what was stated previously on the subject of the inadmissibility of derogations or restrictions to the right to life not expressly provided for by international rules.

Violation of the right to life due to omission by the State has also been found by the ECtHR in some cases in which the State party has failed to execute an international or European arrest warrant issued by another State against an individual held responsible for violations of the right to life.[16] A similar failure to act contrary to the regime examined here has been found in cases where the State on whose territory crimes have been committed does not request the extradition of individuals convicted or accused of having committed crimes to protect the right to life.[17] For the same reasons, it should be noted that a State party to the ECHR, once it has obtained the extradition or transfer of the individual responsible for the violation of the right to life (e.g. in the case of application of treaties on the transfer of prisoners whose conviction is final), is obliged to actually prosecute such an individual or execute the sentence already imposed abroad.[18]

---

[14] See appl. no. 23458/02, paras 189 and 192–194.

[15] See appl. no. 30909/06.

[16] See judgment of 9 July 2019, *Romeo Castaño v. Belgium*, appl. no. 8351/17.

[17] See judgment of 20 October 2009, *Agache and Others v. Romania*, appl. no. 2712/02, para 83. Similar points have been made by the Strasbourg Court with reference to offences constituting violations of the prohibition of torture: see judgment of 23 February 2016, *Nasr and Ghali v. Italy*, appl. no. 44883/09, paras 270–272.

[18] See judgment of 26 May 2020, *Makuchyan and Minasyan v. Azerbaijan and Hungary*, appl. no. 17247/13.

6.2.2 *Extraterritorial or Indirect Application of the International Rules on the Right to Life—Relevance of Climate Change Issues*

The particular importance of the right to life has given rise to the extraterritorial application of the rules that protect it.[19] According to a well-established trend in international case law, it is forbidden to expel or extradite foreigners who risk in the country of final destination (generally the national country of the individuals in question) a threat to their life or being subjected to torture or inhuman or degrading treatment.

The risk assessment carried out, in particular, by the ECtHR is very articulated. Firstly, there is an *objective* examination of the overall situation in the State of final destination regarding the risk of the above-mentioned human rights violations as well as a more localised risk, i.e. concerning those specific parts of the territory where the individual is headed for. Secondly, a *subjective* examination is also conducted, in essence an assessment of the specific risk concerning the individual in question in light, for example, of his or her personal, political, religious beliefs or sexual orientation.

In addition, the territorial State cannot justify the failure to carry out the analysis of the risk faced by the individual in case of deportation or extradition by referring to a supposedly *free* decision of the individual to leave the State—so-called "voluntary return"—especially when in reality these are *forced* decisions, motivated by the unjustified refusal of the State authorities to grant the request for asylum or temporary stay.[20]

In the relevant international practice and case law on human rights, there is a clear tendency to further expand the boundaries of extraterritorial application of the rules protecting the right to life.

In this regard, reference can be made first of all to the case law of the ECtHR which rules out the possibility for the State of residence of the foreigner to deport individuals who risk receiving, in the national State, treatment inadequate to their serious state of ill-health or where the level of such treatment is significantly lower than that offered in the State of residence.[21] In its judgment of 13 December 2016 in *Paposhvili v. Belgium*, the ECtHR (Grand Chamber) laid down the principle that there is a violation of Article 3 ECHR in the case of deportation or removal from the State of a seriously ill individual who cannot receive, in his or her own country, medical treatment that is such as to ensure his or her survival or to exclude a significant worsening of his or her health condition. For the Court it is a matter of verifying, case by case, whether there is a real risk of death or serious deterioration of health of

---

[19] On the relationship between this question and the concept of jurisdiction in human rights treaties, see Chap. 3, Sects. 3.6–3.6.3.

[20] In this respect see ECtHR judgment of 14 November 2019, *N.A. v. Finland*, appl. no. 25244/18, para 57.

[21] In the relevant cases the ECtHR analysed the applicant's situation both under Article 3 (Prohibition of torture) and Article 2 (Right to life).

an individual because of "a serious, rapid and irreversible decline in his or her state of health resulting in intense suffering" or as a result of "a significant reduction in life expectancy".[22]

A further and recent example of extension in practice of the principle of the extraterritorial application of the international rules in the matter of protection of the right to life is the prohibition of deportation of a foreigner in the face of the serious consequences of climate change—rising sea levels, water table pollution, reduction of habitable and cultivable land, etc.—on the living conditions of the individual in question in his or her country of origin. In its *General Comment No. 36* of 30 October 2018, the HRC stated on a general level that environmental degradation, climate change and unsustainable development constitute "some of the most pressing and serious threats to the ability of present and future generations to enjoy the right to life".[23]

In a subsequent individual communication, that same Committee applied in practice the principle according to which the territorial State cannot deport or reject foreigners who in their own country risk suffering the serious consequences of climate change, because in these circumstances the living conditions would become incompatible "with the right to life with dignity".[24] In the case submitted for its examination the HRC did not however find that there was a serious and imminent risk to the living conditions of the individual in question. This because, according to the HRC, the main negative effects of climate change, including the risk of total uninhabitability of the country of origin (Kiribati), would happen within 10–15 years and only in the absence of significant corrective measures by the State concerned "with the assistance of the international community".[25] That said, the Committee's statements on the lack of immediacy of the risk in question, despite the objective and current seriousness of the environmental situation (especially in certain countries) and those on the effectiveness of the hypothetical corrective measures to be adopted (to date totally insufficient), do raise serious doubts. In a very recent individual communication, the HRC, while confirming that "environmental degradation can compromise effective enjoyment of the right to life, and that severe environmental degradation can adversely affect an individual's well-being and lead to a violation of the right to life", has likewise ruled out the violation of the right to life by enhancing the limited and not timely measures to combat climate change adopted by the State.[26]

---

[22] Appl. no. 41738/10, para 183 of the judgment. In *Savran v. Denmark*, appl. no. 57467/15, the ECtHR (Grand Chamber), with judgment of 7 December 2021, reiterated its stance, ruling out that the applicant's expulsion to Turkey had exposed him to a "serious, rapid and irreversible decline in his state of health resulting in intense suffering".

[23] See para 62.

[24] See the decision of 24 October 2019, published on 7 January 2020, in *Teitiota v. New Zealand*, CCPR/C/127/D/2728/2016, para 9.11.

[25] *Id.*, para 9.12.

[26] See the Views of 21 July 2022, *Daniel Billy and Others v. Australia*, CCPR/C/135/D/3624/2019, paras. 8.3–8.8.

Nevertheless, the principle laid down by the HRC has been appropriately applied by domestic courts in cases concerning requests for asylum or temporary protection. Recently, the Italian Court of Cassation, referring extensively to the decision in the above-mentioned *Teitiota* case, affirmed that, when assessing an application for temporary protection on humanitarian grounds, the evaluation of the danger existing in the applicant's country of origin must also be conducted "with specific reference to the particular risk to the right to life and dignified existence arising from environmental degradation, climate change or unsustainable development of the area".[27]

6.2.3 Right to Life and Prohibition of Trafficking of Human Organs

The right to life and the associated right to the protection of human dignity, which will be discussed below,[28] also guarantee the protection of physical and specific parts of the human being. Therefore, the prohibition of trade and trafficking in human organs and tissues derives from these rights. While a violation of the right to life exclusively for the purpose of removing organs—a practice that is quite frequent in some countries in a state of severe poverty—is clearly prohibited, so too is the practice of trading in human organs and tissues for monetary gain and hence not as a donation. The principle in question is enshrined in some regional agreements like the Additional Protocol to the Convention on Human Rights and Biomedicine concerning Transplantation of Organs and Tissues of Human Origin of 24 January 2002. Pursuant to Article 21 of the Protocol "the human body and its parts shall not, as such, give rise to financial gain or comparable advantage". Analogous provisions are contained in the Council of Europe's Convention against Trafficking in Human Organs of 25 March 2015[29] and also in Article 3(2)(c) of the CFREU.

6.2.4 Right to Life, Protection of the Unborn and Abortion

It is debated whether the right to life includes the protection of the unborn child. On the basis of existing international law and the reservations made by some States parties to human rights treaties that include the right to life, unfortunately the answer would appear to be no. There are also those who have noted that the reference in some international instruments of particular importance, such as the UDHR, to persons already born ("all human beings are born free and equal in dignity and rights")[30]

[27] See order no. 5022 of 24 February 2021.

[28] See *infra*, Sect. 6.5.

[29] See Articles 4(1)(b), 4(1)(c) and 7(1) of the Convention.

[30] See Article 1 UDHR.

could be interpreted as excluding the application of international human rights law to the unborn child. In reality, international case law tends not to adopt a specific position on the issue in question, maintaining a substantially neutral stance in this regard and thus leaving States free to include or not the protection of the unborn child within the framework of the right to life. In this regard, in its judgment of 8 July 2004 in *Vo v. France*, the ECtHR (Grand Chamber) stated that "it is neither desirable, nor even possible" to rule on whether the legal situation of the conceived child should be analysed within the framework of Article 2 ECHR, in view of the absence of scientific certainty on the matter and the differences in the domestic laws of the countries that are parties to the ECHR.[31] Consequently, the Court recognises that States parties have a wide margin of appreciation in regulating this matter.

Consistent with this approach, the Strasbourg Court has ruled out any violation of the right to life in connection with the destruction of human embryos carried out in accordance with the rules in force in the relevant national legal system. Specifically, in *Evans v. The United Kingdom*, a request for destruction of the embryos had been made, on the basis of English law, by a woman's ex-partner following the dissolution of their union. In the Court's view, "the embryos created by the applicant … do not have a right to life within the meaning of Article 2 of the Convention".[32]

On the basis of the same arguments, the ECtHR has adopted a neutral position on the question of abortion, not considering it, per se, contrary to the ECHR, but neither the object of an individual right. However, it must be pointed out that, although the choice to regulate recourse to abortion falls within the margin of appreciation afforded to the States parties to the ECHR, this choice is limited in several respects. Firstly, States are required to provide for recourse to abortion at least in cases where, during pregnancy, there is a risk of death or serious damage to the health of the pregnant woman.[33] In addition, national legislation must ensure a fair balance between the various conflicting interests—protection of the unborn child, of the pregnant woman, etc.—and comply with the principle of proportionality. Lastly, national rules on abortion must be effectively applied throughout the national territory, without theoretically lawful conduct like conscientious objection on the part of doctors and medical staff employed in public hospitals[34] or the lack of local facilities for performing abortions acting as a barrier.

In this regard, reference may be made to the non-binding decision on the merits of 10 September 2013 adopted by the European Committee of Social Rights ("ECSR") in *International Planned Parenthood Federation—European Network (IPPF EN) v. Italy*.[35] The ECSR found a violation of Article 11 of the ESCrev concerning the right to health protection due to the high number of conscientious objectors among medical and health personnel in public hospitals, which *de facto* prevented—especially in some parts of Italy—the application of the law on the termination of pregnancy. It

[31] Appl. no. 53924/00, para 85.

[32] ECtHR (Grand Chamber), judgment of 10 April 2007, appl. no. 6339/05, para 56.

[33] In this regard, see also HRC, *General Comment No. 36* of 30 October 2018, para 8.

[34] ECtHR, judgment of 30 October 2012, appl. no. 57375/08, *P. and S. v. Poland*.

[35] Complaint no. 87/2012.

was obviously irrelevant from the standpoint of the State's responsibility whether the violation had been materially committed by national bodies or, as in the present case, by local (regional) bodies.[36]

There are however differing positions on the protection of the unborn child in the international legal system itself. For example, Article 4(1) ACHR states that the right to life "shall be protected by law and, in general, from the moment of conception". The rule in question has been interpreted in a suitably restrictive manner by the IACtHR, holding that "the protection of the right to life under this provision is not absolute, but rather gradual and incremental according to its development", which does not include the protection of the embryo before its implantation in the female uterus,[37] and deeming that legislation of States parties providing for abortion,[38] even if just in exceptional cases (rape or risk of death of the mother), complies with ACHR.

Moreover, given how much domestic legislation on the protection of the rights of the conceived can differ, at the national level there are some cases in which such rights are strongly guaranteed, both at the legislative and case law levels. For example, in the context of the Irish Constitution, the Eighth Amendment adopted on 7 October 1983, amending Article 40 of the Constitution, establishes the principle that the State recognises "the right to life of the unborn, with due regard to the equal right to life of the mother, guarantees in its laws to respect, and, as far as practicable, by its laws to defend and vindicate that right". The matter in question is, moreover, in continuous evolution both at the international and national level, as demonstrated by the fact that in consideration of the developments that have come about within Irish society and with the aim of modifying the content of the above-mentioned amendment, a new law—the Health (Regulation of Termination of Pregnancy) Act 2018—was enacted in 2018, following a popular referendum, which legalises abortion in some specific cases.

6.2.5 Right to Life and the Death Penalty

Unfortunately, it must be conceded that the protection of the right to life does not imply the exclusion in all circumstances of recourse to the death penalty, at least not from the standpoint of general international law. The positions adopted by some States, international organisations and above all many NGOs aimed at incorporating the prohibition of the death penalty into customary law tend to be based on an overly "optimistic" view, failing to take due account of the fact that numerous countries belonging to various geographical areas have laws that provide for the death penalty,

[36] See Article 4(1) ARSIWA according to which "The conduct of any State organ shall be considered an act of that State under international law … whatever its character as an organ of the central Government or of a territorial unit of the State".

[37] See IACtHR judgment of 28 November 2012, *Artavia Murillo et al. ("in vitro fertilisation") v. Costa Rica*, paras 264 and 315.

[38] See Inter-American Commission Resolution No. 23/81 of 6 March 1981 (case 2141), paras 18 ff.

even for minor crimes, although it must be pointed out that many of these laws are rarely applied.

That said, there is a general tendency to limit the imposition of the death penalty by requiring an explicit legal basis and fair sentencing by independent and impartial courts in order to avoid arbitrary executions. In international case law, the imposition of the death penalty will be considered arbitrary, in light of a broad interpretation of international rules protecting the right to life, also when domestic law obliges the courts to impose the death penalty automatically for certain crimes, thus leaving no room for considering the specific circumstances of the case.[39]

In addition, imposing the death penalty on certain categories of particularly vulnerable individuals is considered as a violation of human rights law: minors and pregnant women, as expressly stated in Article 6(5) ICCPR, and the mentally ill. Finally, the death penalty should only be envisaged for the most serious crimes, as provided for in Article 6(2) ICCPR itself and highlighted by the HRC in its *General Comment No. 36* of 30 October 2018.[40]

In that General Comment the HRC stressed that States parties to ICCPR that have abolished the death penalty cannot deport, extradite or otherwise transfer persons to a country in which they are facing criminal charges that carry the death penalty, unless credible and effective assurances against the imposition of the death penalty have been obtained,[41] in line with what has long been affirmed at the European level and in the case law of some abolitionist countries. In this regard, the Italian Constitutional Court declared Article 698, second paragraph, of the Criminal Procedure Code and the law ratifying and executing the extradition treaty between Italy and the United States of 13 October 1983 to be unconstitutional,[42] insofar as they allowed the extradition of Italian citizens for crimes punishable in the United States by the death penalty on condition that adequate guarantees were given regarding the non-imposition of capital punishment. According to the Court, the prohibition of the death penalty and the "values underlying it – first and foremost the essential good of life – require an absolute guarantee", thus ruling out any recourse to the mechanism of diplomatic guarantees between the two countries regarding the non-application of the death penalty.[43]

Again in the said General Comment, the HRC considers as irrevocable any decision to become a party to the Second Optional Protocol to the ICCPR, aiming at the abolition of the death penalty, adopted and proclaimed by UNGA Resolution 44/128 of 15 December 1989.[44] This position appears to be inspired by the position—which finds some support in the literature and which was already endorsed by the HRC in its

[39] In this regard, see the ACtHPRA judgment of 28 November 2019 in *Ally Rajabu and Others v. United Republic of Tanzania*, appl. no. 007/2015, paras 92 ff.

[40] See paras 5, 10, 16 and 33. Similar provisions are contained in Articles 4(2) and 4(5) ACHR.

[41] See paras 30 and 34.

[42] See Article IX of the Treaty.

[43] See judgment no. 223 of 27 June 1996, para 5 of the conclusions on points of law.

[44] See para 34.

General Comment No. 26 of 8 December 1997 on "Continuity of Obligations"[45]—that ratification of a human rights treaty is presumed to be irrevocable where that treaty does not provide for denunciation or withdrawal. In our view, however, that stance appears to be informed by the progressive development of international law.

Much more satisfactory in terms of ruling out the death penalty is the situation existing in some regional areas of human rights protection. While Article 4(3) ACHR prevents the reintroduction of the death penalty in States parties that have abolished it, there is an absolute prohibition of the death penalty in Europe: in the EU on the basis of Article 2(2) of the CFREU and in the CoE through Protocols 6 and 13 to the ECHR. This has led the ECtHR, in its judgment of 2 March 2010, in *Al-Saadoon and Mufdhi v. The United Kingdom*, to affirm that Article 2 ECHR has been amended—in light of the application of the ECHR by the States parties and in consideration of the overall developments in the international legal order—to the effect of prohibiting the death penalty "in all circumstances".[46] The prohibition in question means that it is equally unlawful to deport or remove individuals who risk the death penalty in non-ECHR countries.

It should be noted that both in the period preceding the final affirmation of the prohibition of the death penalty at the European level[47] and in the period following the above-mentioned 2010 judgment in *Al Saadoon and Mufdhi*,[48] the ECtHR has held that the risk of the imposition of the death penalty by a third State also entails the violation—by the State party to the ECHR that deports, extradites or otherwise transfers the individual in question—of the prohibition of inhuman or degrading treatment or punishment in view of the state of fear and distress suffered by individuals facing the death penalty. This demonstrates, once again, the importance of the aspect of indivisibility of human rights,[49] which makes it possible to prohibit harmful conduct in the light of several international norms for the protection of human rights: in this case, the rule on the right to life and the rule on the prohibition of inhuman or degrading treatment or punishment.[50]

6.3 Right to Life, Medically Assisted Procreation and Surrogacy

The right to life has given rise to further so-called fourth generation rights, in particular rights that have arisen as a result of scientific advances in the field of biomedicine.

---

[45] See para 5.

[46] Appl. no. 61498/08, para 120.

[47] See judgment of 7 July 1989 in *Soering v. The United Kingdom*, appl. no. 14038/88.

[48] See para 137 of the judgment.

[49] See Chap. 2, Sect. 2.4.2.

[50] See Chap. 7, Sect. 7.2. The classification of the death penalty as an inhuman or degrading punishment irrespective of how it is actually carried out is further affirmed at the universal level in the abovementioned *General Comment* of 30 October 2018 adopted by the HRC, para 51.

These rights raise a number of highly topical issues concerning, for example, the lawfulness of assisted procreation, genetic engineering, euthanasia, etc. From a legal point of view, the invocation of certain rights in the field of biomedicine, on the one hand, may be in conflict with other human rights such as the right to respect one's religious beliefs, thus raising a delicate problem of coordination between individual or collective rights. On the other hand, the application of these new rights contributes to the redefinition of the notion of the right to life, potentially significantly expanding its sphere of application.

Despite the extreme complexity of the subject in question, we believe that it is possible to deduce from an analysis of international and European law on human rights and biomedicine some prohibitions that seem by now to be well established in practice. Worthy of mention are the prohibition of eugenic practices aimed at selecting the human species, for example, through steps aimed at affecting the sex of the human being,[51] the prohibition of cloning human beings (provided for by the Additional Protocol to the Oviedo Convention on the Prohibition of Cloning Human Beings of 12 January 1998 and by Article 2(3)(d) of the CFREU) and the prohibition of interventions on the human genome on grounds other than for diagnostic or therapeutic reasons,[52] in order to prevent the transmission of certain genetic diseases.

In the following sections a select number of the above issues will be analysed in connection with the right to life even though some of them have been addressed by domestic and international courts also or only in light of other human rights, in particular, the right to private and family life.[53]

6.3.1 Medically Assisted Procreation

At the national level very different approaches have been adopted as regards access to medically assisted procreation techniques. Some States have refrained from adopting a specific regulatory framework, others have taken a liberal approach allowing recourse to "homologous" and "heterologous" techniques of assisted procreation (thus relating to procreation within and outside the couple), while other States have followed a particularly restrictive approach allowing only homologous fertilisation by married or cohabiting couples and even limiting cases of pre-implantation diagnosis with a view to ascertaining the existence only of certain genetically transmissible diseases.

[51] See Article 14 of the Oviedo Convention on Human Rights and Biomedicine of 4 April 1997.

[52] See Article 13 of the Oviedo Convention.

[53] See Chap. 9, Sects. 9.1–9.1.5.

At the ECtHR level[54] worth noting is the Court's judgment of 1 April 2010 in *S. H. and Others v. Austria*, finding that the Austrian legislation allowing homologous fertilisation but prohibiting, save in exceptional cases, heterologous fertilisation was contrary to the principle of non-discrimination under Article 14 ECHR and the right to private and family life under Article 8 ECHR. According to the Court, once States parties to the ECHR decide to allow access to assisted fertilisation procedures, they cannot distinguish between homologous and heterologous fertilisation so as to avoid creating unjustified discrimination against infertile couples, for whom access to homologous fertilisation is obviously of no use.[55]

However, the ECtHR (Grand Chamber), in reviewing the decision taken by the Chamber in the same case,[56] overturned the conclusions reached by the latter and in its judgment of 3 November 2011 held that the choice of a State party to the ECHR to prohibit certain types of medically assisted procreation falls within its margin of appreciation and is therefore not contrary to the right to respect for private and family life, in the light of the significant differences found in the national legal systems and the absence of applicable international conventions on the subject. That said, the Court did issue a "warning" to the effect that this area of law is constantly evolving in relation to scientific developments,[57] thus not excluding the subsequent formation of a European consensus in favour of access to both forms of assisted fertilisation.

Moreover, in its judgment of 28 August 2012 in *Costa and Pavan v. Italy*, the ECtHR declared that the limitations provided for by Italian legislation on the use of pre-implantation diagnosis for assisted reproduction techniques did not comply with the rules on the right to private and family life. The Court's judgment was based mainly on the inconsistency found in the Italian legislation, which, on the one hand, prevented the use of pre-implantation diagnosis for some serious genetic diseases transmissible to the foetus (in this case cystic fibrosis) while, on the other hand, allowed therapeutic abortion for those same diseases under Law No. 194 of 22 May 1978.[58] Consequently, the Court held that the interference with the right to private and family life was disproportionate and therefore unlawful.

Subsequently, in its judgment no. 162 of 9 April 2014 the Italian Constitutional Court struck down the ban on access to heterologous fertilisation for infertile couples due to infringement of several provisions of the Constitution, considering that the prohibition was contrary to the constitutionally guaranteed rights to create a family and to health. In ascertaining the unreasonable nature of the prohibition imposed by the legislator, the Court underlined in particular its discriminatory nature on economic

[54] It should be noted that solutions similar to those adopted by the ECtHR have been reached by the IACtHR in relation to cases of a total prohibition of access to assisted procreation techniques considered contrary to several provisions of the ACHR: judgment of 28 November 2012, *Artavia Murillo et al. v. Costa Rica*, paras 136 ff.

[55] Appl. no. 57813/00.

[56] On the Grand Chamber's jurisdiction on review, see Chap. 4, Sect. 4.1.

[57] On "warning judgments", see Chap. 4, Sect. 4.3.3.

[58] Appl. no. 54270/10, para 62.

grounds since only the wealthiest could travel abroad and undergo heterologous fertilisation techniques.[59]

6.3.2 Surrogacy

European and non-European countries have also adopted very different legislative solutions and practices with regard to surrogacy.[60] Some countries prohibit surrogacy outright—i.e., whether there is a biological link between the conceived child and one of the parents or no biological link at all—while other countries allow access to this technique, sometimes regulating in detail the ways in which an agreement can be reached between the individual or the couple, whether heterosexual or of the same-sex, and the woman carrying the pregnancy.

Even in cases where States do not regulate surrogacy or even prohibit the practice, it is not uncommon for national courts, on the basis of the principle of the best interests of the child and/or the right to establish a family, to consider the parent–child relationship established in countries where surrogacy is permitted as lawful thereby overriding the limit set by the principle of *ordre public* on the recognition of such a relationship created abroad. National courts have sometimes recognised only the lawfulness of the relationship with one of the members of the couple, in particular the one who has a biological link with the child. From this point of view, reference may be made to judgments nos. 824 and 825 of 5 July 2017 issued by the French Court of Cassation, which, on the basis of the principle of the best interests of the child permitted in France the registration of the birth certificate of a child born by surrogacy abroad, a practice prohibited by the French legal system, but exclusively as regards the biological father and hence denying recognition of the parent–child relationship as regards the non-biological mother.

Issues relating to the lawfulness of the use of surrogacy have been examined in depth by the ECtHR and, as in the case of medically assisted procreation, there has been no shortage of conflicting decisions by the Strasbourg Court.

In two judgments of 26 June 2014 in *Mennesson v. France*[61] and *Labassee v. France*,[62] the ECtHR found that France had violated Article 8 ECHR, with particular reference to the failure to respect the right to personal identity of children born abroad on the basis of recourse to surrogacy and who had been denied recognition of any legal status in the French legal system, despite the fact that in both cases the biological fathers of the children were Mr Mennesson and Mr Labassee respectively.

---

[59] See para 13 of the conclusions on points of law.

[60] For a concise analysis of the national rules approved in this regard by the States parties to the ECHR, see the ECtHR advisory opinion of 10 April 2019 based on the mechanism provided for in Protocol No. 16 (see Chap. 4, Sect. 4.1), paras 23–24.

[61] Appl. no. 65192/11.

[62] Appl. no. 65941/11.

In a subsequent judgment of 24 January 2017 in *Paradiso and Campanelli v. Italy*,[63] the ECtHR (Grand Chamber), reversing the conclusions reached in that same case by the Chamber in its judgment of 27 January 2015, held that the prohibition on surrogacy laid down in Italian Law No. 40 of 19 February 2004 was compatible with the ECHR. More specifically, the Court ruled out the application of the right to family life under Article 8 ECHR, giving weight in the case before it to the absence of any biological link between the child and the parents as well as the short period of time that the child had been in the family in question (six months). Consequently, the Court analysed the case exclusively from the less protective aspect of the right to privacy, finding that the respondent State had not violated Article 8.

More recently, the ECtHR (Grand Chamber) expressed its views on surrogacy in the above-mentioned advisory opinion of 10 April 2019,[64] adopted, pursuant to Protocol No. 16 to the ECHR at the request of the French Supreme Court. In that opinion, the Court did not limit itself to conducting a survey of its own case law but appropriately contributed to its development. On the question of the necessity to recognise the parent–child relationship between a non-biological mother and a child born as a result of surrogacy abroad, the Court ruled in the affirmative, attaching particular importance to the principle of the best interests of the child. The ECtHR also left to the discretion of the State authorities the choice of legal instruments, including adoption, through which to achieve recognition of that legal link, on condition that these instruments are applied "promptly and effectively, in accordance with the child's best interests".[65] The principles affirmed by the Court in the opinion were applied by the ECtHR in its decision of inadmissibility of 12 December 2019 in *C v. France* and *E v. France*.[66]

6.3.3 Donation of Embryos and Scientific Research

The sensitive issue of the lawfulness of conduct aimed at the donation of human embryos for scientific research has also been analysed by the ECtHR.

In its judgment of 27 August 2015 in *Parrillo v. Italy*,[67] the ECtHR (Grand Chamber) addressed whether Article 8 ECHR was infringed by national legislation banning the donation for scientific research purposes of embryos resulting from *in vitro* fertilisation. The Court, which analysed the case in question from the specific point of view of the applicant's right to privacy under Article 8 ECHR, ruled that the prohibition was not contrary to that provision of the Convention. More specifically, although the ban on embryo donation constituted an interference with an individual's

---

[63] Appl. no. 25358/12.

[64] Request no. P16-2018-001.

[65] See para 55 of the opinion.

[66] Appl. nos. 1462/18 and 17348/18.

[67] Appl. no. 46470/11.

private life, it could—according to the ECtHR—be regarded as "necessary in a democratic society" in that it is the expression of an appropriate balance between opposing general and individual interests and does not exceed the wide margin of appreciation afforded in this respect to the States parties to the ECHR. From this last standpoint, the Court highlighted both the absence of a European consensus among the States parties on the specific regulation of this matter and the significant discretion granted in this field by existing international instruments such as Article 18 of the Oviedo Convention of 1997.

6.4 End-of-Life Issues: ECtHR Case Law

It is now necessary to examine the questions relating to so-called end-of-life situations, regarding which of particular importance is the lawfulness at the national and international level of both decisions on the interruption of artificial hydration and nutrition in favour of individuals in a permanent and irreversible vegetative state and on recourse to euthanasia.

These issues have been adequately addressed in ECtHR case law. In this regard, it can be briefly noted that the Court recognises a wide margin of appreciation for States in the matter of recourse to forms of interruption of artificial hydration and nutrition as well as euthanasia, both treated very differently by the various members of the CoE.

The particular discretion afforded to the States parties in regulating issues concerning decisions to interrupt artificial nutrition and hydration was affirmed by the ECtHR (Grand Chamber) in its judgment of 5 June 2015 in *Lambert and Others v. France*,[68] wherein it held that an order issued by a domestic court to interrupt the medical treatment at issue did not violate the right to life under Article 2 ECHR. The Court attributes a wide margin of appreciation to the States parties because of the absence of a "European consensus" on regulating cases of interruption and artificial feeding, adding that in the case before it the national rules exhibited sufficient legislative clarity and guaranteed an adequate weighing of the various opposing interests.

More recently, the ECtHR ruled that a decision to suspend artificial ventilation for a new-born child and not to allow him access to experimental treatment whose effectiveness had not been scientifically proven fell within the margin of appreciation afforded to States parties.[69] In its decision the Court thus declared as inadmissible the application filed by the parents who had requested access to experimental treatment for their son, who suffered from a rare genetic disease with an unfavourable prognosis. Taking into account the absence of any concrete prospect of improvement in the infant's state of health, British doctors had decided to suspend artificial ventilation and proceed only with palliative care. The parents contested that decision, demanding

[68] Appl. no. 46043/14.

[69] ECtHR, decision of 27 June 2017, *Gard and Others v. United Kingdom*, appl. no. 39793/17.

that experimental treatment available abroad be given, but the national courts upheld the lawfulness of the doctors' conduct in light of the principle of the best interests of the child. The Strasbourg Court ruled out a violation of Article 2 ECHR, emphasising once again the absence of any European consensus in the matter in question and noting that the British authorities, within a clear national regulatory framework that provides for recourse to the courts in case of doubt about the most appropriate solution to be adopted, had adequately balanced the different interests involved in this case, affording particular importance to the principle of the best interests of the child.

The above approach has been confirmed in a similar case concerning a five-year old child who suffered from acute necrotising encephalopathy and was in a permanent vegetative state with no prospect of improvement: in its decision of 21 April 2021 on inadmissibility in *Parfitt v. United Kingdom*,[70] the Court ruled that the national decisions withdrawing the life-sustaining treatment did not violate the right to life and the right to private and family life, relying again on the principle of the best interests of the child.

Finally, the ECtHR has ruled that some euthanasia practices permitted in a number of States parties to the ECHR are compatible with the right to life. In this context, the Court has stated that the right of every individual to end his or her own existence constitutes an aspect of the right to life, provided that the choice to terminate life is free and informed, in line with the HRC's statement in *General Comment No. 36* of 30 October 2018.[71] The Court added that the individual also has the right to choose the means by which to end life and the time at which to put that decision into practice.[72]

Very recently, the Strasbourg Court reaffirmed its position on euthanasia, stating that the right to life does not prevent the adoption of national laws concerning the decriminalization of the recourse to euthanasia, provided that adequate and sufficient guarantees are established to avoid abuses.[73]

However, it does not follow from the Court's approach, whereby the decision to end one's life is a matter for the personal choice of the individual, that there is a positive obligation on the State to provide for euthanasia in the various forms adopted in practice. The right to assisted suicide is not in fact provided for in most European States and the absence of national rules on the subject is based—according to the Court—on legitimate reasons, in particular to avoid excessive recourse to the practice of assisted suicide.

In short, it would appear that the ECtHR has adopted a position of *reasoned neutrality* in its decisions on end of life, ensuring exclusively that the choices made at the national level are the expression of a rigorous balancing of the conflicting interests and are proportionate to the aim to be achieved. This position of the Court

---

[70] Appl. no. 18533/21.

[71] See para 9.

[72] See respectively the ECtHR judgments of 20 January 2011 in *Haas* v. *Switzerland*, appl. no. 31322/07, para 51, and of 14 May 2013 in *Gross* v. *Switzerland*, appl. no. 67810/10, para 59.

[73] See judgment of 4 October 2022, *Mortier v. Belgium*, appl. no. 78017/17, paras. 138–139.

appears consistent with the similar neutrality it has displayed in questions concerning recourse to abortion, mentioned above.[74]

6.5 The Rights Linked to the Right to Life—The Protection of Human Dignity

The first generation of human rights, amongst which civil rights of a fundamental nature, have developed enormously from both a legislative and case law standpoint that has progressively guaranteed their particularly extensive application, giving rise in some cases to veritable independent rights.

It must be pointed out, however, that it is not always easy to understand when a new human right has been created, originally derived from a fundamental right but subsequently consolidated as an autonomous right, and when by contrast it is a matter of mere applications, albeit of a very extensive nature, of "old" fundamental rights. Similarly, it is not always clear in practice whether derived rights are always to be considered the expression of fundamental rights, such as, for example, the right to life or the right not to be subjected to torture or inhuman or degrading treatment, or whether by contrast they are to be linked to other human rights that may be subject to restrictions by the State on the basis of the principle of balancing general and individual interests.

Bearing in mind the foregoing, a series of other rights that have now acquired significant autonomy also at the legislative level have derived from the right to life. First and foremost, the right to the protection of human dignity, which is certainly to be considered an autonomous right and which indeed complements and completes the protection derivable from the right to life, contributing in turn to the formation of further individual or collective rights.

It should be pointed out that the fact of anchoring the more recent rights to the right to life and human dignity is not only a theoretical exercise without practical effects, but serves to strengthen their protection from a normative point of view. For example, many of the derived rights are contemplated in legal instruments relating to economic, social and cultural rights, considered as aforesaid to be second generation and protected for the most part by so-called progressive obligations.[75] However, if linked to fundamental rights, the derived rights assume greater importance and their regulation, albeit within certain limits, can be based on the more robust rules applying to fundamental rights, enabling the application of obligations with more effective content and that call for immediate respect.

Again with regard to the right to human dignity, it is used not only in connection with the right to life but also with other fundamental rights, complementing and extending their scope of application. For example, on the one hand, the ECtHR has stated that racial discrimination may constitute a violation of human dignity

---

[74] See *supra*, Sect. 6.2.4.

[75] On the content of these obligations, see Chap. 3, Sect. 3.10.

and therefore constitute degrading treatment under Article 3 ECHR.[76] On the other hand, in the judgment delivered by the Grand Chamber on 6 July 2005 in *Nachova and Others v. Bulgaria*, the Court stated, more specifically, that racial violence "is a particular affront to human dignity" and therefore requires from the authorities "special vigilance and a vigorous reaction" so as to use "all available means to combat racism and racist violence".[77]

It is clear from the above that human dignity is now an essential value in the field of human rights protection, playing a *transversal* role—therefore not limited to specific human rights—aimed at strengthening and expanding the scope of application of a plurality of individual or collective rights.

Needless to say, in order to enjoy effective protection, the aforementioned rights linked to certain fundamental rights require not so much observance of negative obligations on the part of the States, which would be often totally ineffective, but rather the observance of a vast range of positive obligations of a general and more specific nature that entail the adoption of numerous national measures, including of a legislative nature, which vary according to the original level of protection of these rights in the individual country examined.

Rights related to the right to life and the right to protection of human dignity include, for example, the right to health, the right to adequate and stable housing, the right to water and the right of access to essential health services.

6.5.1 Right to Health and Right to Access to Essential Medical Services

The right to health is expressly grounded in various specific provisions in an array of conventions, such as Article 12 ICESCR and Article 16 ACHR. It has also been derived from interpretation by the IACtHR, which has thus given concrete effect to the general clause in Article 26 ACHR,[78] e.g. in its judgment of 8 March 2018 in *Poblete Vilches and Others v. Chile*.[79]

The CESCR has in particular specified that the right to health implies the obligation of the State to provide a health system which is effectively available, in terms of facilities and services offered, accessible to all without discrimination, of good quality in relation to the services provided and the skills of health personnel as well

[76] See judgment of 12 July 2005 in *Moldovan and Others v. Romania (no. 2)*, appl. nos. 41138/98 and 64320/01, paras 111 and 113.

[77] Appl. nos. 43577/98 and 43579/98, para 145.

[78] Article 26 (Progressive Development): "The States Parties undertake to adopt measures, both internally and through international cooperation, especially those of an economic and technical nature, with a view to achieving progressively, by legislation or other appropriate means, the full realization of the rights implicit in the economic, social, educational, scientific, and cultural standards set forth in the Charter of the Organization of American States as amended by the Protocol of Buenos Aires".

[79] See paras 100 ff.

as informed by ethical behaviour on the part of doctors and in conformity with any specific cultural needs of the users of such services.[80]

6.5.2 Right to Food and Right to Water

From the right to life and the right to the preservation of human dignity—but in reality also from other human rights derived from the latter, for example the right to health—one can derive the right to food and the right to water, again as rights that have attained an autonomous form and content.

The right to food is already referred to in Article 25(1) UDHR and protected by Article 11 ICESCR. The link between the right to food and other human rights is widely highlighted in international practice. With reference to the relationship between the right to food and the right to health, the UNGA, in its Resolution No. 59/202 of 20 December 2004, declares that the right to food consists in the possibility for each individual to have access "to safe and nutritious food, consistent with the right to adequate food and the fundamental right of everyone to be free from hunger, so as to be able to fully develop and maintain their physical and mental capacities".[81]

Similarly, there is no lack of references to the connection between the right to food and the right to human dignity. In particular, in *General Comment No. 12* of 12 May 1999, on Article 11 (The Right to Adequate Food), the CESCR observed that "the right to adequate food is indivisibly linked to the inherent dignity of the human person".[82]

The right to water is proclaimed in UNGA Resolution 64/292 of 28 July 2010,[83] which recognises "the right to safe and clean drinking water and sanitation as a human right that is essential for the full enjoyment of life and all human rights", calling upon States and international organisations "to provide financial resources, capacity-building and technology transfer, through international assistance and cooperation, in particular to developing countries, in order to scale up efforts to provide safe, clean, accessible and affordable drinking water and sanitation for all".[84]

In its *General Comment No. 15* of 20 January 2003 on Articles 11 and 12 (The Right to Water), the CESCR observes preliminarily that the human right to water "is indispensable for leading a life in human dignity. It is a prerequisite for the realization of other human rights", and defines this right as the right of everyone to "sufficient, safe, acceptable and physically accessible and affordable water for

[80] See *General Comment No. 14* of 11 August 2000 on Article 12 (The Right to the Highest Attainable Standard of Health), para 12.

[81] See para 2.

[82] See para 4 of the General Comment, which also refers to the criteria of quantity and quality of food, considered necessary to define an adequate level of nutrition.

[83] The Resolution also highlights the relationship between the right to water and the right to life, noting that the right to water is "essential for the full enjoyment of life and all human rights": para 1.

[84] See paras 1–2.

personal and domestic uses".[85] The CESCR also stressed that water is required for a range of different purposes, besides personal and domestic uses, to realise many of the ICESCR rights indicated above. According to CESCR, water is for instance necessary to ensure the right to food and the right to health.[86]

Comprehension Check and Tasks

1. What does the right to life protect? (Sect. 6.2)
2. What are the negative and positive obligations of the State with regard to the right to life? Refer in particular to the ECtHR judgments in *McCann* (1995) and *Giuliani and Gaggio* (2011). (Sects. 6.2–6.2.1)
3. The ECtHR has adopted a neutral position on the right to abortion. What does this neutrality consist of and what are the State's obligations with regard to abortion? (Sect. 6.2.4)
4. What are the limits of customary international law on the death penalty? (Sect. 6.2.5)
5. With regard to medically assisted procreation and surrogacy, States have adopted very different legislative solutions and practices. Why is this important for the establishment of a European consensus according to the ECtHR? (Sects. 6.3.1–6.3.2)
6. The ECtHR (Grand Chamber) expressed its views on surrogacy also in its advisory opinion of 2019. In this opinion, did the Court limit itself to confirming its own case law or did it contribute to its development? (Sect. 6.3.2)
7. In end-of-life issues, what is the position of the ECtHR in the *Gard* (2017) and *Parfitt* (2021) cases? (Sect. 6.4)

---

[85] See paras 1–2.

[86] *Id.*, para 6.

Chapter 7
Other Grave Breaches of Human Rights: Prohibition of Genocide, Prohibition of Torture and Inhuman and Degrading Punishment or Treatment, Prohibition of Slavery and Forced Labour and Prohibition of Racial Discrimination and Apartheid

Contents

Abstract The chapter focuses on serious violations of human rights other than the right to life, analysing for example the vast international jurisprudence on the prohibition of genocide and on the prohibition of torture and inhuman and degrading treatment. Some particular aspects of the application of relevant international standards are also examined, including the so-called genocide denial; the conflict between State immunity or State organs immunity and the need to repress grave breaches of human rights; and the formation of new rights arising from the application of international norms on the prohibition of torture—such as the right to hope—or on the prohibition of slavery—as in the case of the prohibition of trafficking in human beings.

P. Pustorino, *Introduction to International Human Rights Law*,
https://doi.org/10.1007/978-94-6265-563-8_7

7.1 Prohibition of Genocide

The prohibition of genocide is contained in a peremptory norm of international law. The relevant obligations of States are therefore *erga omnes*. The *jus cogens* character of the rule that prohibits genocide was confirmed by the ICJ in the judgment of 26 February 2007 in the case concerning the *Application of the Convention on the Prevention and Punishment of the Crime of Genocide*, in which the Court referred to its numerous precedents stressing that "the norm prohibiting genocide was assuredly a peremptory norm of international law (jus cogens)".[1]

The international obligations on genocide prohibit not only State actions aimed at committing this international crime but also omissions by the State in relation to harmful conduct by State organs or private individuals—in particular armed groups or insurrectionary movements—where the State has the capacity to prevent and repress genocide in accordance with the principle of due diligence. In this respect, the interpretation according to which Article I of the Convention on the Prevention and Punishment of the Crime of Genocide of 9 December 1948[2] establishes a positive obligation on the State to prevent genocide committed by other States or private individuals is well established.[3]

The violation of the State's obligation to prevent and suppress acts of genocide committed by individuals was established in the above-mentioned 2007 judgment of the ICJ, with regard to the massacre of thousands of Bosnian-Muslim civilians in 1995 in Srebrenica by Serbian military and paramilitary forces, mostly belonging to the Autonomous Republic of Srpska, one of the two entities of Bosnia and Herzegovina. On the other hand, the Court ruled out the possibility of directly attributing the crime of genocide to Serbia, since the individuals who materially committed the harmful act were not, in the Court's opinion, to be considered *de jure* or *de facto* organs of Serbia.

The failure to attribute to Serbia the conduct of the military and paramilitary forces operating in Srebrenica, as in many other parts of Bosnia and Herzegovina and Croatia, is very puzzling in light of the significant political, military and economic ties between the armed groups in question and the Serbian government. By contrast, as is well known, the ICTY, in ascertaining the individual criminal responsibility of Bosnian Serb soldiers employed in the same military operation, found that an "overall control" had been exercised by the Serbian authorities over the individuals

[1] See *Bosnia and Herzegovina v. Serbia and Montenegro*, in ICJ 2007, pp. 110–111, para 161.

[2] The text of the provision states that the Contracting Parties "confirm that genocide, whether committed in time of peace or in time of war, is a crime under international law which they undertake to prevent and to punish".

[3] See ICJ 2007, p. 221, para 430, according to which "responsibility is however incurred if the State manifestly failed to take all measures to prevent genocide which were within its power, and which might have contributed to preventing the genocide. In this area the notion of "due diligence", which calls for an assessment in concreto, is of critical importance".

responsible for these international crimes and operating in groups that are particularly well organised in military terms.[4]

The violation of the prohibition of genocide on the basis of omission on the part of the State was also established, again in the case of Srebrenica, by the Dutch courts. Leaving aside questions relating to the concurrent responsibility of the UN for the same event, which could not be verified on the merits due to the application by the Dutch courts of the principle of absolute immunity afforded to the UN, with regard to the responsibility of the Netherlands for the Srebrenica massacre both the Court of Appeal of The Hague, in its judgment of 5 July 2011, and the Supreme Court, in its judgments of 6 September 2013, in the cases of *The State of the Netherlands* v. *Nuhanović* and *The State of the Netherlands v. Mustafic-Mujic et al.*, established the civil liability of the Netherlands following the decision to evacuate the refugee camp protected by the Dutch military contingent.

In particular, the Dutch courts emphasised that the Netherlands had the power to prevent the conduct of Bosnian Serb soldiers, but decided not to intervene, abandoning the refugee camp and handing over the civilians to the Serbs. A more recent judgment of the Dutch Supreme Court, issued on 19 July 2019 in a further proceeding related to the Srebrenica case, reaffirmed the applicability of the principle of dual responsibility, of the UN and the Netherlands, for the wrongdoing committed in the case in question, but significantly reduced the Netherlands' *share* of responsibility.[5]

With regard to the content of the prohibition of genocide, it is well established that genocide consists in the intentional killing, destruction or extermination (*mens rea*), in whole or in part, of a national, ethnical, racial or religious group (*actus reus*).[6] From this point of view, again in the above-mentioned 2007 judgment, the ICJ stated that the practice of so-called ethnic cleansing, consisting in the modification of the ethnic composition of the population by using force or intimidation also removing persons of given groups from some specific areas, may constitute an act of genocide if one of the prohibited acts specified in Article II of the 1948 Convention has been committed combined with "the intent to destroy the group as such".[7]

On the other hand, it is highly doubtful that the notion in question includes political or social genocide, consisting in the "mass" killing of members of a given political or social group, as well as cultural genocide, consisting in criminal conduct aimed at the destruction of a culturally defined group. However, it should be noted that some States (Colombia, Costa Rica, Côte d'Ivoire, Ethiopia, Lithuania, Panama, Poland and Slovenia) have included political groups in their domestic definition of genocide, while others (Estonia, Latvia, Lithuania, Peru and Slovenia) have further extended the notion of genocide to include "social" groups.

---

[4] See the judgment of 15 July 1999 of the Appeals Chamber of the ICTY, *Prosecutor v. Duško Tadić*, IT-94-1-A, paras 120–122 and 137.

[5] See the judgment in *The Netherlands v. Stichting Mothers of Srebrenica et al.*, in which the Court applied the criterion of effective control over Dutch military personnel employed in the UNPROFOR mission pursuant to Article 8 of the ARSIWA.

[6] See Article II of the Convention on the Prevention and Punishment of the Crime of Genocide of 1948 and Article 6 of the ICC Statute.

[7] Cit., pp. 122–123, para 190.

These developments in domestic law have been reflected to some extent in international case law. In its judgment of 20 October 2015 in *Vasiliauskas v. Lithuania*,[8] the ECtHR (Grand Chamber) found that the respondent State had violated Article 7 ECHR, which establishes the principle of legality in criminal matters and the consequent principle of non-retroactivity of criminal law,[9] on the ground that the applicant's conviction for genocide—in relation to the killing in 1953, during the Soviet military occupation of Lithuania, of members of a political group represented by the Lithuanian partisans—had been carried out in a manner that did not fall within the notion of genocide existing at the time, thus running counter to the principle of foreseeability of the criminal prohibition.

However, in a more recent decision the Strasbourg Court seems to take a more open stance towards including political groups in the traditional notion of genocide. In its judgment of 12 March 2019, rendered in *Drėlingas v. Lithuania*[10] and concerning a similar conviction for genocide committed against Lithuanian partisans, which took place this time in 1956, the Court considered the broad interpretation of the notion of genocide applied at the national level to be legitimate. The Court stated that on this occasion, and unlike in the aforementioned *Vasiliauskas* case, the Lithuanian courts had shown that the partisans constituted, at the time of the commission of the serious wrongdoing in this case, a national and ethnic group, within the meaning of Article II of the 1948 Convention, because "the partisans had played an essential role when protecting the national identity, culture and national self-awareness of the Lithuanian nation".[11]

In this way, the European Court, while not accepting the view of a formal broadening of the notion of genocide so as to include political groups alongside national, ethnic, racial or religious groups, essentially reaches the same result through a broad interpretation of the notion of national or ethnic group, which can include certain political groups.

7.1.1 Genocide Denial

The commission of the crime of genocide does not exclude the right of everyone to express their opinions, even of an extreme nature, on historical events linked to cases of genocide. Indeed, under certain strict conditions, which will be highlighted below, denial of this crime is even permitted.

An analysis of ECtHR case law shows that the fundamental elements for assessing the conflict between freedom of opinion (which, as explored later in this book,[12] constitutes an essential guarantee for the constitution of a democratic society and

[8] See appl. no 35343/05.

[9] See Chap. 8, Sects. 8.3–8.3.1.

[10] See appl. no. 28859/16.

[11] See para 103 of the Court's judgment.

[12] See Chap. 9, Sect. 9.3.

extends to the protection of "extreme opinions" expressed by the individual) and the prohibition of genocide are the good faith of the author of the opinions and the reliability and objectivity of the news and information available on treating a certain historical event as genocide. In addition, the social and political context in which the denialist opinions are expressed must be assessed. Finally, the particular nature of the crime of genocide is of relevance, which, as stated above, requires the establishment of an *actus reus* consisting in the acts of destruction of a specific group of individuals and a *mens rea* consisting in the specific intention to destroy that group.

On this basis, the ECtHR (Grand Chamber), in its judgment of 15 October 2015 in *Perinçek v. Switzerland*,[13] held that the criminal conviction of a Turkish politician for denying the Armenian genocide of 1915—a crime whose existence and precise qualification is debated among historians—was contrary to Article 10 ECHR although it is not disputed that Turkey did commit other very serious human rights violations against the Armenian population at the time. According to the Court, considering that "the applicant's statements bore on a matter of public interest and did not amount to a call for hatred or intolerance, that the context in which they were made was not marked by heightened tensions or special historical overtones in Switzerland, that the statements cannot be regarded as affecting the dignity of the members of the Armenian community to the point of requiring a criminal-law response in Switzerland, that there is no international-law obligation for Switzerland to criminalise such statements, that the Swiss courts appear to have censured the applicant for voicing an opinion that diverged from the established ones in Switzerland, and that the interference took the serious form of a criminal conviction ... the Court concludes that it was not necessary, in a democratic society, to subject the applicant to a criminal penalty in order to protect the rights of the Armenian community at stake in the present case".[14]

That contrasts with the ECtHR's assessments with reference to historically established crimes of genocide, such as the genocide of the Jews during World War II. In this case, the Court seems to consider that denialist views fall outside the scope of the protection of freedom of expression and opinion, with the effect of holding that national legislation that criminalises this specific form of denialism is consistent with the ECHR subject to the proportionality of the repressive measures adopted, which may be exceeded if excessively severe penalties are imposed on the author of the denials.

More specifically, in the inadmissibility decision of 10 November 2015 in *M'Bala M'Bala v. France*,[15] the Court ruled out that even "disguised" forms of denial of the genocide of the Jews, expressed by the author in the context of a deplorable theatrical performance, can be protected as manifestations of freedom of opinion, representing instead a demonstration of hatred and anti-Semitism in clear support of unacceptable denialist positions. In this decision, the Court pointed out that the applicant had abused the right to freedom of expression in order to pursue aims contrary to the

[13] See appl. no. 27510/08.

[14] See para 280 of the Court's judgment.

[15] See appl. no. 25239/13.

object and purpose of the ECHR,[16] adding that, if such unlawful behaviour were upheld, it would result in "the destruction of Convention rights and freedoms".[17]

In its more recent inadmissibility decision of 8 January 2019 in *Williamson v. Germany*,[18] the ECtHR, basing its reasoning on Article 10 ECHR and not on the aforementioned abuse of rights (Article 17), reiterated its position on the lawfulness of proportionate criminal sanctions against individuals who deny the Holocaust, even where the denials, although originally disseminated abroad, are subsequently made available in the country in which the criminal proceedings for the crime of denial take place.

7.2 Prohibition of Torture and Inhuman and Degrading Treatment: Scope of the International Law Rules

The prohibition of torture is contained in a *jus cogens* rule, as affirmed several times by the bodies charged with scrutinising observance of international human rights conventions[19] and by the ICJ in its judgment of 20 July 2012 in *Questions relating to the Obligation to Prosecute or Extradite*, according to which "the prohibition of torture is part of customary international law and it has become a peremptory norm (*jus cogens*)".[20] The norm containing the prohibition in question therefore contains obligations *erga omnes*.

The prohibition of torture, which is generally associated with the prohibition of inhuman or degrading treatment and punishment, is contained in many universal and regional human rights conventions or acts of a *general* nature, i.e. relating to the protection of numerous individual or collective rights—e.g. Article 5 UDHR, Article 3 ECHR and Article 4 CFREU—as well as in treaties specifically designed to prohibit such harmful conduct.[21]

It is common ground in the literature and in case law that compliance with the prohibition of torture entails a series of negative and positive obligations incumbent on States, both substantive and procedural. Among the most significant of these

[16] The Court found that pursuant to Article 17 ECHR the applicant cannot enjoy the protection of Article 10. According to Article 17 "Nothing in this Convention may be interpreted as implying for any State, group or person any right to engage in any activity or perform any act aimed at the destruction of any of the rights and freedoms set forth herein or at their limitation to a greater extent than is provided for in the Convention".

[17] See para 41 of the decision.

[18] See appl. no. 64496/17.

[19] See, for example, the ECtHR (Grand Chamber) judgment of 21 November 2001 in *Al-Adsani v. The United Kingdom*, appl. no. 35763/97, paras 60–61.

[20] *Belgium v. Senegal*, in ICJ 2012, p. 457, para 99.

[21] See the UN Convention against Torture and Other Cruel, Inhuman or Degrading Treatment or Punishment of 10 December 1984, the Inter-American Convention to Prevent and Punish Torture of 9 December 1985 and the European Convention for the Prevention of Torture and Inhuman or Degrading Treatment or Punishment of 26 November 1987.

positive obligations is a "legislative" one consisting of a duty to enact domestic legislation on the prohibition of torture, whose provisions must be commensurate with the gravity of the conduct in question. A violation of the positive obligation to provide for legislative rules having as their object the prohibition of torture has been ascertained several times by the ECtHR, for example, in the judgments of 7 April 2015 in *Cestaro v. Italy*[22] and of 26 October 2017 in *Blair and Others v. Italy*,[23] both relating to the serious and repeated acts of torture committed by police forces on the margins of the G8 summit in Genoa in 2001 against a number of individuals.

Similar positive obligations are incumbent on the State to prevent and punish violations of the prohibition of torture, including in judicial proceedings, whether committed by State organs or private individuals. It follows that it is possible to establish a breach by the State of the prohibition of torture or inhuman or degrading treatment in cases of injuries committed between private individuals, on the assumption that the State has not taken the necessary measures to prevent or punish such violations of an inter-individual nature.[24]

The concrete application of the prohibition of torture and inhuman or degrading treatment requires, firstly, that a "minimum threshold" of seriousness be identified in order to bring certain instances of harmful conduct within the scope of application of the relevant international rules, and, secondly, that a distinction be drawn between cases qualifying as "torture" and those falling under the prohibition of "inhuman" or "degrading" treatment.

The prohibition of torture applies to both physical and mental suffering and differs from the prohibition of inhuman or degrading treatment in relation to the lower threshold of seriousness required to establish the latter conduct. It should also be noted that the notions of torture and inhuman or degrading treatment are by no means immutable over time, but are conditioned both by the overall development of the international legal regime on human rights and by scientific advances in the determination of the effects of harmful practices on the individual, especially as regards psychological injuries. Consequently, treatment deemed inhuman or degrading today may in the future be classified as acts of torture, as expressly stated by the ECtHR in its judgment of 28 July 1999 in *Selmouni v. France*.[25]

In *Ireland v. The United Kingdom*, decided by judgment of 18 January 1978, the ECtHR clarified that the minimum level of severity to be attained by all violations of Article 3 ECHR cannot be determined in absolute terms but rather in relative terms and "depends on all the circumstances of the case, such as the duration of the treatment, its physical or mental effects and, in some cases, the sex, age and state of health of the victim, etc.".[26] In our view, a violation of the prohibition of torture, as well as of the prohibition of inhuman or degrading treatment, may occur

[22] Appl. no. 6884/11.

[23] Appl. nos. 1442/14, 21319/14 and 21911/14.

[24] On this general aspect of treaty-based human rights provisions, see Chap. 3, Sect. 3.7.

[25] Appl. no. 25803/94, para 101 of the judgment. The question is also relevant in the context of "warning" judgments: see Chap. 4, Sect. 4.3.3.

[26] Appl. no. 5310/71, para 162 of the judgment.

in practice either in light of the application of only one of the above criteria—where it is considered to be of particular importance in the case—or on the basis of the cumulative application of the same criteria, which taken together lead the interpreter to consider that there has been a violation of these prohibitions.

As an example of a case in which, according to the Strasbourg Court, the injuries suffered by the victim did not attain a minimum level of severity, one may cite the decision of 18 June 2009 in *Budina v. Russia*.[27] In that case the Court declared manifestly ill-founded and thus inadmissible the application of a disabled woman who claimed a violation of Article 3 because her State pension was so meagre that it did not allow her to meet her essential needs. While not ruling out the possibility that, in the event of an individual's total economic dependence on public financial support, the State may be held liable as a result of the national authorities' inaction and indifference to the individual's situation of serious need, the Court ruled out the possibility that, in the present case, the State's conduct went beyond the minimum level of severity that could be classified as inhuman or degrading treatment.

As regards the distinction between inhuman and degrading treatment, the Strasbourg Court (Grand Chamber) ruled in its judgment of 11 July 2006 in *Jalloh v. Germany* that treatment has to be considered as *inhuman* "because, inter alia, it was premeditated, was applied for hours at a stretch and caused either actual bodily injury or intense physical and mental suffering". On the other hand, treatment has to be considered *degrading* "when it was such as to arouse in its victims feelings of fear, anguish and inferiority capable of humiliating and debasing them and possibly breaking their physical or moral resistance … or when it was such as to drive the victim to act against his will or conscience".[28] It is therefore legitimate to consider that, from the Court's point of view and despite the obvious connection between the two concepts, the notion of inhuman treatment is based simultaneously on verification of the physical and mental consequences caused to the victim whereas the notion of degrading treatment is mainly concerned with the mental and psychological consequences produced to the detriment of a given individual, which may vary more, compared to what can be ascertained in relation to inhuman treatment, depending on the victim considered and the circumstances of the specific case. In any event, the contiguity of the concepts of inhuman and degrading treatment has sometimes led the ECtHR to find that the State has violated both prohibitions.

In relation to the prohibition of inhuman or degrading treatment, one particular aspect of the prohibition should be stressed, i.e. determining who the victims of any such violations are. While in most cases the victim is exclusively the natural person directly subjected to the harmful conduct, it cannot be ruled out that in some specific circumstances the same unlawful conduct will constitute a violation of the prohibition of inhuman or degrading treatment also against other individuals, for example, the victim's family members who witness—by chance or because of compulsion on the part of the perpetrators of the harmful conduct—the use of such practices and who

---

[27] Appl. no. 45603/05.

[28] Appl. no. 54810/00, para 68 of the judgment.

in turn feel a sense of distress and helplessness such as to entail an independent violation of the prohibition in question.

Finally, as regards the notion of inhuman or degrading punishment, "the suffering or humiliation involved must in any event go beyond that inevitable element of suffering or humiliation connected with a given form of legitimate treatment or punishment".[29] In this regard, it is sufficient to recall the ECtHR leading case,[30] in which the Court condemned the practice of corporal punishment provided for by the law of the respondent State at the time and imposed on the basis of a court order on juveniles responsible for minor offences in the Isle of Man. In particular, the Court held that such punishments were incompatible with the values of "a person's dignity and physical integrity" and therefore violated Article 3 ECHR.[31]

7.2.1 Prohibition of Torture, Rape and Sexual Violence

Following the reasoning of the Strasbourg Court in *Selmouni*, conduct that violated human rights but was previously not considered so detrimental as to fall under the prohibition of torture or inhuman or degrading treatment—e.g. rape—can nowadays be considered as falling within its scope of application. The inclusion of rape, and indeed any sexual violence, within the scope of the prohibition of torture and inhuman or degrading treatment has now been accepted in the case law and practice of the bodies charged with scrutinising the observance of human rights treaties.[32] Whether a specific case falls within the realm of torture or inhuman or degrading treatment depends on the seriousness of the harm, the identity of the victim and the particular aims pursued by the sexual violence, such as discrimination on grounds of sexual orientation, as stated by the IACtHR in its judgment of 12 March 2020 in *Azul Rojas Marín et al. v. Peru*.[33]

On the basis of the above, the ECtHR, in its judgment of 25 September 1997 in *Aydin v. Turkey*, held that the rape of a woman in detention, and thus in a particularly vulnerable condition, associated with "a series of particularly terrifying and humiliating experiences while in custody at the hands of the security forces", constituted an act of torture under Article 3 ECHR.[34]

---

[29] ECtHR, *Jalloh v. Germany*, cit., para 68.

[30] This is the well-known judgment of 25 April 1978 in *Tyrer v. United Kingdom*, appl. no. 5856/72.

[31] See para 33 of the judgment.

[32] See the considerations of ACommHPR in its decision in *Organisation Mondiale Contre la Torture et Ligue de la Zone Afrique pour la Défense des Droits des Enfants et Elèves (pour le compte de Céline) v. Democratic Republic of Congo*, no. 325/06, adopted at the 57th ordinary session of the Commission (4–18 November 2015), paras 61 ff.

[33] The case concerned a case of ill-treatment and sexual violence carried out by police officers against an individual because of his sexual orientation: paras 158 ff.

[34] Appl. no. 23178/94, paras 83–87 of the judgment.

This approach was confirmed by the CAT,[35] which, in its decision of 2 August 2019, held that the rape and other acts of sexual violence to which a woman was subjected during the armed conflict in the former Yugoslavia, where rape constituted a well-known and brutal general practice, are to be classified as acts of torture, having caused her "severe physical and mental pain and suffering and were inflicted intentionally during the armed conflict in the State party in order to punish and intimidate the complainant and to humiliate and degrade her, representing a form of discrimination on the basis of her gender and ethnicity".[36]

7.2.2 Inhuman and Degrading Treatment and Detainees' Conditions

The application of the prohibition of torture and inhuman or degrading treatment or punishment raises particular issues in relation to individuals deprived, albeit lawfully, of their liberty. Unfortunately, it must be emphasised that persons detained on the basis of preventive measures or because they have been sentenced to imprisonment are sometimes subjected to conduct that may amount to torture, whether physical or psychological, or inhuman or degrading treatment.

There are several reasons why the prohibition of torture or inhuman and degrading treatment of detainees may be violated, for example, overcrowding in prison, often associated with other deprivations of essential goods for the life of the prisoner such as scarcity of water, food and air. In addition, situations of solitary confinement for long periods of time, which can amount to acts of psychological torture,[37] are unfortunately not uncommon.

One of the best-known decisions in this respect is the ECtHR judgment of 8 January 2013 in *Torreggiani and Others v. Italy*,[38] which found that the applicants had suffered inhuman and degrading treatment in view of their intolerable living conditions in prison, including the reduced "living" space available to inmates.[39]

In its judgment of 20 October 2016 in *Muršić v. Croatia* the ECtHR (Grand Chamber) further clarified the issue of the minimum space that must be afforded to detainees in order to avoid a violation of the prohibition of inhuman or degrading treatment, stating that, in cases of cells occupied by several individuals, the State is obliged to guarantee that each detainee has a space of at least three square metres. In

[35] On the Committee's powers, see Chap. 5, Sect. 5.2.5.

[36] See para 7.3 of the non-binding decision on the communication in *A. v. Bosnia and Herzegovina*, CAT/C/67/D/854/2017.

[37] See the Report of 14 February 2020 submitted to HRCoun by the Special Rapporteur on Torture and Other Cruel, Inhuman or Degrading Treatment or Punishment, A/HRC/43/49, para 57.

[38] Appl. nos. 43517/09 and others.

[39] The Court also found that the problem of overcrowding in Italian prisons was generalised and therefore structural, thus indicating to the State general measures to correct the situation: see Chap. 4, Sect. 4.3.1.

the event of personal space falling below this standard, in the Court's view there is "a strong presumption" of a violation of Article 3 ECHR, which can only be avoided if the State is able to demonstrate the existence of factors that may compensate for the scarce allocation of personal space, such as the fact that the limitation of personal space is temporary, that sufficient freedom of movement of the detainee outside his or her cell is still granted, etc.[40]

The IACtHR expressed similar views in its judgment of 2 September 2004 in *"Juvenile Reeducation Institute" v. Paraguay*. In particular, the Court condemned the unsustainable conditions of the individuals held in the detention centre, observing that "the subhuman and degrading detention conditions that all the inmates at the Center were forced to endure inevitably affected their mental health, with adverse consequences for the psychological growth and development of their lives and mental health".[41]

While in the above cases, the violation of the prohibition of inhuman and degrading treatment derives mainly from the objective conditions in which the detainees concerned find themselves, irrespective of their particular situation, such as their state of health or their psycho-physical condition, in other cases the violation may arise precisely because of the level of particular suffering and need of the individual detainee.

For example, in its judgment of 11 February 2014 in *Contrada v. Italy (No. 2)*,[42] the ECtHR found a violation of Article 3 ECHR in relation to the violation of the prohibition of inhuman and degrading treatment following a decision by the national authorities to keep a detainee—who had been convicted by the domestic courts for complicity in mafia association—in prison despite the worsening of his state of health. From the Court's reasoning, it seems possible to infer a principle to the effect that keeping a detainee in prison may constitute, per se—regardless of the seriousness of the offences committed by the individual—a violation of the prohibition of inhuman and degrading treatment, where the stay in prison does not allow the individual to have access to the necessary and appropriate treatment for his or her serious and established illness.

This principle was reiterated by the ECtHR in its judgment of 25 October 2018 in *Provenzano v. Italy*, holding that keeping a detainee in a special so-called "hard prison" regime may constitute inhuman and degrading treatment on account of both the individual's serious physical and mental health condition and the latter's progressive deterioration, which, according to the ECtHR, would cast doubt on the applicant's social dangerousness.[43]

It should be added that a violation of the prohibition of inhuman and degrading treatment may also occur where an individual who is in detention, or under the temporary control of state authorities, is subjected to compulsory medical treatment of a non-urgent nature and against his or her will. Classic examples are cases of

---

[40] Appl. no. 7334/13.

[41] See para 168.

[42] Appl. no. 7509/08.

[43] Appl. no. 55080/13, paras 147 ff. of the judgment.

sterilisations of women not warranted on grounds of a medical emergency and carried out in the absence of the consent of the person concerned, or in any case through inadequate means of ascertaining her actual intentions.[44]

However, international human rights law cannot be considered to be violated by mandatory health treatment provided for by national legislation and justified on grounds of public interest such as practice of compulsory vaccination for specific categories of individuals like minors[45] or in relation to the vast majority of the national population as in the recent case of the compulsory vaccination decreed to combat the spread of COVID-19.

7.2.3 Inhuman and Degrading Treatment and End-of-Life Issues

On the basis of what has been said above with reference to end-of-life issues,[46] one may wonder whether the prohibition imposed at the national level on access, under certain specific conditions, to techniques allowing an individual to interrupt his or her life constitutes inhuman or degrading treatment. If in most cases this hypothesis can be ruled out, in view also of the above-mentioned national differences in the regulation of this delicate matter, one cannot rule out that a ban on access to such practices may constitute inhuman or degrading treatment where it is unequivocally demonstrated that maintaining an individual in a permanent and irreversible vegetative state causes prolonged and particularly severe suffering.

7.3 Broad Interpretation of the Prohibition of Torture and Inhuman and Degrading Treatment: The Formation of New Rights

The prohibition of torture and inhuman or degrading treatment has long been used in international case law and practice as an avenue for outlawing conduct that on the basis of a particularly broad interpretation falls within the scope of the prohibition in question.

---

[44] See the ECtHR judgment of 8 November 2011 in *V.C. v. Slovakia*, appl. no. 18968/07, paras 106 ff., and the IACtHR judgment of 30 November 2019 in *I.V. v. Bolivia*, paras 262 ff.

[45] In relation to national policies on the compulsory vaccination of minors, which sometimes provide for sanctions against offenders, both of a financial nature and in the form of a ban as regards access to school services, see recently ECtHR (Grand Chamber) judgment of 8 April 2021, *Vavřička and Others v. Czech Republic*, appl. no. 47621/13 and five other applications.

[46] See Chap. 6, Sect. 6.4.

In this regard reference may be made to the ACommHPR decision in *Interights and Ditshwanelo v. The Republic of Botswana*. The Commission held that the practice of hanging as a method of carrying out the death penalty was contrary to Article 5 ACHPR, which prohibits torture and inhuman or degrading treatment. The ACommHPR did not expressly rule whether the death penalty is contrary to the African Charter, but noted that this specific means of execution of the death penalty "is inhuman and degrading" as it "causes excessive suffering and is not strictly necessary; therefore, it constitutes a violation of Article 5 of the African Charter".[47]

In this regard, as mentioned before,[48] the ECHR system appears to be more advanced since the death penalty is now prohibited in all circumstances. On the basis of this assumption, the ECtHR has also specified that recourse to the death penalty, whatever the method of execution, gives rise to "some physical pain" and "intense psychological suffering" and is therefore incompatible with respect for the right to life and the right not to be subjected to inhuman or degrading treatment.[49]

7.3.1 Right to Hope

The "right to hope" serves as an example of how a broad interpretation of the prohibition of inhuman or degrading treatment seems to have created in practice a new human right. In particular, referring to the trend at the international and European level to provide mechanisms for reviewing life sentences, the ECtHR has brought the right to hope within the scope of the prohibition of inhuman or degrading treatment under Article 3 ECHR. According to the Court, in fact, there is a clear incompatibility between human dignity (reflecting the particular importance of that value in terms of broad interpretation of the rules on human rights)[50] and criminal convictions without any prospect of release of the individual concerned.[51] Moreover, the prospect for release must be a concrete one and the means for achieving it must be clearly set out.[52]

This by now well-settled case law was further confirmed in the ECtHR's judgment of 13 June 2019 in *Marcello Viola v. Italy (No. 2)*.[53] In that decision the Court referred once again the value of the human dignity of the detainee and the need for his possible social reintegration and the prospect of regaining his freedom. In

---

[47] See decision on communication no. 319/06 taken at the 57th regular session of the Commission (4–18 November 2015), para 87.

[48] See Chap. 6, Sect. 6.2.5.

[49] See judgment of 24 July 2014 in *Al-Nashiri v. Poland*, appl. no. 28761/11, para 577.

[50] On this function of human dignity, see Chap. 6, Sect. 6.5.

[51] ECtHR (Grand Chamber), judgment 9 July 2013 in *Vinter and Others v. The United Kingdom*, appl. nos. 66069/09, 130/10 and 3896/10, paras 113 and 123 ff.

[52] ECtHR, judgment of 12 March 2019 in *Petukhov v. Ukraine (No. 2)*, appl. no. 41216/13, paras 168 ff.

[53] Appl. no. 77633/16.

light thereof the Court considered that the prohibition of inhuman or degrading treatment was breached by the national legislation at issue that, for some particularly serious crimes involving a so-called 'irreducible' life sentence, makes a detainee's eligibility for conditional release and other alternative measures to detention (e.g. bonus permits) conditional only on the convicted person's cooperation with the judicial authorities. Having ascertained the structural nature of the shortcomings in the national system, the Court also asked Italy to amend its legislation, guaranteeing in the above-mentioned cases the possibility for reviewing the sentence in the event of the offender's rehabilitation and thus superseding the current regime based on cooperation with the judicial authorities being the sole said condition in order to be eligible for prison benefits and measures other than imprisonment.[54]

7.4 Extraterritorial Application of the Norms on the Prohibition of Torture and Principle of *Non-refoulement*

It has already been pointed out[55] that an analysis of the case law and practice of the bodies charged with scrutinising observance of human rights treaties reveals the existence of the principle that it is forbidden for the State of residence of an alien to deport or extradite that individual to countries where he or she risks being subjected to torture or inhuman or degrading treatment. This principle is expressly established in the most recent international human rights instruments, for example in Article 19(2) CFREU. Consequently, by analogy with what has been observed in relation to the right to life,[56] the authorities of the State of residence of the foreigner are required to carry out a prognostic assessment of the risk for the individual being subjected by State organs or private individuals to torture or inhuman or degrading treatment in the country of final destination on account of the personal, political or religious convictions or sexual orientation of the individual concerned.[57]

In its *General Comment No. 4* of 4 September 2018 on the implementation of Article 3 of the 1984 UN Convention against Torture in the context of Article 22,[58] the CAT first stated that the prohibition of torture and the prohibition of other ill-treatment are "absolute" and "non-derogable".[59] Furthermore, it added that also "[t]he principle of 'non-refoulement' of persons to another State where there are substantial grounds for believing that they would be in danger of being subjected

[54] See paras 141–143 of the judgment.

[55] See Chap. 3, Sect. 3.6.3.

[56] See Chap. 6, Sect. 6.2.2.

[57] See ECtHR, judgment of 17 November 2020 in *B and C v. Switzerland*, appl. nos. 889/19 and 43987/16, paras 54 ff.

[58] Article 22 concerns individual communications which may be submitted to the Committee. On this question, see Chap. 5, Sect. 5.2.5.

[59] See para 8 of the *General Comment*.

to torture is similarly absolute".[60] It would seem, therefore, that the Committee's position is that the peremptory and thus non-derogable nature of the prohibition of torture is reflected in the principle of *non-refoulement*: in other words, on the basis of an evolutionary and coordinated interpretation of the international legal rules, the principle of *non-refoulement* also enjoys the same superior rank of *jus cogens*, albeit limited to cases in which the deported individual risks being subjected to torture.[61]

The CAT then went on to stress, on the one hand, that the principle of *non-refoulement* must be applied "in any territory" under the jurisdiction of each State party and in "any area under its control or authority",[62] as already affirmed by the ECtHR in its judgment of 2 March 2010 in *Al-Saadoon and Mufdhi v. The United Kingdom*,[63] concerning the transfer to the Iraqi authorities, by the British military contingent occupying Iraq at the end of the 2003 Gulf War, of certain Iraqi citizens accused of crimes for which, if convicted, the death penalty could be imposed. On the other hand, the CAT clarified that the diplomatic assurances provided by the States of final destination of the individual and concerning the exclusion of the use of torture or inhuman or degrading treatment "should not be used as a loophole to undermine the principle of *non-refoulement*".[64] However, the CAT did not take a clear contrary position, as would have been desirable in our view, on the inadequacy per se of diplomatic assurances that there will be no torture or inhuman or degrading treatment by the country of final destination of the deported individual.

In view of the absolute and non-derogable nature of the prohibition of torture, the obligation not to deport, extradite or surrender individuals who risk being subjected to torture or inhuman and degrading treatment in the country of final destination must also be respected in cases where such individuals constitute a danger to the security and public order of the State that intends to proceed with the removal.

Worthy of note in this regard is the judgment of the ECtHR (Grand Chamber) of 28 February 2008 in *Saadi v. Italy*[65] concerning the case of a foreign national who, after having served a criminal sentence in Italy, was to be deported and repatriated to the State where he had been sentenced in absentia by a military court to a long prison term for involvement in terrorist activities. The Court held that the deportation was contrary to Article 3 ECHR, given the real risk that the individual might be subjected to torture or inhuman or degrading treatment by the national authorities of the country

---

[60] *Id.*, para 9.

[61] This functional approach between the prohibition of torture and the principle of *non-refoulement* has been recently applied by the Italian Court of Cassation, in the judgment of 26 April 2022, no. 15869, which, on the basis of a detailed analysis of the principle of *non-refoulement*, has stated that "given that the prohibition of torture constitutes a principle of jus cogens and that the non-refoulement constitutes a component - a segment - of the prohibition of torture instrumental to its implementation, it follows that non-refoulement also rises to the level of a peremptory rule, to the extent that, in fact, it is functional to protect the person from treatments considered as torture": para 6.1 of the conclusions on points of law.

[62] See para 10 of the *General Comment*.

[63] See appl. no. 61498/08.

[64] *Id.*, para 20.

[65] Appl. no. 37201/06.

of destination. The Court also stated that, in view of the absolute and non-derogable nature of the prohibition in Article 3, it was not possible to strike a balance between the values and interests protected by that provision and those relating to the protection of national security. Similarly, the Court ruled out increasing, in cases involving the protection of public order and national security, the level of risk generally required—in light of the criteria set out in the Court's case law—for assessing the lawfulness of national measures deporting or extraditing foreigners.

7.5 International Crimes and Universal Criminal Jurisdiction

It has already been mentioned that States have a positive obligation to ascertain and repress, including through legislative measures, conduct that may constitute a violation of the prohibition of torture and inhuman or degrading treatment.[66] From this point of view, several international treaties—for example Article 5 of the 1984 UN Convention against Torture—provide for the *aut dedere aut judicare* principle, which obliges States parties, in light of what is established by their own legislation and of the link between the actual case and the national system (*locus commissi delicti*, citizenship of the perpetrators and of the victims, presence on the territory of the accused individuals, etc.), to prosecute those responsible for such acts or to hand them over to other States with more significant jurisdictional links. The *aut dedere aut judicare* principle was held by the ECtHR to be consistent with the ECHR in the inadmissibility decision of 17 March 2009 in *Ould Dah v. France*.[67] In that case a foreign national had been convicted by the French courts for violation of the prohibition of torture in relation to crimes committed in his own country and against nationals of that country, hence without any specific connection with the French legal system. That conviction was held to be lawful despite the fact that the defendant had been granted an amnesty in his country of origin.[68]

It should also be noted that, according to the ECtHR, although the ECHR does not conflict with the *aut dedere aut judicare* principle in respect of the suppression of international crimes and with the broader principle of universal jurisdiction, the ECHR cannot be interpreted extensively as obliging the Contracting Parties to provide for these principles. In particular, for the Strasbourg Court, the absence of national legislation or case law on the principle of universal jurisdiction for civil claims brought before the courts of the Contracting Parties to the ECHR seeking compensation for damage suffered as a result of acts of torture committed abroad by

[66] See *supra*, Sect. 7.2.

[67] Appl. no. 13113/03.

[68] On the conflict between amnesties and *jus cogens*, see Chap. 3, Sect. 3.2.

organs of third countries does not conflict with the right to access to justice under Article 6(1) ECHR.[69]

In the same case, the Court specifically ruled out the existence of a rule of customary international law on universal civil jurisdiction in respect of acts of torture,[70] while requiring the Contracting Parties to the ECHR "to take account in their legal orders of any developments facilitating effective implementation of the right to compensation for acts of torture", particularly in light of the so-called *forum necessitatis*, which allows the assertion of national jurisdiction for human rights violations committed abroad, provided that there are some "connecting factors" between the dispute and the national forum and there are no "competing" national jurisdictions more closely connected to the case at issue.[71]

7.6 International Crimes, State Immunity and Immunity of State Organs

With regard to the repression of the crime of torture, it is necessary to examine, both in the case of legal proceedings against States and in the case of proceedings against individuals-organs, whether immunity from jurisdiction should be granted to the foreign country and to the individuals responsible for such serious conduct.

7.6.1 State Immunity

With regard to immunity from civil jurisdiction of the foreign State accused of torture and more generally of international crimes, the isolated position—insofar as it is not shared by other national courts—of Italian case law is well known, dating back to the *Ferrini* case decided by the Italian Court of Cassation in its judgment no. 5044 of 11 March 2004. It denied immunity to Germany, which, although acting in the exercise of its official functions ("*jure imperii*"), was responsible for international crimes and the violation of peremptory norms, in particular, the deportation and forced labour of Italian citizens by the Nazi regime during WWII. That principle has been repeated several times in subsequent rulings by the same Court.

This position taken by the Italian courts also had important consequences at the enforcement level, including as regards recognition, for enforcement purposes, of foreign judgments holding Germany responsible for international crimes committed mainly in countries occupied by Nazi troops.

---

[69] ECtHR (Grand Chamber), judgment of 15 March 2018 in *Naït-Liman v. Switzerland*, appl. no. 51357/07. For an examination of the right of access to justice, see Chap. 8, Sect. 8.2.1.

[70] *Id.*, paras 183–187.

[71] *Id.*, paras 218–220.

However, in its judgment of 3 February 2012[72] the ICJ found that Italy had violated the customary rule on State immunity from civil jurisdiction, stating that the rule on State immunity should be applied even when the respondent State is accused of international crimes as well as of having violated *jus cogens* rules during military operations conducted abroad. As regards the question of conflict between the rules on State immunity and those prohibiting serious violations of human rights and international humanitarian law, the ICJ ruled, in a manner which in our view is not completely in line with what is normally the case in legal proceedings, that the international rules on immunity are procedural in nature while *jus cogens* and the rules prohibiting the commission of international crimes are substantive in nature, thus operating at different levels and at different stages of the proceedings before national courts.[73] The Court therefore requested Italy to prevent further legal proceedings against Germany in relation to similar conduct and to revoke the decisions of the national courts already adopted and in conflict with the judgment. Finally, the Court stated that the resolution of the questions concerning the reparation to be granted to the victims of such barbaric actions was a matter for an unlikely negotiation between the two States (in fact never concluded).

It should be pointed out that the position adopted by the ICJ reflects the position expressed in international and national case law that has dealt with the conflict between the rule on the jurisdictional immunity of the State and the *jus cogens* norms protecting fundamental human rights. In this regard, even the case law of the ECtHR, according to which the decision of a court of a Contracting Party to the ECHR that grants immunity from jurisdiction to a foreign State accused of acts of torture committed in its territory does not constitute a violation of the right of access to justice, appears to be well-settled.[74]

The complex German-Italian saga, however, had further and unexpected developments. In its judgment no. 238 of 22 October 2014, the Italian Constitutional Court ruled out the application in the Italian legal system of the customary rule as interpreted by the ICJ. In essence, the Constitutional Court ruled that the fundamental principles of the Italian Constitution, and in particular the right of access to justice under Article 24 and the right to personal dignity under Article 2, prevail over the rule of customary international law on jurisdictional immunity of foreign States.

The Italian Constitutional Court's judgment had a number of consequences. Firstly, it enabled recognition of judgments issued by foreign courts and relating to convictions of States for international crimes, as happened in 2021 when the Italian Court of Cassation recognised a judgment issued by the District Court of NY

[72] See *Jurisdictional Immunities of the State, Germany v. Italy: Greece intervening.*

[73] Indeed, it is well known that the recognition of immunity also depends on the nature of the activities carried out by the foreign State.

[74] In this regard, see the judgment of the Grand Chamber of 21 November 2001 in *Al-Adsani v. The United Kingdom*, appl. no. 35763/97, and the judgment of 14 June 2014 in *Jones and Others v. The United Kingdom*, appl. nos. 34356/06 and 40528/06.

finding Iran, the Iranian central bank and other entities liable for their involvement in the terrorist attack on the Twin Towers in 2001.[75]

Secondly, the legal proceedings pending before the Italian courts concerning the responsibility of Germany for crimes committed during the Nazi regime have been resumed. Accordingly, in its judgment no. 20442 of 28 September 2020 the Italian Court of Cassation *en banc* held—in accordance with the principle affirmed by the Constitutional Court—that the right of access to Italian justice cannot be limited by conduct "which does not express the sovereign function of the foreign State but rather constitutes crimes against humanity, such as deportation, forced labour, massacres". This is because "the clearly criminal nature of such acts prevents them from benefiting from the protective shield of immunity" since such conduct is in contrast with "universal values that transcend the interests of individual State communities and whose true substance consists in an abuse of State sovereignty". For this reason, the Court affirmed Italian jurisdiction over a case concerning the deportation, forced labour and killing of an Italian soldier by Nazi forces.[76]

The German-Italian saga is not over: on 29 April 2022 Germany instituted proceedings before the ICJ against Italy for allegedly failing to respect its jurisdictional immunity as assessed by the ICJ in the 2012 judgment. At the same time, Germany requested provisional measures asking the Court to order Italy to ensure that German properties indicated in the application "are not subjected to a public auction pending a judgment by the Court on the merits" and that "no further measures of constraint are taken by [Italian] courts against German property". On 4 May 2022 Germany withdrew its request for the indication of provisional measures after the adoption by Italy of Decree No. 36 of 30 April 2022 (incorporated in the law of 29 June 2022 No. 79), according to which Italian courts must lift measures of enforcement previously taken, and are barred from taking further measures of constraint against German property used for government non-commercial purposes located on Italian territory. Moreover, the Decree provides for the creation by Italy of a State Fund for the compensation of damages suffered by victims of war crimes and crimes against humanity committed by the Third Reich during World War II in Italy.

Meanwhile, the stance adopted by the Italian courts was expressly cited by the Central District Court of Seoul in its judgment of 8 January 2021[77] in the sad case of the "comfort women" of Korean citizenship, kidnapped and made sex slaves by the Imperial Japanese Army during World War II, a practice widely followed by the Japanese in different parts of Asia in the period 1930–1945 (about 200,000 victims). The Court, which expressly referred to the Italian Constitutional Court Judgment no. 238 of 2014, denied that the Japanese government enjoyed immunity from Korean jurisdiction, relying on the peremptory nature of the international rules violated and

[75] See the judgment of 10 December 2021, no. 39391.

[76] See paras 1.4–1.5 of the judgment.

[77] Case no. 2016 Ga-Hap 505092.

on the constitutional basis of the right of access to justice. Japan was therefore ordered to pay compensation to the relatives of the victims.[78]

More recently, in a case concerning the sinking of a fishing boat in 1943 by a German submarine near Cabo Frio (Rio de Janeiro) that caused the death of ten fishermen, the Brazilian Supreme Court (Supremo Tribunal Federal), in its judgment of 23 August 2021,[79] ruled that the immunity of States from national jurisdiction cannot be recognised in cases of unlawful acts connected to human rights. The decision in question, in which immunity was excluded under the Brazilian Constitution,[80] would appear to have effects even broader than the previous national decisions as it generically refers to human rights violations and not just to gross violations of human rights or international crimes to deny a State's immunity.

7.6.2 State Organs' Immunity

On the question of the immunity of individuals-organs accused of committing acts of torture or other international crimes, a distinction must be drawn between the personal immunities of the State organ, enjoyed by the supreme organs of the State—the head of State, head of government, foreign minister and diplomatic agents—and the functional immunities enjoyed by all State organs.

With regard to personal immunities, it should be noted that the statutes of the ICTY and ICTR, as well as the statute of the ICC, exclude the possibility that personal or functional immunities may prevent the prosecution of those responsible for the international crimes provided for in the respective statutes. On that basis some national courts, which ruled in particular on the *Al-Bashir* case[81] and with specific reference to the violation of the obligation incumbent on the State parties to the ICC statute to arrest and surrender Al-Bashir to the ICC, have held that the regime governing international crimes prevails over the customary international law on personal immunities.[82]

However, it must be conceded that, beyond the special systems of international criminal law referred to above, international and national case law as a whole still seems to be in favour of recognising personal immunity for supreme organs of a State accused of international crimes, as stated by the ICJ in its judgment of 14

[78] However, a subsequent decision of 21 April 2021 (case no. 2016 Ga-Hap 58023), issued by the same Central District Court of Seoul in a case similar to the one reported above, granted immunity from civil jurisdiction to Japan, taking into account the "overall" reparations agreed between Japan and South Korea in the 1965 and 2015 agreements for the numerous acts of misconduct committed by the Japanese military in the 1910–1945 period.

[79] *Recurso extraordinário com agravo no.* 954.858.

[80] See Article 4(II) ("prevalence of human rights"), which is one of the general principles of Brazilian foreign relations.

[81] See Chap. 5, Sect. 5.6.

[82] See the judgments of the Supreme Court of Appeal of South Africa dated 15 March 2016 and the Court of Appeal of Kenya dated 16 February 2018.

February 2002 in the *Arrest Warrant of 11 April 2000* case, relating to the dispute that arose following the request for arrest made by the Belgian judicial authorities against the Foreign Minister of the Democratic Republic of Congo. After having carefully examined State practice, including national legislation and case law, the Court stated that it was "unable to deduce from this practice that there exists under customary international law any form of exception to the rule according personal immunity from criminal jurisdiction and inviolability to incumbent Ministers for Foreign Affairs, where they are suspected of having committed war crimes or crimes against humanity".[83]

On the other hand there would seem to be no shield based on functional immunity for a State organ accused of international crimes, including the prohibition of torture, as recently affirmed in the judgment of 28 January 2021 by the German Federal Court of Justice. Therein it was held that State officials who hold subordinate positions do not enjoy functional immunity under customary international law in foreign criminal proceedings for war crimes or other crimes of concern to the international community as a whole.[84]

That said, there is no shortage of indications to the contrary in case law, especially in relation to disputes concerning the civil liability of officials,[85] as confirmed by the previously mentioned 2014 ECtHR judgment in *Jones and Others v. the United Kingdom*. At the national level worthy of note is the Hague District Court judgment of 29 January 2020 concerning a dispute brought by a Dutch citizen claiming compensation for the crimes allegedly committed in 2014 by Israeli military leaders during an airstrike on Palestinian positions. The Court, which expressly ruled on the basis of general international law, stated that the Israeli military enjoys functional immunity that applies, in the context of domestic disputes, also when the official is accused of international crimes.[86]

It should be finally noted that functional or personal immunity is sometimes denied in national case law in relation to the commission of international crimes or grave breaches of human rights on the basis that the serious harmful conduct in question falls outside the scope of the institutional functions attributed to the official. In this regard, in its judgment no. 39788 of 25 September 2014 in the *Abu Omar* case, the Italian Court of Cassation found that the kidnapping of Abu Omar was entirely extraneous to the functions exercised by foreign State organs—in particular, certain individuals who were, at the same time, US diplomatic agents and CIA officials. In a similar vein, very recently the Supreme Court of the United Kingdom, in the judgment of 6 July 2022 in *Basfar v. Wong*, has extensively interpreted Article 31, para 1c, of the Vienna Convention of 18 April 1961 on Diplomatic Relations, considering

[83] See ICJ 2002, p. 24, para 58.

[84] See appl. no. 3, StR 564/19.

[85] A more significant trend excluding functional immunity can be seen in relation to criminal proceedings.

[86] See para 4.43 of the judgment in *Ziada v. The State of The Netherlands*, case no. C-09-554385. The Hague Court of Appeal, in its judgment of 7 December 2021, upheld the conclusions set out in the first instance decision.

the conduct of a foreign diplomatic agent consisting in trafficking in human beings and slavery towards an individual employed by the diplomatic agent operating in the United Kingdom, in the "commercial activity" of the diplomatic agent, as such falling within one of the exceptions to immunity from jurisdiction in disputes of a civil nature.

7.7 Prohibition of Slavery, Servitude and Forced Labour

The prohibition of slavery and the prohibition of servitude are contained in peremptory norms of international law, while it is doubtful whether the prohibition of forced or compulsory labour is contained in a peremptory norm or in customary international law. The prohibitions in question are sometimes laid down in *ad hoc* legal instruments. In this context, with regard to the prohibition of slavery reference can be made, at the universal level, to the Slavery Convention of 25 September 1926 and the Supplementary Convention on the Abolition of Slavery, the Slave Trade, and Institutions and Practices Similar to Slavery of 7 September 1956. Similarly, with regard to the prohibition of forced labour, it is worth mentioning, in the ILO context, the Forced Labour Convention of 28 June 1930 (No. 29), the Abolition of Forced Labour Convention of 25 June 1957 (No. 105), as well as the Protocol of 2014 to the Forced Labour Convention (1930), which recognises that the prohibition of forced or compulsory labour forms part of the body of fundamental rights.

On the other hand, in some legal instruments the same provision embodies all the above-mentioned prohibitions. In relation to this second approach, one can cite at the universal level Article 8 ICCPR and at the regional level, Article 4 ECHR, Article 6 ACHR and Article 5 CFREU. The latter also outlaws trafficking in human beings.[87] In a broader sense, Article 5 ACHPR states that "[a]ll forms of exploitation and degradation of man, particularly slavery, slave trade … shall be prohibited".

The relevant international conventions, as interpreted by the bodies charged with scrutinising observance of the relevant treaties referred to above, provide for both negative obligations on the part of the State to refrain from resorting to such harmful practices and, above all, positive obligations. In this latter respect, States have respectively the obligation to prevent and repress violations of these rights committed by State organs or private individuals, the "legislative" obligation "to adopt criminal-law provisions which penalise the practices referred to in Article 4" as well as the duty to undertake "effective prosecution of any act aimed at maintaining a person in such a situation", as stated by the ECtHR in its judgment of 26 July 2005 in *Siliadin v. France*.[88]

It is undisputed that slavery today also constitutes a crime against humanity, when committed in an international or non-international armed conflict and "as part of a widespread or systematic attack directed against any civilian population, with

[87] See Article 5(3).

[88] See appl. no. 73316/01, paras 89 and 112 of the judgment.

knowledge of the attack", as provided by Article 7(1), subparas (c) and (g), of the ICC Statute. The prohibition of slavery as an international crime has been interpreted broadly in the case law of international criminal tribunals. In this regard, the ICTY, in the Appeals Chamber judgment of 12 June 2002 issued in the case of *Prosecutor v. Dragoljub Kunarac, Radomir Kovač and Zoran Vuković* applied the prohibition in question to a case of prolonged and unlawful deprivation of liberty against an individual.[89]

Of considerable importance is the distinction, on the one hand, between "slavery" and "servitude", and, on the other hand, between "forced labour" and "compulsory labour". In the *Siliadin* case cited above, the ECtHR, recalling the notion contained in Article 1 of the Slavery Convention of 1926,[90] stated that the classification of certain conduct as slavery requires that it be found that a certain person exercises "a genuine right of legal ownership", thus reducing the victim "to the status of an 'object'".[91] By contrast, for the Court, with regard to the concept of "servitude", "what is prohibited is a particularly serious form of denial of freedom", which arises in instances where "in addition to the obligation to perform certain services for others" there is "the obligation for the 'serf' to live on another person's property and the impossibility of altering his condition".[92]

Although slavery and servitude have obvious similarities, they can be distinguished in the case of slavery on the basis of the more serious degree of the deprivation of the person's liberty as well as in light of the "annihilation" of any form of individual liberty of the enslaved person, so as to make him an "object" at the mercy of the person practising slavery.

With reference to the distinction between forced and compulsory labour, as far back as its judgment of 23 November 1983 in *Van der Mussele v. Belgium*, the Strasbourg Court clarified that the notion of forced labour "brings to mind the idea of physical or mental constraint". Otherwise, the concept of compulsory labour "cannot refer just to any form of legal compulsion or obligation", for instance in the case of "work to be carried out in pursuance of a freely negotiated contract … on the sole ground that one of the parties has undertaken with the other to do that work and will be subject to sanctions if he does not honour his promise". In such cases it is necessary that the work be carried out "under the menace of any penalty and also performed against the will of the person concerned, that is work for which he has not offered himself voluntarily".[93]

Among the exceptions to the prohibition of forced or compulsory labour expressly provided for in Article 4 ECHR, of particular relevance is that relating to work

[89] See cases IT-96-23 and IT-96-23/1-A, paras 116 ff.

[90] Namely, that "slavery is the status or condition of a person over whom any or all of the powers attaching to the right of ownership are exercised".

[91] See para 122 of the judgment.

[92] *Id.*, para 123.

[93] See appl. no. 8919/80, para 34 of the judgment.

sometimes imposed on or required of detainees on a consensual basis.[94] The ECtHR, while noting that the Contracting Parties retain a wide margin of appreciation in this area, has established the principle that prison labour must be taken into account within the framework of national social security legislation, even though it is not mandatory for the State to apply general social security law, in particular with regard to the minimum age for entitlement to a pension.[95]

Both the notions of slavery and servitude, as well as those of forced or compulsory labour, are to be interpreted independently of any concepts established under national legal systems. Moreover, the notions in question are subject to an evolutionary interpretation, meaning that they must take into account both developments in the relevant international legal rules and the effects of prohibited harmful practices, so as to include *modern* forms of slavery or servitude. The factors on the basis of which it is possible to *decipher* the harmful conduct and classify it as a case of servitude or slavery are both of a subjective and objective nature. The former concern, for example, the age, sex and particular vulnerability of the individual subjected to such harmful conduct. The latter concern the level of limitation of personal freedom and, in the context of an employment relationship, working hours, the absence of adequate remuneration and debt bondage, defined as "the status or condition arising from a pledge by a debtor of his personal services or of those of a person under his control as security for a debt, if the value of those services as reasonably assessed is not applied towards the liquidation of the debt or the length and nature of those services are not respectively limited and defined".[96]

7.7.1 Human Trafficking and Prohibition of Slavery

In addition to the *classical* prohibitions of slavery, servitude and forced or compulsory labour, international law today prohibits particular forms of slavery, such as trafficking in human beings, on the basis of specific provisions. Among the treaty-based legal instruments specifically dedicated to prohibiting trafficking in human beings, one can mention the two additional protocols to the UN Convention against Transnational Organised Crime of 15 December 2000: the Protocol to Prevent, Suppress and Punish Trafficking in Persons, Especially Women and Children and the Protocol against the Smuggling of Migrants by Land, Sea and Air. To these must be added,

---

[94] Article 4(3)(a): "For the purpose of this article the term 'forced or compulsory labour' shall not include: (a) any work required to be done in the ordinary course of detention imposed according to the provisions of Article 5 of [the] Convention or during conditional release from such detention".

[95] ECtHR (Grand Chamber), judgment of 7 July 2011 in *Stummer v. Austria*, appl. no. 37452/02, paras 105 ff., ruling out that domestic legislation which does not include working prisoners within the national social security systems established for other workers is contrary to Article 4 ECHR.

[96] See Article 1(a) of the above-mentioned Supplementary Convention of 1956 and more recently the *Report of the Special Rapporteur on contemporary forms of slavery, including its causes and consequences*, transmitted to the Human Rights Council during its 39th session (10–28 September 2018), A/HRC/39/52, para 14.

at the regional level, the CoE Convention on Action against Trafficking in Human Beings of 16 May 2005, and the ASEAN Convention against Trafficking in Persons, Especially Women and Children of 21 November 2015.

Where it is not possible in a given case to apply *ad hoc* rules on the prohibition of trafficking in human beings, the general prohibitions of slavery, servitude and forced or compulsory labour, which may be applied on a subsidiary basis to cases more properly related to trafficking in human beings, are relevant. This interpretation is justified in light of the relationship between general and special rules, with the consequence that, in the absence of specific rules applicable to these particular forms of slavery or servitude, recourse may be had to the general rules.

The ECtHR judgment of 7 January 2010 in *Rantsev v. Cyprus and Russia*[97] can be interpreted in this sense. The Court applied Article 4 ECHR to a case of international trafficking in human beings and exploitation of prostitution, without specifically classifying the conduct in question as slavery, servitude, forced or compulsory labour.[98] Recalling the case law of the ICTY, the ECtHR stated that "the traditional concept of 'slavery' has evolved to encompass various contemporary forms of slavery based on the exercise of any or all of the powers attaching to the right of ownership". In assessing whether a situation amounts to a form of slavery, the ECtHR found that it is necessary to ascertain "whether there was control of a person's movement or physical environment, whether there was an element of psychological control, whether measures were taken to prevent or deter escape and whether there was control of sexuality and forced labour".[99] This legal approach designed to fill the gaps in terms of regulation of the most recent human rights appears to be acceptable and seems to confirm that the rules governing human rights are indivisible and complementary.

The principle established in the *Rantsev* case has been reaffirmed several times by the ECtHR with reference to cases of international trafficking in individuals. For example, in its judgment of 21 January 2016 in *L.E. v. Greece*,[100] the Court stated that the positive obligations of States to prevent and suppress violations of the prohibition of slavery and servitude committed at the inter-individual level also apply in cases of trafficking in human beings. In its subsequent judgment of 25 June 2020 in *S.M. v. Croatia*, the ECtHR (Grand Chamber) further clarified that Article 4 ECHR can be applied to cases of trafficking and exploitation of prostitution occurring exclusively at the national level and without the involvement of specific criminal organisations,[101] in line with Article 2 of the above-mentioned 2005 CoE Convention.

The ECtHR has recently addressed the question of whether judicial proceedings against victims of trafficking in human beings are in conformity with the ECHR, in particular with regard to both the prohibition of slavery and servitude under Article 4 and respect of the right to a fair trial under Article 6. In its judgment of 16 February 2021 in *V.C.L. and A.N. v. The United Kingdom*, the Court established the principle

---

[97] Appl. no. 25965/04.

[98] *Id.*, para 279.

[99] *Id.*, para 281.

[100] Appl. no. 71545/12.

[101] See paras 294–297 of the judgment, appl. no. 60561/14.

that legal proceedings against trafficked individuals, in this case minors, who had committed certain offences and pleaded guilty, are lawful only provided that the State authorities first ascertain their status as victims of trafficking under international law and discharge "the positive obligation to take operational measures to protect" them.[102] It is not enough, as happened in that case, that the national courts limit themselves to checking whether there had been a general abuse of process.

7.7.2 Labour Exploitation, Slavery and Forced Labour

In relation to other modern forms of exploitation of individuals, it is also questionable, as in the case of trafficking in human beings for prostitution, whether certain harmful conduct constitutes slavery, servitude and forced or compulsory labour. This is the case, for example, where intolerable working conditions, although formally accepted by the worker, are associated with equally intolerable conditions of life of the individual, denoting a significant subjection to the employer or the latter's representatives. In the most serious cases of exploitation of workers, it is arguable there is a veritable form of slavery resulting from the exercise of a substantial right of ownership over the individuals in question as well as their "commodification" for the purpose of economic exploitation.

The question of the legal classification of conduct entailing serious labour exploitations has been addressed by the ECtHR with regard to the application of Article 4 ECHR.

In its judgment of 30 March 2017 in *Chowdury and Others v. Greece*,[103] the ECtHR brought within the scope of forced labour, linked to trafficking in human beings, a situation in which some foreign seasonal workers lived and worked in a state of total degradation, without adequate remuneration for the work performed and under the control of armed private guards.[104] The Court once again reiterated the positive obligation of Contracting Parties to the ECHR to establish a legislative and administrative framework relating to the prohibition of forced labour, so as to prevent and suppress unlawful conduct by State organs or private individuals, including by carrying out adequate checks and inspections where there is a suspicion of trafficking in persons and forced labour. For the Court, the States also have a duty to ensure effective investigation and judicial procedures to investigate violations of the prohibition of forced labour.

---

[102] Appl. nos. 77587/12 and 74603/12, para 181.

[103] Appl. no. 21884/15.

[104] In this regard, the Court referred to Article 3(a) of the said UN Protocol to Prevent, Suppress and Punish Trafficking in Persons, Especially Women and Children and Article 4(a) of the CoE Convention of 2005.

7.8 Prohibition of Racial Discrimination and Apartheid—Other Forms of Discrimination

Among the prohibitions contained in general international law, and in our view also in the *jus cogens*, are the prohibition of racial discrimination and the more specific prohibition of apartheid.

The International Convention on the Elimination of All Forms of Racial Discrimination of 21 December 1965 has specified that "the term 'racial discrimination' shall mean any distinction, exclusion, restriction or preference based on race, colour, descent, or national or ethnic origin which has the purpose or effect of nullifying or impairing the recognition, enjoyment or exercise, on an equal footing, of human rights and fundamental freedoms in the political, economic, social, cultural or any other field of public life".[105] In this regard, States parties, on the one hand, have committed to condemning racial discrimination and undertake "to pursue by all appropriate means and without delay a policy of eliminating racial discrimination in all its forms and promoting understanding among all races", if necessary by resorting to legislation.[106] On the other hand, States are obliged to prevent public or private entities from using forms of propaganda or incitement to racial discrimination,[107] by means of a series of legislative, administrative and financial measures and by criminalising the most serious manifestations of a racist character, taking into account, in this regard, the following criteria: the content and form of speech; the economic, social and political climate prevalent at the time the speech was made and disseminated; the position or status of the speaker in society and the audience to which the speech is directed; the reach of the speech, including the nature of the audience and the means of transmission; and the objectives of the speech.[108]

The 1965 Convention also specifically protects the right of everyone, without distinction as to race, colour, or national or ethnic origin, to equality before the law, in relation to the enjoyment of a series of rights expressly set out in the Convention.[109] Moreover, the States parties are obliged to (i) repress, including through the courts, any racial discrimination actually engaged in, providing for the right of victims to just and adequate reparation for any damage suffered as a result of such discrimination, and (ii) to combat the prejudices that lead to racial discrimination, through the use of appropriate measures to be implemented in the fields of teaching, education, culture and information.[110]

---

[105] See Article 1(1) of the 1965 Convention.

[106] *Id.*, Article 2(1).

[107] *Id.*, Article 4.

[108] On these criteria, see CommERD, *General Recommendation No. 35* of 26 September 2013 on Combating Racist Hate Speech, CERD/C/GC/35, para 15.

[109] *Id.*, Article 5.

[110] *Id.*, Articles 6–7. As noted before (see Chap. 5, Sect. 5.2.3), the 1965 Convention established a committee to monitor implementation (CommERD), which has no binding powers and is competent to examine both reports by States parties on measures of compliance with the Convention and inter-State and individual communications.

Already prohibited in general terms on the basis of the 1965 Convention,[111] apartheid is considered by the UN International Convention on the Suppression and Punishment of the Crime of Apartheid of 30 November 1973 as "a crime against humanity" while the inhuman acts resulting from the policies and practices of apartheid and similar policies and practices of racial segregation and discrimination are considered as "crimes violating the principles of international law, in particular the purposes and principles of the Charter of the United Nations, and constituting a serious threat to international peace and security".[112] According to Article II of the 1973 Convention, the conduct covered by the prohibition of apartheid is that carried out "for the purpose of establishing and maintaining domination by one racial group of persons over any other racial group of persons and systematically oppressing them". The conduct in question, regulated at the conventional level above all as a reaction to the segregationist practice followed in South Africa since the 1960s, essentially constitutes an extreme form of racial discrimination.

The 1973 Convention provides for several positive obligations on States parties to adopt all necessary measures, including legislation, to prevent and punish both the individuals directly responsible for acts of apartheid or segregationist policies and those who encourage or support such conduct.[113] It also establishes the principle of universal criminal jurisdiction "by a competent tribunal of any State Party to the Convention which may acquire jurisdiction over the person of the accused or by an international criminal tribunal having jurisdiction with respect to those States Parties which shall have accepted its jurisdiction"[114] for offences falling within the notion of apartheid under Article II of the Convention.[115]

The 1973 Convention also provides for a weak system of monitoring compliance with the provisions thereof, based on the establishment of a Special Committee on Apartheid[116] and on the powers of the former UNCommHR, who was responsible for examining the periodic reports submitted by States parties on the implementation of their obligations under the Convention.[117] These powers are now exercised only by the Special Committee on Apartheid.

The legal framework under examination also includes the right to non-discrimination in general, i.e. on grounds other than race or apartheid, whose specific prohibitions, as we have seen, are embodied in international rules of a superior rank. The distinction between the principle of equality, which prescribes the same treatment for equal cases and situations, and the principle of non-discrimination, which prohibits the adoption of different measures in respect of similar cases and situations unless there are objective reasons for adopting different measures and the latter

---

[111] *Id.*, Article 3.

[112] See Article I of the 1973 Convention.

[113] *Id.*, Articles III–IV.

[114] *Id.*, Article V.

[115] Article XI of the Convention specifies that the conduct referred to in Article II "shall not be considered political crimes for the purpose of extradition".

[116] *Id.*, Article VII.

[117] *Id.*, Articles IX–X.

are proportionate, no longer seems to have a particular practical relevance. As the ECtHR observed in *Napotnik v. Romania* "the right not to be discriminated against in the enjoyment of the rights guaranteed under the Convention is also violated when States, without an objective and reasonable justification, fail to treat differently persons whose situations are significantly different".[118] Also in this case, the actual effect is to discriminate, without justification, the position of individuals or groups of individuals.

Discriminatory measures may consist of acts of commission or omission aimed specifically at *distinguishing*, i.e. aimed overtly at discriminating against certain individuals or groups of them, or of *indirect* discrimination, i.e. formally neutral but in reality having discriminatory effects against specific individuals on account of various objective or subjective factors (age, sex, religion, membership of a social category, etc.), which can only be specifically identified on the basis of an examination of the case in question.

The prohibition of discrimination in general is therefore residual in the international legal order, aiming to prohibit discriminatory practices other than the most serious ones analysed above, and seems to be contained in customary international law. However, in our view it is not correct to assume that all residual discriminations have the same legal standing, since the prohibition of certain forms of discrimination appears to have a more solid foundation in domestic and international practice. This is true, for example, of discrimination based on religious or ethnic grounds, which is already reflected in the oldest international treaties on the protection of religious minorities and is the specific subject of numerous acts of soft law issued by international organisations, such as the Declaration on the Elimination of All Forms of Intolerance and of Discrimination Based on Religion or Belief adopted by the UNGA on 25 November 1981.[119]

Moreover, the anti-discrimination regime contains no shortage of treaty law dedicated to the protection of certain categories of individuals considered particularly vulnerable in terms of their exposure to forms of discrimination. From this point of view, reference can be made to the UN Convention on the Elimination of All Forms of Discrimination against Women of 18 December 1979 and the UN Convention on the Rights of Persons with Disabilities of 13 December 2006, whose preamble states that the discrimination against any person on the basis of disability "is a violation of the inherent dignity and worth of the human person".[120]

Furthermore, some cases of discrimination based on a certain factor or personal or social characteristic, such as the gender of the person concerned, have also been applied in practice as a legal parameter to prohibit other forms of gender discrimination, such as those against homosexuals and transsexuals.

---

[118] ECtHR judgment of 20 October 2020 in *Napotnik v. Romania*, appl. no. 33139/13, para 73.

[119] See Resolution no. 36/55.

[120] See para *h* of the preamble of 2006 Convention. On the competences of CommEDAW and CED, see Chap. 5, Sects. 5.2.4 and 5.2.6.

Finally, as noted for the more serious forms of discrimination highlighted above, it is natural that effective protection of the rights deriving from the principle of non-discrimination in general requires compliance with both negative obligations on the part of States and, above all, obligations of a positive nature, which imply, where necessary, recourse to administrative and legislative measures aimed at eliminating discrimination against specific categories of individuals and preventing the emergence of future discrimination as highlighted by the HRC in its *General Comment No. 28* of 29 March 2000[121] and repeatedly by the IACtHR, for example in its judgment of 26 February 2016[122] and more recently in its judgment of 15 July 2020.[123] In the latter decision, the Court made it very clear that "the right to equality" has two dimensions. The first is a formal dimension that establishes equality before the law; the second is a material or substantial dimension that requires the adoption of positive measures of promotion in favor of groups that have historically been discriminated against or marginalized. For the Court, this dimension of the right to equality serves "to correct existing inequalities, to promote the inclusion and participation of historically marginalized groups, and to guarantee to disadvantaged individuals or groups the effective enjoyment of their rights and, in short, to provide individuals with the real possibility of achieving material equality".[124]

Comprehension Check and Tasks

1. What is the ECtHR's approach in balancing freedom of thought and genocide denial? (Sect. 7.1.1)
2. What are the factors on the basis of which the ECtHR distinguishes between torture and inhuman and degrading treatments? (Sect. 7.2)
3. What is the right to hope and what are the effects of its application? (Sect. 7.3.1)
4. Focus on the recent developments on international crimes and State immunity (Sect. 7.6.1)

[121] Article 3 (The Equality of Rights Between Men and Women), para 3.

[122] See the judgment in *Duque v. Colombia*, para 92.

[123] See the judgment in *Workers of the Fireworks Factory in Santo Antônio de Jesus and their Families v. Brazil*, paras 186–199.

[124] *Id.*, para 199.

References

ICJ (2002) Judgment of 14 February 2002 in the Arrest Warrant of 11 April 2000. ICJ Reports
ICJ (2007) Judgment of 26 February 2007 in the case concerning the Application of the Convention on the Prevention and Punishment of the Crime of Genocide. ICJ Reports
ICJ (2012) Judgment of 20 July 2012 in Questions relating to the Obligation to Prosecute or Extradite. ICJ Reports

Chapter 8
Right to Liberty and Security, Right to a Fair Trial and Principle of No Punishment Without Law

Contents

Abstract The chapter discusses a number issues concerning the application of international rules on the right to liberty and security, e.g. in relation to enforced disappearances and extraordinary renditions; the right to a fair trial, which is connected to a series of other human rights, e.g. the right of access to justice; and the principle of no punishment without law, which requires compliance with the principle of non-retroactivity of criminal norms and raises problems in relation to the repression of international crimes.

8.1 Right to Liberty and Security, Enforced Disappearances and Extraordinary Renditions

The right to liberty and security has very ancient normative roots. It would seem to derive from the institution of *habeas corpus* contemplated, albeit in primitive forms, in the *Magna Charta Libertatum* of 15 June 1215,[1] promulgated by the King of England. This legal instrument provided for a series of substantive and procedural guarantees in favour of individuals accused of certain crimes and aimed at limiting the arbitrariness of public power.

[1] See clause 39.

P. Pustorino, *Introduction to International Human Rights Law*,
https://doi.org/10.1007/978-94-6265-563-8_8

The notions of "liberty" and "security", although formally distinct, are generally referred to jointly in the universal and regional legal instruments covering this right, such as, for example, Article 3 UDHR, Article 9 ICCPR, Article 5 ECHR, Article 5 CFREU and Article 7 ACHR. As the ECtHR stated in its judgment of 13 January 2009 in *Nikolaishvili v. Georgia*, "the expression 'liberty and security of person' in Article 5 § 1 must be read as a single right and that, consequently, 'security' should be understood in the context of 'liberty'".[2]

The respect of the right to liberty and security implies the prohibition of any form of arrest, detention or deprivation of liberty carried out by the public power and having an arbitrary character. It should be noted that the violations in question are based on "an act of a State having a continuing character",[3] which therefore ceases only when the personal liberty of the individual is restored, without prejudice to the right of the person to compensation for the damage suffered as a result of the violation.

The guarantees provided for in the international rules on liberty and security apply to any deprivation of personal liberty, including of a temporary nature and even when it occurs outside the traditional places where people are generally deprived of their liberty, such as detention centres. The ECtHR, with the aim of distinguishing measures entailing deprivation of personal liberty from those of mere restrictions on liberty of movement and with specific reference to preventive measures adopted at the criminal level, noted that "the starting-point must be his or her specific situation and account must be taken of a whole range of factors such as the type, duration, effects and manner of implementation of the measure in question".[4]

In relation to the scope of application of the international rules protecting the right to personal liberty and security, the rules in question apply to both unlawful conduct attributable to the State and violations of an inter-individual nature, thus obliging the State to prevent and repress, including through measures of a legislative nature, violations committed between private individuals on the basis of the oft-mentioned principle of due diligence.[5]

Article 5 ECHR specifies the guarantees, both substantive and procedural, which must be respected by Contracting Parties to ensure the observance of the right to personal liberty. These guarantees imply compliance by the State with various positive and negative obligations.

The *primary* guarantee contained in Article 5 is that restrictions of personal liberty must be in accordance with national law, thereby ruling out any arbitrariness at the root of the measures adopted. However, a restrictive measure, even if formally provided for by national law, can still be considered at odds with international rules

---

[2] Appl. no. 37048/04, para 52 of the judgment.

[3] See Article 14(2) ARSIWA: "The breach of an international obligation by an act of a State having a continuing character extends over the entire period during which the act continues and remains not in conformity with the international obligation".

[4] Grand Chamber, judgment of 23 February 2017, *De Tommaso v. Italy*, appl. no. 43395/09, para 80.

[5] See Chap. 3, Sect. 3.7.

and standards on human rights. Firstly, the provisions established by the law must be "accessible"—and therefore easily knowable by the addressees of the rule—and "foreseeable", i.e. clear in terms of content and effects of the cases contemplated and of the penalties provided for in order "to allow the person—if need be, with appropriate advice—to foresee, to a degree that is reasonable in the circumstances, the consequences which a given action may entail".[6] These requirements are to be scrutinised, both in normal and emergency situations, for example in cases of armed conflict, international or non-international, or simple internal tensions and disorder of a certain gravity, which often lead the States involved in these situations to adopt special legislation through which both the right to personal liberty and other human rights are significantly restricted. Secondly, the application of national law must be in accordance with the principles of necessity of the measures of deprivation of liberty, which must thus be functional to the protection of general or particular interests, and proportionate to the aim pursued.

Among the other guarantees provided for by Article 5 ECHR, worth mentioning is the right of the arrested or detained individual to be informed promptly, in a language which he or she understands, of the reasons for his arrest and of any charge against him, the right to be brought promptly before a judge or other officer authorised by law to exercise judicial power and to be entitled to trial within a reasonable time or to be released pending trial, and the linked right to take proceedings by which the lawfulness of his detention shall be decided speedily by a court and his release ordered if the detention is not lawful.[7]

8.1.1 Enforced Disappearances and the Right to Truth

With regard to the application of the right to personal liberty and security, some practices that constitute flagrant and very serious violations of this right are particularly important: enforced disappearances and extraordinary renditions. The two types of violations are sometimes linked, since enforced disappearances consist of abductions and kidnappings carried out by national or foreign State bodies whereas extraordinary renditions are the handing over of the individuals concerned to agents of foreign countries, who generally transfer these individuals to third countries and often to secret locations for the purpose of interrogating and detaining them without any time limit and often without providing them with any legal guarantee.

Enforced disappearances of individuals are thus often *internal* to the State that carries out the kidnapping and abduction, i.e. without the involvement of foreign State organs and without the victims being subsequently handed over to the authorities of third countries. However, in some cases, the internal operations of enforced disappearance of individuals are carried out on the basis of information obtained through cooperation between the intelligence services of several countries, thus attributing a

[6] ECtHR, judgment of 16 April 2019, *Alparslan Altan v. Turkey*, appl. no. 12778/17, para 103.

[7] See Article 5(2), (3) and (4).

certain *internationality* to this harmful conduct, as happened in relation to the infamous "Condor" operation launched in the early 1970s and based on the cooperation between the secret services of some Latin American countries, governed at the time by dictatorial regimes, with the aim of identifying and kidnapping their political opponents.

It follows that enforced disappearance implies, in the majority of cases, *chain* violations of fundamental rights: the right to personal liberty and security, the right to life, the right not to be subjected to torture or inhuman or degrading treatment, etc.

Today, there are universal and regional treaties specifically dedicated to prohibiting enforced disappearances. At the regional level, mention may be made of the Inter-American Convention on Forced Disappearance of Persons of 9 June 1994, developed within the framework of the OAS, and, at the universal level, the International Convention for the Protection of All Persons from Enforced Disappearance ("ICPPED") of 20 December 2006. The latter provides for a number of substantive and procedural obligations, such as a general obligation not to commit these violations and the obligation to prohibit them at the national level by means of specific criminal law provisions. There is also a positive procedural obligation to investigate cases of disappearance and to inform the relatives of the disappeared person of the outcome of such investigations.

The evolution of international case law on enforced disappearances seems to have gradually contributed to the formation of a new human right, although not endowed with normative autonomy: the "right to truth", which is held by the relatives of disappeared persons and whose violation persists—since it is an unlawful State conduct having a continuing character—until the moment in which the relatives of the victim obtain clear and exhaustive information on the fate of their relative and the identification of those responsible for such violations. The right to the truth has been developed especially in the case law of the IACtHR, starting with the judgment of 29 July 1988 in *Velásquez-Rodríguez v. Honduras,* in which the Court stated that the "duty to investigate facts of this type continues as long as there is uncertainty about the fate of the person who has disappeared. Even in the hypothetical case that those individually responsible for crimes of this type cannot be legally punished under certain circumstances, the State is obligated to use the means at its disposal to inform the relatives of the fate of the victims and, if they have been killed, the location of their remains".[8]

The ECtHR has endorsed the IACtHR's approach and found Contracting Parties to the ECHR liable for violating the right to life, with regard to the substantive and procedural obligations set out in Article 2,[9] and the right not to be subjected to inhuman or degrading treatment, in view of the distress caused to relatives by the disappearance of their relatives. The Strasbourg Court thus censured the State's inaction and the lack of cooperation between the State authorities and the relatives of the victims in order to inform them of the events concerning the missing person.[10]

---

[8] See para 181 of the judgment.

[9] On the content of these obligations, see Chap. 6, Sects. 6.2–6.2.1.

[10] In this regard, see the ECtHR's judgment of 10 February 2011, *Dudarovy v. Russia*, appl. no. 5382/07, para 113.

While the holder of the right to truth is generally a restricted group of individuals, coinciding with the close relatives of the victims of enforced disappearances, in international case law it is even affirmed that, in some cases of enforced disappearances involving a number of individuals, the holder may also have a collective dimension justified by the circumstance that not only the relatives of the victims but also the national population as a whole are entitled to know the fate of the numerous individuals affected by such dreadful conduct, sometimes in historical circumstances of key importance for the country concerned.[11]

8.1.2 *Extraordinary Renditions*

In relation to harmful conduct amounting to extraordinary rendition, the *international* aspect of the State behaviour in question is always a peculiar factor, as mentioned above. In some cases, the involvement of the authorities of third countries may exist right from the moment of the planning of the rendition and the subsequent kidnapping of the individual in question, who is therefore transferred to detention centres, sometimes secret, located in the territory of the same foreign country that took part in the kidnapping or in areas under its authority, or of other States that are willing to detain these individuals. It even happens in practice that the victim, once interrogated and tortured by agents of a given country, is subsequently handed over to the authorities of other countries and subjected to the same harmful treatment in order to extract further confessions and information.

At the international level, the fact that the unlawful practices in question are contrary to numerous human rights standards has been highlighted by several international bodies charged with scrutinising the observance of human rights conventions. In ECtHR case law, reference should be made to the Grand Chamber judgment of 13 December 2012 in *El-Masri v. The Former Yugoslav Republic of Macedonia*,[12] in which the Court found that the respondent State had violated Articles 3 (prohibition of torture and of inhuman or degrading treatment), 5 (right to liberty and security), 8 (right to respect for private and family life) and 13 (right to an effective remedy). The applicant was forcibly disappeared by the Macedonian authorities and subsequently handed over to American CIA agents. He was then transferred to Afghanistan to a detention camp controlled by the US military, where he was subjected to numerous human rights violations.

---

[11] This approach was followed by the ECtHR in its judgment of 24 May 2011, *Association "21 December 1989" and Others v. Romania*, appl. no. 33810/07, in which the Court found that the respondent State had breached its obligation to conduct adequate investigations "in view also of the importance to Romanian society of knowing the truth about the events of December 1989", relating to the well-known 1989 uprising: para 194.

[12] Appl. no. 39630/09.

The previously mentioned *Abu Omar*[13] case was also examined by the Strasbourg Court. In its judgment of 23 February 2016 in *Nasr and Ghali v. Italy*,[14] the Court found that Italy had violated the same convention provisions mentioned above in relation to the *El-Masri* case, noting in particular that, although an adequate judicial investigation had been conducted at the national level and the perpetrators had been convicted, the government had not ensured execution of the sentence and, moreover, the President of the Republic had issued pardons to certain US citizens who were responsible for both the enforced disappearance and the subsequent handover of Abu Omar. Additionally, according to the Court, the main purpose of the Italian government's secrecy in this case was to hinder the establishment of the truth and the conviction of those responsible.

8.1.3 Right to Liberty and Measures Against COVID-19

As noted above[15] the national measures adopted, albeit through very different instruments in terms of form and substance, by almost all States of the international community to deal with the pandemic caused by the spread of COVID-19 have significantly affected the free exercise of a number of human rights.

Among the numerous cases submitted to international courts and bodies, it is worth mentioning the position recently expressed by the ECtHR regarding the compatibility of some national measures to counter the spread of COVID-19 and the right to liberty and security. In the decision of inadmissibility of 20 May 2021 in *Terheş v. Romania*,[16] the Court ruled out that the lockdown measures lasting just under two months adopted by the Romanian authorities constituted a deprivation of liberty within the meaning of Article 5 ECHR. Such in light both of the general nature of those measures, which were not aimed at specific individuals, and the limited nature of the restrictions imposed, which on various grounds allowed individuals to leave their homes temporarily thereby ensuring that the measures did not reach the level of intensity from the point of view of the restriction of personal rights that could be equated with forms of house arrest.

The compatibility with the ECHR of the national measures adopted to reduce the spread of Covid-19, in particular the mandatory use of protective masks and the related financial penalty in case of non-compliance, was very recently ascertained by the Strasbourg Court in the inadmissibility decision of 19 May 2022 in *Makovetskyy v. Ukraine*.[17]

---

[13] See Chap. 7, Sect. 7.6.2.

[14] Appl. no. 44883/09.

[15] See Chap. 3, Sect. 3.9.

[16] Appl. no. 49933/20.

[17] See appl. no. 50824/21.

8.2 Right to a Fair Trial

The right to a fair trial is very well regulated, covering both access to and the proper functioning of the trial and the overall organisation of the national judicial system, which must ensure that judicial proceedings are carried out correctly, effectively and in a manner independent from other powers of the State, in particular the executive branch.

At the universal level the right in question is, for example, provided for in Article 14 ICCPR while at the regional level in Article 6 ECHR and in Article 47 CFREU. The latter provision has a particularly wide scope of application, establishing that "[e]veryone whose rights and freedoms guaranteed by the law of the Union are violated has the right to an effective remedy before a tribunal", thus not limited, as established by the above-mentioned Article 6 ECHR, to disputes concerning "civil rights and obligations or of any criminal charge" against the defendant.

The right in question is not confined to the limited scope of the specific rules on fair trial but is linked to numerous other guarantees that are now autonomous in law and supplement the content of the right to a fair trial, such as the right to an effective remedy before a national court. It follows that, even in some older legal instruments, the right to a fair trial is *split* into several rules, as is the case with Articles 10 and 11 UDHR. It is therefore common practice for bodies charged with scrutinising the observance of human rights treaties to assess the fairness of national trials in light of several international norms covering the various fair trial guarantees.

It should also be pointed out that, although these guarantees are now embodied in a series of general and specific principles and norms, it is certainly possible that the unfairness of trials, especially in the criminal sphere, can be deduced from an overall examination of the specific features of judicial proceedings at the national level.

In principle, there is no reason to rule out the application of the right to a fair trial in relation to any national judicial proceeding which has the characteristics to be defined as such—in terms of organisation, structure and competence of the judicial body—and in which the personal rights of the individual or his obligations are adjudicated on in final terms in various legal fields (excluding only interim proceedings or proceedings of an exclusively provisional nature). However, while the application of the right to a fair trial to criminal and civil proceedings, including enforcement proceedings, is accepted in practice, its application to administrative proceedings is more controversial, while the application of the right to a fair trial is generally excluded for tax proceedings due to the public nature of the relevant disputes. In the words of the ECtHR, "tax matters still form part of the hard core of public-authority prerogatives, with the public nature of the relationship between the taxpayer and the community remaining predominant".[18]

In the matter of the application of due process guarantees to judicial proceedings, the classification at the national level of a given issue or dispute as belonging to one or other of the respective spheres of law—civil, criminal, administrative, etc.—is not binding on an international court. On the basis of the method of autonomous

[18] Judgment of 12 July 2001 rendered in the case of *Ferrazzini v. Italy*, appl. no. 44759/98, para 29.

interpretation of the terms used in human rights conventions, an international court may reject the national classification and thus consider that the said question or dispute is to be brought within a different legal framework.

This is particularly relevant with regard to certain disputes considered, at the national level, to be of a public nature, such as those relating to public sector employment, which may concern the individual rights of the worker, especially of a financial nature, and therefore, at the international level, will be considered to enjoy the guarantees of a fair trial. And likewise with regard to the *competing* areas of criminal and administrative law. In this latter area of application, on the one hand, States tend to remove jurisdiction in certain matters from the criminal courts with a view to attributing it to administrative courts, in order to *dilute* the substantive and procedural guarantees of criminal law enjoyed by individuals involved in these cases. On the other hand, there is no lack of cases of *duplication* of criminal and administrative proceedings against the same individuals and for the same wrongdoing. For this reason, in a 1976 leading case[19] the ECtHR stated that it wished to proceed autonomously in classifying the issues at stake in the national judicial proceedings, taking into account, in particular, for the purposes of the classification of a proceeding as criminal or merely disciplinary, the very nature of the wrongdoing, beyond what is formally established at national level, as well as the degree of severity of the penalty, in terms of duration, content and effects.[20]

As mentioned above, the right to a fair trial comprises a number of guarantees and rights, some of which have attained a particular degree of autonomy also in terms of their being the subject matter of specific rules in human rights conventions. In this regard, it must be pointed out that, while some of the additional rights that can be linked to the right to a fair trial must be applied *across the board* to the various judicial proceedings, others must be applied only to certain proceedings, especially those of a criminal nature, which require, as can be easily understood, a more detailed body of stronger safeguards.

Among the best-known guarantees in connection with the right to a fair trial are those relating to the principle of *ne bis in idem*, which prohibits the State from trying an individual for the same acts for which he has previously faced trial culminating in a final judgment, regardless of its outcome—acquittal or conviction. In this regard it is necessary to focus "on those facts which constitute a set of concrete factual circumstances involving the same defendant and inextricably linked together in time and space, the existence of which must be demonstrated in order to secure a conviction or institute criminal proceedings".[21]

The prohibition of *ne bis in idem* does not, however, prevent the State from imposing, for the same acts and on the same individuals, different penalties that are

---

[19] See the judgment of 8 June 1976, *Engel and Others v. The Netherlands*, appl. nos. 5100/71 and others, para 82.

[20] For a more recent confirmation of this approach of the Court, see the judgment of 10 December 2020, *Edizioni Del Roma società cooperativa a.r.l. and Edizioni Del Roma s.r.l. v. Italy*, appl. nos. 68954/13 and 70495/13, paras 39 ff.

[21] ECtHR, judgment of 4 March 2014, *Grande Stevens and Others v. Italy*, appl. no. 18640/10 and others, para 221, on the application of Article 4 of Protocol No. 7 to the ECHR.

"the product of an integrated system enabling different aspects of the wrongdoing to be addressed in a foreseeable and proportionate manner forming a coherent whole, so that the individual concerned is not thereby subjected to injustice" following the joint imposition of those penalties.[22]

Finally, it should be pointed out that the prohibition of *ne bis in idem* operates with respect to proceedings before the courts of the same State (principle of national *ne bis in idem*). Whereas it would seem to have no place—subject to the application of special rules, for example, on the basis of international agreements or for specific legal systems like the EU one[23]—with respect to proceedings before the courts of different countries (principle of international *ne bis in idem*).[24]

8.2.1 Right to a Fair Trial and Access to Justice

Among the main rights that make up the overall content of the right to a fair trial is the right to effective access to justice, which appears to be functional to the exercise of many other jurisdictional rights. Respect for the right in question means that the State may not create obstacles of a substantive or procedural nature, whether economic (such as excessive costs for lodging an appeal) or of another nature (such as laying down excessively short time limits for initiating legal proceedings or for challenging a decision already adopted) that are unjustified and disproportionate with regard to the need, albeit legitimate, to protect general interests, such as the speed of legal proceedings and legal certainty.

The right of access to justice does not exhaust its effects in the context of the judicial proceedings at issue: where the individual has succeeded in obtaining a favourable ruling in terms of establishing his rights, in particular in the area of civil litigation, the State is thereafter obliged to ensure the correct and full execution of the decision taken by the national courts. As the ECtHR stated in its judgment of 19 March 1997 in *Hornsby v. Greece*, the right to a court "would be illusory if a Contracting State's domestic legal system allowed a final, binding judicial decision to remain inoperative to the detriment of one party. It would be inconceivable that Article 6 para 1... should describe in detail procedural guarantees afforded to litigants—proceedings that are fair, public and expeditious—without protecting the implementation of judicial decisions... Execution of a judgment given by any court must therefore be regarded as an integral part of the 'trial' for the purposes of Article 6".[25]

---

[22] ECtHR (Grand Chamber), judgment of 15 November 2016, *A and B v. Norway*, applications nos. 24130/11 and 29758/11, para 122.

[23] Article 50 CFREU provides that: "No one shall be liable to be tried or punished again in criminal proceedings for an offence for which he or she has already been finally acquitted or convicted within the Union in accordance with the law".

[24] For this distinction, see Italian Court of Cassation judgment no. 33564 of 24 July 2019, para 2 of the conclusions on points of law.

[25] Appl. no 18357/91, para 40 of the judgment.

The right of access to justice can be subject to limitations for reasons mainly related to compliance with international rules, e.g. on immunity from civil jurisdiction granted in favour of foreign States and international organisations, or in order to comply with domestic rules on immunity of national parliamentarians, provided that, in the latter case, immunity is restricted to activities carried out in the context of the parliamentarian's official duties.

With specific regard to the limitation of the right of access to justice on grounds of the need to respect the immunity of foreign States and international organisations, criticism has been levelled against international case law, in particular that of the ECtHR. As noted earlier with regard to the former,[26] the Strasbourg Court has found no violation of Article 6(1) even in cases where national courts upheld the immunity of foreign States in proceedings relating to their civil liability for the commission of international crimes.[27] As regards the immunity of international organisations, the Court applies the principle of equivalent protection. Under this approach, the immunity is considered compatible with the right of access to justice provided the plaintiffs have at their disposal, under the internal rules of the organisation, "reasonable alternative means to protect effectively their rights under the Convention".[28] However, while the Court generally assumes the adequacy of such alternative remedies, they are often difficult for the individual to access and, in any case, not very effective. In addition, the Court has not applied this approach consistently. In the previously mentioned *Mothers of Srebrenica* case, where the immunity of the UN was at issue and no alternative means existed under UN internal rules, the Court stated that it did not follow that "in the absence of an alternative remedy the recognition of immunity is *ipso facto* constitutive of a violation of the right of access to a court".[29]

8.2.2 Right to a Fair Trial and Other Linked Rights

A further important guarantee supplementing the general content of the right to a fair trial is the right to an independent, impartial and legally constituted court. In this context, the issue of the independence of the judiciary from other powers of the State, in particular the executive, is critical. In this respect, of key importance is the method of appointment, the length of the term of office and the fact that a judge is not removable, even if only in relation to certain cases submitted to him. This means that he may not be replaced at the discretion of the executive power. Consequently, any measure of temporary suspension from the exercise of judicial office or dismissal of

[26] See Chap. 7, Sect. 7.6.1.

[27] In this regard, see the previously mentioned judgment the ECtHR (Grand Chamber) judgment of 21 November 2001, *Al-Adsani v. The United Kingdom*, appl. no. 35763/97.

[28] ECtHR (Grand Chamber) judgment of 18 February 1999, *Waite and Kennedy v. Germany*, appl. no. 26083/94, para 68.

[29] ECtHR (Grand Chamber) judgment of 11 June 2013, *Stichting Mothers of Srebrenica and others v. The Netherlands*, appl. no. 65542/12, para 164.

judges may not be arbitrary but must be justified on the basis of the commission of criminal offences, or of serious disciplinary misconduct or on the grounds of lack of adequate professional competence.[30]

Equally relevant is the assessment of the impartiality of the judge that has jurisdiction to resolve the domestic dispute. This assessment is based both on a *subjective* criterion—personal and professional interests or the existence of preconceived opinions of the judge in relation to the dispute submitted to him for adjudication—and on an *objective* criterion, consisting of facts from which it may be inferred that the court or a judge is actually biased, or that there is a risk of bias, such as the composition of the court or an inadequate statement of reasons for the decisions adopted, in relation to the facts of the dispute.

In relation to each of the above-mentioned aspects—independence and impartiality—both the judges' professional character and the detailed national rules on the incompatibility of the judicial function in specific situations that do not allow the free exercise of judicial power should ensure, at least in principle, compliance with the international rules on the right to a fair trial.

As recently stated by the ECtHR in its judgment of 20 May 2021, in *Beg S.p.A. v. Italy*,[31] the respect of the criteria of independence and impartiality of the adjudicating body must be ensured also when the dispute in question is referred, by legislative provision or by mutual agreement of the parties, to an arbitration panel.

Among the other rights that apply to the various judicial proceedings falling within the scope of the right to a fair trial is the right of the litigants to have their dispute discussed and decided in public hearings, so that the proceedings are conducted in a manner which is *visible* and accessible to the public, in order to preserve the relationship of trust between the national community and the administration of justice. However, reasons of efficiency and economy of judicial proceedings, security, protection of particularly vulnerable individuals or other reasons based on objective justifications may exclude or limit, also with regard to certain stages of the proceedings, the application of this specific guarantee.

A further general guarantee of a fair trial is the right of everyone to have his or her case heard, and the related judicial proceedings conducted, within a reasonable time, irrespective of the outcome. In this regard, the ECtHR, on the basis of particularly well-established case law, has stated that the reasonableness of the length of the proceedings depends on several factors, such as the complexity of the dispute, the relevance and sensitivity of the interests at stake—including therefore the seriousness of any offences committed—as well as the conduct of the parties to the dispute and of the national court, e.g. in terms of inaction or lack of activity of those same parties (including at the stage of adoption or enforcement of the national decision), or in terms of mistakes made by the parties or the court which have led to a significant increase in the length of the proceedings.

Turning now to the rights that specifically applies to criminal proceedings, reference must be made first of all to the presumption of innocence, which must be

[30] In this regard, see IACtHR judgment of 16 February 2021, *Cordero Bernal v. Peru*, para 72.

[31] See appl. no. 5312/11, paras 125 ff.

translated into procedural and substantive rules consistent with this guarantee and relating in particular to the burden of proof. Consequently, it is the prosecution that must prove the accused's guilt, which cannot be assumed by obliging the accused to prove his innocence *a priori*. In the words of the HRC, in its *General Comment No. 32* of 23 August 2007 on Article 14 (Right to Equality before Courts and Tribunals and to a Fair Trial), the presumption of innocence, "which is fundamental to the protection of human rights, imposes on the prosecution the burden of proving the charge, guarantees that no guilt can be presumed until the charge has been proved beyond reasonable doubt, ensures that the accused has the benefit of doubt, and requires that persons accused of a criminal act must be treated in accordance with this principle".[32]

Further essential safeguards applicable in criminal matters are the right to equality of arms between the prosecution and the defence and, more specifically, the rights of defence of the accused, which are often set out in detail in the various international legal instruments. Of particular relevance in this respect are the right to defend oneself in person—which includes the right to be present at the various stages of judicial proceedings, even if the individual in question has decided to remain in absentia in the early stages of the proceedings—or to have recourse to a lawyer of one's choice. The latter guarantee presupposes the right to seek legal advice promptly, unless there are "compelling reasons"—e.g. reasons of national security—justifying a temporary delay in access to a lawyer.[33] It also implies the possibility to consult one's lawyer periodically, even if the accused is in custody, as well as to benefit from legal aid if the individual in question does not have sufficient financial means. In relation to this specific guarantee, the State is required to guarantee effective legal aid, without the State being able to confine itself to provide the indigent person with mere formal access to a legal aid lawyer.

Also of great importance are the right to be promptly informed of criminal charges—which implies an obligation on the part of the national authorities to ensure that the accused has a true understanding of the nature and content of the offences that he is charged with—and the right to adequate time and means for defence, which must be modulated according to the nature and complexity of the domestic legal case and which includes the right of access to the documentation available to the prosecution, subject to the existence of proven needs to protect national security.

Likewise, the right to present exculpatory testimony and to cross-examine witnesses used by the prosecution and the right to an interpreter where the individual does not know the language used in the proceedings must be respected, not only in relation to the oral stage of the proceedings but also in relation to the written stage, for example, with regard to the translation of judicial documents. In this regard, the ECtHR has rightly specified that, during questioning, the interpreter is required to maintain a neutral position, consisting of translating acts or statements, without

---

[32] See CCPR/C/GC/32, para 30.

[33] In this regard, see the considerations of the Grand Chamber of the ECtHR in its judgment of 13 September 2016, *Ibrahim and Others v. The United Kingdom*, appl. nos. 50541/08 and others.

being able to take an active role or to empathise with the person questioned in order to induce him to make statements prejudicial to his position.[34]

Further, mention must be made of the right of appeal, which allows an individual whose guilt has been established at first instance to appeal to a higher court to challenge the conviction, and of the right not to be tried or punished twice for the same offence, provided for in Articles 2 and 4 of Protocol No. 7 to the ECHR.

Finally, it should be noted that the international rules on the right to a fair trial do not appear to be incompatible, at least in principle, with national legislation which allows a reduction—at times significant—of certain fair trial guarantees for some types of offence, on the basis of specific conditions which vary according to the domestic legislation under consideration. However, the legitimacy of such regulatory mechanisms is subject, on the one hand, to the accused's consent, as is the case e.g. for summary proceedings for establishing the accused's criminal liability; on the other hand, to an appropriate balance being struck between the general interest of the State in speedy legal proceedings and the individual's interest in enjoying at least the fundamental guarantees inherent in the right to a fair trial.

8.3 Principle of Legality and of Non-retroactivity of Criminal Law

The principle of legality and the linked principle of non-retroactivity of criminal law are ancient and well rooted safeguards against arbitrariness from, above all, the executive power of the State with respect to its own citizens. Therefore, these principles appear to be closely linked to the already examined right to liberty. Thus, the principle of legality prohibits the arrest, detention or conviction of individuals except on the basis of a law already in force at the time of the commission of the conduct allegedly constituting a criminal offence.

There are many national constitutions, even dating back a long time, which provide for observance of the principle of legality, especially in the criminal field. For this reason, the normative origin of the principle of legality must be considered to lie in a general principle of domestic law. This confirms, firstly, that general principles of domestic law can play an important role in filling normative gaps in the international protection of human rights and, secondly, that such principles, while originating in national legal systems, can *migrate* into more traditional international sources, thus being incorporated into treaty law and customary norms.[35]

At the international level, the principle of legality is reflected, with varying wording, both in universal legal instruments such as in Article 11(2) UDHR and in Article 15 ICCPR as well as in regional instruments such as in Article 9 ACHR, in Article 7 ECHR and in Article 49 CFREU. The latter rule also brings within the

[34] On this aspect affecting the fairness of the proceedings, see the ECtHR judgment of 24 January 2019, *Knox v. Italy*, appl. no. 76577/13.

[35] On the current function of general principles of domestic law, see Chap. 3, Sect. 3.3.

scope of the principle of legality the question of proportionality between the offence committed and the penalty provided for at the national level, stating that the "severity of penalties must not be disproportionate to the criminal offence".[36]

The principle of legality in criminal matters requires particularly rigorous application in view of the importance of the values it seeks to protect: the liberty of the individual and the rule of law. For this reason, the principle in question is considered non-derogable both under Article 4(2) ICCPR and Article 15(2) ECHR.

The principle examined here applies to criminal matters, a notion which, as has already been stated with respect to other human rights applicable in the criminal field, is autonomous of the one adopted at the national level. Consequently, a national provision or decision which excludes the criminal nature of the offence or sanction imposed on an individual is reviewed by international judicial bodies on the basis of the criteria of the actual nature of the sanction and its level of severity. Such an international review can *attract* into the criminal sphere national legal rules that label certain conduct or sanctions as administrative—e.g. certain crime prevention measures—which, due to the nature, content and level of severity of the sanctions adopted, should instead be subject to the guarantees afforded for criminal matters, as in the case of the confiscation of assets belonging to individuals found guilty of particularly serious crimes.

The principle of legality protects both the aspect relating to the foreseeability of one's conduct as criminal and the determination of the penalties provided for the violation, on the basis of the well-known principle *nullum crimen, nulla poena sine lege*. The principle in question therefore includes the more specific principle of non-retroactivity of criminal law, which prohibits both the retroactive application of criminal rules against the individual and broad or analogical interpretations of the rules to the detriment of the accused compared to the scope expressly provided for in the legislation.[37] Also contrary to international law is any attempt to apply national legislation or adopt practices that seek to modify the penalty already imposed on the offender to the latter's detriment, for example, by extending the period of imprisonment originally set in the final decision on the basis of new criminal law provisions applied retroactively.

It should be pointed out that the prohibitions in question are to be considered *one-way*. This means that the principle of non-retroactivity is in no way incompatible with a retroactive application of criminal law that improves the offender's situation. This is the case, for example, where criminal law provisions more favourable to the convicted person are applied after the commission of the offence or after the final conviction, as expressly provided for in the aforementioned Articles 15(1) ICCPR, 9(1) ACHR and 49(1) CFREU. The principle in question (*lex mitior*) may even lead to the individual's release from prison if the offence he was convicted of is abolished.

One can seemingly rule out that the principle of non-retroactivity of criminal law may apply to statutes of limitations. Therefore, limitation periods may be changed

---

[36] Article 49(3).

[37] In this regard, see the judgment of 17 May 2010 adopted by the ECtHR (Grand Chamber), *Kononov v. Latvia*, appl. no. 36376/04, para 185.

by national law, with the consequent retroactive application of the rules but always ensuring a proper balance between the principles of legality and non-retroactivity of criminal law and the interest of the State in extending the limitation periods for certain particularly serious offences. Consequently, an excessive or unjustified extension of limitation periods, where it results in the retroactive application of those periods to certain individuals, may be contrary to the principles examined here.

The particular relevance of the principle of legality in criminal law also seems to constitute, albeit within certain limits, a *bulwark* against the retroactive application of EU law provisions, as demonstrated by the well-known *Taricco* case on which the CJEU has ruled twice.[38] In its ruling of 5 December 2017, the Court essentially allowed an exception to the general principle of the primacy of EU law—according to which national rules must be disapplied when they conflict with directly applicable EU law—stating that if the national court considers that the obligation to disapply the national provisions "conflicts with the principle that offences and penalties must be defined by law, it would not be obliged to comply with that obligation, even if compliance with the obligation allowed a national situation incompatible with EU law to be remedied".[39]

It should be pointed out that compliance with the principle of legality must be ensured not only on a formal level, for example, through the enactment of a law, but also on a substantive level, thus requiring the State to word the criminal prohibitions and provide for the relevant penalties in a manner consistent with the principle on accessibility and foreseeability, so as to meet the requirement that the criminal law be knowable by the community and not to raise doubts for the addressees of the law as to the criminal implications of certain conduct and the type and extent of the penalties laid down.

The criterion of the foreseeability of the law must be respected both where the criminal prohibition is addressed to the population as a whole, e.g. in the case of common crimes, which can therefore be committed by any individual, and in the case of offences which can only be committed by specific categories of individuals, as in the case of offences which presuppose the offender's status as a public official.

It should also be added that the criterion of the foreseeability of legislative provisions is flexible in the sense that it has to be applied in relation to the complexity of the legal rules. In this way, if the text of the law appears to be very technical in nature and therefore difficult to understand, the legislator is required to be particularly clear in setting out the content and effects of the criminal rules. On the other hand, in the application of the foreseeability criterion, elements of a "subjective" nature, concerning the particular qualities and characteristics of the individual involved in a criminal case, may be taken into account, albeit within certain limits. Consequently, it is legitimate to consider that a legal practitioner has a greater capacity to understand legal texts and is therefore endowed, more than other individuals, with the qualities necessary to "foresee" what is laid down in the criminal rule.

---

[38] See the judgments of the Grand Chamber of 8 September 2015, C-105/14, and 5 December 2017, C-42/17, respectively.

[39] See para 61 of the judgment.

Furthermore, the foreseeability of the law must be observed not only with reference to written rules but also in relation to the case law where it supplements the content of the norm—in "a need for elucidation of doubtful points and for adaptation to changing circumstances"[40]. And all the more so when case law endorses evolving interpretations of criminal rules, as in the case of the offence of external complicity with a mafia-type organisation, which in the Italian system traces its roots to case law, as also noted by the ECtHR in its judgment of 14 April 2015 in *Contrada v. Italy (No. 3)*, according to which "*il n'est pas contesté entre les parties que le concours externe en association de type mafieux constitue une infraction d'origine jurisprudentielle*".[41] In these cases, what needs to be ascertained is whether the *new* case law on the point is well-settled in the national legal system before the occurrence of the conduct with criminal implications, so as to meet the aforementioned requirements of foreseeability and therefore knowledge of the criminal law.

For the same reasons, the criterion of the foreseeability of criminal precepts and penalties must also be observed when the domestic law refers to other legal rules in order to complement the criminal prohibition (so-called legislation by reference). As noted by the ECtHR in its advisory opinion of 29 May 2020,[42] delivered under the previously mentioned mechanism in Protocol No. 16 to the ECHR,[43] the criterion in question also operates where the legal rules referred to by the criminal law under consideration are constitutional and are therefore presumed to be more easily known at the national level.

8.3.1 Principle of Legality in Criminal Matters and International Crimes

Article 7(2) ECHR provides that respect for the principle of legality "shall not prejudice the trial and punishment of any person for any act or omission which, at the time when it was committed, was criminal according to the general principles of law recognised by civilised nations". In essence, this provision allows the courts of Contracting Parties to the ECHR to try individuals accused of international crimes, even in the absence of national rules prohibiting the commission of such serious crimes, on the basis of the general principles of law derivable from the national legal systems of the same Contracting States and of third States and, on the basis of the practice of applying this rule, in light of the relevant international law rules. This provision was, for example, applied by the ECtHR (Grand Chamber) in its judgment

[40] See ECtHR (Grand Chamber), judgment of 17 September 2009, *Scoppola v. Italy (No. 2)*, appl. no. 10249/03, para 100.

[41] Appl. no. 66655/2013, para 66 of the judgment.

[42] See *Use of the "Blanket Reference" or "Legislation by Reference" Technique in the Definition of an Offence and the Standards of Comparison between the Criminal Law in Force at the Time of the Commission of the Offence and the Amended Criminal Law*, request no. P16-2019-001.

[43] See Chap. 4, Sect. 4.1.

of 22 March 2001 in *Streletz, Kessler and Krenz v. Germany*,[44] with reference to crimes committed by certain officials of the former German Democratic Republic.

Although the wording of Article 7 suggests that there is a derogation from the general principle of legality in criminal law with regard to the repression of international crimes, the ECtHR has held that the possibility for Contracting Parties to try those responsible for these crimes, even those dating from the period of World War II, is in conformity with the principle of legality, representing a particular application of it and not a derogation or exception.

According to the Court, in fact, "Article 7 § 1 can be considered to contain the general rule of non-retroactivity" and "Article 7 § 2 is only a contextual clarification of the liability limb of that rule, included so as to ensure that there was no doubt about the validity of prosecutions after the Second World War in respect of the crimes committed during that war... It is thus clear that the drafters of the Convention did not intend to allow for any general exception to the rule of non-retroactivity. Indeed, the Court has held in a number of cases that the two paragraphs of Article 7 are interlinked and are to be interpreted in a concordant manner".[45]

However morally understandable the provision and its application may be, moreover limited to the repression of international crimes, it is arguable that it represents a real derogation from the principle of legality in the criminal sphere, which recalls the controversy—not without foundation—concerning the conduct of the Nuremberg trials of certain Nazi criminals, which were conducted on the basis of legal rules established (or specified) mainly at the end of the Second World War, as well as by courts whose independence is open to question. From this point of view, it is appreciable that the rule in question has had a rather limited application by the national courts of the Contracting Parties to the ECHR, both in *quantitative* terms—i.e. with regard to the number of legal proceedings actually initiated relying on the aforementioned legal basis—and above all in *qualitative* terms, given that it has been applied in relation to the very serious crimes committed by the Nazi regime during the Second World War and subsequently by members of certain communist regimes in Eastern Europe and, more recently, in the context of the armed conflict in the former Yugoslavia.[46]

In this regard, it is our opinion that, at least for crimes dating back in time and therefore lacking, at the time of the events, detailed regulation at the international and domestic level, reference to the legal parameters constituted by international law and the general principles of domestic law does not ensure an adequate level of clarity and foreseeability, especially as regards the penalties to be imposed. These reflections also make it clear how important it is for States to adopt specific legislation prohibiting the commission of international crimes—if necessary modifying the national rules

---

[44] Applications nos. 34044/96, 35532/97 and 44801/98.

[45] ECtHR (Grand Chamber), judgment of 18 July 2013, *Maktouf and Damjanović v. Bosnia and Herzegovina*, appl. nos. 2312/08 and 34179/08, para 72.

[46] On the recent application of Article 7 ECHR to a case concerning international crimes committed, through both acts of commission and omission, by a high-ranking Croatian police officer against Serb prisoners during the international and non-international armed conflicts in the former Yugoslavia, see ECtHR judgment of 20 January 2022, *Milanković v. Croatia*, appl. no. 33351/20.

on the basis of treaties that they have ratified—in order, on the one hand, to preserve the principle of legality and, on the other hand, to provide the national courts with the necessary legal instruments to punish these very serious violations of international law.

Comprehension Check and Tasks

1. What are the States' obligations with regard to the right to liberty and security? (Sect. 8.1)
2. Focus on the right to truth and its content (Sect. 8.1.1)
3. What are the criteria indicated in the international case law to assess the independence and impartiality of a judge in the context of the right of access to justice? (Sect. 8.2.1)
4. What is the specific scope of application of the principle of legality in criminal matters? (Sect. 8.3)

Chapter 9
Right to Respect for Private and Family Life, Freedom of Thought, Conscience and Religion, Freedom of Expression and Freedom of Assembly and Association

Contents

Abstract The chapter addresses the international rules on the rights to respect for private and family life, to freedom of thought, conscience, and religion, to freedom of expression and to freedom of assembly and association. These have been the subject of expansive interpretation in international case law, especially that of the ECtHR, in order to encompass the protection of new rights or categories of individuals, such as the protection of personal data, the right to be forgotten, the protection of same-sex couples or the right of access to the Internet. Finally, the chapter examines, by referring to the relevant case-law, possible conflicts either between human rights or between human rights and state interests. Relevant examples are the conflict between freedom of religion and the need to guarantee the security of the State, which has been discussed in the case law on the Islamic veil, or the issues concerning the display of the crucifix in public schools.

P. Pustorino, *Introduction to International Human Rights Law*,
https://doi.org/10.1007/978-94-6265-563-8_9

9.1 Right to Respect for Private and Family Life

The right to respect for private and family life is protected in numerous universal and regional human rights treaties, although the content of the various norms are not always identical and there are various rules specifically concerning the protection of the family.[1] Furthermore, Article 12 UDHR, Article 17 ICCPR and Article 11(2) ACHR also expressly prohibit harm to the honour and reputation of any individual, while the CFREU, in addition to establishing the protection of the right to private and family life, provides for an *ad hoc* rule on the protection of the individual's personal data.[2]

As already noted for other human rights, the right to respect for private and family life constitutes a sort of *container* into which a series of additional rights and guarantees have converged, some of which have arisen as a result of the application of the relevant international norms to *modern* problems and circumstances, stemming both from the evolution of new technologies and from developments in civil society. Moreover, several issues falling within the scope of the international law rules on private and family life have already been analysed earlier in this book, especially with reference to the right to life, considered in light of the new techniques used in the field of assisted procreation, surrogacy, etc.[3]

Effective protection of the right to private and family life implies compliance by States not so much with *negative* obligations, that is, not to engage in harmful conduct, but more with *positive* obligations—that is, to adopt specific action—a number of which relate to legislative measures designed to fill gaps in national law or to strengthen the domestic level of protection. The rules on the protection of private and family life are generally *vertical* in their application, concerning interference by State bodies with private individuals. However, in some very serious cases of violation of the right in question, for example, in the previously mentioned cases of domestic violence against women or minors,[4] an examination of case law reveals a *horizontal* application of these rules too, which obliges the State to prevent and repress the violations in question committed at the inter-individual level.

The right to private and family life belongs to the category of rights that can be restricted.[5] Accordingly, interference with private and family life is lawful on condition that it is provided for by law and justified by general interests—such as national security, the maintenance of public order, the prevention of crime, the protection of health, etc.—or by individual or collective interests such as the protection of other rights of individuals or groups of persons.

The balancing of these rights and interests must be carried out not only a *priori,* in particular at the time of the approval of the national legislation aiming to reconcile the

---

[1] In this regard, Article 23 ICCPR.

[2] See Articles 7 and 8 CFREU.

[3] See Chap. 6, Sects. 6.3–6.3.3.

[4] See Chap. 3, Sect. 3.7.1.

[5] See Chap. 3, Sect. 3.9.

various opposing requirements, but also *ex post* bearing in mind the specific circumstances of the case at issue and the actual methods of State intervention. Therefore, the natural margin of appreciation that States enjoy in the matter of balancing the various interests at stake is widened or reduced by the international bodies charged with scrutinising observance of human rights treaties, having regard to the various factors and elements specific to the case in question.

In particular, the nature, general scope, duration and purpose of the restrictive measures adopted by the State, as well as their effects on the individuals targeted by those measures, are taken into account. In addition, State measures restricting private and family life are sometimes assessed in light of similar measures taken by other States in analogous situations—in particular countries belonging to the same treaty system—in a comparative perspective aimed at identifying a *common denominator* within the system in question.

In the well-established practice of the bodies in charge of scrutinising the observance of numerous human rights treaties, the lawfulness of an interference with an individual's private and family life is thus analysed in light of the principles of the necessity of State intervention and the proportionality of the measures actually adopted, making ample reference to the several factors and elements mentioned above.

9.1.1 Notion of Private Life

The overall concept of private life and family life is autonomous at the international level from its counterpart at the national level. Moreover, the two constituent notions cannot be regarded as *watertight compartments* for the purposes of assessing the facts of the case because State conduct often affects the private and family life of one or more individuals at the same time.

It should be stressed that the concept of private and family life also guarantees the protection of places and goods belonging both to the personal sphere, e.g. the home of the individual and his family, and to the individual's occupational sphere, thus including adequate protection of postal or electronic correspondence as well as telephone conversations and the individual's own conduct at work. Therefore, a worker's behaviour may be monitored only in accordance with the principles of necessity and proportionality, for example in order to prevent or punish criminal or disciplinary wrongdoing committed by employees, and provided that the surveillance measures are limited in time, are used only for those purposes by the employer and are subject to judicial or administrative review to verify their legality.[6]

It should also be noted that the specific right to privacy protects the personal, physical and mental sphere of the individual, and comprises both an *internal* intimate aspect of the person and an *external* aspect consisting of the right of each individual

[6] In this regard, see ECtHR (Grand Chamber) judgment of 17 October 2019, in *López Ribalda and Others v. Spain*, appl. nos. 1874/13 and 8567/13.

to develop and maintain personal and social relationships with individuals and with the community as a whole, thus including not only lasting relationships with certain persons but also sporadic and short-term relationships.

Among the most current issues in matters of protection of privacy, in relation to which a conflict often arises with respect to real or presumed general interests of the State (for example, with reference to the general interest to safeguard the national security or to prosecute particularly serious crimes), is the right not to be subjected to unjustified interception or surveillance. These activities are carried out by means of telephone, electronic or satellite systems and are designed both to intercept communications of a private nature and to pinpoint the presence of a person in a certain place. The protection of the individual's right to privacy applies not only when the interception or surveillance are carried out in private places but also when they take place in public places or places open to the public.

In this respect, international case law tends to distinguish the above-mentioned interception and surveillance according to their level of interference with the individual's right to privacy. This distinction is particularly relevant for the purpose of examining the proportionality of the restrictive measures adopted by the State. In this sense, the ECtHR has held that the satellite monitoring system known as GPS (Global Positioning System) involves a lower level of interference than visual and acoustical surveillance systems. According to the Court, "GPS surveillance is by its very nature to be distinguished from other methods of visual or acoustical surveillance which are, as a rule, more susceptible of interfering with a person's right to respect for private life, because they disclose more information on a person's conduct, opinions or feelings".[7]

Those targeted by State interception and surveillance activities may be both individuals and a plurality of persons. The means employed may include sophisticated *bulk interception* systems, i.e. systems monitoring specific places or specific persons (including the websites visited by the individual in question) that enable a very large and indiscriminate number of communications between several individuals to be intercepted.

In the cases referred to above the State is first of all required to regulate by law the interference with the right to privacy, ensuring the clarity and therefore the foreseeability of the relevant legal provisions. While foreseeability of the law is naturally attenuated in relation to certain surveillance and interception measures pursued at State level like bulk interception, nevertheless it is necessary for the State to provide for rules of sufficient clarity and precision as to their content and scope of application so as to avoid arbitrariness on the part of the public or private bodies responsible for implementing them.

In addition, the State must demonstrate, both at the legislative level and at the level of actual implementation of domestic rules, the necessity and proportionality of the measures adopted ensuring a proper balance between individual and general interests opposed to the right to privacy, such as those concerning the prevention of serious crimes (for example, in the field of countering organised crime or international

[7] See judgment of 2 September 2010 in *Uzun v. Germany*, appl. no 35623/05, para 52.

terrorism) or the protection of the health of the population in the case of a significant health emergency (as in the case of national measures adopted to cope with the spread of COVID-19). More specifically, an analysis of ECtHR case law reveals some specific criteria that can be used to verify the lawfulness of any conduct interfering with the free enjoyment of the right to privacy. These criteria are modulated differently depending on the various surveillance and interception measures implemented at the national level.

With specific regard to the assessment of covert surveillance measures, the ECtHR has identified some minimum safeguards that the State must respect in order to avoid abuses of power by national authorities. They consist in "the nature of the offences which may give rise to an interception order; a definition of the categories of people liable to have their telephones tapped; a limit on the duration of telephone tapping; the procedure to be followed for examining, using and storing the data obtained; the precautions to be taken when communicating the data to other parties; and the circumstances in which recordings may or must be erased or the tapes destroyed".[8]

The need for the State to comply with the above-mentioned safeguards in relation to the various surveillance systems that may affect the right to privacy was reiterated with regard to mass interception mechanisms. In this context, the Court emphasised, on the one hand, the need to provide a certain and foreseeable legislative framework as a basis for surveillance measures, and, on the other hand, the importance of establishing checks and balances, including judicial ones, to verify the correct application and, if necessary, modify the measures restricting the privacy of a number of individuals.

In its judgment of 25 May 2021 the ECtHR (Grand Chamber) ruled in the well-known case of *Big Brother Watch and Others v. The United Kingdom*, finding that the national rules in force at the time on the bulk interception of electronic communications and the acquisition of personal data were inconsistent with the right to private and family life. On a general level, it was stated that "in order to minimise the risk of the bulk interception power being abused, the Court considers that the process must be subject to 'end-to-end safeguards', meaning that, at the domestic level, an assessment should be made at each stage of the process of the necessity and proportionality of the measures being taken; that bulk interception should be subject to independent authorisation at the outset, when the object and scope of the operation are being defined; and that the operation should be subject to supervision and independent ex *post facto* review".[9]

Finally, it is necessary to specify that compliance with the rules and conditions on the basis of which it is lawful to undertake interception or to monitor individual and collective conduct operates both in the case where the activities in question are carried out directly by the State or by private companies on behalf of the State, as well as with regard to the activities of the intelligence services of foreign States which subsequently share that information with other countries.

---

[8] See the inadmissibility decision of 29 June 2006 in *Weber and Saravia v. Germany*, appl. no. 54934/00, para 95.

[9] Appl. nos. 58170/13, 62322/14 and 24969/15, para 350 of the judgment.

Furthermore, in case of transmission, by a Contracting State to foreign States or international organisations, of material obtained by bulk interception, in the above-mentioned *Big Brother Watch* case the ECtHR stated that the transmission "should be limited to such material as has been collected and stored in a Convention compliant manner and should be subject to certain additional specific safeguards pertaining to the transfer itself. First of all, the circumstances in which such a transfer may take place must be set out clearly in domestic law. Secondly, the transferring State must ensure that the receiving State, in handling the data, has in place safeguards capable of preventing abuse and disproportionate interference. In particular, the receiving State must guarantee the secure storage of the material and restrict its onward disclosure. This does not necessarily mean that the receiving State must have comparable protection to that of the transferring State; nor does it necessarily require that an assurance be given prior to every transfer. Thirdly, heightened safeguards will be necessary when it is clear that material requiring special confidentiality—such as confidential journalistic material—is being transferred. Finally, the Court considers that the transfer of material to foreign intelligence partners should also be subject to independent control".[10]

9.1.2 *Notion of Family Life*

The notion of family life in the case law and practice of the bodies charged with scrutinising the observance of human rights treaties is influenced by developments in civil society and, accordingly, by the different types of family union that exist today. Apart from the natural inclusion of the family formed by marriage, family unions formed in the absence of marriage are also protected, as is the family formed on the basis of the relationship between parents and their natural or adopted children. And even limited protection is given to *sui generis* family relationships such as between grandparents and grandchildren or between brothers and sisters, provided that the emotional and family bond is genuine and particularly intense.[11]

The protection of family life extends to families formed by foreigners permanently residing abroad. It follows that the deportation of foreigners who have formed family groups in other countries is subject to a specific assessment from the point of view of respect for family life.[12] For the ECtHR, among the criteria to be used in order to verify the lawfulness of measures to deport and hence separate a foreigner from

[10] *Id.*, para 362.

[11] On the family relationship between grandparents and grandchildren, see recently the ECtHR judgment of 14 January 2021, *Terna v. Italy*, appl. no. 21052/18, paras 63–64.

[12] On the balance between the needs of protection of the public interest in the prevention of crime and the protection of private and family life of the individual, see recently the judgment of the UK Supreme Court of 16 July 2021, UKSC 30, *Sanambar v. Secretary of State for the Home Department*, paras 47 ff., which considers it lawful to deport a foreigner both because he is responsible for numerous crimes in the United Kingdom and because of the possibility of his reintegration in the country of origin, Iran.

his family unit are "the nature and seriousness of the offence committed by the applicant; the duration of the applicant's stay in the country from which he is going to be expelled; the time which has elapsed since the commission of the offence and the applicant's conduct during that period; the nationalities of the various persons concerned; the applicant's family situation, such as the length of the marriage; other factors revealing whether the couple lead a real and genuine family life; whether the spouse knew about the offence at the time when he or she entered into a family relationship; and whether there are children in the marriage and, if so, their age. Not least, the Court will also consider the seriousness of the difficulties which the spouse would be likely to encounter in the applicant's country of origin, although the mere fact that a person might face certain difficulties in accompanying her or his spouse cannot in itself preclude expulsion".[13]

In the subsequent Grand Chamber judgment of 18 October 2006 in *Üner v. The Netherlands*, the ECtHR considered it appropriate to make explicit two criteria that it considered implicit in those identified in *Boultif*: "the best interests and well-being of the children, in particular the seriousness of the difficulties which any children of the applicant are likely to encounter in the country to which the applicant is to be expelled; and the solidity of social, cultural and family ties with the host country and with the country of destination". In relation to this last criterion, the Court affirmed, correctly in our view, that "the longer a person has been residing in a particular country, the stronger his or her ties with that country and the weaker the ties with the country of his or her nationality will be".[14]

The same rules protecting the family life of a foreigner permanently residing abroad ensure the right to reunification for family members who are outside the country where the foreigner lives. In this matter, however, the territorial State's margin of appreciation is wide and linked to the State's right to admit foreigners to its territory, without prejudice to special legal regimes—for example, EU law—and the application of specific international human rights principles, in particular, the principle of *non-refoulement*.[15]

However, the State is obliged to strike a balance between the general and individual interests at stake, with the effect that unreasonable and disproportionate conduct, both with regard to respect for the right to family reunification and with regard to procedural aspects such as excessive time limits for applying for reunification,[16] must be regarded as contrary to human rights law.

[13] See ECtHR judgment of 2 August 2001 in *Boultif v. Switzerland*, appl. no. 54273/00, para 48.

[14] Appl. no. 46410/99, para 58 of the judgment.

[15] On this principle, see Chap. 7. Sect. 7.4.

[16] In this regard, see ECtHR (Grand Chamber), judgment of 9 July 2021, *M.A. v. Denmark*, appl. no. 6697/18.

9.1.3 Right to Image, Reputation and Personal Identity

Among the additional rights to be included in the concept of private and family life is the right to the protection of image and privacy of the person and his family. The protection of this right is generally attenuated in the case of the fame of the person in question and on condition that there is a general interest in the dissemination of certain images or news, but also taking into account the type of images depicting the person or information provided to the public.

The right to the protection of reputation and honour is also part of an individual's private life. This right may be subject, on the basis of a number of criteria developed in international case law, to a balancing act in the event of conflict with the right to freedom of opinion and expression by journalists or other individuals, more about which below.[17]

The right to private life also comprises the right to personal identity, which includes the protection of the human embryo obtained through *in vitro* fertilisation, given that "the embryos contain the genetic material of the person in question and accordingly represent a constituent part of that person's genetic material and biological identity",[18] as well as the right to know one's origins, including one's biological origins, although the specific aspect of the disclosure of the identity of the biological parents must be balanced by the State with the individual right of the latter to remain anonymous, as established in the ECtHR judgment of 25 September 2012 in *Godelli v. Italy*.[19]

The right to private life also includes the right to a name, sometimes protected by specific international rules.[20] It represents an essential element for the identification of the person, both within the specific context of the family unit and above all within the framework of national society. On the one hand, it includes the right to preserve one's name, thus excluding unjustified measures to change one's name by the State.

The right to a name also implies respect for the right of parents to choose their children's names without however tolerating discrimination between men and women in national laws, for example, by mandating at birth, even against the will of both parents, the paternal surname, as stated by the ECtHR in its judgment of 7 January 2014 in *Cusan and Fazzo v. Italy*.[21]

---

[17] On this issue, see Chap. 9, Sects. 9.3–9.3.2.

[18] ECtHR (Grand Chamber), judgment of 27 August 2015, *Parrillo v. Italy*, appl. no. 46470/11, para 158.

[19] See appl. no. 33783/09.

[20] See Article 18 ACHR.

[21] Appl. no. 77/07, para 67 of the judgment.

9.1.4 *Protection of Personal Data and the Right to Be Forgotten*

Other rights that fall within the private sphere of the individual and that have become established as a result of the development of new information technologies include the right to the protection of one's personal data and the so-called right to be forgotten.

On the subject of the protection of personal data, reference should be made to the CoE Convention for the Protection of Individuals with regard to Automatic Processing of Personal Data of 28 January 1981, no. 108, as amended by the Protocol of 10 October 2018. The Convention requires that personal data be acquired, collected and used with the consent of the person concerned, or on the basis of the law, and provided that the legislation is endowed with the usual requirements of clarity and foreseeability and ensures an adequate balancing of the general and particular interests with regard to the collection and processing of personal data. From this point of view, what matters is, on the one hand, the nature and content of the personal data acquired, which, save in exceptional circumstances provided for by law, cannot include the sensitive data of the individual; on the other hand, the use of these data, which must be strictly linked to the purpose for which they are obtained from the individuals, or to the general purposes laid down by law, and in any event in accordance with the principle of proportionality.

The right to the protection of personal data must also be *modulated* having regard to both the age of the individual and any special needs he may have, for example, by requiring special protection for minors or persons with disabilities.

It should be made clear that, while individuals are entitled to the protection of their personal data collected and used by third parties, they are also entitled to have access to certain information lawfully collected by national authorities such as that on their state of health or that recorded in civil registers concerning them.

The importance of the right to the protection of personal data, which must also be guaranteed in relation to the collection and use of such data through IT tools—for instance with regard to information and data collected in the numerous online archives managed by public and private operators and often accessible via the web—has given rise in practice to a new form of individual or collective guarantee: the right to informational self-determination, which allows "individuals to rely on their right to privacy as regards data which, albeit neutral, are collected, processed and disseminated collectively and in such a form or manner that their Article 8 rights may be engaged".[22]

Linked to the right to protection of personal data is the right to be forgotten, which implies the right to request the removal of both information on facts that date back in time and no longer correspond to the current profile of the person concerned, including personal data for which the individual did not originally consent to the processing of or subsequently withdrew consent, or where the data acquired are no longer necessary for the private or public purposes for which they were collected.

---

[22] On this right, see the ECtHR (Grand Chamber) judgment of 27 June 2017, *Satakunnan Markkinapörssi Oy and Satamedia Oy v. Finland*, appl. no. 931/13, para 137.

It seems clear that, also in this case, States are required to balance the need to protect the privacy and reputation of the individual with the competing needs of the general public to be informed of facts or situations, even if compromising (for example, pertaining to criminal proceedings or convictions), which concern a given individual, taking into account, among other things, the identity of the person who is considered to be the victim of the violation, the relevant facts (including when they happened), the method of information and the effects on individuals of the dissemination of news concerning past events.[23]

These considerations also seem to be in line with the CJEU's decision in the well-known *Google Spain* case. In its judgment of 13 May 2014, the Grand Chamber of the Court had to rule on the interpretation of Directive 95/46/EC of the European Parliament and of the Council of 24 October 1995 on the protection of individuals with regard to the processing of personal data and on the free movement of such data[24] in light of Articles 7–8 CFREU. In so doing the Court observed that from the examination of the Directive it follows "that even initially lawful processing of accurate data may, in the course of time, become incompatible with the directive where those data are no longer necessary in light of the purposes for which they were collected or processed. That is so in particular where they appear to be inadequate, irrelevant or no longer relevant, or excessive in relation to those purposes and in light of the time that has elapsed".[25]

The need to weigh up the right to be forgotten with the freedom of expression and information, in light, *inter alia*, of the criteria of the harm sustained by the individual seeking the anonymisation of his identity in the electronic archive of a newspaper and the passage of time since the original publication in the print edition of the same newspaper (20 years in the case at issue), has recently been reaffirmed by the ECtHR in its judgment of 21 June 2021 in *Hurbain v. Belgium*.[26] In that case it was held there was no violation of the freedom of expression of a publisher of a daily newspaper, which had been ordered by the national courts to anonymise the article in its electronic archive mentioning the full name of a driver who not only served a sentence of final conviction for a deadly road accident but also had been rehabilitated.

Finally, two further clarifications should be made. Firstly, the right to be forgotten does not prevent the State from collecting and using information, albeit of a historical nature, relating to the criminal conduct of an individual and his personal data (DNA profile, fingerprints, photographs, etc.), for the purpose of preventing and suppressing further criminal offences by the individual in question or by third parties, provided

[23] For an application of these criteria, see ECtHR judgment of 28 June 2018, *M.L. and W.W. v. Germany*, appl. nos. 60798/10 and 65599/10.

[24] The Directive has been repealed by Regulation 2016/679 of the European Parliament and of the Council of 27 April 2016 on the protection of natural persons with regard to the processing of personal data and on the free movement of such data.

[25] Case C-131/12, para 93.

[26] Appl. no. 57292/16. The applicant requested that the case be referred to the Grand Chamber. On 11 October 2021 the Grand Chamber panel of five judges decided to refer the case to the Grand Chamber pursuant to Article 43 ECHR.

that there are both time limits for the retention and use of such information and also guarantees of periodic review of the need to retain the personal data, as confirmed by the ECtHR in its judgment of 13 February 2020 in *Gaughran v. The United Kingdom*.[27] Secondly, with reference to the use of personal data by private entities like the operators of social media networks, although it is extremely difficult for the State to ensure compliance with the right to be forgotten, the regulatory parameter to be applied in this matter is the principle of due diligence. It follows that the State is required to take all the preventive and repressive measures at its disposal to ensure compliance with this right, also at the level of inter-individual relations.

9.1.5 Protection of Same-Sex Couples

In accordance with developments in various national legal systems and in civil society as a whole, the question has arisen—often in connection with the prohibition of discrimination between heterosexual and homosexual unions—of including same-sex relationships within the framework of the right to respect for private and family life. As was well underlined in general terms by the CommEDAW in *Rosanna Flamer-Caldera v. Sri Lanka*, "whatever the form of a family, the treatment of women in the family both at law and in private must accord with the principles of equality and justice for all people".[28]

Overcoming a previous approach that included same-sex relationships only in the notion of private life and valuing the legislative and social developments in the field of protection of stable same-sex couples, the ECtHR, in its judgment of 24 June 2010 in *Schalk and Kopf v. Austria*, considered "it artificial to maintain the view that, in contrast to a different-sex couple, a same-sex couple cannot enjoy 'family life' for the purposes of Article 8. Consequently, the relationship of the applicants, a cohabiting same-sex couple living in a stable de facto partnership, falls within the notion of 'family life', just as the relationship of a different-sex couple in the same situation would".[29] The Court therefore included same-sex unions of a stable nature within the notion of family.

Subsequently, the ECtHR (Grand Chamber), in its judgment of 7 November 2013 in *Vallianatos and Others v. Greece*, opened up further in favour of the protection of family relationships of a homosexual nature, limiting the importance of the said condition of stability of the family union and thus guaranteeing similar protection to

---

[27] Appl. no. 45245/15.

[28] See the decision of 21 February 2022, CEDAW/C/81/D/134/2018, para 9.7. In this case, concerning the criminalization of same-sex conduct between consenting adults in the Sri Lankan legal system, the CommEDAW clarified that "decriminalization of consensual same-sex relations is essential to prevent and protect against violence, discrimination and harmful gender stereotypes": para 9.4.

[29] Appl. no. 30141/04, para 94 of the judgment.

homosexual couples who, "for professional and social reasons" and therefore on the basis of an adequate justification, are not permanently cohabiting.[30]

A further significant development in the ECtHR's case law took place with the judgment of 21 July 2015 in *Oliari and Others v. Italy*, in which the Court censured the absence in the national legal system of a legal framework allowing for recognition and protection of same-sex relationships, thus finding a violation of Article 8 ECHR. In particular, the Court criticised the serious shortcomings of the Italian legal system in this area, pointing out, *inter alia*, the gap between social reality, in which same-sex unions widely exist and are accepted, and the absence of effective legal protection for them. The Court highlighted the rapid development in the recognition of the rights of same-sex couples, albeit through different legal instruments—marriage, civil partnerships, etc.—both within the framework of the legal systems of the CoE member countries and at the universal level.

Of significant importance is ample attention given by the ECtHR in *Oliari* to the US Supreme Court judgment handed down just a month before[31] whereby on the basis of the principle of non-discrimination the latter Court held that "same-sex couples may exercise the fundamental right to marry in all States, and that there was no lawful basis for a State to refuse to recognise a lawful same-sex marriage performed in another State on the ground of its same-sex character".[32]

For these reasons, the ECtHR found a failure to comply with the positive obligations deriving from Article 8 ECHR referred to above, also requiring the State "to implement, under the supervision of the Committee of Ministers, appropriate general and/or individual measures to fulfil its obligations to secure the right of the applicants and other persons in their position to respect for their private and family life".[33] This, in accordance with the well-established case law according to which the Court, in the event of systematic or generalised violations, may require the adoption of general measures (including legislative ones) or measures of an individual nature in order to resolve the situation created in the case at issue and prevent similar situations from arising.[34]

Recently, the Strasbourg Court, in its judgment of 13 July 2021 in *Fedotova and Others v. Russia*, reaffirmed the positive obligation of Contracting Parties to the ECHR to provide a legal framework that guarantees the recognition of same-sex relationships, rejecting the respondent State's argument that a majority of Russians disapprove of same-sex unions. In the Court's commendable opinion, "[i]t would be incompatible with the underlying values of the Convention, as an instrument of the

---

[30] Appl. nos. 29381/09 and 32684/09, para 73 of the judgment.

[31] US Supreme Court judgment of 26 June 2015 in *Obergefell and Others v. Hodges, Director, Ohio Department of Health and Others.*

[32] Appl. nos. 18766/11 and 36030/11, para 65 of the ECtHR judgment.

[33] See para 200 of the judgment.

[34] On this issue, see Chap. 4, Sect. 4.3.1. On the basis of the ruling of the ECtHR, the Italian Parliament approved Law No. 76 of 20 May 2016 on the regulation of civil unions, including those between persons of the same sex.

European public order, if the exercise of Convention rights by a minority group were made conditional on its being accepted by the majority".[35]

The Strasbourg Court, in light of an express provision contained in Article 12 ECHR according to which the right to marry is reserved to "men and women", has, on the other hand, ruled out the possibility that Contracting Parties are obliged to allow same-sex couples to marry,[36] while pointing out that the laws of Contracting States that allow same-sex marriage are not to be considered contrary to the ECHR.

9.2 Freedom of Thought, Conscience and Religion

The right to believe in a particular religion and to freely profess and express one's religious convictions, in public or in private, constitutes the main aspect of freedom of thought, conscience and religion. The right in question may be exercised individually or collectively, acquiring in particular a *simple* collective dimension, where it is invoked by a plurality of individuals bound by equal religious sentiments but without the use of specific places in which such activities are carried out, or an *institutional* one, where it is exercised through bodies or in places of a religious nature.

As pointed out by the ECtHR,[37] this right has an *internal* intimate dimension, which pertains to the private sphere of the individual, and an *external* dimension, which concerns the external manifestations of one's religious opinions and ideas.

Universal and regional human rights treaties, as interpreted in practice, protect all forms of belief or religion, including less widespread religions in accordance with the principle of religious pluralism, provided that they are based on religious views "that attain a certain level of cogency, seriousness, cohesion and importance", as observed by the ECtHR in interpreting the State's obligation to guarantee the right to education while respecting the religious and philosophical convictions of a student's parents.[38]

As noted in relation to many other human rights, it is clear that the effective observance of the right to religious freedom implies respect by the State for both negative obligations to refrain from interfering in the free exercise of that right and above all positive obligations aimed at concretely allowing each individual to freely manifest their beliefs and opinions on religious matters.

The need to protect freedom of conscience and religion does not prevent the State from showing a preference for certain religions, even to the extent of endorsing a *State religion*, provided, on the one hand, that the members of the national community—citizens or foreigners—are free to profess other religious faiths and, on the other hand, that the precepts of the State religion are not incompatible with the freedom

---

[35] See appl. nos. 40792/10, 30538/14 and 43439/14, para 52.

[36] See the above-mentioned judgment in *Schalk and Kopf v. Austria*, para 108.

[37] See the judgment of 25 May 1993 in *Kokkinakis v. Greece*, appl. no. 14307/88, para 31.

[38] See the judgment of 25 February 1982 in *Campbell and Cosans v. The United Kingdom*, appl. nos. 7511/76; 7743/76, para 36. On the right to education, see Chap. 11, Sect. 11.3.

to believe in other religions and with other human rights such as the right not to be discriminated against on religious grounds. According to the ECtHR those limits are exceeded in the case of the introduction of Islamic law (Sharia) in a Contracting Party to the ECHR because Sharia "is incompatible with the fundamental principles of democracy, as set forth in the Convention".[39]

Religious freedom encompasses both the right to change one's religious beliefs, as established by Article 18 UDHR and Article 10(1) CFREU, the right not to believe (thus maintaining a position of atheism or agnosticism), the right not to reveal one's religious beliefs in public and the right not to be pressured or coerced into maintaining or changing one's religious beliefs.

As noted by the HRC in its *General Comment No. 22* of 30 July 1993, "the freedom to 'have or to adopt' a religion or belief necessarily entails the freedom to choose a religion or belief, including the right to replace one's current religion or belief with another or to adopt atheistic views, as well as the right to retain one's religion or belief".[40]

Naturally the right to change one's religious beliefs and to accept other faiths is completely at odds with the national legislation and practices of some radical Islamic states, under which the crime of apostasy, particularly in the case of abandoning the Islamic religion, is punished with severe penalties and sometimes even the death penalty. Similarly, it is contrary to the right to religious freedom for the State to refuse to issue identity documents or civil status documents to individuals who profess religions other than those permitted by the State, or in any case to oblige them to adhere to one of those religions even if only for the purpose of issuing such documents thereby preventing them from declaring their adherence to the other religions that they actually practice.[41]

An examination of the ECtHR's case law further shows that Contracting Parties to the ECHR also have a positive obligation to ensure peaceful coexistence between the various religions practised at the national level and mutual tolerance among their adherents as well as vis-à-vis those who do not have a religious faith. Hence an obligation to prohibit conduct of a blasphemous nature insofar as it is based on gratuitously offensive or unsubstantiated statements and is likely to spread hatred and intolerance towards a particular religion and those who practice a religious faith.[42]

The right to religious freedom has been applied in various ways in the case law and practice of the international bodies charged with scrutinising the observance

[39] ECtHR (Grand Chamber) in its judgment of 13 February 2003 in *Refah Partisi (the Welfare Party) and Others v. Turkey*, appl. nos. 41340/98 and others, para 123.

[40] See para 5.

[41] See the ACommHPR Report of 17 February 2016 in *Hossam Ezzat & Rania Enayet (Represented by Egyptian Initiative for Personal Rights & INTERIGHTS) v. Arab Republic of Egypt*, Communication No. 355/07, finding a breach of Article 8 of the ACHPR by Egyptian legislation, subsequently amended (Report, para 140), which obliged adherents of religions other than Islam, Judaism or Christianity to declare their adherence to one of these religions in order to obtain documents on their marital status: para 138.

[42] See the judgment of 25 October 2018 in *E.S. v. Austria*, appl. no. 38450/12, paras 43–44 and 52–53.

of human rights treaties, both as regards the right in question and related rights, such as the right to education[43] or the right to freedom of opinion and expression, confirming what stated earlier in this book about the indivisibility of human rights.[44] However, there is a certain *fluctuation* in the resolution of cases concerning religious freedom submitted to the said bodies, with conflicting rulings not just between those established by different treaties but even between bodies established by the same treaty. In this regard, particular attention should be paid to the disputes that have arisen over the use of religious symbols, both by individuals, such as the Islamic headscarf, and by public bodies, such as the display of crucifixes in some public schools.

9.2.1 Islamic Veil

In relation to the question of the Islamic veil, as aforesaid ECtHR case law has so far ruled out the possibility that the ban on wearing the full veil (niqab) in public places imposed by some of the Contracting Parties to the ECHR is contrary to the right to religious freedom.[45] The conclusions reached by the Court in the cases referred to are, in our opinion, valid insofar as the national laws in question appear to be the expression of an adequate balance between the general interest in State security—and in light of safeguarding the principle of State neutrality in the religious sphere—and the individual interest in the use of certain religious symbols.

However, the HRC ruled differently on the same issue in two separate non-binding decisions in which extensive reference was made to the above-mentioned ECtHR case law, finding that the respondent State had violated the right to religious freedom—in that the national legislation in question did not comply, according to the Committee, with the principles of necessity and proportionality—and the right not to be discriminated against on religious grounds because of the ban on wearing the full veil in public places or places open to the public.[46]

With a view to reaching some common ground among the international bodies charged with scrutinising the observance of human rights treaties, the ECtHR has now adopted a partially different position from its previous one. Indeed, in its judgment of 18 September 2018 in *Lachiri v. Belgium*, the Court found a violation of the right to religious freedom in relation to a case concerning the use of an Islamic headscarf (hijab), essentially covering just the hair and the nape of the neck and which the applicant intended to wear during a judicial hearing, stressing that the headscarf was not a full veil and noting that the woman in question was not a public official and was therefore not required to comply with the obligation of "*discrétion dans*

[43] See Chap. 11, Sect. 11.3.

[44] See Chap. 2, Sect. 2.4.2.

[45] See Chap. 4, Sect. 4.3.3.

[46] See the views of 17 July 2018, respectively in *Yaker v. France*, CCPR/C/123/D/2747/2016, paras 8.1 ff., and *Hebbadj v. France*, CCPR/C/123/D/2807/2016, paras 7.1 ff.

l'expression publique de ses convictions religieuses".[47] Furthermore, the Court stated that the conduct actually engaged in by the person in question could not be considered disrespectful or constitute an obstacle to the exercise of judicial functions,[48] with the result that religious freedom was violated. In this regard, it should be noted that the distinction between the niqab and the hijab seems correct, while the distinction between civil servants and ordinary citizens is more dubious, and lends itself, in our opinion, to discretionary interpretations by domestic courts.

9.2.2 Crucifix and Religious Ceremonies

A similar situation of uncertainty regarding the assessment of legislation adopted or practices followed at the national level in matters of religion occurred in the case of *Lautsi and Others v. Italy*,[49] concerning the lawfulness of displaying a crucifix in an Italian public school. The case was analysed by the Strasbourg Court in light of the right to education of minors. Overturning the conclusions reached by the Chamber of the Court in its judgment of 3 November 2009, the Grand Chamber of the Court, in its judgment of 18 March 2011, held that the measure adopted by the Italian authorities concerning the affixing of the crucifix fell within the margin of appreciation granted to Contracting Parties to the ECHR, a margin which, according to the Court, was particularly wide in light of the absence of a "European consensus" among the contracting States on the use of religious symbols in State schools. It should be noted that in the 2011 judgment the ECtHR found that the crucifix was a "passive" religious symbol because its display was not associated with indoctrination of pupils in State schools since there was no compulsory teaching of the Christian religion. Moreover, according to the Court, there was adequate tolerance on the part of the national education authorities towards other religious beliefs and symbols, some of which were regularly used by pupils.

More recently, in its judgment of 20 October 2020 in *Perovy v. Russia*, the ECtHR maintained a similar position to that adopted in the *Lautsi* case on the issue of the compulsory participation by certain pupils in a religious blessing ceremony held on the occasion of the start of the school year. In this case, too, the Court stressed the lack of proselytising intent on the part of the State authorities in order to exclude the violation of the right to religious freedom and the right to education.[50]

[47] See appl. no. 3413/09, para 44 of the judgment.

[48] *Id.*, para 46.

[49] Appl. no. n. 30814/06.

[50] Appl. no. 47429/09, paras 65–66 and 76 of the judgment.

9.2.3 Post-mortem Examinations and Religious Convictions

In the recent case of *Polat v. Austria*[51] the ECtHR found that a post-mortem examination carried out by the national health authorities on a baby's body against the mother's will was incompatible with the freedom of religion and the right to respect for private and family life.

The Court ascertained that the post-mortem examination was carried out in accordance with national law, which does not require the consent of the relatives of the deceased individual, and that the national rules pursue a legitimate interest in so far as they are founded on the interests of the development of science and protection of public health, in particular where there are diagnostic doubts as to the death of the person. That said, the Court found that the national authorities had failed to strike a correct balance between, on the one hand, the needs of science and the protection of public health and, on the other hand, the applicant's rights to prevent certain examinations of the body of a deceased person because they were contrary to her religious convictions. More specifically, the Court stated that the applicant's views had not been considered when the national decision had been made, neither by hospital personnel nor by the domestic courts, concluding that the decision to perform a post-mortem examination on the applicant's child against her will and against her religious convictions had been an unjustified interference with her right to manifest her religion and her family life.[52]

9.3 Freedom of Opinion and Expression

The right to freely express one's ideas and opinions has legal roots going back a long way, sometimes incorporated into national constitutions of long standing. It constitutes an essential *barrier* against the arbitrariness of public power and the establishment and maintenance of dictatorial regimes that tend to eliminate or significantly reduce the expression of ideas contrary to those advocated by such regimes.

At an international level freedom of opinion and expression has a legal basis in numerous instruments of a universal and regional nature. At a universal level these include Article 19 UDHR and Article 19 ICCPR. On a regional level mention can be made of Article 10 ECHR, Article 11 CFREU, which specifically protects "the freedom and pluralism of the media",[53] and Article 13 ACHR, which expressly prohibits the prior censorship of freedom of thought and expression.[54]

---

[51] Judgment of 20 July 2021, appl. no. 12886/16.

[52] The Court also found that the failure by the national authorities to disclose to the applicant adequate information regarding the extent of the examination carried out on the corpse of the baby had been a further violation of the same rights.

[53] See Article 11(2) of the Charter.

[54] See Article 13(2) and (3) of the Convention.

It is therefore not surprising that the assertion that "freedom of expression constitutes one of the essential foundations of a democratic society" resonates in the case law of the bodies charged with scrutinising observance of human rights treaties.[55] It must be added that the free exercise of the right to manifest one's ideas and opinions also makes it possible, from the perspective of the indivisibility and coordination of the various human rights,[56] to exercise a further right closely linked to freedom of opinion and expression: the right to participate, individually or collectively, in the cultural, political and social life of one's country of birth or residence as the case may be.

It should also be pointed out that freedom of expression and, even more so, freedom of opinion have a *positive* and a *negative* dimension since they protect both the right to express one's own ideas and opinions, which obviously implies the freedom not to manifest one's own convictions, and the right to have access to those of others. These rights can be exercised in both individual and collective form.

Similarly to what has been observed with regard to religious freedom, the collective form of freedom of expression may be manifested in a *simple* setting, through forms of expression involving several individuals in a spontaneous and unorganised manner, or in an *institutionalised* setting, in the context of bodies and places dedicated to the dissemination of the most diverse forms of expression and art such as theatres, acting or painting schools, as well as through instruments aimed at spreading ideas and information such as newspapers and radio and television, and now also the Internet. The negative dimension of the collective exercise of the right is particularly important given that, at least in theory, it is the entire national community that has an interest in learning about different ideas, opinions and artistic and cultural expressions.

The scope of the right in question covers any form of expression, even those of a non-conventional nature, in as much as they are not commonly accepted by the general public. For example, certain artistic forms of expressing one's ideas that may be at odds with the common sense of art and culture operating in a given historical and social context. Similarly, minority or extreme opinions, based on highly questionable arguments in terms of historical, political, economic, social and other reconstructions, fall within the scope of freedom of opinion.

This can be deduced from the ECtHR (Grand Chamber) judgment of 23 September 1998 in *Lehideux and Isorni v. France*, in which the criminal conviction of two individuals who had published in the newspaper *Le Monde* an article aimed at rehabilitating, at least in part, the figure of Marshal Pétain, head of the Vichy Government in France, commonly described as a "collaborator" of the Nazi occupation regime in France during WWII, was considered to be in conflict with the right to freedom of opinion. In this regard, the Court stated that, although the historical reconstruction carried out by the applicants was highly dubious, they had not crossed the *external* limit of freedom of opinion, since "it does not appear that the applicants attempted to

---

[55] ECtHR (Grand Chamber), judgment of 23 September 1994 in *Jersild v. Denmark*, appl. no. 15890/89, para 31.

[56] On this feature of human rights, see Chap. 2, Sect. 2.4.2.

deny or revise what they themselves referred to in their publication as 'Nazi atrocities and persecutions' ... In describing Philippe Pétain's policy as 'supremely skilful', the authors of the text were rather supporting one of the conflicting theories in the debate about the role of the head of the Vichy government, the so-called 'double game' theory".[57]

According to the ECtHR, the scope of freedom of expression is even wider with regard to an individual's political opinions. In its judgment of 11 June 2020 in *Baldassi and Others v. France*, the Court stated that by their very nature political opinions and actions—relating in this case to forms of boycott of products from Israel in support of the Palestinian cause—are polemical and often virulent but that this does not diminish the public interest in their dissemination provided that such opinions do not constitute an incitement to violence, hatred or intolerance.[58]

International law on freedom of opinion and expression envisages that the right may be subject to certain restrictions on condition that they are provided for by law—which, as for restrictions on other human rights, must be accessible and foreseeable—and are functional to the protection both of important collective interests such as State security, public order, the protection of health or morals, and of significant individual rights and interests such as the honour and reputation of individuals. The bodies charged with scrutinising the observance of human rights treaties use a two-fold test in order to verify the lawfulness of restrictions imposed by the State (including criminal convictions of a custodial nature or concerning the payment of fines): (i) the necessity of State interference, which must be justified by the protection of the general or individual interests referred to above, and (ii) the proportionality of the measures taken, the latter analysed in terms of the nature, content, duration and effects on the addressees of the decisions or actions implemented at State level. This approach is also followed with regard to the assessment of disciplinary sanctions imposed on State officials, including judges, when they make unfounded allegations deemed to be damaging to the reputation of others.[59]

As mentioned above, the *external* limit to freedom of expression and opinion lies in the prohibition of incitement to violence, hatred and racial discrimination. In such cases, not only the inhibition of the expression of opinion but also a possible restrictive measure of a criminal nature can be considered—depending on the circumstances of the case and in accordance with the principle of proportionality—to comply with human rights law. In this regard, the need to prohibit by law any advocacy of national, racial or religious hatred that constitutes incitement to discrimination, hostility or violence, is expressly provided for in Article 20(2) ICCPR and, in similar terms, by Article 13(5) ACHR.

In its judgment of 2 September 2021 in *Sanchez v. France*,[60] the ECtHR therefore found that the criminal conviction of a French politician (at the time a local councillor who was standing for election to national Parliament) for inciting hatred or violence

[57] Appl. no. 24662/94, para 47 of the judgment.

[58] See appl. nos. 15271/16 and six others, para 79 of the judgment.

[59] ECtHR judgment of 8 December 2020 in *Panioglu v. Romania*, appl. no. 33794/14.

[60] Appl. no. 45581/15.

against a group of people or an individual due to their religion was not incompatible with freedom of opinion and expression. What is puzzling about the content of the judgment is that the conviction did not emanate from the applicant's own speech but rather from his failure to take prompt action in deleting the comments that others wrote under his Facebook public account, on the assumption that the applicant had been under a duty to monitor the content of the statements published by others in his profile. The Court sought to justify the broad interpretation under consideration by stating that politicians have a particular responsibility in combating hate speech, that the comments made in the present case had been clearly unlawful and that some comments had been visible even weeks after they had been posted. However, in our opinion the Court's position does not appear to be entirely defensible because it obliges some individuals who use social media platforms only for professional purposes, without pursuing commercial aims, to engage in a complex exercise of constantly monitoring the contents of the statements of other individuals.

9.3.1 Obligation of States and Horizontal Application of Human Rights Norms on Freedom of Thought

The issues relating to respect for freedom of opinion and expression, including the delicate aspect of achieving a balance between this right and other individual or collective rights or interests of a general nature, are particularly complex. Therefore, in order to comply with the relevant international standards, the State must comply with both negative and, above all, positive obligations, the latter aimed at making the freedom in question effective and striking a correct balance with other relevant rights and interests. As regards the content of the positive obligations, there are both specific ones, concerning particular aspects of freedom of opinion and expression, and general ones. These are designed to establish an overall system of protection for all those who wish to participate in public debates, guaranteeing them the possibility of freely expressing their views even if contrary to those advocated by the national authorities or the majority of public opinion.[61]

Finally, the scope of some of the above-mentioned positive obligations extends to inter-individual relations, thus requiring the State, firstly, to guarantee the free exercise of freedom of opinion and expression between private individuals; and, secondly, to prevent and repress, on the basis of the oft-mentioned principle of due diligence, the attacks on the freedom in question carried out by individuals through traditional means of dissemination of their opinions or through modern means of electronic communication in the form of social media (Facebook, Twitter, etc.). The specific obligation of the State to criminalise conduct or statements of a discriminatory nature or which may constitute forms of incitement to hatred and violence in relations between private individuals was reaffirmed by the ECtHR in its judgment of

[61] In this regard see ECtHR judgment of 14 September 2010 in *Dink v. Turkey*, appl. nos. 2668/07 and others, para 137.

14 January 2020 in *Beizaras and Levickas v. Lithuania*, a case that concerns hateful statements and serious threats made by a number of individuals against a same-sex couple who had posted photographs displaying affection on Facebook, without the State authorities having deemed it appropriate to investigate the perpetrators.[62]

9.3.2 Freedom of Information and Protection of the Press

Although often hinging on the same rule to protect freedom of opinion and expression, a separate assessment must be made with regard to freedom of information, with particular reference to the protection of journalists and the pluralism of information.

Freedom of information, to an even greater extent than the general freedom of opinion and manifestation of thought, takes on a dual dimension consisting of the *positive* right to inform and the *negative* right to be informed about facts and events of public interest.

With regard to the fundamental role played by journalists in ensuring effective respect for freedom of information, it must be said that, in international human rights case law, journalists are commonly referred to as the "watchdogs" of public opinion, as they perform what is considered to be an indispensable function to counteract the executive power in particular. Accordingly, journalists constitute an essential element for the creation and maintenance of a democratic and pluralist society. Consequently, the State is under a duty not only to observe negative obligations, consisting of duties to refrain from hindering the free exercise of journalistic activities, but also to observe positive obligations aimed at rendering effective the performance of the functions carried out by journalists, protecting their work from any unjustified attacks from public authorities or private individuals.[63]

The protection of journalists implies the protection of their sources, which is directly linked to freedom of information, especially freedom of the press. As noted by the ECtHR (Grand Chamber), the protection of journalistic sources "is one of the basic conditions for press freedom ... Without such protection, sources may be deterred from assisting the press in informing the public on matters of public interest. As a result the vital public-watchdog role of the press may be undermined and the ability of the press to provide accurate and reliable information may be adversely affected".[64] Consequently, sources of a confidential nature must not be disclosed by the journalist unless fundamental interests of the State such as the prevention and prosecution of certain particularly serious crimes, are at stake.[65] From the recent ECtHR case law it emerges that even the anonymity of the authors of comments posted on the websites of newspapers, although not included in the

---

[62] See appl. no. 41288/15, para 110.

[63] ECtHR judgment 10 January 2019 in *Khadija Ismayilova v. Azerbaijan*, appl. nos. 65286/13 and 57270/14, paras 158 ff.

[64] Judgment of 27 March 1996 in *Goodwin v. The United Kingdom*, appl. no. 17488/90, para 39.

[65] ECtHR judgment 6 October 2020 in *Jecker v. Switzerland*, appl. no. 35449/14.

journalistic sources, must be protected, balancing this interest with other general or particular interests, such as the right to reputation of third parties.[66]

The margin of appreciation granted to journalists in reporting facts and making personal comments is therefore particularly broad, even when it is established that the publication of their work in the press or online may harm the reputation of others. The margin of appreciation is even more significant where the person affected by the journalistic activities has achieved a level of fame—for example, because he or she is an actor, a politician or even a national judge dealing with disputes of particular importance for the national community[67]—as to have to endure a higher degree of criticism and provocation compared to that which would *ordinarily* be suffered by any other individual, as stated by both the IACtHR[68] and the ACtHPRA.[69]

The ECtHR itself applied this principle to a case in which the information and images published concerned a well-known person who, after retiring from political life in his country, was considering resuming political activities. Assessing the lawfulness of the action in light of the right to private and family life of the person in question under Article 8 ECHR, the Court held that in this case there remained a public interest in knowing certain information of an economic nature relating to the individual in question and his family[70] and that the State had struck an appropriate balance between freedom of information and the right to privacy.[71]

In order to ascertain in practice whether the measures to restrict journalists' freedom of information are lawful, it is thus necessary to balance the right in question against the right to reputation and honour of the offended individuals, which must be brought within the framework of the right to privacy.[72] The criteria used by the ECtHR in order to ascertain the adequacy of such a balance consist of: (a) the good faith of the journalist, who may well make mistakes unconsciously or even by forcing the interpretation of certain facts or news, without this implying having acted in bad faith or with the sole aim of offending an individual;[73] (b) the level of seriousness of the attack on the reputation of others, which implies examination of the content,

---

[66] See judgment of 7 December 2021, *Standard Verlagsgesellschaft mbH v. Austria (no. 3)*, appl. no. 39378/15.

[67] In the case of criticism of the work of a national court, the ECtHR has noted that such criticism, however harsh, must not undermine public confidence in the exercise of justice: see recently the judgment of 9 March 2021, *Benitez Moriana and Iñigo Fernandez v. Spain*, appl. nos. 36537/15 and 36539/15, paras 47–49.

[68] See the judgment of 2 July 2004 in *Herrera-Ulloa v. Costa Rica*, para 129.

[69] See the judgment of 5 December 2014 in *Lohé Issa Konaté v. Burkina Faso*, para 155.

[70] See the inadmissibility decision of 25 June 2019, *Zu Guttenberg v. Germany*, appl. no. 14047/16, para 27.

[71] *Id.*, para 33.

[72] See *supra*, Sect. 9.1.3.

[73] In order to verify the good faith of the journalist, the national authorities are required in particular to check whether there is a connection between the facts reported and their knowledge by the public, on the one hand, and the value judgments expressed by the journalist concerning those facts, on the other, which may also be expressed in a particularly provocative manner. In this regard see recently ECtHR judgment of 21 February 2021, *Tuşalp v. Turkey*, appl. no. 32131/08.

forms and duration of that attack; (c) the negative effects produced on the private and family life of the offended individual; and (d) the actual interest of the community in knowing the journalist's information and opinions on a specific story.

In this regard, it can be said that the application of these criteria almost always reaffirms journalistic freedom, except in the instances mentioned above of incitement to violence, hatred and racial discrimination or in the case of gratuitously offensive and unsubstantiated statements. This is reflected, for example, in the ECtHR's judgment of 30 October 2018 in the case of *Kaboğlu and Oran v. Turkey* concerning repeated attacks by Turkish journalists on two university lecturers for the views they expressed on minority rights. According to the Court, not only did the articles written by the journalists constituted hate speech, even containing physical threats against the individuals in question, and thus fell outside the scope of the protection of journalists' freedom of opinion, but they "were geared to repressing their intellectual personality, inspiring in them feelings of fear, anguish and vulnerability capable of humiliating and debasing them and of breaking their will to defend their ideas".[74]

With the exception of hate speech, there is also a well-established tendency to exclude the lawfulness—on human rights law grounds—of criminal sanctions of a custodial or financial nature, or disciplinary measures (such as long-term suspension from professional activity) that are disproportionate for journalists who have infringed the right to honour and reputation of others, even in cases where the criminal or disciplinary sanctions are not actually applied or are temporarily suspended. Excessive awards of damages obtained in civil proceedings against journalists responsible for harming the reputation of others are similarly considered contrary to the freedom of the press because a judgment of that type "is also capable of discouraging the participation of the press in debates over matters of legitimate public concern and has a chilling effect on the freedom of expression and of the press".[75]

The particularly restrictive approach adopted in this respect by the bodies charged with scrutinising observance of human rights treaties appears to be justified by the fact, which is well highlighted by the international courts involved, that, when it comes to the protection of individual journalists, the *value* to be safeguarded is not only the opinion of the individual journalist but the freedom of the press and information as a whole, which as aforesaid contributes decisively to the maintenance of the democratic life of States and cannot therefore be hindered by the *threat* of excessive criminal or civil measures.

9.3.3 Information Pluralism

Freedom of information encompasses the protection of pluralism of information, which extends to all means of informing and disseminating ideas and opinions.

[74] Appl. nos. 1759/08, 50766/10 and 50782/10, para 87 of the judgment.

[75] See recently ECtHR judgment of 27 July 2021, *Sic - Sociedade Independente de comunicaçäo v. Portugal*, appl. no. 29856/13, para 69.

Pluralism of information implies, on the one hand, distinguishing between the owners and/or licence holders of sources and means of information and, on the other hand, the diversification of the actual content of the information disseminated to the public. It seems clear that the two aspects are closely linked since pluralism in the ownership of newspapers and television generally entails pluralism in the content offered. It is equally clear that effective pluralism of information can only be ensured through the State's compliance with positive obligations, including those of a legislative nature, which also ensure an adequate *separation* between political and economic power.

With specific reference to the pluralism of information in the audio-visual sector, reference should be made to ECtHR (Grand Chamber) judgment of 7 June 2012 in *Centro Europa 7 S.r.l. and Di Stefano v. Italy*,[76] a case concerning the unjustified delay in allowing the actual use of certain television frequencies by a company that had long since been allocated the frequencies following a lengthy regulatory and judicial process at the national level. In this context, the Court made a number of general points of particular importance in the field of pluralism of information. First of all, it stated that "there can be no democracy without pluralism".[77] Furthermore, the Court compiled a sort of *ranking* in terms of respect for pluralism of information, pointing out that audio-visual media had a more immediate and effective impact on public opinion compared to the traditional printed media and therefore stressing that "[t]he audio-visual media, such as radio and television, have a particularly important role in this respect. Because of their power to convey messages through sound and images, such media have a more immediate and powerful effect than print ... The function of television and radio as familiar sources of entertainment in the intimacy of the listener's or viewer's home further reinforces their impact".[78]

Consequently, the Court highlighted the inadequacy, in order to guarantee the pluralism of the sources and contents of information, of compliance with simple negative obligations of the State not to interfere in the choices of operators of the audio-visual sector, emphasising the need to comply with positive obligations, among which that "to put in place an appropriate legislative and administrative framework to guarantee effective pluralism", especially in a situation in which pluralism is already strongly affected by dominant positions, as found in the case at issue.[79]

Finally, in a different political and cultural context and much more problematic also from the point of view of respect for freedom of information, the IACtHR expressed similar views on the subject of pluralism of information in its judgment of 22 June 2015 in *Granier et al. (Radio Caracas Television) v. Venezuela.* After recalling the collective dimension of the right to information, which includes the "collective right to receive any information whatsoever and to have access to the thoughts expressed by others",[80] the Court stated that "the plurality of the media and news constitutes an effective guarantee of freedom of expression, and the State has a

[76] Appl. no. 38433/09.

[77] See para 129 of the judgment.

[78] *Id.*, para 132.

[79] *Id.*, para 134.

[80] See para 136 of the judgment.

duty to protect and ensure this under Article 1(1) of the Convention, by minimizing restrictions to information and encouraging a balanced participation, and by allowing the media to be open to all without discrimination". In line with what was stated by the ECtHR, the IACtHR also pointed out that "freedom of expression may also be affected without direct State intervention. This may occur, for example, when, owing to the existence of monopolies or oligopolies in the ownership of the media, a practice is established of mechanisms aimed at preventing the communication and circulation of ideas and opinions".[81]

9.3.4 Right of Access to the Internet

In recent times, it has been debated whether the right of access to the Internet constitutes an autonomous human right in itself, irrespective of the connection with other individual or collective rights. Indeed, there is no shortage of national legislation, such as that passed in Estonia and Finland respectively, as well as constitutional rules, such as Article 16(2) of the Ecuadorian Constitution providing for universal access to information and communication technologies, which seems to include the right to online access.

The constitutional courts of some countries have also adjudicated on this matter. However, the relevant decisions appear to link the right of access to the Internet to freedom of expression and opinion as well as to the right to participate in the democratic life of one's country. This is how one can interpret French Constitutional Council judgement no. 580 of 10 June 2009 assessing the constitutionality of Law No. 669 of 19 May 2009 on the dissemination and protection of creations on the Internet, insofar as it states that the right to access the Internet is a manifestation of freedom of expression and participation in democratic life.[82]

Even more significant are the conclusions reached by the *Sala Constitucional* of the Supreme Court of Costa Rica in its judgment no. 12790 of 30 July 2010 in *Guzmán v. Ministerio de Ambiente, Energía y Telecomunicaciones, Ministerio de la Presidencia*: in stating the right of access to the Internet of great importance for the exercise of other human rights, it also ruled that it is to be considered an autonomous human right.[83]

More recently, a similar approach has been followed by the High Court of Kerala in its judgment of 19 September 2019. After noting that a prohibition of access to the web constitutes a violation of a specific human right, it went on to specify that "the right to have access to the Internet becomes the part of right to education as well as the right to privacy".[84]

---

[81] *Id.*, paras 142–143.

[82] See para 12 of the judgment.

[83] See Part VI of the judgment.

[84] In *Faheema Shirin R. K. and Others v. State of Kerala and Others*, para 13.

Notwithstanding the important developments in case law mentioned above, there arguably is no autonomous human right of access to the Internet in international law as it currently stands, even if one were to seek a legal basis in a general principle of domestic law. This statement should in no way obscure the fact that access to the Internet today constitutes an indispensable complement to the effective enjoyment of a series of human rights, such as freedom of expression and opinion, freedom of religion, the right to education and the right to participate in the democratic life of one's own country or of third countries, in line with what has been affirmed on the subject of the indivisibility and interdependency of human rights.[85] Therefore, international human rights law can be considered as applicable to the various forms of expression of thought, opinions and religious beliefs manifested through the Internet. As well noted by HRCoun in its resolution of 5 July 2012, "the same rights that people have offline must also be protected online, in particular freedom of expression, which is applicable regardless of frontiers and through any media of one's choice".[86]

In view of how instrumental Internet access is in relation to numerous human rights, it follows that States may not, without adequate justification, hinder the use of electronic communication tools by the population as a whole or discriminate against certain groups of individuals with regard to access to the Internet.

Therefore, the not infrequent *individual* or *collective* suspension of access to the Internet—i.e. barring individuals or entire national communities from gaining access—is at odds with human rights law when not based on grounds of necessity and carried out in accordance with the principle of proportionality. This is what can be deduced from the ECtHR's judgment of 18 December 2012 in *Yildirim v. Turkey*, in which the Court highlighted "the importance of Internet sites in the exercise of freedom of expression" and, recalling its previous case law, stated that "[i]n the light of its accessibility and its capacity to store and communicate vast amounts of information, the Internet plays an important role in enhancing the public's access to news and facilitating the dissemination of information in general".[87]

More recently the ECtHR has been at pains to underline that access to the Internet is increasingly seen as a right ("*est de plus en plus considéré comme un droit*") and that there have been calls for the development of effective policies to ensure universal access to the Internet ("*des appels ont été lancés pour que soient élaborées des politiques efficaces visant à assurer l'accès universel à Internet*").[88]

Finally, it should be noted that recourse to the Internet is *ambivalent*, in the sense that, on the one hand, it allows the free exercise of the right to express one's thoughts, information or religious beliefs; on the other hand, it cannot undermine the

---

[85] See Chap. 2, Sect. 2.4.2.

[86] See Resolution No. 20/8, para 1.

[87] Appl. no. 3111/10, para 48 of the judgment. In relation to the case at hand, the Court ruled that the temporary blocking of a website used by a university lecturer and, subsequently, the total blocking of his access to the Internet—measures decided by the Turkish authorities to prevent the lecturer's dissemination of texts considered offensive to the memory of Atatürk—are to be considered contrary to the right to freedom of expression.

[88] Judgment of 9 February 2021 in *Ramazan Demir v. Turkey*, appl. no 68550/17, para 33.

right to one's image, honour and reputation, as well as the right to property, including intellectual property.

From this point of view, there is a need for adequate supervision by the State, including with regard to the numerous activities carried out by private individuals online, combining free access to the Internet and protection of other rights that may be harmed by an inadequately regulated use of the Internet. That is evident in relation to the now frequent recourse to fake news on the Internet, which may pursue—especially if carried out on a large scale—political or economic purposes or simply aim to offend the honour and reputation of others through the spreading of false news. Clearly, there is a particularly urgent need for international regulation of the use of the Internet and its limits, regulation that for now appears to be almost non-existent, except for a few guidelines adopted by private bodies, often themselves involved in using the Internet for economic purposes. Hence, they are guidelines that do not afford any independent and impartial role on the regulation of the complex legal issues involved.

9.4 Freedom of Assembly and Association

Among the other rights that may be restricted by the State, either to protect general interests such as security, public order and public health or to protect individual or collective rights, one can mention freedom of peaceful assembly and association, which includes the freedom to form and join trade unions for the protection of one's professional interests, as well as freedom of movement. The restrictions to which these freedoms may be subject are well exemplified by the stringent measures adopted in the 2020–2022 period by several States in response to the global health emergency caused by COVID-19.

Freedom of assembly and association must obviously be exercised collectively and is provided for at the universal level in Article 20 UDHR and Articles 21 and 22 ICCPR, and at the regional level in Article 11 ECHR, Articles 15 and 16 ACHR, Articles 10 and 11 ACHPR and Article 12 CFREU.

Both rights under consideration include a *positive* and a *negative* dimension, in the sense that, on the one hand, a group of individuals may decide to associate or congregate, subject to particular derogations aimed at limiting, but not prohibiting outright, the right of association of public officials carrying out "sensitive" activities, such as members of the armed forces and the police.[89] On the other hand, the State may not oblige certain categories of individuals to assemble and especially to associate as a necessary precondition for the recognition of certain rights and privileges recognised at the national level.

[89] That Article 11 ECHR is infringed by legislative measures containing an absolute prohibition for members of the armed forces to join trade unions for the purpose of protecting their rights at work was affirmed by the ECtHR in its judgments of 2 October 2014 in *Matelly v. France*, appl. no. 10609/10, and *ADEFDROMIL v. France*, appl. no. 32191/09.

With specific regard to the right of association, it may be freely exercised in relation to both the form that the group takes, i.e. on the basis of a legally recognised association or a mere unincorporated association, and the objectives pursued by the group, which may for example include political aims with the related establishment of political parties or movements. The internal limits to the establishment of an association are generally that the purposes pursued are not contrary to the fundamental principles of the domestic legal system and the law governing associations, provided that the national rules are in line with what has been established at the international level on freedom of association and assembly.

Similarly, the right of peaceful assembly may be exercised in a multitude of ways in practice, and the holders of this right are not only the actual participants in a meeting but also the organisers.[90] Moreover, there are no *quantitative* limits on the number of participants in a meeting, nor are there *qualitative* limits pertaining to the reasons why a group of individuals should meet. Neither are there any *temporal* limits since participants may meet for a long time or for a very short period.

Moreover, the meeting may take place in public or private places and may be organised in advance and in detail through traditional forms of notice of call to participants or may take place spontaneously using modern forms of communication like e-mail, WhatsApp or Twitter. For this reason, in its judgment of 19 November 2019 in *Obote v. Russia*, the ECtHR included flash mobs within the scope of freedom of peaceful assembly,[91] i.e. a sudden gathering of a group of individuals, generally organised by instant messaging services, for the purpose of carrying out brief demonstrative, protest or recreational actions. In the case at issue, the Court criticised the conduct of the respondent State, which had interrupted the meeting and imposed a fine on the participants (which the ECtHR held to be of a criminal nature) on the premise that there had been no prior authorisation from the national authorities for the holding of the event and that national public order had been jeopardised, which the ECtHR considered not to be the case in view of the peaceful conduct and the very small number of participants at the meeting.

As mentioned above, the freedom of assembly and many other human rights were deeply limited, in the period 2020-2022, by the numerous national measures adopted to limit the spread of COVID-19. With judgment of 15 March 2022 in *Communauté genevoise d'action syndicale (CGAS) v. Switzerland*,[92] the ECtHR has recently stated that the national measures of the respondent State, however justified by reasons of protection of public health, were excessive and thus disproportionate in consideration of the blanket nature, the significant length of the ban on organizing and participating in public events and the nature and severity of the penalties in case of violations. Moreover, according to the ECtHR, the domestic courts had not conducted an effective judicial review of the measures complained of during the relevant period.

---

90 In this regard, see the ECtHR judgment of 19 November 2019 in *Razvozzhayev v. Russia and Ukraine* and *Udaltsov v. Russia*, appl. nos. 75734/12 and two others, para 287.

91 Appl. no. 58954/09, para 35 of the judgment.

92 Appl. no. 21881/20.

Consequently, Switzerland had overstepped the margin of appreciation afforded to it in the present case and thus violated Article 11 ECHR.

9.5 Freedom of Movement

Freedom of movement is protected at the universal level in Article 13 UDHR and Article 12 ICCPR and at the regional level in the Article 2 of Protocol No. 4 to the ECHR, Article 22 ACHR and Article 12 ACHPR.

In short, this right relates to the freedom of individuals or a plurality of them to move within the territory of the national State or other States, provided, in the latter case, that residence abroad has been obtained in a legal manner and thus without breaching domestic immigration law. Freedom of movement includes the right to reside in a given place and to leave one's own country or a foreign State, as well as the right to return to the national country or to "his own country",[93] a broad term that includes countries other than those of which the individual is a citizen and with which special ties have been formed.

As noted by the HRC in its decision of 6 April 2018 in *Deepan Budlakoti v. Canada*: "the scope of 'his own country' is broader than the concept of 'country of his nationality'. It is not limited to nationality in a formal sense, that is, nationality acquired at birth or by conferral; it embraces, at the very least, an individual who, because of his or her special ties to or claims in relation to a given country, cannot be considered to be a mere alien. The Committee recalls its jurisprudence in which it has stated that there are factors other than nationality which may establish close and enduring connections between a person and a country, connections which may be stronger than those of nationality. It has noted that the words 'his own country' invite consideration of such matters as long-standing residence, close personal and family ties and intentions to remain, as well as the absence of such ties elsewhere".[94]

Both freedom of assembly and association[95] and freedom of movement must be protected by the State in which individuals wish to exercise those freedoms against violations committed either by State bodies or by private individuals.[96]

---

[93] See Article 12(4) ICCPR.

[94] See CCPR/C/122/D/2264/2013, para 9.2 of the decision.

[95] See *supra*, Sect. 9.4.

[96] With regard to freedom of movement, see HRC *General Comment No. 27* of 2 November 1999, para 6.

Comprehension Check and Tasks

1. What is the right to be forgotten and what are the limitations to its scope of application? (Sect. 9.1.4)
2. Focus on the developments in international case law on the protection of same-sex couples (Sect. 9.1.5)
3. Is the freedom to wear the Islamic veil unlimited or are there any limits and, if so, based on what factors? (Sect. 9.2.1)
4. What does the horizontal application of human rights norms entail in the context of the protection of freedom of opinion and expression? (Sect. 9.3.1)
5. What does effective pluralism mean and what are the States' obligations to achieve this aim? (Sect. 9.3.3)
6. Is the right of access to the Internet a real and autonomous human right? (Sect. 9.3.4)

Chapter 10
Refugees' Rights, Right to Citizenship and Other Political Rights

Contents

Abstract The chapter focuses on the content and judicial application of the international rules on the protection of refugees and migrants, also discussing forms of subsidiary or temporary protection, and on the right to citizenship, examining the relevant case law concerning the limits to the deprivation of citizenship in EU law and international human rights law.

10.1 Rights of Refugees and Migrants

International law provides some protection for refugees. The most relevant universal legal instrument is the Geneva Convention Relating to the Status of Refugees of 28 July 1951. The subsequent Protocol of 31 January 1967 eliminated the anachronistic temporal and geographical limitations of the Geneva Convention, which had restricted its application to events occurring before 1951 in Europe.

In short, the main requirement for refugee *status* is a well-founded fear of persecution for reasons of race, religion, nationality, membership of a social group or in light of the political opinions of the individual concerned. Further requirements are that the individual be outside his country of origin and the absence of protection from that country.

Causes of persecution have been interpreted broadly in practice, for instance to include persecution based on an individual's sexual orientation within the framework of persecution motivated by membership of given social group. That ensures today the protection of homosexuals.

Persecution is generally committed by State bodies, but the protection provided by the 1951 Convention—in line with the oft-mentioned developments in horizontal

P. Pustorino, *Introduction to International Human Rights Law*,
https://doi.org/10.1007/978-94-6265-563-8_10

application of human rights rules—is also afforded where the persecution is by private individuals, based on observance of the principle of due diligence. The territorial State is thus obliged to prevent and repress wrongdoing of an inter-individual nature.

The fundamental principle in refugee protection is that of *non-refoulement*. Although originating in Article 33 of the 1951 Convention,[1] this principle has acquired the status of a customary rule of international law and has progressively broadened its scope of application, prohibiting the return or expulsion of individuals who risk being subjected to torture or inhuman or degrading treatment in their State of origin.[2] As mentioned above, this well-established trend is widely reflected in the case law and practice of the bodies in charge of scrutinising observance of various international human rights conventions.

The principle of non-refoulement is applicable not only when applicants for refugee status are already on the national territory—and for this purpose it is irrelevant whether they entered the State legally or illegally—or in the territorial sea, but also when they have been received, albeit temporarily, by public State vessels (such as navy ships operating on the high seas) or at international airports, since these locations are considered areas of State jurisdiction.[3] Therefore, the reconstruction carried out by the ECtHR (Grand Chamber) in its judgment of 23 February 2012 in *Hirsi Jamaa and Others v. Italy* appears to be correct: that was a case concerning a rescue at sea carried out by an Italian navy vessel, which had transferred migrants from Libya on board only to then subsequently hand them over to the Libyan authorities. Consequently, in the Court's opinion, "in the period between boarding the ships of the Italian armed forces and being handed over to the Libyan authorities, the applicants were under the continuous and exclusive *de jure* and *de facto* control of the Italian authorities".[4]

According to an expansive interpretation that does not however seem to correspond to the current state of general international law, the principle of non-refoulement should apply also in cases where the applicant for refugee status turns to foreign embassies abroad seeking diplomatic asylum.

In its advisory opinion on the *Institution of Asylum and its Recognition as a Human Right in the Inter-American System of Protection* of 30 May 2018, the IACtHR ruled out that the American Convention provides for an individual's right to obtain diplomatic asylum at the embassies of States parties to the Convention. However, it stated that the principle of non-refoulement operates in this matter and applies also in the case where the individual is inside the embassy and therefore under the jurisdiction of the foreign State.[5] The Court further stated that in such cases the

[1] Article 33(1): "No Contracting State shall expel or return ("*refouler*") a refugee in any manner whatsoever to the frontiers of territories where his life or freedom would be threatened on account of his race, religion, nationality, membership of a particular social group or political opinion."

[2] See Chap. 7, Sect. 7.4.

[3] On the notion of jurisdiction contained in human rights treaties, see Chap. 3, Sects. 3.6–3.6.3.

[4] Appl. no. 27765/09, para 81 of the judgment.

[5] (*Interpretation and Scope of Articles 5, 22.7 and 22.8 in relation to Article 1(1) of the American Convention on Human Rights*), OC-25/18, paras 167, 177 e 189.

embassy State is not obliged to grant refugee status even if the conditions for such recognition are met but "that there remain other obligations on the State to take diplomatic measures, including the request to the territorial State to issue a laissez-passer, or other measures under its authority and, in accordance with international law, to ensure that applicants' convention rights are guaranteed".[6]

On the contrary, in its inadmissibility decision of 5 May 2020 in *M.N. and Others v. Belgium*, the ECtHR (Grand Chamber) ruled out the existence of State jurisdiction in relation to a request for a temporary visa, functional to a subsequent asylum application, made by Syrian citizens at the Belgian Embassy in Lebanon. The Court distinguished the case at issue from a situation involving the expulsion or refoulement of individuals who are "on the territory of the State concerned—or at its border ...—and thus clearly fall within its jurisdiction".[7]

International law does not allow a State to circumvent the obligation of non-refoulement by, for example, carrying out naval interdiction operations—whether of a national nature or in coordination with other States or international organisations—aimed at preventing vessels carrying individuals who may claim refugee status from entering its territorial sea. This prohibition applies, in our view, even where *contact* between the navy of the State in question and the rescue vessels is deliberately avoided precisely in order not to trigger national jurisdiction.

In fact, as noted by the IACommHR in its decision of 13 March 1997 in *The Haitian Centre for Human Rights et al. v. United States*, the non-refoulement obligation knows no "geographical limitations".[8] More clearly, the ECtHR, in the above-mentioned *Hirsi Jamaa* case, ruled that "the removal of aliens carried out in the context of interceptions on the high seas by the authorities of a State in the exercise of their sovereign authority, the effect of which is to prevent migrants from reaching the borders of the State or even to push them back to another State, constitutes an exercise of jurisdiction within the meaning of Article 1 of the Convention which engages the responsibility of the State in question under Article 4 of Protocol No. 4",[9] concerning the prohibition of collective expulsions.

This unlawful conduct may also occur on the basis of the application of bilateral cooperation agreements between States in the field of combating illegal immigration, as occurred with regard to the agreements concluded between Italy and Libya between 2000 and 2017. In such instances complicity between States can also occur where a State aids or assists another State in the commission of an internationally wrongful act within the meaning of Article 16 ARSIWA.[10]

---

[6] *Id.*, para 198.

[7] Appl. no. 3599/18, para 120 of the decision.

[8] See Case 10.675, Report No. 51/96, para 157 of the decision.

[9] See para 180 of the judgment.

[10] Article 16 (Aid or assistance in the commission of an internationally wrongful act): "A State which aids or assists another State in the commission of an internationally wrongful act by the latter is internationally responsible for doing so if: (a) that State does so with knowledge of the circumstances of the internationally wrongful act; and (b) the act would be internationally wrongful if committed by that State".

With specific reference to the protection of migrants by sea, there are a number of international conventions—the International Convention for the Safety of Life at Sea of 1 November 1974, the International Convention on Maritime Search and Rescue of 27 April 1979[11] and the UN Convention on the Law of the Sea of 10 December 1982[12]—that oblige States to provide for and implement measures to rescue individuals whose lives are in danger and to accompany them in the shortest possible time to a "place of safety", without unwarranted excuses about national security and combating illegal immigration being able to impede compliance with those obligations by the domestic authorities.

The connection between the above-mentioned international obligations and those relating to the recognition of refugee status is well highlighted in Italian Supreme Court of Cassation judgment no. 6626/2020 of 20 February 2020, which specifies that States are under a duty to rescue shipwrecked persons and take them to a safe port so that they can "apply for international protection under the 1951 Geneva Convention, which certainly cannot be done on the ship"[13] that rescued them.

Moreover, once the asylum seeker is on the territory of the State, the latter is obliged to ensure effective access to the means provided at the national level to apply for refugee status. In particular, according to the above-mentioned 2018 advisory opinion of the IACtHR, the territorial State is under a duty, *inter alia*, to put in place adequate procedures to verify fulfilment of the requirements for obtaining refugee status, to afford effective access to these procedures by asylum seekers and also to ensure that these procedures comply with the essential guarantees of due process, adapting, if necessary, the application of the procedures to special needs, such as the presence of particularly vulnerable persons like minors among asylum seekers.[14]

The protection of applicants for refugee status and migrants in general extends to cases where the individuals concerned are temporarily transferred to reception and assistance centres in which the territorial State has also to observe more stringent obligations in order to protect vulnerable individuals, like minors.[15] From the point of view of respect for human rights, a number of Contracting Parties to the ECHR have been repeatedly found to be in breach of their conventional obligations on account of the inadequate treatment afforded to individuals in reception centres (or hotspots as they are often called).[16]

[11] See Chapter III of the Convention.

[12] See Article 98 of the Convention.

[13] See para 9 of the conclusions of points of law.

[14] See paras 99 and 122 of the advisory opinion.

[15] See ECtHR, judgment of 18 November 2021, *M. H. and Others v. Croatia*, appl. nos. 15670/18 and 43115/18, paras 183 ff.

[16] In its judgment of 15 December 2016 in *Khlaifia and Others v. Italy*, appl. no. 16483/12, the ECtHR (Grand Chamber) found both a breach of Article 5 (right to liberty and security), in relation to the arbitrary nature of the deprivation of liberty of migrants in the absence of an adequate legal basis for the restrictive measures, and of Article 13 (right to an effective remedy), due to the non-existence of judicial review mechanisms to challenge the legality of such measures. By judgment of 3 October 2019 in *Kaak and Others v. Greece*, appl. no. 34215/16, the ECtHR found a violation

In addition to the right not to be returned and the rights of first aid mentioned above, refugees must be assured further substantive and procedural rights specifically provided for in the 1951 Geneva Convention and sometimes extended to refugee children (e.g. the right to education) like the issuance of personal and travel documents. They must also not be discriminated against—compared to nationals of the State granting refugee status—in matters of religious freedom, public education and the application of labour and social insurance legislation.

On the other hand, the treatment of refugees is *benchmarked* as against that reserved for ordinary foreigners in relation to other activities such as access to public housing for the destitute or the purchase of movable and immovable property.

It should finally be noted that the special framework established by the 1951 Convention is *in addition* to general human rights law. It follows that refugees also enjoy all the human rights covered by treaty-based and customary law, unless derogated from by special refugee legislation affording broader protection than general human rights rules.

10.1.1 Subsidiary and Temporary Protection

The legislation governing the granting of refugee status must be distinguished from the legal frameworks provided for at the international and EU level granting "subsidiary" or "temporary" protection to certain individuals. Those rules are less favourable from both a *quantitative* and a *qualitative* point of view insofar as they envisage fewer and shorter-lasting rights than those granted to the holder of refugee status. Subsidiary protection is generally granted where the individual risks being subjected to the death penalty, torture or inhuman or degrading treatment in the country of final destination if expelled from the country in which he or she has applied for protection or where the individual is in a very serious health condition. Temporary protection is generally granted to persons fleeing from countries that are embroiled in international or non-international armed conflicts, as in 2022 for Ukrainian people, or where serious natural or man-made disasters have occurred.

Just as the notion of refugee has been broadly interpreted, likewise the granting of temporary protection has been extended by legislation and case law to categories of individuals who did not originally and formally fall within the scope of that notion. In its judgment no. 25143 of 10 November 2020, the Italian Supreme Court of Cassation stated that the severe climatic conditions of the country of origin must be assessed for the purpose of granting international protection, where such conditions affect the right to health of the individual under consideration and relegate him to a "condition of inescapable poverty".[17] This interpretation, which is to be welcomed, would seem to be progressively becoming established in national case law, as demonstrated

of Article 5(4) ECHR with regard to the right of migrants to challenge in court the lawfulness of expulsion orders issued against them.

[17] See paras 6.5 and 7(c) of the conclusions on points of law.

by Court of Appeal of Bordeaux judgments nos. 20BX02193 and 20BX02195 of 18 December 2020, which granted the request for renewal of temporary stay on French territory for health reasons of a Bangladeshi national suffering from a serious chronic respiratory disease, linked to a situation of allergic asthma, which required daily artificial ventilation treatment. According to the Court, given that the level of atmospheric pollution in Bangladesh is one of the highest in the world and that, as a result, the mortality rate of individuals suffering from respiratory diseases is much higher than in France, having regard also to the lack of health resources and equipment in the country of origin, the applicant would thus be exposed to a risk of worsening health and premature death in case of expulsion.[18]

10.2 Right to Citizenship

Within the framework of political rights, legal scholars have long discussed the existence of the right to citizenship understood as the "political and legal bond that connects a person to a specific State".[19] The right in question is generally exercised in an individual form, but there is no reason why it cannot take on a collective dimension, for example in the case of a *mass* granting or withdrawal of citizenship, instances sometimes linked to cases of succession of States as a consequence of international armed conflicts often entailing the modification of national law on citizenship.

In general international law there would seem to be no human right as such to citizenship, although there is no lack of universal[20] and regional[21] legal instruments providing for such a right. Without prejudice to what will be stated below, granting and revoking citizenship still seems to fall within the exclusive purview of States. Equally discretionary is the State's choice of criteria for granting citizenship, on the basis of *jus sanguinis*, *jus soli* or a combination of these criteria.

The wide margin of appreciation granted to the State in matters of citizenship is, however, limited within the framework of certain special regulatory frameworks such as EU law, which provides for the automatic granting of European citizenship and other related rights to citizens of EU Member States, in application of what is defined in the literature as *jus tractum* since the status of European citizen is derived from the status of citizen of one of the EU Member States.

Similarly, in light of conventional law (European Convention on Nationality of 6 November 1997 and Convention on the Reduction of Statelessness of 30 August 1961, which supplements the Convention Relating to the Status of Stateless Persons of 28 September 1954), all States must make an effort to limit cases of statelessness

[18] See para 4 of the judgment.

[19] See IACtHR judgment of 8 September 2005 in *Girls Yean and Bosico v. Dominican Republic*, para 137.

[20] See Article 15(1) UDHR.

[21] See Article 20 ACHR.

and must not adopt an arbitrary or discriminatory approach in the granting and withdrawal of citizenship. That holds true both in normal situations and in extraordinary situations (such as the aforementioned cases of succession of States, which can lead to the loss of original citizenship), as recommended by the UNGA in its resolution of 9 February 1996.[22]

A greater openness in favour of the right to acquire and maintain nationality can be seen, again on foot of international conventions, in relation to specific categories of individuals like minors[23] and the disabled.[24]

Turning now to State practice, it is arguable that there was a violation of the principles of non-discrimination and non-arbitrariness as a result of the behaviour adopted in relation to citizenship that occurred following the approval in Myanmar in 1982 of a law that linked the notion of citizenship to being members of the "national race". Citizenship was thus expressly restricted to certain specific ethnic groups, whose members are therefore entitled to *full* citizenship, while other individuals, such as in particular members of the Rohingya ethnic group, are entitled to lesser rights and may also be deprived of citizenship. Similar concerns regarding discrimination against certain national communities of the Islamic faith have been raised with reference to the content of the recent Indian Act of 12 December 2019 which amended the previous legislation of 1955.

With regard to case law dealing with the acquisition of citizenship in the wake of succession of States, worth mentioning in connection with the dissolution of the former Yugoslavia is ECtHR (Grand Chamber) judgment of 26 June 2012 in *Kurić and Others v. Slovenia*.[25] The case concerned procedures for the acquisition of citizenship established by Slovenia, which allowed individuals permanently residing on Slovenian territory to apply for Slovenian citizenship but only within a short period of time and without the State being able to provide assurances as to the addressees' actual knowledge of these short time limits. The Court stated that even in the absence of a right to citizenship provided for in the ECHR, the challenged procedures were contrary to the right to private and family life insofar as the national law did not fulfil the requirements of foreseeability of the domestic rules and the measures adopted did not comply with the principles of necessity and proportionality. The procedures were also found to breach the principle of non-discrimination between the various groups of individuals on the basis of their national origin.

Finally, it must be pointed out that major issues may arise with regard to cases of facilitated granting of national citizenship, where that citizenship implies the awarding of further rights that go beyond the national level and involve other States. This complex situation has arisen, for example, following the enactment of laws in Cyprus and Malta enabling citizenship to be acquired on foot of significant economic

---

[22] See A/RES/50/152, para 16.

[23] See Article 24(3) ICCPR and Articles 7(1) and 8(1) of the Convention on the Rights of the Child of 20 November 1989.

[24] See Article 18 of the Convention on the Rights of Persons with Disabilities of 13 December 2006.

[25] Appl. no. 26828/06.

and financial investments in the two countries. Indeed, these practices risk undermining the overall balance of the EU legal framework on European citizenship, considering that the granting of citizenship of an EU Member State implies as aforesaid the automatic granting of EU citizenship, with the attribution of a series of rights in favour of the EU citizen that can be exercised in any EU Member State.

For this reason, on 20 October 2020 the European Commission launched infringement proceedings against Cyprus and Malta, arguing that the granting by these Member States of their citizenship in exchange for a pre-determined payment or investment and without a genuine link with the Member States concerned is not compatible with the principle of sincere cooperation enshrined in Article 4(3) TEU and also undermines the integrity of the status of EU citizenship provided for in Article 20 TFEU.

It should also be pointed out that cases of particularly *generous* granting of an additional citizenship over and above an already existing original citizenship may give rise to the international responsibility of the State that unjustifiably confers citizenship, for example in the absence of historical, territorial or cultural ties with the individuals benefiting from the measures in question. In these cases it is arguable that there is a violation of the principle of non-interference in the internal affairs of the State that the individuals were already lawfully and originally citizens of.

In some cases, the violation of the principle of non-interference through the *exorbitant* granting of citizenship by a State is linked to situations of international armed conflict between the countries concerned. A case in point is the conflict between Russia and Ukraine following Russia's annexation of Crimea in 2014, Russian support for the independence of some regions in Eastern Ukraine, in particular Donetsk and Luhansk (recognised by Russia as autonomous States on 21 February 2022) and Russia's aggression against Ukraine started on 24 February 2022. In this context, the measures adopted by Russia entailing the almost automatic granting—except for an opt-out mechanism basically unused in practice—of Russian citizenship to Ukrainian citizens residing in Crimea appear obviously unlawful insofar as linked to the illegal military annexation. And likewise the measures approved by Russia aimed at facilitating the acquisition of Russian citizenship by *all* Ukrainian citizens, not only those residing in the four recently annexed regions of Donetsk, Luhansk, Kherson and Zaporizhzhia.[26]

10.2.1 Deprivation of Citizenship and Its Limits

It was pointed out in the previous section that, in matters of withdrawal of citizenship, States must seek to avoid situations of statelessness and must not engage in arbitrary or discriminatory conduct.

---

[26] See the *Presidential Executive Order* of 11 July 2022, No. 440, by the President of the Russian Federation.

The case law on national measures depriving individuals of citizenship concerns mainly situations in which the individual was involved in terrorist activities and situations in which the individual committed fraud in the process of acquiring citizenship.

With regard to the first situation, at the outset it should be noted that some national laws, mainly in the English-speaking world, have recently introduced the principle of the loss of citizenship in the case of terrorist activities carried out by the individual. That legislation is applied in practice in a rather broad way, giving the executive power ample discretion in the adoption of decisions to deprive one of citizenship, as evident in the judgment of 26 February 2021 handed down by the UK Supreme Court in *R (on the application of Begum) v. Special Immigration Appeals Commission.*

The practice of withdrawing citizenship on grounds of commission of terrorist offences was considered by the ECtHR to be in conformity with the ECHR, albeit under certain conditions, in the inadmissibility decision of 9 March 2017 in *K2 v. The United Kingdom.*[27] The Court affirmed that the measure taken by the State was not contrary to the principles of necessity and proportionality, but pointed out that in the case before it the individual, although deprived of his British citizenship, still retained that of another State. It follows that where the deprivation of nationality implies the creation of a situation of statelessness, or where the national measures are considered excessive (for example because they do not take adequate account of the family and social ties established by the individual in the territory of the State or the particular duration of the link of nationality acquired by the individual concerned), the measures in question could be considered contrary to international human rights law.

In a more recent decision concerning French legislation on the withdrawal of citizenship for individuals responsible for acts of terrorism, the ECtHR confirmed its position on the compatibility of such measures with the right to private and family life on condition they are provided for by law and are proportionate. In particular, the Court pointed out that "terrorist violence is in itself a grave threat to human rights" and considered lawful the respondent State's conduct, noting that "as a result of their actions, such individuals may no longer enjoy the specific bond conferred on them by the nationality of the country in which they reside". This was also because the terrorist acts "show that their attachment to France and its values is of little importance for them in the construction of their personal identity".[28]

With reference to the second situation mentioned above concerning fraud committed during the process of acquisition of citizenship, worthy of mention is the well-known ECJ judgment of 2 March 2010 in *Rottmann v. Freistaat Bayern.*[29] The Court held that EU law was not infringed by withdrawing the applicant's only

[27] Appl. no. 42387/13.

[28] See the judgment of 25 June 2020 in *Ghoumid and Others v. France*, appl. nos. 52273/16 and 4 others, para 50. At the same time, the Court found that the measures depriving the applicants of their French nationality did not in any event give rise to a situation of statelessness in view of the applicants' maintenance of other nationalities.

[29] See case C-135/08.

EU Member State citizenship thereby making him stateless on grounds of fraud committed when obtaining German nationality through failing to disclose a criminal record in another Member State. Consistent with what can be deduced from ECtHR case law,[30] the CJEU did however add that any decision on withdrawal of citizenship must observe the principle of proportionality, taking into account the consequences for the situation of the individual concerned by the measure in question.

Finally, deprivation of citizenship also has negative effects on the protection of human rights from a different and in some ways opposite point of view. It poses greater difficulties for the *former* national State when the latter seeks to prosecute individuals deprived of citizenship for the serious crimes committed by them. This is because the bond of citizenship also constitutes a relevant head of jurisdiction for the purpose of trying the aforementioned individuals. The question has quite recently arisen for some members of ISIS (Islamic State in Iraq and the Levant) who have had their citizenship withdrawn by several countries, thus making it more difficult to prosecute the crimes that they have committed in their home States or abroad.

10.3 Other Political Rights

Turning quickly to an examination of the main political rights other than the right to citizenship, these are the right to vote and stand for election, to political association and active political participation in the public life of the country of citizenship or residence. In this regard, it must be admitted, in line with what has been said about the right to citizenship, that States are reluctant to consider the political rights in question as human rights, to be granted as such to every human being since the rights are often linked to the possession of a specific national citizenship or in any case to the establishment of stable and effective residence in the territorial State.

Emblematic in this regard is Article 16 ECHR on the prohibition of interpreting certain rules of the Convention[31] "as preventing the High Contracting Parties from imposing restrictions on the political activity of aliens". Consequently, although the provisions of some international conventions like Article 21 UDHR provide for certain political rights in favour of any individual, other such provisions like Article 25 ICCPR restrict those rights to nationals of the states under consideration. As noted by the HRC in its *General Comment No. 25* of 12 July 1996: "In contrast to other rights and freedoms recognised by the Covenant (which are ensured to all individuals within the territory and subject to the jurisdiction of the State), Article 25 protects the rights of 'every citizen'".[32]

[30] On the relevance of the principle of proportionality in relation to the deprivation of citizenship, see ECtHR judgment of 22 December 2020 in *Usmanov v. Russia*, appl. no. 43936/18.

[31] In particular Articles 10, 11 and 14 ECHR.

[32] See para 3.

Comprehension Check and Tasks

1. In which cases and in which spaces is the principle of *non-refoulement* applicable? (Sect. 10.1)
2. Are the policies of States aiming to intercept, stop and sometimes hand over to foreign authorities migrants, before they enter the territorial sea, lawful? (Sect. 10.1)
3. Which are the States' obligations on the deprivation of citizenship? (Sect. 10.2.1)

Chapter 11
Economic, Social and Cultural Rights

Contents

Abstract The chapter focuses on so-called second generation human rights, i.e. economic, social, and cultural rights. Among economic rights, particular attention is given to the right to property, which has been interpreted in an expansive way in international, and especially ECtHR, case law. Among cultural rights, the right to education is specifically addressed, also in relation to the possible conflict with other human rights—e.g. the parents' religious convictions.

11.1 Right to Property

Economic, social and cultural rights are considered to be more recent, second-generation rights.[1] Their legal framework is predominantly based on obligations to be progressively achieved, which therefore affords greater discretion to the State as to when and how to realise the rights concerned.[2]

Among economic rights, the right to property stands out. In international law it originated from the practice of protecting the investments of foreign individuals or companies abroad in order to limit the power of the territorial State to nationalise or expropriate foreign assets. In particular, a number of preconditions have gradually become established, the fulfilment of which are necessary in order to legitimise State measures that wholly or partially deprive foreign persons of their property, namely, public interest and non-discrimination between foreigners of different nationalities. There are also conditions that need to be met at a later stage, in particular, the granting of compensation, which was defined in declarations dating back to the

[1] See Chap. 6, Sect. 6.1, on the classification of human rights.

[2] On the nature and content of progressive obligations, see Chap. 3, Sect. 3.10.

P. Pustorino, *Introduction to International Human Rights Law*,
https://doi.org/10.1007/978-94-6265-563-8_11

nationalisations of the first decades of the last century as needed to be "prompt, adequate and effective". Compliance with those requirements is further bolstered by the right of foreign investors to sue in the national courts, so as to be able to contest any domestic measures that do not comply with international law.

The notion of property has become very broad as a result of human rights treaties including provisions for respect for property or more generally for the assets of a natural or legal person. It encompasses rights in movable property, such as ownership of shares or bonds issued by private companies or the State, rights in immovable property, rights in intellectual property—the latter already expressly protected in Article 27(2) UDHR and more recently in Article 17(2) CFREU—and certain claims the entitlement to which is ascertained by law or by national or international courts, included arbitration tribunals such as the International Chamber of Commerce,[3] such as rights of a social security nature[4] or severance payments, whether linked to contribution paid by beneficiaries or entirely dependent on public funds. Also encompassed are rights in matters of succession, statutory or contractual indemnities for goodwill, tax exemptions[5] etc.

The gradual expansion of the scope of the right to property, especially in light of ECtHR case law, has implied an albeit limited protection of an individual's legitimate expectations of an economic nature. From this point of view, both the position prior to the acquisition of property and the position afterwards concerning its actual enjoyment are protected. The former includes the application for registration of a trademark or patent provided that the application is adequately founded on the provisions of the domestic legislation on the registration of trademarks and patents.[6] The latter incudes devaluation of a real estate asset following withdrawal of a building licence already granted[7] or the non-implementation of a TV broadcasting licence. In all these cases, the ECtHR emphasised the current and definite economic value of the legal situations involving legitimate expectation of an economic character.

In the area of property rights, the State is bound to respect both negative obligations of non-interference in the enjoyment and use of assets belonging to private persons and positive obligations aimed at guaranteeing the effective observance of the right in question, even when the infringement is committed by private persons. In the latter case, the usual principle of due diligence concerning the prevention and repression by the State of inter-individual violations applies, which implies the provision of an adequate legal framework to protect the right to property.

---

[3] See recently the ECtHR judgment of 30 June 2022, *BTS Holding v. Slovakia*, appl. no. 55617/17, paras 62 ff.

[4] On these property rights, see the ECtHR (Grand Chamber) judgment of 24 April 2006 in *Stec and Others v. The United Kingdom*, appl. nos. 65731/01 and 65900/01.

[5] For a case concerning exemption from payment of a property tax, see recently ECtHR, judgment of 5 April 2022, *Assemblée Chrétienne Des Témoins de Jéhovah d'Anderlecht and Others v. Belgium*, appl. no. 20165/20, para. 41.

[6] In this regard, see the ECtHR (Grand Chamber) judgment of 11 January 2007 in *Anheuser-Busch Inc. v. Portugal*, appl. no. 73049/01, para. 78.

[7] On this issue, see the ECtHR judgment of 29 November 1991 in *Pine Valley Developments Ltd and Others v. Ireland*, appl. no. 12742/87.

In the ECHR system, Article 1 of Protocol No. 1 states that "every natural or legal person is entitled to the peaceful enjoyment of his possessions". The norm in question, according to the ECtHR's established case law, contains three different but interconnected provisions: respect for the right to property; regulation of cases of deprivation of property; and State regulation of the use of property, which must be in the general interest. It should be noted that the words used in those provisions have an autonomous meaning compared to those used at the national level. This has allowed the ECtHR to adopt decisions that differ from those made in the same cases at the national level.

Depending on the seriousness of the damage caused to an individual's property, the ECtHR has classified national measures affecting private property as either deprivation of private property or national regulation of the use of property.

Of particular importance is the Strasbourg Court's case law on limits to measures of deprivation of private property. In this context, the ECtHR has assessed the lawfulness of both measures of expropriation of individual assets and national legislation underlying the nationalisation of entire industrial sectors or economic reforms, which have inevitably had a significant impact on the property rights of the whole or a substantial part of the national community.

In this respect the ECtHR has found against not only formal measures of deprivation or severe limitation of property rights but also measures of various kinds that essentially produce the same result, equating the latter with the former. In this regard the Court stated, on the basis of a teleological interpretation of Article 1 of Protocol No. 1, that "[s]ince the Convention is intended to safeguard rights that are 'practical and effective', it has to be ascertained whether the situation complained of amounted nevertheless to a de facto expropriation".[8]

The specific conditions for the deprivation of property pursuant to Article 1 of Protocol No. 1 are the pursuit by the State of purposes based on needs of public interest, lawfulness (including the requirement that the applicable domestic law is accessible and foreseeable in its application) and compliance with international law, which requires the State to grant compensation to the individual deprived of property. In addition, both the measures of deprivation of property and those regulating the use of property must be in line with the principle of proportionality and hence apt to strike a fair balance between the competing national or individual interests.

With particular regard to the public interest, the ECtHR affords a wide margin of appreciation to the State, especially in cases of legislative measures of a general nature having a significant impact on the national economy. In any event, measures that are unreasonable and particularly disproportionate in relation to the objectives pursued are considered not to be in accordance with the public interest and the principle of proportionality, and may even be classified as veritable acts of an arbitrary nature. That said, the ECtHR has held that certain national austerity measures, for example a reduction in the pensions of certain public sector employees, comply with Article 1 of Protocol No. 1 insofar as rooted in the serious economic difficulty of the State and

[8] ECtHR judgment of 24 June 1993 in *Papamichalopoulos and Others v. Greece*, appl. no. 14556/89, para. 42.

provided that the measures adopted were necessary and proportionate to the objective to be achieved, having regard to their limited duration and in any case valuing the interests of the individual. In that respect it has been held that the State must not cause excessive prejudice to the property rights of the individual, for example, as a result of the excessive taxation of certain severance payments[9] or where those targeted by the measures are deprived of the necessary means of economic support.[10]

Finally, a deprivation of property must be followed up by compensation, generally in full for *isolated* expropriations. Whereas for nationalisations or socio-economic reforms (all the more so if they are measures aimed at radically changing the structure of the national economy, transforming it for example from a planned economy to a market economy),[11] account is taken—including for the purpose of assessing proportionality of the State's action—of various interests of a general nature that may entail a reduction in the amount of compensation on condition that an appropriate balance between general and special interests is ensured in the case. In other words, both as regards the existence of the public interest and the determination of the compensation to be paid to the private individuals deprived of their property, the State has a wider margin of appreciation as to the choice of the measures to be adopted and their content where it must carry out wide-ranging and complex reforms. In such cases, therefore, the ECtHR generally limits itself to checking a reasonable balance between the various interests involved.

11.2 Right to Work

Among social rights, there are numerous pertaining to labour. This particular category of rights unequivocally demonstrates that various human rights can have an individual and collective dimension as regards entitlement thereto and their concrete implementation.[12]

Labour rights, like other human rights, are strengthened in their protection by certain important principles including that of non-discrimination, which prohibits direct and indirect discrimination committed also in the field of employment[13] and which is widely included in the legal instruments adopted to protect workers' rights.

Labour rights are broad *containers* into which a series of more specific rights, now autonomous in law, have long since converged. They cover the entire labour sphere: access to employment, regulation of the employment relationship and termination of employment.

---

[9] On this issue, see the ECtHR judgment of 14 May 2013 in *N.K.M. v. Hungary*, appl. no. 66529/11.

[10] See the ECtHR's inadmissibility decision of 4 July 2017 in *Mockienė v. Lithuania*, appl. no. 75916/13.

[11] On this distinction, see the ECtHR judgment of 22 June 2004 in *Broniowski v. Poland*, appl. no. 31443/96.

[12] See Chap. 2, Sect. 2.6.

[13] See Chap. 7, Sect. 7.8.

Of particular relevance in the field of labour protection is the extensive activity carried out by the International Labour Organisation ("ILO"), which was founded in 1919 and subsequently became a specialised agency of the UN. Worth noting is the statement in the Philadelphia Declaration approved by the General Conference of the Organization on 10 May 1944 on the aims and objectives of the ILO and annexed to its new Constitution adopted on 9 October 1946, which states that "labour is not a commodity" and that "the war against want requires to be carried on with unrelenting vigour within each nation, and by continuous and concerted international effort in which the representatives of workers and employers, enjoying equal status with those of governments, join with them in free discussion and democratic decision with a view to the promotion of the common welfare".[14] It also provides, in a particularly far-sighted manner, that all human beings, irrespective of race, creed or sex, have the right to pursue both their material well-being and their spiritual development in conditions of freedom and dignity, of economic security and equal opportunity.[15]

From an *operational* standpoint, the Philadelphia Declaration also calls upon the Organisation to promote the implementation, in ILO member countries, of programmes aimed at achieving "(a) the full employment and the raising of standards of living; (b) the employment of workers in the occupations in which they can have the satisfaction of giving the fullest measure of their skill and attainments and make their greatest contribution to the common wellbeing; ... (d) policies in regard to wages and earnings, hours and other conditions of work calculated to ensure a just share of the fruits of progress to all, and a minimum living wage to all employed and in need of such protection; (e) the effective recognition of the right of collective bargaining, the cooperation of management and labour in the continuous improvement of productive efficiency, and the collaboration of workers and employers in the preparation and application of social and economic measures; (f) the extension of social security measures to provide a basic income to all in need of such protection and comprehensive medical care; (g) adequate protection for the life and health of workers in all occupations; (h) provision for child welfare and maternity protection; (i) the provision of adequate nutrition, housing and facilities for recreation and culture; (j) the assurance of equality of educational and vocational opportunity".[16]

Based on the provisions of its Constitution and the Philadelphia Declaration, the ILO has developed a wide range of conventions on the protection of numerous aspects of work or specific categories of workers considered particularly vulnerable, open to ratification by member countries. In addition, on 18 June 1998 the ILO Declaration on Fundamental Principles and Rights at Work was approved. Despite some obvious shortcomings in terms of individual and collective rights in the field of work, for example, regarding the health and safety of workers in the workplace, that declaration sets out the fundamental rights in the field of work that must be respected by all members of the Organisation, whether or not they have ratified the relevant conventions protecting these rights. These fundamental rights relate to

---

[14] See Article I(a) and (d) of the Declaration.

[15] *Id.*, Article II(a).

[16] *Id.*, Article III(a)-(j).

freedom of association and effective recognition of the right to collective bargaining, the elimination of forced or compulsory labour, the abolition of child labour and the elimination of discrimination in respect of employment and occupation.

Labour rights have been included in several other legal instruments of a universal and regional nature. At a universal level, of note is Article 23 UDHR, which protects the right of everyone respectively: to work, to free choice of employment, to just and favourable conditions of work and to protection against unemployment; to equal pay for equal work without any discrimination; to just and favourable remuneration ensuring for himself and his family an existence worthy of human dignity; to form and to join trade unions for the protection of his interests.

Also of note are Articles 6-8 ICESCR.[17] Article 6 recognises the right to work "which includes the right of everyone to the opportunity to gain his living by work which he freely chooses or accepts". The same provision states that the devising of national programmes and policies to achieve the full realisation of this right should ensure the objectives of a "steady economic, social and cultural development and full and productive employment under conditions safeguarding fundamental political and economic freedoms to the individual".

Article 7 protects the right of everyone "to the enjoyment of just and favourable conditions of work", which includes, *inter alia*: the right to fair wages and equal remuneration for work of equal value without distinction of any kind, in particular women being guaranteed conditions of work not inferior to those enjoyed by men, with equal pay for equal work;[18] the right to safe and healthy working conditions, which requires the State to take effective measures to prevent accidents and occupational diseases; equal opportunity for everyone to be promoted in their employment to an appropriate higher level, subject to no considerations other than those of seniority and competence; the right to rest, leisure and reasonable limitation of working hours and periodic holidays with pay, as well as remuneration for public holidays.

Article 8 provides a further list of individual and collective labour rights. More specifically, the individual right to form and join trade unions is protected, subject to limitations prescribed by law and necessary, in a democratic society, for the protection of national security, public order or the protection of the rights and freedoms of others. Other rights are specifically collective in nature and consist in the right of trade union associations to form federations or organisations, national and international, and to freely function, subject to the limitations already highlighted with regard to the individual right to form trade unions. Finally, the right to strike, to be exercised in accordance with the national laws of the country concerned, should be considered as a right that can be exercised both individually and collectively.

At the regional level, the ECHR does not expressly provide for the protection of social rights, which have however been taken into account by the ECtHR in the

[17] Also relevant is Article 9 of the Covenant, which protects the right of everyone to social security, including social insurance, e.g. concerning benefits in case of temporary unemployment of the worker.

[18] The equal nature of work must be ascertained through both objective and subjective factors, such as working conditions, skills and the specific responsibilities and efforts required of the worker.

interpretation of several rights explicitly protected in the Convention such as the right not to be discriminated against, the right to private and family life, the right to property and the right to education.

Again within the framework of the CoE, worthy of mention is the European Social Charter ("ESC"), adopted in 1961 and revised in 1996 ("ESCrev"). Part I lays down a series of general principles on the protection of employment concerning both the protection of all workers and that of certain categories of workers considered to be more vulnerable, namely, children, pregnant women, the disabled and migrant workers. Part II sets out the specific rights enjoyed by workers.

However, the overall effectiveness of the ESC and the aim of uniform application by the Contracting Parties are compromised by the provisions of Part III. Firstly, it is provided that respect for the principles set out in Part I constitutes only a policy objective "to be pursued by all appropriate means both national and international in character". Secondly, it is provided that each Contracting Party is bound only by a limited number of the articles included in Part II, some of which from a specific list and others from among the remaining articles that the State may choose.[19] Needless to say, this *à la carte* system is as cumbersome as it is ineffective.

Part IV, which on this point refers back to the provisions of the ESC (1961), is dedicated to the setting up of a supervisory mechanism centred on sending the Secretary General of the Council of Europe a report at two yearly intervals on the state of implementation of Part II of the Social Charter.[20] The reports are also to be communicated to the national organisations that are members of the international organisations of employers and trade unions that have consultative status at the Council of Europe. Moreover, the "Contracting Parties shall forward to the Secretary General any comments on the aid reports received from these national organisations, if so requested by them".[21] The examination of the State reports is now entrusted to the European Committee of Social Rights ("ECSR"), which, in its final report—made public although not binding—assesses the conformity of the conduct and legislation of the Contracting Parties with the Charter's provisions.[22] The reports of the Contracting Parties and the conclusions of the ECSR are submitted for examination to a Governmental Committee, which may make suggestions to the CMCoE regarding the adoption of recommendations on situations or issues of non-compliance with the ESC.[23]

It should be noted that the Charter provides for a system of collective complaints, already introduced by the Additional Protocol of 1995 relating to the ESC and extended to the application of the ESCrev. In short, this system allows international

[19] See Article A(1) of Part III, which requires the Contracting Party to bind itself in respect of six of the nine articles referred to—considered to be of particular importance in the system of the Charter—as well as to indicate other rules, totalling a minimum of sixteen articles, with which it must ensure compliance.

[20] ESC (1961), Article 21.

[21] *Id.*, Article 23.

[22] *Id.*, Article 24.

[23] *Id.*, Articles 27-29.

and national employers' and workers' organisations and NGOs with consultative status at the CoE to lodge a complaint against a Contracting Party regarding non-compliance with the provisions of the Charter. The complaint is assessed by the ECSR, which, in its concluding non-binding report, rules on the violation of the Charter by the Contracting Party and forwards the report, which is made public, to the CMCoE and the Parliamentary Assembly of the Council of Europe. In turn, the CMCoE may make recommendations to the Contracting Party, which is obliged to indicate, in the State Report submitted under Article 21 ESC (1961), the measures taken to address the CMCoE's recommendations.[24]

Finally, an examination of EU law would fall outside the scope of this chapter on the discussion of internationally protected labour rights. Suffice it to say that the CFREU, in addition to reinforcing the protection of the rights of the EU citizens, through the provision of freedom to seek employment, to move, to exercise the right of establishment and to provide services in any Member State, contemplates a series of rights granted to any worker. Included are the right to engage in work and to pursue a freely chosen or accepted occupation, the right to equality between men and women in matters of employment, work and pay, as well as the right to information and consultation within the undertaking, the right of collective bargaining and action, and the right of access to placement services. The CFREU also provides specific protection with regard to unjustified dismissal or dismissal for reasons of maternity, fair and just working conditions, social security and social assistance, the prohibition of child labour and the protection of young people at work.[25]

11.3 Right to Education

The main cultural rights are the right to education and the right to participate in the cultural life of the country in which the individual resides or of which he is a citizen. A number of international legal instruments, in particular the ICESCR, contain varying provisions on the protection of the right to education[26] and the right of each individual to take part in cultural life and to enjoy the benefits of scientific progress and its applications respectively.[27]

The right to education is essential for the construction of the personality of the individual and hence for the exercise of most human rights, which require adequate awareness and cultural knowledge as in-depth as possible in order to be able to effectively enjoy them. In this regard Article 26(2) UDHR—and analogously Article 13(1) ICESCR—specifies that education "shall be directed to the full development of the human personality and to the strengthening of respect for human rights and

[24] See Articles 1–12 of the 1995 Additional Protocol.

[25] See Articles 15, 23 and 27–34 CFREU.

[26] See Articles 13–14 of the Covenant.

[27] *Id.*, Article 15(1)(a) and (b).

fundamental freedoms", in line with what has often been said about the indivisibility and coordination of the various human rights.

In order for it to be effectively enjoyed, the right to education requires that States comply with a number of positive obligations aimed at guaranteeing the individual, first and foremost access to the basic education system, consisting of public primary education, which must be compulsory, free and provided in a non-discriminatory manner. As for higher education, including university education, the State cannot be expected to provide it equally free of charge and for the benefit of all, but higher education must be accessible to all on the basis of merit, with easier access for the less well-off, for example, through the provision of scholarships.

In addition, the State is required to establish, in terms of the general organisation of the education system and teaching, an adequate quality of education, which includes the obligation to provide teaching and educational programmes that ensure the complete and objective education of students, thus excluding forms of indoctrination based on political or religious conceptions prevailing in the State in question. This implies the need to offer a broad educational panorama, guaranteeing both *original* pluralism, i.e. the possibility of choosing different educational paths according to the different needs and characteristics of the individual, and *internal* pluralism, concerning the dissemination of different theories and opinions in relation to the interpretation of certain elements or facts being taught, for example with regard to controversial historical and political events.

Finally, special measures must be taken to assure access to education for vulnerable groups of students, such as members of minorities or indigenous peoples and individuals with disabilities, for whom an inclusive education system must be guaranteed to ensure their integration into society. For this reason, on the one hand, States are obliged to effectively provide for specific support in ordinary schools for individuals with disabilities in order to avoid situations of discrimination against them.[28] On the other hand, where it is not possible to include the individual with a disability in ordinary education in view of the particular seriousness and characteristics of the illness, the State is not precluded from having recourse to educational establishments specialised in the treatment of certain disabilities.[29]

According to Article 2 of Protocol No. 1 to the ECHR, the State, in the performance of its functions in matters of education and teaching, must respect the religious and philosophical convictions of the parents of students. This particular conformation of the right to education raises two particularly important legal questions. The first relates to the previously mentioned potential conflict between, on the one hand, the religious convictions of the student's parents and, on the other hand, the religious views most widely held at the national level, which may result in the State authorising the use of symbols belonging to a particular religion in public places, as in the case of the display of crucifixes in some public schools.[30]

---

[28] See the ECtHR judgment of 10 September 2020 in *G.L. v. Italy*, appl. no. 59751/15.

[29] On this issue, see the ECtHR's inadmissibility decision of 24 January 2019 in *Dupin v. France*, appl. no. 2282/17.

[30] See Chap. 9, Sect. 9.2.2.

The second potential conflict situation is *internal* to the student's family and relates to the incompatibility between the parents' *radical* religious convictions, which may even exclude an individual's right to receive a school education or to receive it within the limits of those convictions, and the child's right to a complete and *neutral* education. In both cases the State is obliged to strike an appropriate balance between the opposing requirements, which however "must not conflict with the fundamental right of the child to education".[31] Therefore, in the event of a conflict that cannot be resolved by interpretation, the child's right to education must prevail over the parents' right to impose a particular education.

11.4 Right to Cultural Goods—The Principle of Common Heritage of Mankind

The existence of a right of access to and enjoyment of cultural goods is widely debated in the literature, especially among experts in public and constitutional law, thus anchoring the various legal situations to specific constitutional provisions that explicitly or implicitly refer to them.

In the international legal system, the protection of cultural goods of particular artistic, religious and historical importance is ensured both in peacetime and in wartime, since there is an advanced special legal framework on the protection of such assets during non-international and international armed conflicts.

In the specific context of human rights, the growing awareness of the importance of the protection of cultural goods has led to a by-now consolidated trend aimed, on the one hand, at limiting the right of individual and collective ownership of cultural goods of great importance, for example by providing for the right of the State to monitor their effective state of conservation and maintenance and sometimes even a right of pre-emption in case of sale of such property between private parties. On the other hand, numerous obligations on the part of the State have been laid down with regard to the protection, conservation and free access to cultural goods. These State obligations also have the objective, as already noted,[32] of preserving cultural heritage for the benefit of future generations.

The expression "national cultural good" is used, albeit in a broad sense, to mean an asset that is an expression of the cultural, religious and historical identity of a country and a given national community. This notion has been enriched at the international level, giving rise to the concept of the common heritage of mankind, which, at the same time, complements and goes beyond the national level of protection.

The common heritage of mankind includes both goods of exclusively national origin and relevance, i.e. relating to single countries and well-defined internal communities, and "transnational" goods, i.e. of importance for national communities

[31] ECtHR judgment of 25 February 1982 in *Campbell and Cosans v. The United Kingdom*, appl. nos. 7511/76 and 7743/76, para. 36.

[32] See Chap. 6, Sect. 6.1.

belonging to different countries. In the latter case, such communities may be populations spread out over several countries or inhabiting in delimited parts of them (e.g. minorities). For example, goods of a religious nature and places of worship, although located in a given country, are often relevant for large communities of individuals present in many countries.

The notion of common heritage of mankind covers both tangible and intangible assets, such as the manifestations and expressions of human ingenuity, art and cultural traditions, which can be realised through forms of expression other than those of a physical or material nature and which, moreover, are constantly changing due to the effects of scientific progress and its concrete artistic and cultural applications.

The principle of common heritage of mankind gives rise to precise legal obligations for States, some of which are already provided for in the well-known UNESCO Convention Concerning the Protection of the World Cultural and Natural Heritage of 16 November 1972 and subsequently incorporated into more specific conventions. In particular, there are State obligations of a procedural nature, consisting, on the one hand, of the duty of cooperation between States in order to guarantee the protection and conservation of common heritage of mankind and, on the other hand, of an albeit rudimentary centralised system for monitoring compliance with the substantive obligations incumbent on the States parties to the various international treaties.

In turn, the substantive obligations for the protection of property falling within the concept of common heritage of mankind are aimed at protecting and preserving the assets in question by laying down specific obligations concerning the prevention of harmful situations caused by man or natural events and the repression of violations. The legal framework in question also applies to cases of damage to these assets committed between individuals, requiring the State to prevent, on the basis of the abovementioned principle of due diligence, violations committed between private individuals and to prosecute those responsible.

Comprehension Check and Tasks

1. What are the assets covered by the right to property? (Sect. 11.1)
2. How is the role of the ILO relevant for the development of the right to work? (Sect. 11.2)
3. What is the ESC? (Sect. 11.2)
4. What are the States' obligations concerning the right to education? (Sect. 11.3)

Chapter 12
Right to Self-determination of Peoples, Right to Development and Right to a Clean and Healthy Environment

Contents

Abstract On the basis of domestic and international case law, including the relevant judgments and advisory opinions of the International Court of Justice, this chapter examines so-called third generation human rights, i.e. the right to self-determination of peoples, the right to development and the right to a clean and healthy environment (including its implications in matters of climate change).

12.1 Right to Self-determination

It has often been pointed out that individual entitlement to a human right does not rule out the possibility that the same right may also be invoked by a number of individuals or by specific social, religious or political groups. There are, however, some human rights that are held only by collective entities, coinciding with the entire national population or a specific part of it. The most significant examples are the right to self-determination of peoples and the right to development, although for the latter right invocation by individuals belonging to specific national communities cannot be ruled out, at least in theory.

From the point of view of the historical evolution of human rights, the advent of the principle of self-determination of peoples marks a very significant development in the international protection of human rights in terms of flanking the individual dimension of human rights with a collective one. Until the consolidation of the principle of self-determination, the collective dimension was marginal and limited mainly to certain group rights of minorities.

P. Pustorino, *Introduction to International Human Rights Law*,
https://doi.org/10.1007/978-94-6265-563-8_12

The principle in question, defined by the ICJ as "a fundamental human right",[1] operates within the framework of opposition between a State (national government or foreign power) and a people, be it a national population as a whole (represented, in the case of a foreign military occupation, by a national liberation movement) or a minority or indigenous peoples within a country.

The historical origin of the principle is commonly traced back to US President Woodrow Wilson's *Fourteen Points* indicated in 1918, which was incorporated in substance into Articles 1 and 55 of the UN Charter. It is a customary principle which, as stated by the ICJ, provides for obligations *erga omnes* and constitutes "one of the essential principles of contemporary international law".[2] When exactly that principle came into being within the framework of general international law is however disputed. The question of *timing* is of great importance since the principle of self-determination is not retroactive in nature and therefore cannot call into question territorial arrangements dating back in time and sometimes made in total disregard of the needs and wishes of national populations.

In its already mentioned advisory opinion of 2019 on the *Legal Consequences of the Separation of the Chagos Archipelago from Mauritius in 1965*, the ICJ observed that the well-known resolution of 14 December 1960, No. 1514 (XV), on the Granting of Independence to Colonial Countries and Peoples, "represents a defining moment in the consolidation of State practice on decolonization",[3] thus assuming that, at least since 1960 and with specific reference to decolonisation cases, the principle of self-determination has been established as a principle of customary nature.

In its judgment of 28 January 2021 on the *Dispute Concerning Delimitation of the Maritime Boundary Between Mauritius and Maldives in the India Ocean*, the International Tribunal on the Law of the Sea ("ITLOS"), drew the consequences, in our view correctly, of what was indicated by the ICJ in its 2019 advisory opinion, maintaining that "Mauritius can be regarded as the coastal State in respect of the Chagos Archipelago for the purpose of the delimitation of a maritime boundary even before the process of the decolonization of Mauritius is completed. In the Special Chamber's view, to treat Mauritius as such State is consistent with the determinations made in the Chagos arbitral award, and, in particular, the determinations made in the [ICJ] Chagos advisory opinion".[4]

As a legal principle, the principle of self-determination has two dimensions: external and internal. The principle of external self-determination applies to colonies, to territories forcibly occupied by a foreign power and to those subject to racist or apartheid regimes. In these cases self-determination constitutes a right for the peoples in question, as underlined by the ICJ in its advisory opinion of 22 July 2010 on the *Accordance with International Law of the Unilateral Declaration of Independence*

---

[1] ICJ 2019, para 144.

[2] See ICJ 1995, p. 102, para 29. The *erga omnes* character of the obligations in the matter of self-determination of peoples is reaffirmed by the ICJ in ICJ 2004, pp. 171–172, para 88, and p. 199, para 156.

[3] Cit., para 150.

[4] Preliminary Objections Judgment, *Mauritius v. Maldives*, para 250.

in Respect of Kosovo.[5] Therefore, in those instances, peoples under colonial domination, foreign occupation or subject to a racist regime have the right to acquire or regain independence from a foreign power or to demand the removal of the governmental regime of a racist nature.

That said, in certain situations the ascertainment of the will of the people, as a determining factor for the exercise of external self-determination, poses particular difficulties. This is so, for example, where the population whose will must be ascertained has been *imported* from the mother country, as happened in the case of the Falklands/Malvinas, claimed by Argentina on the basis of the criterion of geographical contiguity with Argentine territory but with an almost exclusively British population. Consequently, the inhabitants have repeatedly expressed their desire to remain under the sovereignty of the United Kingdom, as demonstrated by the last referendum held in March 2013.

Furthermore, the will of the people must be expressed freely, without any conditioning by the authorities of the territorial State or foreign States. Where the conditioning takes place on the basis of military occupation or control by foreign powers, as occurred in relation to the referendum held in Crimea on 16 March 2014, which was in fact under Russian military control at the time, that constitutes a violation of both the prohibition on the use of force and the principle of self-determination of peoples, resulting in the unlawfulness of the procedure for ascertaining the will of the people, as noted by the UNGA in its resolution of 27 March 2014, No. 68/262, on the Territorial Integrity of Ukraine.[6] Similarly unlawful under international law would have been the referendum which should have taken place on 17 July 2022 in South Ossetia (a separatist region in Georgia under the Russian military control) on the request for annexation to the Russian Federation. In May 2022 plans for the referendum were scrapped by the South Ossetian authorities, at least for the time being. Similar considerations of unlawfulness are valid for the referendums of September 2022 on the annexation by Russia of some territories of Donbass (Donetsk and Lugansk), of Kherson and Zaporizhzhia, as again noted by the UNGA in the resolution of 12 October 2022 (A/RES/ES-11/4).

Apart from the cases expressly referred to by the ICJ, external self-determination does not involve a right of the population. The result is that international law is essentially *neutral* in those residual cases and the principle of effectiveness for the consolidation of the possible territorial change under consideration is important. In these cases, it is necessary in particular to strike a balance between the principle of self-determination of peoples, and hence respect for the will of the people, and the principle of territorial integrity of the State, which implies not only the right of the

---

[5] "During the second half of the twentieth century, the international law of self-determination developed in such a way as to create a right to independence for the peoples of non-self-governing territories and peoples subject to alien subjugation, domination and exploitation". In ICJ 2010, p. 436, para 79.

[6] For these reasons the UNGA underscored that "the referendum held in the Autonomous Republic of Crimea and the city of Sevastopol on 16 March 2014, having no validity, cannot form the basis for any alteration of the status of the Autonomous Republic of Crimea or of the city of Sevastopol": para 5 of the resolution.

State to preserve its territorial boundaries but also the duty to protect the territory and the national population residing therein.

Coordination between the two above-mentioned principles is fairly straightforward in cases where there is prior or subsequent acceptance by the territorial sovereign of the results of a properly held popular consultation on the request for independence, as was the case for the referendum on independence held in East Timor on 30 August 1999 in the wake of the very serious human rights violations committed by the Indonesian authorities in that territory.

Needless to say, despite prior acceptance by the national government of the future outcome of the popular referendum on the detachment of part of the national territory, the local population is free to speak out against it and thus decide not to vote in favour of independence, as was the case for the referendum held in Scotland in 2014 and agreed with the government of the United Kingdom under the Edinburgh Agreement of 2012. And likewise for the two referendums, held in 2018, 2020 and 2021 in New Caledonia and agreed with the French government in light of the Nouméa Agreement of 1998.

Where there is no consent of the national government to external self-determination, a conflict arises between the principle of self-determination and the principle of the territorial integrity of the State, as happened in Quebec, Kosovo and, more recently, Catalonia. With particular reference to Quebec, the Canadian Supreme Court, in its advisory opinion of 20 August 1998 on *Reference Re Secession of Quebec*, ruled out the lawfulness of secession, indicating however that if it is requested by the local population,[7] the central government must take note of it and negotiate an agreed solution, which does not necessarily have to lead to secession.[8]

In the same opinion, the Supreme Court referred to a controversial hypothesis of secession, conceived as a *remedy* to gross violations of human rights and of the principle of internal self-determination itself, more about which below. According to the Court, "when a people is blocked from the meaningful exercise of its right to self-determination internally, it is entitled, as a last resort, to exercise it by secession".[9] Remedial secession is based on two specific conditions: (1) the unjustified withdrawal of autonomy granted in the past by the central government (as happened in Kosovo); (2) gross violations of human rights, also amounting to international crimes, committed by the central government against the local population.[10]

---

[7] According to the very balanced opinion of the Court: "The continued existence and operation of the Canadian constitutional order could not be indifferent to a clear expression of a clear majority of Quebecers that they no longer wish to remain in Canada. The other provinces and the federal government would have no basis to deny the right of the government of Quebec to pursue secession, should a clear majority of the people of Quebec choose that goal, so long as in doing so, Quebec respects the rights of others" (para 151 of the opinion).

[8] *Id.*, para 103.

[9] *Id.*, para 134.

[10] *Id.*, para 135, where the Court states that even assuming that the remedial secession "is sufficient to create a right to unilateral secession under international law, the current Quebec context cannot be said to approach such a threshold".

Although designed to *react* to a violation of principles and norms of particular weight in the international legal order, remedial secession would not yet seem to be accepted in international law, as implicitly stated by the ICJ in the above-mentioned advisory opinion of 2010 on the issue of Kosovo independence. Therein the Court stressed that "whether, outside the context of non-self-governing territories and peoples subject to alien subjugation, domination and exploitation, the international law of self-determination confers upon part of the population of an existing State a right to separate from that State is, however, a subject on which radically different views were expressed by those taking part in the proceedings and expressing a position on the question. Similar differences existed regarding whether international law provides for a right of 'remedial secession' and, if so, in what circumstances".[11]

Finally, as regards its *internal* dimension, the principle of self-determination of peoples has undergone less development, so that it can only be considered protected under specific international treaties, such as the ICCPR and the ICESCR.[12] We believe, however, that the essential core of the principle of internal self-determination is now protected at the level of general international law, thus obliging each State to recognise for its people the essential guarantees of democracy, freedom and the rule of law, as demonstrated, albeit not with effective results, by the recent phenomenon of the "Arab Spring".

The application of the right to internal self-determination implies the holding by the State of free elections at regular intervals, in which all citizens—and also foreigners if so provided by national law[13]—without discrimination of any kind, including any ethnic components existing at the national level,[14] are called upon to elect their political representatives. The obligation of States to organise free periodic elections by secret ballot is expressly recognised in the UDHR,[15] the ICCPR,[16] Protocol No. 1 to the ECHR,[17] the ACHR,[18] and most recently in the ASEAN Declaration on Human Rights of 18 November 2012.[19]

---

[11] Cit., p. 438, para 82.

[12] See Article 1 of both legal instruments.

[13] On political rights as human rights, see Chap. 10, Sect. 10.3.

[14] In its judgment of 29 October 2019 in *Baralija v. Bosnia and Herzegovina*, appl. no. 30100/18, the ECtHR found that the rules governing elections in Bosnia and Herzegovina, based on the exclusive protection of the three national ethnic groups (Bosnian, Croat and Serb), were discriminatory.

[15] See Article 21(3).

[16] See Article 25(b).

[17] See Article 3.

[18] See Article 23(1)(b).

[19] See Article 5(2).

12.2 Right to Development and the Concept of Sustainable Development

The right to development is considered by the UNGA as "an inalienable human right by virtue of which every human person and all peoples are entitled to participate in, contribute to, and enjoy economic, social, cultural and political development, in which all human rights and fundamental freedoms can be fully realised".[20]

From the examination of the UNGA Resolution, it is clear that the right to development is one vested in the entire national community. However, at least in principle, it also has an individual dimension insofar as "every human person" holds that right. In a similar sense, Article 22 ACHPR establishes, on the one hand, that "[a]ll peoples shall have the right to their economic, social and cultural development" and, on the other hand, that "States shall have the duty, individually or collectively, to ensure the exercise of the right to development".

In the ASEAN Declaration on Human Rights of 2012 it is indicated that the right to development is "an inalienable human right by virtue of which every human person and the peoples of ASEAN are entitled to participate in, contribute to, enjoy and benefit equitably and sustainably from economic, social, cultural and political development", thereby establishing a series of commitments by ASEAN Member States in order to reduce poverty, protect the environment and affirm, also at the international level, fair and sustainable economic and trade relations.[21]

The right to development also appears to be instrumental to the attainment of other human rights, especially economic, social and cultural rights. From this point of view, article 26 ACHR provides that the State Parties "undertake to adopt measures, both internally and through international cooperation, especially those of an economic and technical nature, with a view to achieving progressively, by legislation or other appropriate means, the full realisation of the rights implicit in the economic, social, educational, scientific, and cultural standards set forth in the Charter of the Organization of American States as amended by the Protocol of Buenos Aires".

In our view, while it is difficult to invoke it as a human right on its own, the right to development can find fertile application when interpreted in conjunction with other human rights. In this sense, the right to development can constitute a normative parameter of use in *reinforcing* the scope of more concrete human rights whose violation can easily be ascertained in a given case. As much can be deduced from the practice of the ACommHPR, in relation to the application of the above-mentioned Article 22 of the African Charter to cases concerning the violation of the right to food and adequate nutrition[22] as well as to cases concerning the violation of several rights belonging to indigenous peoples, in the wake of national measures of forced

[20] See Article 1 of the Resolution on the Right to Development of 4 December 1986, No. 41/128.

[21] See paras 35–37 of the Declaration.

[22] See the Decision of the ACommHPR of 27 October 2001 in *Social and Economic Rights Action Center (SERAC) and Center for Economic and Social Rights (CESR) v. Nigeria*, Communication no. 155/96.

relocation of members of these communities in order to commercially exploit the lands they have occupied since time immemorial.[23]

The notion of the right to development has been supplemented, relatively recently, by the word *sustainable*, which, according to the ICJ, expresses the "need to reconcile economic development with protection of the environment".[24] It should also be noted that lately the sustainability of development is not limited to the merely environmental aspects mentioned in numerous acts adopted within the framework of the UN, for example, the 1992 Rio Declaration on Environment and Development,[25] but extends to economic and social aspects. As noted in the solemn Declaration contained in the UN document on *Transforming Our World: the 2030 Agenda for Sustainable Development*, "We are committed to achieving sustainable development in its three dimensions – economic, social and environmental – in a balanced and integrated way".[26] In this sense, one must avoid the excesses of *unbridled* economic development, which can undermine the global environmental balance and contribute to the economic and social impoverishment of various countries and populations.

12.3 Right to a Healthy Environment

The evolution that has occurred in the recognition of the principle of sustainable development, mentioned in the previous section, has facilitated the gradual establishment of an individual and collective human right to a healthy environment, which is expressly provided for in certain international legal instruments on human rights[27] or derived by interpretation mainly from the right to life, the right to health and the right to private and family life.[28]

Recently, the HRCoun in Resolution 48/13 of 5 October 2021 has solemnly recognised "the right to a safe, clean, healthy and sustainable environment as a human right" that is also important for the enjoyment of other human rights. The HRCoun has also encouraged UN Member States: (a) to build capacities for the efforts to protect the environment and to enhance cooperation with other States, the UN system, other international organizations, and relevant non-State actors on the implementation of this right; (b) to share good practices in fulfilling human rights obligations relating to

[23] See the Decision of 25 November 2009 in *Centre for Minority Rights Development (Kenya) and Minority Rights Groups International on behalf of Endorois Welfare Council v. Kenya*, Communication no. 276/2003.

[24] See ICJ 1997, pp. 77–78, para 140.

[25] See principles 3 and 4 of the Declaration.

[26] See A/RES/70/1, para 2.

[27] See Article 24 ACHPR and Article 11 of the Additional Protocol to the American Convention on Human Rights in the Area of Economic, Social and Cultural Rights of 17 November 1988.

[28] In relation to the right to private and family life, the ECtHR has repeatedly stated that, when an individual is directly and seriously affected by severe environmental harm such as noise or other pollution, an issue might arise under Article 8 ECHR: see recently the judgment of 14 October 2021, *Kapa and Others v. Poland*, appl. nos. 75031/13 and others.

the enjoyment of the right to a safe, clean, healthy and sustainable environment; and (c) to adopt policies for the enjoyment of the right in question, including the respect for biodiversity and ecosystems.[29]

The right to a healthy environment implies respect by the State not only of negative obligations to refrain from adopting decisions that compromise the free enjoyment and balance of the natural habitat, but above all of positive obligations of a substantive and procedural nature consisting in conduct aimed both at protecting the environment with preventive measures and at intervening subsequently in order to eliminate environmental damage and preserve the environment also for future generations. This entails a duty to carry out appropriate environmental impact assessments prior to and following the construction of environmentally *invasive* works, a duty to restore the original state of the environmentally damaged places and a duty to inform the populations concerned of both the possible damage to the environment and the corrective measures adopted or to be adopted.

The aforementioned positive obligations on environmental protection also operate where the violations, or the risk of such violations, originate from private parties due to the State's failure to comply with the oft-mentioned principle of due diligence, as affirmed by the HRC in the previously mentioned *General Comment No. 36* of 30 October 2018 on the right to life, according to which "[i]mplementation of the obligation to respect and ensure the right to life, and in particular life with dignity, depends, inter alia, on measures taken by States parties to preserve the environment and protect it against harm, pollution and climate change caused by public and private actors".[30]

Serious violations of the human right to a healthy environment, where they significantly affect the safety and health of individuals, may in fact imply a violation of the right to life, both in substantive and procedural terms. For example, where the State fails to carry out an effective and complete investigation into the causes and effects of environmental disasters which may compromise the health and physical and mental integrity of human beings, or where it does not adequately inform public opinion in general and, more specifically, the populations directly affected by environmental disasters of such investigations and any corrective measures.

That the State has positive obligations in relation to environmental violations committed between private individuals is widely confirmed both in ECtHR case law (for example in the judgment of 24 January 2019 in *Cordella and Others v. Italy*[31]) and in IACtHR case law (for example in the judgment of 6 February 2020 in *Indigenous Communities of the Lhaka Honhat (Our Land) Association v. Argentina*).

---

[29] See paras 1 and 3 of the Resolution. The UNGA, in its resolution of 28 July 2022, no. 76/300, para 1, has also recognized "the right to a clean, healthy and sustainable environment as a human right".

[30] See para 62. For a concrete application of the principle of due diligence in the HRC's practice, see the views of 25 July 2019 in *Portillo Cáceres v. Paraguay*, CCPR/C/126/D/2751/2016, paras 7.1–7.9, on the violation by the respondent State of the right to life and the right to private and family life on account of the State's repeated failure to act in relation to the serious environmental damage caused to the applicants by private industries.

[31] Appl. nos. 54414/13 et 54264/15, paras 158 ff. of the judgment.

In that latter decision, the IACtHR pointed out that "the States have the obligation to establish adequate mechanisms to monitor and supervise certain activities in order to ensure human rights, protecting them from actions of public entities and also private individuals.[32]

12.4 Protection of the Environment and Climate Change

On the subject of environmental protection, the existence of specific positive obligations of States under human rights law has recently been affirmed also in national case law and with particular reference to the negative effects of climate change on the natural environment and on national communities.

In this regard, worth mentioning above all is the leading case of *The State of the Netherlands (Ministry of Economic Affairs and Climate Policy) v. Stichting Urgenda* decided by the Dutch Supreme Court in a judgment issued on 20 December 2019. That judgment established the positive and *individual* obligation of the State to reduce by at least 25%, compared to 1990 levels, the polluting emissions produced by the Netherlands by 2020. The Court based its reasoning both on Articles 2 and 8 ECHR—concerning respectively the right to life and the right to private and family life—and on the relevant ECtHR case law,[33] deriving therefrom the positive obligation of the State to take appropriate decisions and actions in case of a real and imminent risk of environmental degradation for the persons under its jurisdiction. The Court also referenced certain non-mandatory acts adopted by the *Intergovernmental Panel on Climate Change* (IPCC) in the framework of the annual conferences of the States parties to the UN Framework Convention on Climate Change of 9 May 1992,[34] thus demonstrating, on a more general level, the relevance of soft law for the development of international environmental law.[35]

The Dutch Supreme Court ruling in question also seems to have created a positive *trickle-down* effect in other jurisdictions, with the aim of inducing not only their governments but also multinational corporations to reduce the causes of climate change produced by human activities.

In its judgment of 3 February 2021, the Administrative Tribunal of Paris found that the French Government had failed to take the necessary measures for the progressive reduction of anthropogenic greenhouse gases, contrary to the obligations assumed by France both under the Paris Agreement of 12 December 2015 and the UN Framework Convention on Climate Change of 1992, and under the corresponding rules adopted by the European Union.[36] Before determining the specific measures intended to

[32] See para 207. On the relevance of this judgment also to the protection of indigenous peoples, see Chap. 13, Sect. 13.4.3.

[33] See paras 5.2.2–5.2.4 of the judgment.

[34] *Id.*, para 5.4.3.

[35] On the specific relevance of soft law in the field of human rights, see Chap. 3, Sect. 3.11.

[36] See paras 18 ff. of the judgment, nos. 1904967, 1904968, 1904972 and 1904976/4-1.

prevent the worsening of the ecological damage, however, the Court ordered the French Government to carry out a rapid supplementary investigation ("*supplément d'instruction*") so as to acquire all the elements useful for the resolution of the case.

A somewhat similar approach was adopted in the recent judgment delivered on 21 June 2021 by the Brussels Court of First Instance in the *Klimaatzaak* case.[37] Having ascertained that the Belgian central and local authorities had detailed knowledge of the certain risk of dangerous climate change for the country's population, the Court found that those authorities had failed to take the necessary measures to protect the applicants' right to life and right to private and family life as required by Articles 2 and 8 of the ECHR. The Court therefore held that both the federal government and the three federal regions were individually responsible for the lack of climate governance. However, the request for a court order mandating a specific reduction of environmentally harmful emissions within a certain time limit was not granted, on grounds that both the question of the gradualness of emission limitations and the internal distribution of reductions between central government and the regions has to be the subject of a political agreement between the parties concerned, which also takes into account Belgium's contribution to the reduction of polluting emissions at the global level.

Finally, in its judgment of 26 May 2021 in *Vereniging Milieudefensie et al. v. Royal Dutch Shell Plc,* the Hague District Court ordered the oil company Shell to reduce all carbon dioxide resulting from its global activities—including those stemming from the combustion of oil-and-gas products by its customers—by 45% by 2030, in comparison to 2019 levels. While applying Dutch law, as the law deemed applicable on the basis of Articles 4 and 7 of Regulation No 864/2007 of the European Parliament and of the Council of 11 July 2007 on the Law Applicable to Non-contractual Obligations (Rome II), the Court referred extensively to international human rights treaties and in particular to norms on the right to life, the right to health and the right to private and family life in order to establish, within the limits referred to above, a "duty of care" on the part of the multinational corporation.[38]

Comprehension Check and Tasks

1. What is the external dimension of the principle of self-determination? (Sect. 12.1)
2. Do you agree with the reasoning of the Canadian Supreme Court in *Reference Re Secession of Quebec*? (Sect. 12.1)
3. What are the human rights relevant for the protection of the environment in case of the absence of specific environmental rights? (Sect. 12.3)
4. Focus on the recent developments in the national case law on climate change and human rights (Sect. 12.4)

[37] See *Klimaatzaak ASBL v. Belgium*, judgment no. 2015/4585/A.

[38] See paras 4.4.1–4.4.10.

References

ICJ (1995) Judgment of 30 June 1995, Portugal v. Australia, East Timor. ICJ Reports
ICJ (1997) Judgment of 25 September 1997 in Gabćikovo-Nagymaros Project, Hungary v. Slovakia. ICJ Reports
ICJ (2004) Advisory Opinion of 9 July 2004 on the Legal Consequences of the Construction of a Wall in the Occupied Palestinian Territory. ICJ Reports
ICJ (2010) Advisory opinion of 22 July 2010 on the Accordance with International Law of the Unilateral Declaration of Independence in Respect of Kosovo. ICJ Reports
ICJ (2019) Advisory opinion of 25 February 2019 on the Legal Consequences of the Separation of the Chagos Archipelago from Mauritius in 1965. ICJ Reports

Chapter 13
Human Rights, States and Non-state Actors

Contents

Abstract The chapter examines the role played in the field of human rights by states and non-state actors, such as those operating in the framework of international and non-international armed conflicts (e.g. insurgents and national liberation movements, natural persons, minorities and indigenous peoples). The chapter highlights both their increasing importance in international law and the specific needs of protection from the point of view of human rights. In addition, the legal regime concerning multinational corporations is analyzed, together with the tendency, recently followed by some national courts, to ascertain their responsibility under both national and international law for serious violations of human rights.

13.1 States and International Organisations

The fundamental role played by States and, more recently, by international organisations in the international affirmation of human rights has already been extensively highlighted in this work.

P. Pustorino, *Introduction to International Human Rights Law*,
https://doi.org/10.1007/978-94-6265-563-8_13

With reference to the steps taken by States, it was mentioned before[1] that their contribution to the *passage* from the national to the international level of protection of human rights was the most significant one. That said, the role of States appears also to be decisive for the purposes of the formation of general and conventional norms on human rights and their application within national legal systems. And in a more limited form, in terms of contributing to ascertaining violations via judicial means, through the inter-State application mechanisms established by certain international conventions.

Likewise of importance is the function vested in international organisations, which, as noted with regard to the UN,[2] engage in valuable work in preparing binding and non-binding legal instruments and detecting violations of human rights, including through the establishment of numerous monitoring systems operating within the organisations concerned or within the framework of conventions drawn up by them.

It should also be pointed out that while most human rights violations are attributable to States and some non-State actors, there are nevertheless cases of serious violations of fundamental human rights committed by international organisations alone or jointly with States. From this point of view, it is not disputed that international organisations are bound to respect the norms of *jus cogens*, including therefore those on human rights, as well as certain customary norms whose content is consistent with the nature and activities carried out by the organisations, and finally of course the norms contained in the treaties ratified by them. In its judgments of 21 September 2005 in the *Al Barakaat*[3] and *Kadi*[4] cases, the former Court of First Instance of the European Communities stated that it was "empowered to check, indirectly, the lawfulness of the resolutions of the Security Council in question with regard to *jus cogens*, understood as a body of higher rules of public international law binding on all subjects of international law, including the bodies of the UN, and from which no derogation is possible".

With regard to the relationship between international organisations and treaty-based law, it must be noted that although accession by international organisations to human rights agreements is still limited, examples do exist, albeit limited only to certain kinds of organizations. For example, the UN Convention on the Rights of Persons with Disabilities of 13 December 2006 authorises both the formal confirmation (i.e., an act corresponding to that of ratification by States) by signatory regional integration organisations and the accession by any regional integration organisation that has not signed the Convention.[5]

The general importance of issues concerning the responsibility of international organisations, including therefore responsibility for violations of international human rights, is confirmed by the approval in 2011 by the ILC of the Draft Articles on the

---

[1] See Chap. 1, Sect. 1.1.

[2] See Chap. 5.

[3] Case T-306/01, para 277.

[4] Case T-315/01, para 226.

[5] See Article 43 of the Convention.

Responsibility of International Organizations ("ARIO"), which largely follows the content of the better known 2001 ARSIWA, which will be discussed in Chap. 14.

13.2 National Liberation Movements, Insurgents and Terrorist Groups

The growing importance of non-State actors in the international legal order is well-known. Indeed, it constitutes one of the most significant recent developments in international law, affecting the general characteristics of the international legal system as well as the structure and content of fundamental principles such as international subjectivity, i.e. legal personality, and the procedures for the creation of rules of international law, in particular customary and conventional law.

The legal regime governing non-State actors has been extensively discussed in the literature, with particular reference to their obligations under international human rights law and international humanitarian law. The main legal basis on which it is considered legitimate to apply certain international norms to some particularly effective and stable non-State actors is their international legal personality, sometimes recognised rather generously in the literature or in practice.

Given that only a small number of non-State actors possess a non-controversial international legal personality, further legal grounds have been sought to justify the application of at least some international norms to non-State actors, especially those operating in the framework of international and non-international armed conflicts: national liberation movements, insurgents and armed groups. Among the most widely subscribed theories in the literature is one that emphasises, in relation to insurrectional movements and armed groups with a significant political-military structure and organisation, the element of control exercised over the territory and the resident population—regardless of whether the entities possess international legal personality. Thus, according to the opinion of Special Rapporteur Philip Alston, concerning the examination of the long and bloody civil war in Sri Lanka, when an armed group exercises "[a] significant control over territory and population and has an identifiable political structure", it is necessary that it respects human rights.[6]

Other positions stress the importance of the aims pursued by national liberation and insurrectional movements, noting that they intend to take over—or reassume—the government of the State under foreign military occupation or subject to insurrection. For this reason, these entities are obliged to abide by the same international rules that apply to the very State government which they oppose. A further argument

---

[6] See Commission on Human Rights, Civil and Political Rights, Including the Question of Disappearances and Summary Executions. Extrajudicial, Summary or Arbitrary Executions, *Report of the Special Rapporteur, Philip Alston*, Addendum, Mission to Sri Lanka (28 November–6 December 2005), 22 December 2004, E/CN.4/2005/7, para 76.

is that armed groups that are stable, organised and operating in the context of a non-international armed conflict, are obliged to respect the rules of general international law and treaties ratified by the State on whose territory the conflict occurs.

In our opinion, it is possible to apply part of the international legal regime on human rights to non-State actors involved in international and non-international armed conflicts, when they are endowed with a detailed organisational structure of a political and military nature. First, it seems unquestionable that *jus cogens* human rights norms can be applied to them. In this regard, the Commission of Inquiry on the Syrian Arab Republic, established by the HRCoun to investigate violations of human rights and international humanitarian law committed by the various parties to the conflict on Syrian territory, noted that "at a minimum, human rights obligations constituting peremptory international law (*ius cogens*) bind States, individuals and non-State collective entities, including armed groups", stressing that "[a]cts violating *ius cogens* – for instance, torture or enforced disappearances – can never be justified".[7]

As regards which other international human rights norms of a customary and conventional nature are applicable to non-State actors involved in armed conflicts, that determination cannot be made *a priori.* Rather it depends both on the circumstances of the case and content of the relevant international norms, especially where those norms presuppose the existence of structures or organs of particular stability, which are often absent in the political and military organisation of the numerous non-State entities involved in armed conflicts. From this point of view, the existence of the effective capacity of the entities in question to respect certain human rights rules is therefore essential.

It follows that, in most cases, the observance of human rights law must be limited to the fundamental rights of the individual—protected at the level of general international law—and the essential core of the conventional norms applicable to the State involved in the conflict and thus to the non-State actors participating in that conflict. Moreover, the application of human rights norms during an armed conflict cannot be *uniform,* in the sense of expecting the same customary and conventional norms to apply to all non-State actors operating during armed conflicts, but varies according to their specific organisation, structure and political and military capacity.

Moving from the general to the specific, it is now necessary to dwell on national liberation movements and insurgents, which are commonly regarded as subjects of international law. The examination of these two entities is of particular importance in the context of international human rights protection because, on the basis of the above criteria, it is possible in our view to apply a significant part of human rights law to them.

It should first be noted that drawing a distinction between the two entities is not easy since a war of national liberation is carried out by armed groups and/or by one or more insurrectional movements. However, a national liberation movement is generally of a much longer duration in terms of time and, above all, its aim is precisely

---

[7] See Report of 22 February 2012, A/HRC/19/69, para 106.

to *liberate* the national territory from colonial domination, foreign occupation or a racially motivated regime.

In relation to this specific aim, considered legitimate and worthy of protection at the international level, national liberation movements bear various obligations and rights under international law. Among which, the previously mentioned principle of self-determination of peoples.[8] In this regard, the Protocol Additional to the Geneva Conventions of 12 August 1949, and relating to the Protection of Victims of International Armed Conflicts (Protocol I, 8 June 1977), provides that armed conflicts include those "in which peoples are fighting against colonial domination and alien occupation and against racist regimes in the exercise of their right of self-determination, as enshrined in the Charter of the United Nations and the Declaration on Principles of International Law concerning Friendly Relations and Co-operation among States in accordance with the Charter of the United Nations".[9]

In our opinion, even for insurrectional movements that are particularly effective and long-lasting (hence very few), the question of the relationship with the principle of self-determination of peoples arises. As matters currently stand it is not possible to equate a stable and effective insurrectional movement with national liberation movements in terms of their international status—although there is a tendency in this direction, limited to insurgents fighting against dictatorial and brutal government regimes, as happened recently in Libya and Syria. It should also be pointed out that the principle of self-determination of peoples, with regard to insurgents fighting particularly brutal governments, would not be vested in the insurrectional governments but in the insurrectional people, insofar as they are actually identifiable, and self-determination could be invoked both against the government in power and against the insurrectional government itself. Admittedly, practice is very scarce in this regard and concerns both the aforementioned claims of insurgent people against brutal governments, and similar claims made against the insurrectional movement and consisting of the failure of the insurrectional government to comply with basic principles and rules of democracy, rule of law and fundamental human rights, which form an integral part of the principle of internal self-determination.

It should be noted that the above also applies to insurrectional movements, or particularly organised and stable associations of a terrorist nature, such as ISIS (Islamic State in Iraq and the Levant). Indeed, ISIS is known to have exercised quasi-sovereign powers over large areas of territory formally belonging to Iraq and Syria, going so far as to proclaim itself to be a caliphate on 29 June 2014 with the aim of assuming power in several States. The vast control of national territories and the sophisticated political and military organisation of ISIS obliged that entity to comply with numerous international human rights rules, while the organisation in question has distinguished itself for methods and means that are brutal as well as contrary to the most basic rules of justice and human dignity.

---

[8] See Chap. 12, Sect. 12.1.

[9] See Article 1(4) of the Protocol.

13.3 Natural Persons

The role played by natural persons in international law has also been referred to several times in this work.[10]

In light of the indisputable importance of the individual in the international legal order, some scholars maintain that the individual has now acquired international legal personality, full or limited depending on the theory espoused. Whereas other scholars express the traditional view that the individual continues to be only the beneficiary of international rules addressed solely to States or international organisations.

The school of thought that rules out international legal personality holds, in particular, that the individual does not participate in the life of international relations and is not involved, except in a very marginal way, in the functions of creation, ascertainment and coercive enforcement of international law. However, that is not entirely true. Individuals and generally a number of non-State actors participate, albeit indirectly, in the formation of certain international norms, having for instance access to international conferences in which they *pressure* States and international organisations into asserting their positions on the content of the international rules adopted in those frameworks. There are also numerous international conventions, including human rights ones, that establish substantive rights in favour of natural and legal persons.

This consolidated tendency can also be witnessed in the specific field of the rules of international law concerning environmental protection, as demonstrated by the analysis of the Aarhus Convention on Access to Information, Public Participation in Decision-Making and Access to Justice in Environmental Matters of 25 June 1998. In application of the principle of participatory democracy, that Convention recognises the rights of individuals and communities to participate in national decisions concerning the protection of the environment, to access environmental information and to obtain judicial protection of these substantive rights.[11] Again in the field of environmental protection, but in a very different regional and cultural context, a similar approach is followed by the Escazú Regional Agreement on Access to Information, Public Participation and Justice in Environmental Matters in Latin America and Caribbean of 4 March 2018, which entered into force on 22 April 2021.

In addition, natural and legal persons participate in a very significant way in the control of the respect of international law, through the submission of applications or petitions to courts and non-judicial bodies operating at the international level. Of importance here is the principle of the State's consent to accept individual applications before courts or bodies operating within the framework of human rights. Although still found in some conventions, this principle is outdated in others, like the ECHR, which allow for the *automatic* submission of applications by individuals from the moment of ratification of the treaty without therefore requiring the State to accept *ad hoc* the jurisdiction of the international court to receive that type of application.

---

[10] See, e.g., Chap. 1, Sect. 1.3.

[11] See Articles 4–9 of the Convention.

On the other hand, it must be conceded that the participation of natural persons in the phase of coercive implementation of international law is essentially absent.

With specific regard to the obligations of individuals deriving from international law, the latter are the direct addressees of the norms on international crimes, which allow international courts and tribunals, both temporary (ICTY and ICTR) and permanent (ICC) to try individuals accused of genocide, war crimes and crimes against humanity.[12] To some extent, even mandatory acts adopted by bodies of international organisations and addressed to non-State actors, such as *smart sanctions* implemented by the UNSC against natural and legal persons,[13] are indicative of the increasing importance of individuals at the international level.

The granting of international legal personality to individuals depends on valuing one or more of the functions performed by them internationally. In our opinion, the increasing importance of the individual in terms of forming international norms and ascertaining their existence, including judicially, tends to weigh in favour of the existence of international legal personality. Moreover, if the decisive *test* to rule out international legal personality for individuals must be based, on the one hand, on their limited ability to contribute to the creation of international rules and, on the other hand, on the objective absence of any role in the enforcement of those same rules, that very test would imply the non-existence of the international legal personality of several States of modest or very limited legal capacity at the international level.

Finally, it should be noted that some legal scholars are of the view that granting international legal personality to individuals or in any case acknowledging the indisputable position of natural persons in the current international legal system would have a *revolutionary* effect in terms of the structure of the international community and would entail a significant reduction in the powers of the State both within its own territory and in relations with other States, for example, with regard to the aforementioned overcoming of the reserved domain of the State at least for serious violations of human rights.[14] In this regard, we believe that there is no doubt that the increased relevance of natural persons in their individuality and as members of different collective entities has significantly affected the structure and functioning of the international community. However, this does not imply a radical reversal of the trend with regard to the predominantly *State-centric* nature of international society, which remains largely based on relations—sometimes backed up by force—of an interstate nature.

[12] More recently, with the amendments to Article 8a of the Statute of the ICC, the crime of aggression is now prosecutable on the basis of conventional rules different from those applicable to the other crimes.

[13] See Chap. 5, Sect. 5.5.

[14] See Chap. 1, Sect. 1.1.

13.4 Minorities and Indigenous Peoples

It has already been mentioned that minorities and indigenous peoples are, above all, holders of the right of self-determination of peoples.[15] It is worth recalling that what is involved here is internal self-determination, which therefore does not call into question the territorial integrity of the State where these groups of individuals reside and which rather demands respect for the essential guarantees of democracy, freedom, the rule of law and participation in the life of the country where the minorities and indigenous peoples live, including the right to participate in free and periodic elections.

When analysing the international legal framework for the protection of minorities and indigenous peoples, we believe that the principle of internal self-determination is the main legal parameter around which all the other guarantees owed to these peoples revolve. It is even arguable that this regime is nothing more than a set of more specific principles and rules whose function is to supplement and enrich the content of the fundamental principle of internal self-determination.

13.4.1 Minorities

With regard to minorities, it should be noted that the applicable legal instruments grant powers and rights to members of minorities[16] and only to a limited extent to minorities as such. This is due to a number of historical and legal reasons.

First of all, it should be stressed that the international protection of minorities predates the protection of human rights. The protection of minorities, in particular religious minorities, dates back to the sixteenth century, with the conclusion of several international treaties, mostly bilateral, aimed at preventing wars between States, which were motivated, often speciously, by the need to protect members of minorities, considered to be discriminated against and sometimes actually persecuted for their religious beliefs. For instance, in Europe, the Treaty of Cavour between Emanuele Filiberto of Savoy and the Waldensians on 5 June 1561 put an end to the revolt of the latter religious minority, which had adhered to the Lutheran Reformation. The Treaty established the principle of freedom of worship for the Waldensians, including the right to profess their religious beliefs without discrimination. Outside Europe, there was the 1535 treaty between King Francis I of France and Suleiman the Magnificent, Sultan of the Ottoman Empire, which covered several areas of cooperation: military, commercial and religious. It was established, among other things, that the French

[15] See Chap. 12, Sect. 12.1.

[16] Emblematic in this sense is the text of Article 27 of the ICCPR, which attributes to persons belonging to ethnic, religious or linguistic minorities "the right, in community with the other members of their group, to enjoy their own culture, to profess and practise their own religion, or to use their own language".

were free to practise their religion in the Ottoman Empire and a Christian place of worship was built in Constantinople.[17]

The regime for the protection of minorities, especially religious minorities, received a further boost following the conclusion of the Congress of Vienna in 1815 and then, above all, at the end of World War I, with the provision of an—albeit rudimentary—centralised system for monitoring compliance with certain treaties on minority rights by the League of Nations.

Since World War II, the protection of minority groups has been progressively absorbed into the broader normative context of human rights, as set out in Article 1 of the Framework Convention for the Protection of National Minorities of 1 February 1995, drafted by the CoE.[18] In recent times, however, the legal regime governing minorities has regained a certain normative autonomy within the overall framework of human rights protection. The clear correlation between the special rules on minorities and general human rights law opens the way to applying international human rights law to minorities. From this point of view, the relationship, already analysed with regard to the connection between human rights and international humanitarian law[19] and concerning general and special law, comes to the fore again, both in terms of application of the two normative spheres as alternatives and of joint application depending on the circumstances of the case at issue.

The reference to human rights law at large may also serve as a *corrective tool* to exclude or limit the negative effects, with respect to fundamental principles on the rights of individuals, of the exclusive use of the special rules on minorities. This can be inferred from the conclusions reached by the ECtHR (Grand Chamber) in its judgment of 19 December 2018 in *Molla Sali v. Greece*.[20] In that decision the ECtHR affirmed the principle according to which certain rules contained in Sharia law governing relations between members of an Islamic minority (which modified the effects of a will drawn up in accordance with Greek law by a member of the minority) conflicted both with the general principle of non-discrimination—since the effect of the Sharia rule was to discriminate against the testator's wife—and with the principle that allows members of a minority to opt out of the minority legal regime under Article 3(1) of the above-mentioned 1995 Convention for the Protection of National Minorities.[21]

There is another reason of operational nature which explains why instruments designed to protect minorities grant rights mainly to individual members of the minority group. The reason lies in the practical difficulty of enforcing the rights

[17] The treaty in question is also an expression of the aforementioned capitulations regime: see Chap. 1, Sect. 1.2.

[18] "The protection of national minorities and of the rights and freedoms of persons belonging to those minorities forms an integral part of the international protection of human rights, and as such falls within the scope of international co-operation".

[19] See Chap. 3, Sect. 3.8.

[20] Appl. no. 20452/14.

[21] "Every person belonging to a national minority shall have the right freely to choose to be treated or not to be treated as such and no disadvantage shall result from this choice or from the exercise of the rights which are connected to that choice".

granted at a collective level to minorities and, in part, to indigenous peoples. In fact, as mentioned above,[22] among the conditions for the admissibility of individual applications or petitions submitted to bodies charged with scrutinising the observance of certain human rights treaties is that applicants will have to prove that they are a "victim" of a violation of one of the rights protected by the treaty. This requirement can only be met if the violation is committed against specific individuals belonging to the minority, as stated by the ECtHR in the inadmissibility decision of 25 May 2000 in *Noack and Others v. Germany*,[23] in which the Court ruled out the status of victim for an association established for the protection of the rights of a minority but not specifically injured as regards one of the rights protected by the ECHR.

We now come to some substantive aspects of minority protection.

In this regard, it is necessary to begin by dwelling on the specific concept of minority, which necessarily takes on a *territorial* nature, in the sense that the same group may be considered a minority within a certain State but may not have the characteristics of a minority in another State, where, for example, the settlement is very small in number or the members lack the cohesion and solidarity necessary to claim protection of their cultural, ethnic, linguistic or religious identity.

Apart from the aforementioned principle of internal self-determination and the principle of non-discrimination, the general principles applicable to the protection of minorities include the prohibition of their total *assimilation* into national society in a manner that would entail disregarding the specific characteristics of minorities. Of course, *integration* of minority groups into society can be considered as legitimate.

With regard to the regime for the protection of minorities, the particular importance of the positive obligations of States must also be stressed. These are essential to ensure effective protection of minority groups and indigenous peoples.

Among the most significant positive obligations of States found in the instruments for the protection of minorities, mention should be made of the obligation to respect the identity and cultural diversity of minorities residing in the national territory, which is a corollary of the prohibition of assimilation of minorities in the national context, implying the destruction of their ethnic, linguistic and religious traditions. The obligation in question is contained in general terms in Article 27 ICCPR and in more specific terms in Article 5(2) of the 1995 Framework Convention for the Protection of National Minorities.[24] This latter provision was referred to by the ECtHR in its judgment of 8 December 2009 in *Muñoz Diaz v. Spain*,[25] in which the Court stated, in a case concerning the protection of the religious traditions of members of the Roma minority, that "there is an emerging international consensus among the Contracting States of the Council of Europe recognising the special needs

---

[22] See Chap. 4, Sect. 4.2, with reference to individual applications lodged with the ECtHR.

[23] Appl. no. 46346/99.

[24] "Without prejudice to measures taken in pursuance of their general integration policy, the Parties shall refrain from policies or practices aimed at assimilation of persons belonging to national minorities against their will and shall protect these persons from any action aimed at such assimilation".

[25] Appl. no. 49151/07.

of minorities and an obligation to protect their security, identity and lifestyle (... in particular the Council of Europe's Framework Convention for the Protection of National Minorities), not only for the purpose of safeguarding the interests of the minorities themselves but to preserve a cultural diversity that is of value to the whole community".[26]

Finally, it must be pointed out that the determination of further rights of minorities and their members—for example, on the use of the minority language in relations with public authorities, as well as on the preservation of their identity in the field of education (including the study of minority language and culture)[27]—or the effective application of these rights in concrete cases, may depend on various factors. Those include the number of members of minorities compared to the totality of the national population or the specific population of the places where the minorities reside, the historical origin of the settlement, their actual roots in the territory and their particular customs and traditions. Those factors may require a greater effort on the part of some territorial States to respect them. Consequently, the territorial State is not precluded from treating members of certain minority groups differently and more favourably, provided that this treatment is justified by objective reasons relating to a particular minority established at the national level.

13.4.2 Indigenous and Tribal Peoples

Turning now to examine the rules protecting indigenous peoples, it should be noted that they appear to be more limited than those concerning minorities. The reason for this is also practical, as indigenous peoples are mainly located in specific geographic areas. Therefore, it is logical that the constitutions of States with large and recognised indigenous populations, such as some States in South and Central America (Argentina, Bolivia and Brazil), are more generous in terms of protection.

Compared to minorities, the legal regime established in favour of indigenous peoples appears to be more oriented towards enhancing the collective profiles of the substantive and procedural rights at stake. This is due, on the one hand, to the tendency of indigenous peoples themselves to claim their rights in a predominantly collective form, for example with reference to the right of ownership of territories inhabited since time immemorial because "[t]he indigenous and tribal peoples have a community-based tradition relating to a communal form of collective land ownership; thus, land is not owned by the individual but by the group and its community".[28] On the other hand, of note is the greater propensity for some regional systems for the protection of human rights, in particular the American one,[29] to accommodate

[26] See para 60 of the judgment.

[27] See respectively Articles 10 and 12 of the Framework Convention of 1995.

[28] See IACtHR judgment of 8 October 2015 in *Garífuna Community of Triunfo de la Cruz and its Members v. Honduras*, para 100.

[29] See Chap. 4, Sect. 4.4.1.

claims from groups of individuals or NGOs representing indigenous peoples and their rights.

The most important universal legal instrument of a binding nature for the protection of indigenous peoples is the Indigenous and Tribal Peoples Convention of 27 June 1989, No. 169, which followed the Convention of 26 June 1957, both of which were developed within the framework of the ILO. In line with what has already been said with regard to minorities, the special legal regime on indigenous peoples is to be considered complementary to human rights law at large, which can therefore be applied to these groups of individuals. For this reason, Article 3(1) of the 1989 Convention states that "[i]ndigenous and tribal peoples shall enjoy the full measure of human rights and fundamental freedoms without hindrance or discrimination".

Also relevant, although non-binding, is the Declaration on the Rights of Indigenous Peoples, adopted on 13 September 2007 by the UNGA, which is widely referred to in the relevant practice on the subject. At the regional level, particularly in the OAS system, reference can be made to the American Declaration on the Rights of Indigenous Peoples of 15 June 2016.

The ILO Convention of 1989 distinguishes between tribal and indigenous peoples. The former are those "whose social, cultural and economic conditions distinguish them from other sections of the national community, and whose status is regulated wholly or partially by their own customs or traditions or by special laws or regulations". The latter are those "who are regarded as indigenous on account of their descent from the populations which inhabited the country, or a geographical region to which the country belongs, at the time of conquest or colonisation or the establishment of present State boundaries and who, irrespective of their legal status, retain some or all of their own social, economic, cultural and political institutions".[30]

Because of the objective difficulties in classifying an indigenous or tribal people, the Convention adopts the rather simplistic but difficult to replace principle of "self-identification", where identification is carried out by the peoples themselves.[31] It is clear that the process of self-identification is a necessary but not sufficient step to considering that a group of individuals can classify itself as an indigenous population since the territorial State is entitled to check, on the basis of the notion provided for in the 1989 Convention or in other legal instruments, including national ones, whether that status corresponds to the commonly accepted notion of indigenous or tribal people.

In regard to the identification of the concept of indigenous populations, the ACtHPRA, referring to many international sources and studies, considered that the relevant factors to take into account are "the presence of priority in time with respect to the occupation and use of a specific territory; a voluntary perpetuation of cultural distinctiveness, which may include aspects of language, social organisation, religion and spiritual values, modes of production, laws and institutions; self-identification as well as recognition by other groups, or by State authorities

[30] See Article 1(1) and (2) of the Convention.

[31] *Id.*, Article 1(3): "Self-identification as indigenous or tribal shall be regarded as a fundamental criterion for determining the groups to which the provisions of this Convention apply".

that they are a distinct collectivity; and an experience of subjugation, marginalisation, dispossession, exclusion or discrimination, whether or not these conditions persist".[32]

Indigenous peoples are granted the same rights as those already analysed with regard to minorities, such as the right to the protection of cultural identity, the effective respect of which implies the observance of the right of indigenous peoples to be consulted in decisions concerning them and which may affect their way of life and cultural traditions.[33] The right to enjoy their own culture implies respect for a number of other rights linked to it, such as the right of the indigenous population to raise animals according to their cultural tradition, as recently affirmed by the Supreme Court of Norway in *Statnett SF et al. v. Sør-Fosen Sijte and Others*, concerning the construction of a wind power plant in the territories inhabited by an indigenous people.[34] While balancing the right of the Sami population to practice their culture with the right to a good and healthy environment, the Court found a violation of Article 27 ICCPR, which recognises "the right [of persons belonging to ethnic, religious or linguistic minorities], in community with the other members of their group, to enjoy their own culture". According to the Court, the granting of licences for the construction of wind power plant interfered with the reindeer herders' right to enjoy their own culture, stating that there were other—and for the reindeer herders less intrusive—development alternatives and thus avoiding a collision between environmental interests and the reindeer herders' right to enjoy their own culture.[35]

Further rights of indigenous peoples are the right of access to education and, as far as possible, the right to use their indigenous language during schooling.[36] It should be noted that the correlated obligations of the territorial State appear greater when compared to those examined with reference to minorities, with the provision of a further series of positive obligations of a substantive and procedural nature aimed at making the protection of indigenous peoples more effective. From this point of view, it is established that "[s]pecial measures shall be adopted as appropriate for safeguarding the persons, institutions, property, labour, cultures and environment of the peoples concerned"[37] and that "[t]he social, cultural, religious and spiritual values

---

[32] See the judgment of 26 May 2017, *African Commission on Human and Peoples' Rights v. Republic of Kenya*, appl. no. 006/2012, para 107.

[33] See for instance HRC, *General Comment No. 23* of 8 April 1994 on Article 27 (Rights of Minorities), CCPR/C/21/Rev.1/Add.5, para 7, according to which "culture manifests itself in many forms, including a particular way of life associated with the use of land resources, especially in the case of indigenous peoples. That right may include such traditional activities as fishing or hunting and the right to live in reserves protected by law".

[34] See judgment of 11 October 2021.

[35] For a decision of similar content, but based exclusively on domestic law, see Kenyan Environment and Land Court (Meru), judgment of 19 October 2021, in *Mohamud Italrakwa Kochale et al. v. Lake Turkana Wind Power Ltd and Others*, which ruled that the title deeds of the land, on which the windmills necessary to develop a wind power farm were built, were unlawful.

[36] *Id.*, respectively Articles 5–6 and 26–28 of the 1989 Convention.

[37] *Id.*, Article 4(1).

and practices of these peoples shall be recognised and protected, and due account shall be taken of the nature of the problems which face them both as groups and as individuals".[38]

Of particular importance is the obligation to take into account, albeit within certain limits, the particular *modus vivendi* of indigenous peoples, including with regard to the criminal justice system for violations committed by their members, provided that it is compatible "with the national legal system and internationally recognised human rights".[39] This has led some States to adopt laws, or tolerate practices, which allow indigenous peoples to investigate and punish certain crimes, when committed among members of the indigenous population and occurring within specific parts of the national territory, sometimes referred to as 'indigenous reserves', which are regulated by a rudimentary legal system set up by the indigenous communities themselves. In this regard, there is no shortage of problematic cases of double jeopardy, within the framework of indigenous rules and State regulation,[40] which may envision different solutions depending on the autonomy granted to the indigenous legal system in the national one.

The Convention also dedicates numerous provisions to the protection of some specific rights of indigenous peoples, such as those over the land they inhabit,[41] non-discriminatory treatment in access to employment and regulation of the employment relationship—if necessary, again, through the adoption of "special measures"[42]—as well as rights in social security and health services[43] and in education.[44]

13.4.3 Indigenous Peoples, Use of Territory and Protection of the Environment

With regard to the effective protection of the rights of indigenous peoples, the right to ownership or exclusive use of a given territory is of great importance in view of the strictly functional link between the maintenance of the cultural and religious identity of indigenous communities and the territory they have inhabited since time immemorial. This connection was already highlighted in Article 13(1) of the 1989 Convention and has been extensively emphasised by the IACtHR, which has stressed

---

[38] *Id.*, Article 5(a).

[39] *Id.*, Article 9(1).

[40] A recent case of double jeopardy is currently before the US Supreme Court, in *Denezpi v. United States*, and concerns the possibility for a federal court to prosecute a Navajo citizen, already tried for the same conduct by the Ute Mountain Ute Tribe's Court of Indian Offenses which convicted him of the tribal-law offense of assault and battery, for the violation of the federal-law offence of aggravated sexual abuse.

[41] *Id.*, Articles 13–19.

[42] *Id.*, Article 20(1).

[43] *Id.*, Articles 24–25.

[44] *Id.*, Articles 26–31.

the religious and spiritual significance of the relationship between indigenous peoples and the lands they inhabit. For the Court, the relationship between indigenous peoples and their traditional lands can be expressed in different ways and "may include traditional use or presence, through spiritual or ceremonial ties; sporadic settlements or cultivation; traditional forms of subsistence such as seasonal or nomadic hunting, fishing or gathering; use of natural resources associated with their customs or other elements characteristic of their culture".[45]

Very recently and in a similar vein, the ACtHPRA stated that "the protection of rights to land and natural resources remains fundamental for the survival of indigenous peoples". At the same time, the Court stressed that "granting indigenous people privileges such as mere access to land is inadequate to protect their rights to land. What is required is to legally and securely recognise their collective title to the land in order to guarantee their permanent use and enjoyment of the same".[46]

National courts,[47] sometimes referring to international human rights norms and specific legal instruments for the protection of indigenous peoples, have in some cases upheld the validity of particular titles to property claimed by indigenous peoples. What is involved are not written titles, which indigenous peoples generally lack, but ones based on unwritten rules and on possession and use over time. Consequently, courts have sometimes not only awarded pecuniary compensation for unlawful conduct against the indigenous peoples but have also ordered the restitution of the lands permanently acquired or temporarily occupied by the national State through the well-known phenomenon of *land grabbing*, or by private entities like multinational corporations. The courts considered unlawful the economic exploitation activities carried out in these territories by national or foreign companies in flagrant violation of the substantive rights (right to property, right to life, right to food, right to water, etc.) and procedural rights of the indigenous peoples, like the latter's right to be involved in the decision-making processes carried out at the national level concerning the alienation or use of their territories.

The particular importance for indigenous peoples of the territories in which they live has been highlighted also in terms of environmental protection. In its judgment of 6 February 2020 in *Indigenous Communities of the Lhaka Honhat (Our Land) Association v. Argentina*, the IACtHR stressed the particular vulnerability of indigenous peoples "that, essentially, depend economically or for their survival on environmental resources [, such as] from the marine environment, forested areas and river basins. Hence, pursuant to human rights law, States are legally obliged to confront these

[45] Judgment of 27 June 2012 in *The Kichwa Indigenous People of Sarayaku v. Ecuador*, para 148 (see also para 212).

[46] See the judgment of 23 June 2022 (Reparations), *African Commission on Human and Peoples' Rights v. Republic of Kenya*, appl. no. 006/2012, paras 109–110.

[47] In national case law see the judgment of the Constitutional Court of South Africa of 15 October 2003, the order of the Supreme Court of Nigeria of 14 November 2004, the judgment of the Supreme Court of Botswana of 3 December 2006 and the judgment of the Supreme Court of Belize of 18 October 2007.

vulnerabilities based on the principle of equality and non-discrimination".[48] Similarly, the HRC in the views of 21 July 2022, in *Daniel Billy and Others v. Australia*, noted that for indigenous peoples "the enjoyment of culture may relate to a way of life which is closely associated with territory and the use of its resources, including such traditional activities as fishing or hunting", assessing the inadequacy of the national measures—also in terms of the delay in adopting such measures—designed to protect the indigenous population from the effects of climate change, and thus ascertaining the violation of Article 27 of the ICCPR.[49]

13.5 Multinational Corporations

Multinational corporations ("MNCs") are those entities that operate in several countries, usually through companies having a legal personality distinct from the parent company, but controlled by it in various ways and to different extents, generally on the basis of shareholder and/or management control, such as approval of the budget, appointment of directors, etc. For this reason, the parent company and the subsidiaries constitute a single entity in economic terms but generally not from a strictly legal standpoint.

At the national level, individual companies operating in the territory of a State are required to comply with the domestic law of that country. In the event of a breach of national rules by the subsidiary—and also by the parent company where it can be shown that it exercises particularly close control over the associated company—there may be either criminal or civil liability of the individuals who materially committed the harmful act, or of the company as a legal entity independent of natural persons. In the latter respect, while the criminal liability of a corporation has long been established in *common law* systems, in *civil law* systems it was considered that the criminal liability of a corporation conflicted with the principle of *societas delinquere non potest* and the related fundamental principle that criminal liability is personal. This restrictive approach is gradually being superseded in domestic law.

At the international level, the regulation of the activities of MNCs and their accountability is still at an embryonic stage of development. One of the most problematic aspects is the requirement, commonly felt at the international level, that the companies in question respect at least fundamental human rights. However, the efforts of the international community to force MNCs to adhere to these international standards have so far been rather disappointing.

In short, it can be said that the attempt to regulate the activities of MNCs has mainly taken the form of the adoption of various codes of conduct approved by several universal or regional international organisations, such as the 1992 Guidelines of the International Bank for Reconstruction and Development (World Bank), the 2000 Guidelines adopted by the Organisation for Economic Co-operation and

[48] See para 209 of the judgment.

[49] See CCPR/C/135/D/3624/2019, para 8.14.

Development, which have been progressively updated (the latest update was in 2011) and which provide for an, albeit weak, system of monitoring their application through the National Contact Points. Also worthy of note is the Tripartite Declaration of Principles concerning Multinational Enterprises and Social Policy adopted by the ILO in 1977, which has also been updated several times (most recently in 2017).

Further codes of conduct are the Norms on the Transnational Corporations and Other Business Enterprises with Regard to Human Rights, adopted in 2003 by the UN Sub-Commission on the Promotion and Protection of Human Rights, which provides for a series of legal obligations applicable in various regulatory areas (social security, protection of workers' health, environmental and consumer protection, etc.). Moreover, the Guiding Principles on Business and Human Rights adopted in 2011 by HRCoun, which consist of a set of guidelines for States and companies to prevent, address and remedy human rights abuses committed in business operations.

There are also initiatives by individual MNCs or by groups of them to adopt their own rules of conduct that respect human rights, or to voluntarily adhere to some legal rules and principles. One of the earliest examples of this, during the period of apartheid in South Africa, is the Sullivan Principles, which prohibit discriminatory conduct against black people in employment relationships. A special international initiative was the adoption of the UN Global Compact, launched in 1999, which created a worldwide network of States, international organisations, NGOs, MNCs and civil society representatives.

Some of the above-mentioned initiatives can be framed within the so-called corporate social responsibility, according to which especially large MNCs *self-limit* themselves, voluntarily adhering to virtuous practices and conduct in compliance with the essential principles of human rights protection.

These attempts to regulate the activities of MNCs have several shortcomings. The legal instruments are not compulsory and lack effective and independent control for monitoring adherence to the established rules, with actual compliance ultimately being left to the goodwill of the MNCs themselves.

13.5.1 US Case Law

Particularly relevant is the trend that emerged from US case law concerning the obligation of foreign MNCs to respect certain international human rights standards in the context of their activities abroad and to the extent that a connection with US territory could be discerned. The legal basis through which US civil jurisdiction over foreign MNCs has been established is the extraterritorial application of the Alien Tort Statute ("ATS"), concerning violations "of the law of nations or a treaty of the United States".

One of the best-known judgments in this regard is the decision of 18 September 2002 by the US Court of Appeals for the Ninth Circuit in *Doe v. Unocal Corporation et al.*, in which the Court asserted its jurisdiction to try the defendant companies for complicity in gross human rights violations—torture, rape, mass murder and forced labour—committed during the construction of an oil pipeline in Myanmar.

The judgment in question has been followed in subsequent US case law. In this regard, reference can be made to the judgment of 19 March 2003, adopted by the US District Court for the Southern District of New York in *The Presbyterian Church of Sudan v. Talisman Energy, Inc.* concerning the assertion of the jurisdiction of US courts over serious human rights violations committed by a Canadian multinational company against certain religious communities in Sudan, and the judgment of 30 January 2009 by the US Court of Appeals for the Second Circuit in *Abdullahi v Pfizer, Inc.* concerning the establishment of US jurisdiction to adjudicate on the responsibility of the pharmaceutical company for having tested an antibiotic against meningitis on hundreds of African children, without obtaining the informed consent of the parents and causing the death of several children.

This trend was reversed in the judgment of the Court of Appeals for the Second Circuit of 17 September 2010 in *Kiobel and Others v. Royal Dutch Petroleum Co et al.,* upheld by the US Supreme Court in its decision of 17 April 2013. In that latter decision, the Court stated that there was a presumption of "extraterritorial" inapplicability of the ATS, not only where the conduct adversely affecting foreign MNCs occurs exclusively outside the United States but also where the conduct in question "touches and concerns" US territory. In this last case, a connection of "sufficient force" with that territory must be established.

The principle of exclusion of US jurisdiction in similar cases has been confirmed in several decisions of the Supreme Court.[50] Most recently, in the judgment of 17 June 2021 in *Nestlé USA, Inc. v. Doe and Others,* concerning the alleged responsibility of Nestlé for having purchased, processed and sold cocoa derived from some farms in Ivory Coast. The owners of these farms, who received technical and financial resources from Nestlé in exchange for the exclusive right to purchase their cocoa, were accused of gross violations of human rights like kidnapping and child labour.

13.5.2 UK, Canadian and Dutch Case Law

In a departure from recent US case law, courts in other countries—Canada, the Netherlands and the United Kingdom—have lately held that they have jurisdiction to adjudicate on the liability of MNCs, particularly those headquartered in the said countries, for serious human rights violations committed by local companies operating abroad and controlled by their parent company. For example, in its judgment of 10 April 2019 in *Vedanta Resources PLC and Another v. Lungowe and Others*, the UK Supreme Court found that English jurisdiction existed in a case concerning serious

[50] See, for instance, the judgment of 24 April 2018, *Jesner and Others v. Arab Bank, Plc*, concerning the Jordanian Bank's alleged responsibility for the conduct of its agents for having used its New York branch for illegal financial transactions, including money laundering, which benefited Hamas, causing or facilitating its terrorist acts committed abroad.

environmental damage and violation of the right to health committed in Zambia by a local mining company controlled by its London-based parent company. The Court found that the operations of the local company had been carried out under the control of the parent company, which had not only drafted the environmental standards applicable to the subsidiary's activities, but also ensured their implementation at the local level by carrying out "training, monitoring and enforcement" activities.[51]

The Canadian Supreme Court, in its judgment of 28 February 2020 in *Nevsun Resources Ltd. v. Gize Yebeyo Araya and Others*, found that Canadian jurisdiction existed in relation to violations of the prohibitions on forced labour, slavery and inhuman or degrading treatment, respectively, invoked by a number of individuals who had been forced to work in Eritrea at a mine owned by a company majority-owned (60%) by the Canadian company Nevsun. Of particular importance are the Court's statements that, while some norms of customary international law "are of a strictly interstate character and will have no application to corporations", other norms prohibit certain conduct "regardless of whether the perpetrator is a State". It follows, in the Court's view, that it is by no means unequivocal that MNCs enjoy, in the current state of international law, a "blanket exclusion under customary international law from direct liability for violations of 'obligatory, definable, and universal norms of international law'",[52] as can be seen with regard to the rules of international law cited in the case at issue.

Likewise the Netherlands has witnessed a notable judgment on the merits against a multinational company in the judgment of 29 January 2021 issued by The Hague Court of Appeal in *Four Nigerian Farmers and Friends of the Earth v. Shell Petroleum.* In its decision the Court held that the parent company, Royal Dutch Shell, was liable for breach of the "duty of care" with regard to the serious economic and environmental damage caused by its subsidiary, Shell Petroleum Development Company, following the leakage of oil from several pipelines and an oil well in Nigeria.

13.5.3 MNCs and States' Responsibility

With regard to liability for harmful conduct engaged in by MNCs, the application of the legal regime of international State responsibility can also be explored. The liability of the national State of the parent company of an MNC—and, at least hypothetically, of the various national States of the associated companies having independent legal personality—as well as the liability of the territorial State in which the various companies operate may be established where these companies operate as *de jure* State bodies (think of influential MNCs controlled in whole or in part by

[51] See para 61 of the judgment. In a similar vein, see the most recent judgment of the Supreme Court of the United Kingdom of 12 February 2021, *Okpabi and Others v. Royal Dutch Shell Plc and Another*.

[52] See paras 105 and 113 of the judgment.

States)[53]—or *de facto* State bodies on the basis of the well-known criterion of natural or legal persons "acting on the instructions of, or under the direction or control" of a State.[54]

Moreover, it is arguable that both the national States of the MNCs and even more so the States in which they actually operate can be held responsible for not having prevented and repressed the harmful conduct of companies on the basis of the principle of due diligence. For national States, the application of the principle of due diligence seems to imply an obligation to regulate—also at the criminal law level—the conduct of companies operating abroad and therefore to demand compliance by these entities with both domestic rules and international rules protecting human rights applicable extraterritorially.

For States in whose territories MNCs operate, in addition to the principle of due diligence, the notion of jurisdiction established in human rights treaties may also apply,[55] with the effect that the territorial State is obliged to ensure compliance with human rights norms also covering violations committed at the inter-individual level by MNCs, as stated by the HRC in *General Comment No. 36* of 30 October 2018 on the right to life. For the HRC, "States parties must take appropriate measures to protect individuals against deprivation of life by ... foreign corporations operating within their territory or in other areas subject to their jurisdiction. They must also take appropriate legislative and other measures to ensure that all activities taking place in whole or in part within their territory and in other places subject to their jurisdiction, but having a direct and reasonably foreseeable impact on the right to life of individuals outside their territory, including activities undertaken by corporate entities based in their territory or subject to their jurisdiction, are consistent with article 6, taking due account of related international standards of corporate responsibility and of the right of victims to obtain an effective remedy".[56]

13.5.4 MNCs and Individual Criminal Responsibility

Finally, it is necessary to verify the application of the regime on international crimes to the perpetrators of serious violations of human rights committed through the work of MNCs. This form of liability exists both in the case of crimes committed by

[53] The problem in such cases is to verify what degree of State control is considered sufficient to trigger the application of the rules on state attribution of MNCs' conduct. In this respect, in our view it is necessary to verify not only the formal elements of State control, for example in terms of ownership of the company concerned, but also the actual impact of the state on the concrete choices made by the company.

[54] See Article 8 ARSIWA.

[55] On this notion, see Chap. 3, Sects. 3.6–3.6.3.

[56] See para 22. Positive signs in this direction come from recent national legislation (France in 2017 and Germany in 2021) which requires large companies operating on national territories to identify and prevent human rights violations and environmental damage in their operations, making companies liable if they fail to meet these obligations.

specific individuals and in the case of joint criminal enterprises through which a group of individuals, pursuing the same criminal design and using complex forms of cooperation, commits one or more international crimes.

International case law has long considered it to be legitimate to punish criminal conduct committed, including by legal persons, through the establishment of joint criminal enterprises, as already envisaged by the US Nuremberg Military Tribunals against some employees of German companies accused of participating in forced labour programmes and acts of dispossession of public and private property, as well as companies producing war material or chemicals used in concentration camps.

The specific hypotheses of joint criminal enterprises and the level of participation deemed necessary for the purposes of criminal responsibility were defined by the ICTY in the decision of 15 July 1999 adopted by the Appeals Chamber in *Prosecutor v. Duško Tadić*[57] and since implemented by other international criminal courts. In its judgment of 30 January 2015 in *Prosecutor v. Vujadin Popović, Beara, Nikolić, Miletić and Pandurević,* the ICTY (Appeals Chamber) further clarified the cases in which it is possible to establish participation in a joint criminal enterprise and thus convict its members, laying down the principle that it is not essential that the participants in the criminal association have materially taken part in the commission of international crimes, it being sufficient that they be part of the criminal enterprise and share the "common purposes".[58]

National case law also seems to be progressively accepting the possibility of establishing individual criminal responsibility for international crimes committed jointly by natural or legal persons. With regard to the complicity of a French multinational company (the company Lafarge, now LafargeHolcim) with certain terrorist organisations operating in Syria during the non-international armed conflict begun in 2011, the French Court of Cassation, in its judgment no. 868 of 7 September 2021, drew a distinction between complicity in common crimes and complicity in the commission of crimes against humanity, noting that for the latter it is sufficient: (a) for the accomplices to know of the harmful conduct engaged in by the main perpetrators; (b) the facilitation in terms of the preparation or material commission of the crimes, highlighting in this regard the seriousness of such acts and therefore the need to punish those responsible.[59]

Some recent statutes of courts operating at the international level establish jurisdiction over international crimes committed by legal persons. In this respect, reference may be made to the provision contained in the Protocol of 27 June 2014 on amendments to the ACtJHR Statute, not yet in force, which extends the jurisdiction of the Court to crimes committed by legal persons other than States, specifying that this form of criminal liability is additional and not alternative to that of natural persons who are the material perpetrators or accomplices of the same crimes.[60]

---

[57] See paras 185 ff. of the decision, IT-94-1-A.

[58] See IT-05-88, paras 805 ff.

[59] See paras 60 ff.

[60] See Article 46, subparagraph *C,* of the Protocol, in particular paras 1 and 6. On the statute of the ACtJHR, see Chap. 4, Sect. 4.4.2.

Confirming the tendency to verify the criminal liability of legal entities before international courts, one may cite the position taken by the Appeals Panel of the Special Tribunal for Lebanon ("STL") in its decision of 2 October 2014 in the case of *Prosecutor v. New TV S.A.L. Karma Mohamed Tahsin Al Khayat*. On the basis of an extensive interpretation of the rules of the Statute and the Rules of Procedure and Evidence and also referring to legislative and case law developments on the subject of the criminal liability of legal entities, the Tribunal stated that the notion of "person" relevant for the purposes of establishing the conduct of contempt and obstruction of justice includes both natural persons and legal persons.[61]

13.6 Non-governmental Organisations

Although they do not have international legal personality, NGOs play a particularly active role in various sectors of international law. Those operating in the field of human rights must be recognised as performing a key function. They play an important role in the drafting of international norms or the amendment of existing ones by *persuading*, sometimes very effectively, States and international organisations—where they sometimes have observer status, which allows them to take part, albeit in a limited way, in the activities of the organisations. For example, by participating in intergovernmental conferences, where they can often make oral or written submissions regarding their positions on the issues being discussed.

However, the most significant function performed by NGOs in the human rights framework relates to reporting on State activities deemed to constitute serious human rights violations. These complaints can be of an *isolated* nature concerning individual violations or of a *systematic* nature concerning a series of violations of different human rights. In the latter case, there is no shortage of annual and general reports on the overall state of human rights by the best-known and most structured human rights NGOs like Amnesty International, Human Rights Watch, etc. There are also numerous reports on the overall state of observance of human rights in a given country, which, on the one hand, have a significant informative value, and, on the other hand, are of practical use as they are sometimes referred to in judicial proceedings in order to strengthen the arguments of the bodies charged with scrutinising the observance of human rights treaties by States.

In addition, in certain treaty-based human rights systems, NGOs play an important role in monitoring compliance with conventional rights. From this point of view, some such systems grant NGOs—both on the basis of the *substantive* law of the legal systems involved and the *procedural* rules of the bodies established to scrutinise compliance—the right to intervene in court, even in the advanced stages of judicial

[61] See the *Decision on Interlocutory Appeal Concerning Personal Jurisdiction in Contempt Proceedings*, STL-14-05/PT/AP/ARI26.1, paras 31 ff.

proceedings[62] or the more limited role of *amicus curiae*. That is in order to acquire from NGOs information and elements useful for the resolution of disputes submitted to the aforementioned bodies, without however the possibility for an NGO to be a party to the disputes.

In certain treaty-based systems, NGOs are also recognised as having genuine *locus standi*, allowing them, under certain conditions, to bring actions on behalf of interests or rights of a collective nature. In this regard, reference has already been made to the litigation procedure relating to the ACtHPRA.[63] The right to bring actions before the ACtHPRA is granted to NGOs considered particularly qualified and having consultative status before the ACommHPR, provided that the respondent State has made a prior declaration of acceptance of the Court's jurisdiction to receive such applications.[64] It should be noted that the standing of NGOs "accredited to the African Union or to its organs" has been confirmed by the Protocol of 1 July 2008 establishing the Statute of the ACtJHR, which has not yet entered into force.[65]

NGOs perform a similar function within the framework of the collective complaints system established by the ESC, which, although not resulting in binding decisions, does confer to NGOs with consultative status at the CoE the right to lodge a complaint with the ECSR against a Contracting Party concerning non-compliance with the rules of the ESC.[66]

Comprehension Check and Tasks

1. Why is the connection between indigenous peoples and the lands that they have inhabited from time immemorial so important for them? (Sect. 13.4.3)
2. Are MNCs obliged to respect international human rights law and on what legal basis? (Sect. 13.5)
3. What legal developments can one discern from Canadian, Dutch and English case law? (Sect. 13.5.2)
4. The norms on the international responsibility of States are relevant in order to assess States' responsibility for the conduct of MNCs. Focus on the main legal problems concerning this issue. (Sect. 13.5.3)

---

62 Article 61(1) of the Rules of Court of the ACtHPRA, in the latest version approved on 1 September 2020, provides that "under exceptional circumstances, the Court may grant leave for an Application for intervention to be filed after the close of pleadings".

63 See Chap. 4, Sect. 4.4.2.

64 See respectively Article 5(3) and Article 34(6) of the 1998 Protocol establishing the ACtHPRA.

65 See Article 30, subparagraph f.

66 On the competences of the ECSR, see Chap. 11, Sect. 11.2.

Chapter 14
International Responsibility of States for Violations of Human Rights

Contents

Abstract The chapter analyses the legal regime and the most relevant issues regarding state responsibility for violation of human rights. Firstly, it examines the significant impact of human rights law and practice on the law of state responsibility and, in particular, on responsibility for serious breaches of peremptory norms. By examining numerous cases, including the most recent ones, the chapter discusses a number of relevant issues, including the possibility for States not directly affected by serious violations of human rights to adopt countermeasures against the responsible State, as well as the doctrines of humanitarian intervention and responsibility to protect.

14.1 *Erga Omnes* Nature of International Obligations on Human Rights and Effects on State Responsibility

The regime of State responsibility for violations of human rights is conditioned by the particular nature of obligations in this area of international law and by the specific object and purpose of both primary human rights norms and secondary norms on international responsibility.

It should first be noted that the *disruptive* force of human rights law and practice has been amply confirmed in the general framework of the international responsibility of the State. Indeed, the current regime of international responsibility of the State, thus

P. Pustorino, *Introduction to International Human Rights Law*,
https://doi.org/10.1007/978-94-6265-563-8_14

applicable to any violation of international obligations, is significantly affected by developments in the framework of human rights protection. This impact, as also noted in other parts of this work, has not however radically or *revolutionarily* transformed the structure and particular features of the international legal system. Rather, it has integrated itself into that system and has modified some significant aspects of it.

This is reflected, for example, in the fact that, in matters of State responsibility for violations of human rights, the element of damage to other States is often absent since the violation is generally committed against nationals of the offending State. This specific feature of the human rights regime has influenced the entire body of rules concerning State responsibility, resulting in the elimination of harm of an inter-State nature, at least from the *formal* standpoint of the constituent elements of the international wrongdoing. In *practice*, the damage caused is still very relevant to the issue of reparations for the violation committed.

The view that the effective addressees of human rights norms are individuals is also well established. This particular aspect was discussed in the previous chapters in relation to the issue of the international legal personality of individuals.[1] Consequently, while international norms generally protect State interests and thus imply a reciprocity in terms of rights and obligations between States, human rights law seeks to protect absolute and universally recognised international values thereby entailing obligations *erga omnes*. That is, obligations undertaken by a given State vis-à-vis the entire international community or a plurality of specifically identified States, e.g. States parties to an international convention (so-called obligations *erga omnes partes*).

As indicated by the ICJ in its advisory opinion of 28 May 1951 on *Reservations to the Convention on the Prevention and Punishment of the Crime of Genocide*, the 1948 Convention "was manifestly adopted for a purely humanitarian and civilizing purpose". For that reason, the Court observed that "[i]n such a convention the contracting States do not have any interests of their own; they merely have, one and all, a common interest, namely, the accomplishment of those high purposes which are the *raison d'être* of the convention". It follows, according to the Court's reasoning, that "in a convention of this type one cannot speak of individual advantages or disadvantages to States, or of the maintenance of a perfect contractual balance between rights and duties".[2]

More specifically, the ICJ itself, in its judgment of 5 February 1970 in *Barcelona Traction, Light and Power Company, Limited*, stated that *erga omnes* obligations "are the concern of all States" and, from the point of view of their legal basis, specified that some of these obligations are contained in rules of general international law—and today, we might add, in rules of *jus cogens*[3]—while other *erga omnes* obligations are contemplated in treaty provisions.[4]

---

[1] See Chap. 13, Sect. 13.3.

[2] In ICJ 1951, p. 23.

[3] On peremptory rules, see Chap. 3, Sect. 3.1.

[4] See (New Application: 1962) *Belgium v. Spain*, second phase, in ICJ 1970, p. 32, paras 33–34.

The approach followed by the ICJ regarding the non-reciprocal nature of obligations contained in human rights treaties is widely shared by the bodies in charge of scrutinising the observance of individual and collective rights protected in universal and regional conventions. For example, the HRC has pointed out, when assessing objections to reservations made to the ICCPR and its additional protocols, that human rights treaties "are not a web of inter-State exchanges of mutual obligations. They concern the endowment of individuals with rights. The principle of inter-State reciprocity has no place".[5]

14.2 *Aggravated* State Responsibility for Violations of Peremptory Norms

Violations of international norms that impose obligations *erga omnes* imply a regime of *aggravated* responsibility at an international level, which is reflected in the ARSIWA.

The system of aggravated responsibility has to do, first of all, with the States that may invoke the violation of rules imposing obligations *erga omnes*. According to customary international law, any State—not just the injured State—is entitled to invoke the responsibility of another State.[6] In the case of treaty rules, the violation may be invoked by all the parties to the treaty.[7]

In addition, the rules on aggravated responsibility also impact on the consequences of violations of *erga omnes* obligations. From this point of view, the ARSIWA provide that, respectively, all States of the international community or States parties to specific treaties (such as human rights treaties)—depending on the customary or conventional character of the norm containing *erga omnes* obligations—may request from the responsible State the cessation of the internationally wrongful act as well as assurances and guarantees of non-repetition.[8]

The same rule contained in the ARSIWA provides that *omnes* may also request that the responsible State perform the obligation of reparation "in the interest of the injured State or of the beneficiaries of the obligation breached". Reparation may thus be sought by a State not specially affected in favour of another State, e.g. the State specially affected, or, more likely, in favour of the injured individuals. However, it must be conceded that there is a dearth of State practice in this area.

One of the most significant consequences of the violation of *erga omnes partes* obligations lies in the possibility for any contracting party to invoke the responsibility of a State party to the treaty for the violation of the provisions at issue. In this sense, some human rights treaties provide, as we have seen in several parts of this work, for inter-State redress mechanisms irrespective of the existence of a specific interest of

[5] See *General Comment No. 24* of 4 November 1994, para 17.

[6] See ARSIWA, Article 48(1)(b).

[7] *Id.*, Article 48(1)(a).

[8] *Id.*, Article 48(2)(a) and (b).

the claimant State in invoking the violation, for example, the violation of the rights of the claimant State's nationals and the consequent occurrence also of damage of an inter-State nature.

In addition, Article 41 ARSIWA provides that, in the case of a serious violation of peremptory rules of international law, which consist of a narrow category of rules providing for obligations *erga omnes*, States shall not recognise as lawful a situation created by a serious breach of a peremptory norm nor render aid or assistance in maintaining that situation.

It should be pointed out that the question of the violation of *erga omnes* obligations is without prejudice to the *consensual* principle, which applies to the submission of a dispute to an arbitral or judicial body and which consists in the acceptance, by the parties to the dispute, of the jurisdiction of the adjudicatory body to settle that dispute. This position seems to be consistent with the different nature of the international rules that come into play in the context of this issue. The rules containing obligations *erga omnes* are substantive in nature whereas those concerning jurisdiction are procedural. However, on the basis of an extensive interpretation of the conventional regime on *erga omnes* obligations, there seems to be a consolidated tendency in practice to allow *omnes partes* to apply to international courts on the basis of rather general jurisdiction clauses, mainly concerning disputes arising from the interpretation and application of human rights conventions.

The above-mentioned approach, which is to be welcomed as it contributes to the judicial scrutiny of violations of obligations *erga omnes*, was applied by the ICJ in its judgment of 20 July 2012 in *Questions relating to the Obligation to Prosecute or Extradite*, with reference to the jurisdiction clause contained in Article 30(1) of the UN Convention against Torture and Other Cruel, Inhuman or Degrading Treatment or Punishment of 1984. According to the Court, States parties "have a common interest to ensure, in view of their shared values, which acts of torture are prevented and that, if they occur, their authors do not enjoy impunity". This implies not only that "the obligations in question are owed by any State party to all the other States parties to the Convention", but also "the entitlement of each State party to the Convention to make a claim concerning the cessation of an alleged breach by another State party".[9]

The possibility for a State party to bring an action against another State party considered responsible for the violation of *erga omnes partes* obligations also exists where, in the same case, there are States specially affected by such violations. For example, the national States of individuals who are victims of the violation or States directly affected by violations perpetrated by a State. The question has recently arisen with regard to the mass exodus to Bangladesh of individuals belonging to the Rohingya minority persecuted in Myanmar on ethnic and religious grounds. In this regard, the principle of dual standing to bring legal action invoking the violation of obligations *erga omnes partes*—by the specially affected State and by the other

[9] The Court has added that "[i]f a special interest were required for that purpose, in many cases no State would be in the position to make such a claim. It follows that any State party to the Convention may invoke the responsibility of another State party with a view to ascertaining the alleged failure to comply with its obligations *erga omnes partes* ... and to bring that failure to an end": see *Belgium v. Senegal*, in ICJ 2012, pp. 449–450, paras 68–69.

States parties to the Convention in question—was affirmed by the ICJ in its order of 23 January 2020 in *Application of the Convention on the Prevention and Punishment of the Crime of Genocide*[10] concerning the alleged commission of acts of genocide by Myanmar against the Rohingya minority.

14.3 Developments Regarding the Individual Right to Reparation for Serious Violations of Human Rights

It is questionable whether individuals, in terms of general international law—and therefore outside of specific legal systems stemming from a treaty that provides for individual redress mechanisms—can invoke State responsibility for human rights violations and seek redress for the harm suffered.

In any case, there is a tendency, that is gradually becoming established in practice, to contemplate the right in question, but limited to gross violations of human rights and international humanitarian law, where, in the latter case, international crimes are committed. Indicative in this regard is the UNGA resolution of 16 December 2005 on the Basic Principles and Guidelines on the Right to a Remedy and Reparation for Victims of Gross Violations of International Human Rights Law and Serious Violations of International Humanitarian Law. The non-binding resolution refers to the numerous conventions on human rights and international humanitarian law that expressly provide for this right and recommends that States respect these norms and transpose them into national law. More specifically, the resolution recalls a number of positive obligations of States, such as "to take appropriate legislative and administrative and other appropriate measures to prevent violations", to investigate "violations effectively, promptly, thoroughly and impartially", to provide "those who claim to be victims of a human rights or humanitarian law violation with equal and effective access to justice" and also to provide "effective remedies to victims, including reparation".[11]

Furthermore, the resolution provides that, in cases of gross violations of international human rights law and serious violations of international humanitarian law constituting international crimes, States "have the duty to investigate and, if there is sufficient evidence, the duty to submit to prosecution the person allegedly responsible for the violations and, if found guilty, the duty to punish her or him", and to this end "where so provided in an applicable treaty or under other international law obligations, States shall incorporate or otherwise implement within their domestic

[10] See *Gambia v. Myanmar*, para 41. It should be noted that Bangladesh could not bring the case before the ICJ in this instance because at the time of ratification of the Genocide Convention it had adopted the following declaration to the jurisdiction clause contained in Article IX: "For the submission of any dispute in terms of this article to the jurisdiction of the International Court of Justice, the consent of all parties to the dispute will be required in each case". Myanmar had obviously not expressed its specific consent to the submission of the dispute to the ICJ by Bangladesh.

[11] Para 3 (a–d).

law appropriate provisions for universal jurisdiction".[12] States are therefore invited to provide the right to an equal access to an effective judicial remedy for the victims of a gross violation of international human rights law or of international humanitarian law in order to obtain and "adequate, effective and prompt reparation".[13]

Again in the realm of soft law, mention should be made of the resolution of 30 August 2015 adopted by the Institut de droit international at the Tallinn session on "Universal Civil Jurisdiction with Regard to Reparation for International Crimes". It envisages that victims of international crimes have the right "to an effective access to justice to claim reparation" and the linked right "to appropriate and effective reparation from persons liable for the injury". With regard to which State enjoys jurisdiction, it indicates that a court should exercise jurisdiction over claims for reparation by victims of international crimes provided that "no other State has stronger connections with the claim, taking into account the connection with the victims and the defendants and the relevant facts and circumstances", unless the victims do not have available remedies in the courts of States with stronger connections.[14]

Of more significance on the subject of the progressive affirmation of the individual right to reparation for serious human rights violations is some case law. The right in question was recognised by the ECtHR (Grand Chamber) in the previously mentioned judgment of 15 March 2018 in *Naït-Liman v. Switzerland*[15] on the subject of access to the courts of a State party to the ECHR for the purpose of seeking reparation for the violation of the prohibition of torture committed by organs of foreign States abroad.[16] In the judgment, it is stated that the right of victims of acts of torture to obtain redress and to fair and adequate compensation "is firmly embedded, as such, in general international law".[17]

Lastly, in our opinion, it must be ruled out that there are other *special* consequences of committing human rights offences. However, this does not detract from the fact that some of the consequences of internationally wrongful acts are invoked and applied especially in matters of human rights violations: for example, the appropriate assurances and guarantees of non-repetition of unlawful acts, which, although provided

---

[12] *Id.*, paras 4–5.

[13] *Id.*, paras 12–15.

[14] See Articles 1(1), 1(2) and 2(1) of the resolution. It also indicates, on the one hand, that "courts shall be considered to provide an available remedy if ... they are capable of dealing with the claim in compliance with the requirements of due process and of providing remedies that afford appropriate and effective redress"; on the other hand, that "[t]he court where claims for relief by victims have been brought should decline to entertain the claims or suspend the proceedings ... when the victims' claims have also been brought before: a) an international jurisdiction, such as the International Criminal Court; b) an authority for conciliation or indemnification established under international law; or c) the court of another State having stronger connections and available remedies within the meaning of the foregoing paragraphs": Article 2(2) and (3).

[15] Appl. no. 51357/07.

[16] See Chap. 7, Sect. 7.6.2.

[17] See para 108 of the judgment.

for by the ARSIWA,[18] are of limited foundation in practice. Worthy of mention in this regard are human rights violations resulting from the existence of systemic and structural problems in the national legal systems of the ECHR Contracting Parties, which leads to the indication by the ECtHR of general measures that the State responsible is obliged to apply in order not to repeat certain harmful conduct and to solve the structural problem ascertained by the Court.[19]

14.4 Individual and Collective Countermeasures for Serious Violations of Human Rights

In the event of a breach of *erga omnes* obligations by a State, it is undisputed that the State specially affected by the breach may adopt non-forcible countermeasures against the infringing State. On the other hand, the possibility for States not specially affected by the violation of an *erga omnes* obligation to adopt countermeasures against the State responsible is much more doubtful. In fact, if the option of resorting to measures implying the use of force against the State responsible for such violations can definitely be ruled out in that it would contrast with the *jus cogens* principle that prohibits the use of force in international relations, the issue of the option of adopting non-forcible countermeasures, for example of an economic nature, is more problematic.

This course of action is ruled out by the ARSIWA. However, some legal scholars believe that the recourse to non-forcible countermeasures by States not specially affected by violations of obligations *erga omnes* is an option. In support of that view one can cite the resolution of 27 August 2005 approved by the Institut de droit international at the Krakow session on "Obligations and rights erga omnes in international law", which specifies that, in case of "a widely acknowledged grave breach of an obligation *erga omnes*", all the States to which the obligation is owed "are entitled to take non-forcible counter-measures under conditions analogous to those applying to a State specially affected by the breach".[20]

On this point, it should be noted that current practice in this field appears to be rather limited and mainly concerns sanctions adopted by the UNSC already discussed above[21] and less so unilateral sanctions adopted by States. In this respect, it should be noted that in some cases, for example in relation to the Libyan crisis, the economic sanctions adopted by the UNSC against the Gaddafi regime followed in the wake of and complemented unilateral sanctions imposed by some Western States.

---

[18] See Article 30(b) ARSIWA, which indicates that such assurances and guarantees of non-repetition must be provided by the responsible State "if circumstances so require".

[19] See Chap. 4, Sect. 4.3.1.

[20] See Article 5(1)(c) of the resolution.

[21] See Chap. 5, Sect. 5.4.

A similar attitude, consisting of both economic embargoes and targeted sanctions against members of the ruling government regime, has been adopted by some States against countries which, although responsible for serious human rights violations, have not been subject to sanctions by the UNSC due to the exercise of the right of veto by the former Soviet Union in particular, and later by Russia or the United States.

This has been the case recently with regard to the very serious human rights violations committed by the Syrian regime during the international and non-international armed conflict in the country, which have resulted in sanctions by States and international organisations, including the EU.

In addition, unilateral sanctions have been adopted by several countries (Canada, Mexico, Panama, the United States and Switzerland) against members of the Venezuelan government and the State as a whole since 2015, especially in the period 2018–2020, in relation to serious violations of human rights and the principle of democracy (the latter with reference to the blatant irregularities observed in the 2018 general elections), for the specific purpose of hindering the sale of oil and the transfer of funds in favour of the ruling government.

More recently, between 2020 and 2021, the EU adopted sanctions against the Belarusian government and individuals with high political or military responsibility for numerous human rights violations, including the failure of President Lukashenko's regime to respect the right to hold free and fair elections. On 2 December 2021 the Council of the EU adopted the fifth package of sanctions over continued human rights abuses and the instrumentalisation of migrants, targeting members of the judicial branch, high-ranking political officials of the Lukashenko regime, as well as companies (such as Belavia Airlines), and other entities that have helped incite and organise illegal border crossings through Belarus to the EU.[22]

Even more recent and robust economic and financial sanctions have been adopted by several Western States and international organisations against Russia and Belarus for the aggression against Ukraine on 24 February 2022, which also caused very serious violations of human rights and international humanitarian law, including international crimes.

Going back in time, the "Siberian gas pipeline" case is another well-known instance of sanctions adopted by States not directly affected by serious human rights violations. In that case unilateral economic sanctions consisting of embargoes on certain high-technology products and measures to suspend certain international agreements were adopted following the establishment of a state of siege and the imposition of martial law in Poland in 1981, for which Western States held the former Soviet Union primarily responsible in view of the significant Soviet interference with the decisions of the Polish authorities. Economic sanctions were also imposed by some Western States in the late 1990s against the military junta in Myanmar on the

[22] Similarly, the OAS took measures against Venezuela itself and against Nicaragua at the end of 2021, due to the serious violations of human rights and the principle of representative democracy by the regime in power.

grounds of violations of numerous human rights, such as the prohibition of forced or compulsory labour.

Also relevant on the subject of reactions to serious violations of human rights is the practice of other international organisations of a regional nature adopted on foot of their respective statutes, albeit sometimes interpreted broadly, but not on the basis of general international law. In this regard, reference can be made above all to the practice of several regional organisations operating in the African region—in particular the African Union under Article 30 of the Constitutive Act of the AU[23]—of suspending membership due to the overthrow of government and the consequent violation of numerous human rights of the civilian population.

Very recently, Russia's aggression against Ukraine led to the former's suspension from the CoE and, shortly thereafter, to its expulsion.[24]

In view of both the limited practice examined above and the fact that most of the non-forcible countermeasures taken against States responsible for serious violations of human rights have been applied in the framework of special systems of a conventional nature, thus outside the scope of general international law, in the current state of international law there is arguably no *obligation* for States not specially affected to adopt non-forcible countermeasures. That said, it is arguable that States have the *option* to adopt such countermeasures, provided that the State responsible has committed very serious human rights violations in breach of peremptory norms of international law.

14.5 Humanitarian Intervention and Responsibility to Protect

Finally, it must be examined whether recourse to humanitarian intervention is admissible in international law as a further exception to the prohibition of the use of force, in addition to the *traditional* exceptions of self-defence and the use of force authorised by the UNSC. Recently, the notion of humanitarian intervention has been flanked by the doctrine of responsibility to protect.

Humanitarian intervention is defined as action taken by one or more States in a foreign territory to protect the entire civilian population, or a territorially, ethnically or religiously defined part thereof, following serious violations of human rights and the commission of international crimes, including the crime of genocide, by the government in power. It is clear that the use of humanitarian intervention implies, under certain conditions, the use of force by the intervening States.

---

[23] "Governments which shall come to power through unconstitutional means shall not be allowed to participate in the activities of the Union".

[24] See Resolution CM/Res(2022)2 on the Cessation of the Membership of the Russian Federation to the Council of Europe adopted by the CMCoE on 16 March 2022, according to which it was decided "in the context of the procedure launched under Article 8 of the Statute of the Council of Europe, that the Russian Federation ceases to be a member of the Council of Europe as from 16 March 2022".

The literature advocating the existence of a customary norm (already formed or in the process of being formed, depending on the various scholarly views expressed) envisaging recourse to humanitarian intervention tends to significantly limit the scenario of the use of force, considering it to be the *last resort* in the event of failure of measures not involving the use of force and only in the wake of very serious violations of human rights, as happened in the case of Kosovo discussed below.

In some regional systems, particularly in the AU framework, there are specific provisions that can be used to support the doctrine of humanitarian intervention. More specifically, in the Protocol adopted on 9 July 2002 and relative to the Establishment of the Peace and Security Council of the African Union, it is stated "the right of the Union to intervene in a Member State pursuant to a decision of the Assembly in respect of grave circumstances, namely war crimes, genocide and crimes against humanity, in accordance with Article 4(h) of the Constitutive Act".[25] However, this is a case provided for in a specific treaty-based system.

In quite recent times the most significant armed intervention, justified both by some Western States and by NATO on the basis of the doctrine of humanitarian intervention, is that of the massive aerial bombardment carried out in 1999 against Serbia and motivated by the serious human rights violations committed by the Serbian regime against the Kosovar population of Albanian origin.

On that occasion the UK government defined the content and limits of the humanitarian intervention also in relation to possible subsequent actions. This position was then reiterated with reference to the limited military intervention regarding Syria conducted in 2018 by the UK, together with France and the US, and motivated by the alleged use of chemical weapons by the Assad regime against the civilian population considered contiguous to the positions of the Syrian insurgents.

The conditions which, according to the position of the UK, justify the use of force "on an exceptional basis" as a humanitarian intervention and in order "to alleviate overwhelming humanitarian suffering" are: (i) convincing evidence, generally accepted by the international community as a whole, of extreme humanitarian distress on a large scale, requiring immediate and urgent relief; (ii) it must be objectively clear that there is no practicable alternative to the use of force if lives are to be saved; and (iii) the proposed use of force must be necessary and proportionate to the aim of relief of humanitarian suffering and must be strictly limited in time and in scope to this aim.

These conditions are cumulative in nature and hence must all be fully met both at the time of the decision to intervene and during the military operation. As mentioned above they were reiterated in relation to the aerial bombardment conducted in 2018 against the Syrian regime by the UK, in coordination with France and the US. However, these two countries also invoked other more vague and generic grounds of justification, such as the protection of national security, the need to prevent the spread and future use of chemical weapons—this specific basis was also cited by the UK with regard to its own intervention—or the need to respond with appropriate force to the use of chemical weapons against the civilian population. This specific

[25] See Article 4, subparagraph j.

justification would seem to refer to the notion of forcible counter-measure or armed retaliation, which, as mentioned in the previous section hereof, are prohibited under international law.

Leaving aside the shaky foundations of the doctrine of humanitarian intervention in the international legal order, with regard to the 2018 intervention and despite the assurances of the UK government that the conditions for recourse to humanitarian intervention were met, it is arguable that the conditions in question were not actually fulfilled at all. This is because, confining ourselves to examining just one of the conditions set by the British government, the targeted and brief intervention did not produce—and in fact has not since produced—any benefit for the civilian population. On the contrary, it only worsened its general plight.

A certain openness in favour of humanitarian intervention, but within the scope of the UNSC's competence, can be seen in the final report of 2 December 2004 adopted by the High Level Panel on Threats, Challenges and Change set up by the UN Secretary General to reform the UN Charter, a reform that never took place. In that report the existence of an "emerging norm" is identified that would allow the UNSC—and only it—to authorise "military intervention as a last resort in the event of genocide and other large-scale killing, ethnic cleansing or serious violations of international humanitarian law which sovereign Governments have proved powerless or unwilling to prevent".[26]

In light of the above, it must be conceded that there is no general practice and *opinio juris ac necessitatis* of the international community as a whole underpinning humanitarian intervention given that any such move is based exclusively on special treaty-based systems and on some declarations or concrete actions carried out by a few Western States, which often take different positions in relation to both the notion of humanitarian intervention accepted by them and the ways in which that action is undertaken. As a result, humanitarian intervention still remains contrary to the principle prohibiting the use of force and the principle of non-intervention in the internal affairs of a State.

A clear position against the possibility of humanitarian intervention was taken by the Group of 77 (bringing together more than 130 States) in the 2000 Declaration of the South Summit, which states that "[w]e reject the so-called 'right' of humanitarian intervention, which has no legal basis in the United Nations Charter or in the general principles of international law".[27]

The responsibility to protect is a broader but much vaguer concept than humanitarian intervention. That said, the precondition for reliance on the responsibility to protect is the same as for humanitarian intervention: serious violations of human rights and international humanitarian law against the civilian population.

However, the responsibility to protect does not necessarily imply the use of force but is based, first and foremost, on the principle that the primary responsibility to protect civilians from massive human rights violations rests with the State exercising sovereignty. As much was stated by the UNSC during the armed conflict in Libya,

[26] See UNGA A/59/565, para 203.

[27] See para 54 of the Declaration adopted at the Summit of 10–14 April 2000.

where, in the preamble of its Resolution No. 1970 of 26 February 2011, it referred to "the Libyan authorities' responsibility to protect its population". However, in the preamble of the subsequent Resolution No. 1973 of 17 March 2011, it added that all parties to the armed conflict "bear the primary responsibility to take all feasible steps to ensure the protection of civilians". The reference to the UNSC's responsibility to protect is repeated in subsequent resolutions concerning situations of armed conflict or serious disturbances occurring in a country, such as the one in the Democratic Republic of the Congo.[28]

Secondly, in the event of a breach of the territorial State's obligation to protect its civilian population, the responsibility to protect provides for recourse to diplomatic means to protect the population threatened by such harmful conduct.

Thirdly, the use of force is envisaged but must be authorised by the UNSC on the basis of Chapter VII of the UN Charter. These gradual steps are, for example, contemplated in the most significant document on the responsibility to protect, which *crystallises* its content and limits of application: the resolution approved by the Heads of State and Government participating in the World Summit Outcome, held in New York in 2005, which devotes a specific part to the responsibility to protect.[29]

In our view, the responsibility to protect, on the one hand, does not add anything to the international obligations already incumbent on States, e.g. the obligation to protect their population in times of peace as well as in times of war, i.e. during international or non-international armed conflicts. On the other hand, one cannot rule out that the doctrine of the responsibility to protect may even end up *harming* the very notion of humanitarian intervention, which, although not provided for in international law, is nevertheless reflected, as noted, in some limited elements of practice. In fact, it could well be that a doctrine as broad and general as that relating to the responsibility to protect, which in any case does not exclude recourse to the use of force, could end up *watering down* the notion of humanitarian intervention, making its possible but not currently foreseeable establishment at the international level more problematic.

As for the relationship between the responsibility to protect and the UNSC, the impression is that when the Council decided to refer, explicitly or implicitly, to this doctrine, it did so *ad abundantiam* and not as a definite and exclusive basis for its action. In fact, the UNSC acts on the basis of the UN Charter, which gives it a wide margin of discretion in the exercise of its functions and in applying the rules of the Charter. It certainly does not need to justify its decisions on foot of a doctrine of doubtful validity in international law.

[28] See preamble to Resolution No. 409 of 27 March 2018.

[29] See A/RES/60/1.

Comprehension Check and Tasks

1. What is the general impact of human rights law on the rules governing the international responsibility of States? (Sect. 14.1)
2. What is meant by the *erga omnes* character of human rights obligations and what is the difference between *erga omnes* obligations grounded in international customary law and in treaties? (Sects. 14.1–14.2)
3. Focus on *aggravated* State responsibility for violations of peremptory rules on human rights. (Sect. 14.2)
4. On the basis of customary international law, can States not specially affected by serious violations of human rights adopt countermeasures? (Sect. 14.4)
5. Focus on the notion of humanitarian intervention and take a position on its validity under international law. (Sect. 14.5)

References

ICJ (1951) Advisory opinion of 28 May 1951 on Reservations to the Convention on the Prevention and Punishment of the Crime of Genocide. ICJ Reports

ICJ (1970) Belgium v. Spain, second phase. ICJ Reports

ICJ (2012) Judgment of 20 July 2012 in Questions relating to the Obligation to Prosecute or Extradite. ICJ Reports

Table of Cases and Table of UN Treaty Bodies' Comments and Decisions

Table of Cases

Permanent Court of International Justice (PCIJ):

- *Mavrommatis Palestine Concessions, Greece v. United Kingdom*, Judgment of 30 August 1924
- *Nationality Decrees Issued in Tunis and Morocco*, Advisory Opinion of 7 February 1923

International Court of Justice (ICJ):

- *Accordance with International Law of the Unilateral Declaration of Independence in Respect of Kosovo*, Advisory Opinion of 22 July 2010
- *Application of the Convention on the Prevention and Punishment of the Crime of Genocide* (*Bosnia and Herzegovina v. Serbia and Montenegro*), Judgment of 26 February 2007
- *Application of the Convention on the Prevention and Punishment of the Crime of Genocide, The Gambia v. Myanmar*, Order of 23 January 2020
- *Application of the International Convention on the Elimination of All Forms of Racial Discrimination* (*Georgia v. Russian Federation*), Order of 15 October 2008
- *Armed Activities on the Territory of the Congo* (*Democratic Republic of the Congo v. Uganda*), Judgment of 19 December 2005
- *Arrest Warrant of 11 April 2000* (*Democratic Republic of the Congo v. Belgium*), Judgment of 14 February 2002
- *Avena and Other Mexican Nationals* (*Mexico v. United States of America*), Judgment of 31 March 2004
- *Barcelona Traction, Light and Power Company, Limited* (New Application: 1962), *Belgium* v. *Spain*, Second Phase, Judgment of 5 February 1970
- *East Timor*, *Portugal v. Australia*, Judgment of 30 June 1995
- *Gabčikovo-Nagymaros Project*, *Hungary v. Slovakia*, Judgment of 25 September 1997
- *Jadhav*, *India v. Pakistan*, Judgment of 17 July 2019

P. Pustorino, *Introduction to International Human Rights Law*,
https://doi.org/10.1007/978-94-6265-563-8

- *Jurisdictional Immunities of the State, Germany v. Italy (Greece Intervening)*, Judgment of 3 February 2012
- *LaGrand, Germany v. United States of America*, Judgment of 27 June 2001
- *Legal Consequences for States of the Continued Presence of South Africa in Namibia (South West Africa) notwithstanding Security Council Resolution 276 (1970)*, Advisory Opinion of 21 June 1971
- *Legal Consequences of the Construction of a Wall in the Occupied Palestinian Territory*, Advisory Opinion of 9 July 2004
- *Legal Consequences of the Separation of the Chagos Archipelago from Mauritius in 1965*, Advisory Opinion of 25 February 2019
- *Legality of the Threat or Use of Nuclear Weapons*, Advisory Opinion of 8 July 1996
- *Questions relating to the Obligation to Prosecute or Extradite, Belgium v. Senegal*, Judgment of 20 July 2012
- *Reservations to the Convention on the Prevention and Punishment of the Crime of Genocide*, Advisory Opinion of 28 May 1951
- *South West Africa, Ethiopia v. South Africa, Liberia v. South Africa*, Second Phase, Judgment of 18 July 1966

European Commission of Human Rights (ECommHR):

- *Austria v. Italy*, Decision of 11 January 1961, appl. 788/60

European Court of Human Rights (ECtHR):

- *Ada Rossi and Others v. Italy*, appl. nos. 55185/08 and others, Decision of Inadmissibility of 16 December 2008
- *ADEFDROMIL v. France*, appl. no. 32191/09, Judgment of 2 October 2014
- *Agache and Others v. Romania*, appl. no. 2712/02, Judgment of 20 October 2009
- *Al-Adsani v. The United Kingdom*, appl. no. 35763/97, Grand Chamber, Judgment of 21 November 2001
- *Al-Dulimi and Montana Management Inc. v. Switzerland*, appl. no. 10593/08, Judgment of 21 June 2016
- *Al-Jedda v. The United Kingdom*, appl. no. 27021/08, Grand Chamber, Judgment of 7 July 2011
- *Al-Nashiri v. Poland*, appl. no. 28761/11, Judgment of 24 July 2014
- *Alparslan Altan v. Turkey*, appl. no. 12778/17, Judgment of 16 April 2019
- *Al-Saadoon and Mufdhi v. The United Kingdom*, appl. no. 61498/08, Judgment of 2 March 2010
- *Anheuser-Busch Inc. v. Portugal*, appl. no. 73049/01, Grand Chamber, Judgment of 11 January 2007
- *A and B v. Norway*, applications nos. 24130/11 and 29758/11, Grand Chamber, Judgment of 15 November 2016
- *Assemblée Chrétienne Des Témoins de Jéhovah d'Anderlecht and Others v. Belgium*, appl. no. 20165/20, Judgment of 5 April 2022
- *Association "21 December 1989" and Others v. Romania*, appl. no. 33810/07, Judgment of 24 May 2011

- *Aydin v. Turkey*, appl. no. 23178/94, Judgment of 25 September 1997
- *B and C v. Switzerland*, applications nos. 889/19 and 43987/16, Judgment of 17 November 2020
- *Baldassi and Others v. France*, appl. nos. 15271/16 and six others, Judgment of 11 June 2020
- *Banković and Others v. Belgium and 16 Other States*, appl. no 52207/99, Grand Chamber, Decision of Inadmissibility of 12 December 2001
- *Baralija v. Bosnia and Herzegovina*, appl. no. 30100/18, Judgment of 29 October 2019
- *Beg S.p.A. v. Italy*, appl. no. 5312/11, Judgment of 20 May 2021
- *Beizaras and Levickas v. Lithuania*, appl. no. 41288/15, Judgment of 14 January 2020
- *Belcacemi and Oussar v. Belgium*, appl. no. 37798/13, Judgment of 11 July 2017
- *Benitez Moriana and Iñigo Fernandez v. Spain*, appl. nos. 36537/15 and 36539/15, Judgment of 9 March 2021
- *Big Brother Watch and Others v. The United Kingdom*, Grand Chamber, appl. nos. 58170/13, 62322/14 and 24969/15, Judgment of 25 May 2021
- *Blair and Others v. Italy*, appl. nos. 1442/14, 21319/14 and 21911/14, Judgment of 26 October 2017
- *Boultif v. Switzerland*, appl. no. 54273/00, Judgment of 2 August 2001
- *Broniowski v. Poland*, appl. no. 31443/96, Judgment of 22 June 2004
- *Budina v. Russia* appl. no. 45603/05, Decision of Inadmissibility of 18 June 2009
- *Burmych and Others v. Ukraine*, appl. no. 46852/13, Grand Chamber, Judgment of 12 October 2017
- *Campbell and Cosans v. The United Kingdom*, appl. nos. 7511/76 and 7743/76, Judgment of 25 February 1982
- *Carter v. Russia*, appl. no. 20914/07, Judgment of 21 September 2021
- *Centre for Legal Resources on behalf of Valentin Câmpeanu v. Romania*, appl. no. 47848/08, Judgment of 10 July 2014
- *Centro Europa 7 s.r.l. and Di Stefano v. Italy*, appl. no. 38433/09, Grand Chamber, Judgment of 7 June 2012
- *Cestaro v. Italy*, appl. no. 6884/11, Judgment of 7 April 2015
- *Chiragov and Others v. Armenia*, appl. no. 13216/05, Grand Chamber, Judgment of 16 June 2015
- *Chowdury and Others v. Greece*, appl. no. 21884/15, Judgment of 30 March 2017
- *Communauté genevoise d'action syndicale (CGAS) v. Switzerland*, appl. no. 21881/20, Judgment of 15 March 2022
- *Contrada v. Italy (No. 2)*, appl. no. 7509/08, Judgment of 11 February 2014
- *Contrada v. Italy (No. 3)*, appl. no. 66655/2013, Judgment of 14 April 2015
- *Cordella and Others v. Italy*, appl. nos. 54414/13 and 54264/15, Judgment of 24 January 2019
- *Costa and Pavan v. Italy*, appl. no. 54270/10, Judgment of 28 August 2012
- *Cusan and Fazzo v. Italy*, appl. no. 77/07, Judgment of 7 January 2014
- *Cyprus v. Turkey*, appl. no. 25781/94, Grand Chamber, Judgment of 12 May 2014
- *C v. France*, appl. no. 1462/18, Decision of Inadmissibility of 12 December 2019

- *Dareskizb Ltd v. Armenia*, appl. no. 61737/08, Judgment of 21 September 2021
- *De Tommaso v. Italy*, appl. no. 43395/09, Grand Chamber, Judgment of 23 February 2017
- *Dink v. Turkey*, appl. nos. 2668/07 and others, Judgment of 14 September 2010
- *Drėlingas v. Lithuania*, appl. no. 28859/16, Judgment of 12 March 2019
- *Dudarovy v. Russia*, appl. no. 5382/07, Judgment of 10 February 2011
- *Dupin v. France*, appl. no. 2282/17, Decision of inadmissibility of 24 January 2019
- *E v. France*, appl. no. 17348/18, Decision of Inadmissibility of 12 December 2019
- *Ebrahimian v. France*, appl. no. 64846/11, Judgment of 26 November 2015
- *Edizioni Del Roma società cooperativa a.r.l. and Edizioni Del Roma s.r.l. v. Italy*, appl. nos. 68954/13 and 70495/13, Judgment of 10 December 2020
- *El-Masri v. The Former Yugoslav Republic of Macedonia*, appl. no. 39630/09, Grand Chamber, Judgment of 13 December 2012
- *Engel and Others v. The Netherlands*, appl. nos. 5100/71 and others, Judgment of 8 June 1976
- *E.S. v. Austria*, appl. no. 38450/12, Judgment of 25 October 2018
- *Evans v. The United Kingdom*, appl. no. 6339/05, Grand Chamber, Judgment of 10 April 2007
- *Fabris and Parziale v. Italy*, appl. no. 41603/13, Judgment of 19 March 2020
- *Fedotova and others v. Russia*, appl. nos. 40792/10, 30538/14 and 43439/14, Judgment of 13 July 2021
- *Ferrazzini v. Italy*, appl. no. 44759/98, Judgment of 12 July 2001
- *Gard and Others v. United Kingdom*, appl. no. 39793/17, Decision of Inadmissibility of 27 June 2017
- *Gaughran v. The United Kingdom*, appl. no. 45245/15, Judgment of 13 February 2020
- *Georgia v. Russia (II)*, appl. no. 38263/08, Grand Chamber, Judgment of 21 January 2021
- *Ghoumid and Others v. France*, appl. nos. 52273/16 and 4 others, Judgment of 25 June 2020
- *G.I.E.M. S.r.l. and Others v. Italy*, application nos. 1828/06 and 2 others, Grand Chamber, Judgment of 28 June 2018
- *Giuliani and Gaggio v. Italy*, appl. no. 23458/02, Grand Chamber, Judgment of 24 March 2011
- *G.L. v. Italy*, appl. no. 59751/15, Judgment of 10 September 2020
- *Godelli v. Italy*, appl. no. 33783/09, Judgment of 25 September 2012
- *Goodwin v. The United Kingdom*, appl. no. 17488/90, Grand Chamber, Judgment of 27 March 1996
- *Goodwin Christine v. The United Kingdom*, appl. no. 28957/95, Grand Chamber, Judgment of 11 July 2002
- *Grama and Dîrul v. Republic of Moldova and Russia*, applications nos. 28432/06 and 5665/07, Judgment of 15 October 2019
- *Grande Stevens and Others v. Italy*, appl. nos. 18640/10 and others, Judgment of 4 March 2014

- *Gross* v. *Switzerland*, appl. no 67810/10, Judgment of 14 May 2013
- *Grzęda v. Poland*, appl. no. 43572/18, Decision of 18 February 2021
- *Haas v. Switzerland*, appl. no. 31322/07, Judgment of 20 January 2011
- *Hassan v. The United Kingdom*, appl. no 52207/99, Grand Chamber, Judgment of 16 September 2014
- *Hirsi Jamaa and Others v. Italy*, appl. no. 27765/09, Grand Chamber, Judgment of 23 February 2012
- *Hirst v. The United Kingdom (No. 2)*, appl. no. 74025/01, Grand Chamber, Judgment of 6 October 2005
- *Hornsby v. Greece*, appl. no 18357/91, Judgment of 19 March 1997
- *Hurbain v. Belgium*, appl. no. 57292/16, Judgment of 21 June 2021
- *Ibrahim and Others v. The United Kingdom*, appl. nos. 50541/08 and others, Grand Chamber, Judgment of 13 September 2016,
- *Ilaşcu and Others v. Moldova and Russia*, appl. no. 48787/99, Grand Chamber, Judgment of 8 July 2004
- *Mammadov v. Azerbaijan*, appl. no. 15172/13, Judgment of 22 May 2014
- *Mammadov v. Azerbaijan*, appl. no. 15172/13, Grand Chamber, Judgment of 29 May 2019
- *Ireland v. The United Kingdom*, appl. no. 5310/71, Judgment of 18 January 1978
- *Ismayilova v. Azerbaijan*, appl. nos. 65286/13 and 57270/14, Judgment 10 January 2019
- *Jalloh v. Germany*, appl. no. 54810/00, Grand Chamber, Judgment of 11 July 2006
- *Jaloud v. The Netherlands*, appl. no. 47708/08, Grand Chamber, Judgment of 20 November 2014
- *Jecker v. Switzerland*, appl. no. 35449/14, Judgment of 6 October 2020
- *Jersild v. Denmark*, Grand Chamber, appl. no. 15890/89, Judgment of 23 September 1994
- *Jones and Others v. The United Kingdom*, appl. nos. 34356/06 and 40528/06, Judgment of 14 January 2014
- *K2 v. The United Kingdom*, appl. no. 42387/13, Decision of Inadmissibility of 9 March 2017
- *Kaak and Others v. Greece*, appl. no. 34215/16, Judgment of 3 October 2019
- *Kaboğlu and Oran v. Turkey*, appl. nos. 1759/08, 50766/10 and 50782/10, Judgment of 30 October 2018
- *Kapa and Others v. Poland*, Judgment of 14 October 2021, appl. nos. 75031/13 and others
- *Khlaifia and Others v. Italy*, appl. no. 16483/12, Grand Chamber, Judgment of 15 December 2016
- *Knox v. Italy*, appl. no. 76577/13, Judgment of 24 January 2019
- *Kokkinakis v. Greece*, appl. no. 14307/88, Judgment of 25 May 1993
- *Kononov v. Latvia*, appl. no. 36376/04, Grand Chamber Judgment of 17 May 2010
- *Kurić and Others v. Slovenia*, appl. no. 26828/06, Grand Chamber, Judgment of 26 June 2012
- *Kurt v. Austria*, appl. no. 62903/15, Judgment of 15 June 2021
- *Labassee v. France*, appl. no. 65941/11, Judgment of 26 June 2014

- *Lachiri v. Belgium*, appl. no. 3413/09, Judgment of 18 September 2018
- *Lambert and Others v. France*, appl. no. 46043/14, Grand Chamber, Judgment of 5 June 2015
- *Lautsi v. Italy*, appl. no. 30814/06, Judgment of 3 November 2009
- *Lautsi and Others v. Italy*, appl. no. n. 30814/06, Grand Chamber, Judgment of 18 March 2011
- *L.E. v. Greece*, appl. no. 71545/12, Judgment of 21 January 2016
- *Lehideux and Isorni v. France*, appl. no. 24662/94, Grand Chamber, Judgment of 23 September 1998
- *López Ribalda and Others v. Spain*, appl. nos. 1874/13 and 8567/13, Grand Chamber, Judgment of 17 October 2019
- *M.A. v. Denmark*, appl. no. 6697/18, Grand Chamber, Judgment of 9 July 2021
- *Makovetskyy v. Ukraine*, appl. no. 50824/21, Decision of Inadmissibility of 19 May 2022
- *Makuchyan and Minasyan v. Azerbaijan and Hungary*, appl. no. 17247/13, Judgment of 26 May 2020
- *Maktouf and Damjanović v. Bosnia and Herzegovina*, appl. nos. 2312/08 and 34179/08, Grand Chamber, Judgment of 18 July 2013
- *Mamatkulov and Askarov v. Turkey*, appl. nos. 46827/99 and 46951/99, Grand Chamber, Judgment of 4 February 2005
- *Marcello Viola v. Italy (No. 2)*, appl. no. 77633/16, Judgment of 13 June 2019
- *Matelly v. France*, appl. no. 10609/10, Judgment of 2 October 2014
- *M'Bala M'Bala v. France* appl. no. 25239/13, Decision of Inadmissibility of 10 November 2015
- *McCann and Others v. The United Kingdom*, Grand Chamber, appl. no. 18984/91, Judgment of 27 September 1995
- *Mennesson v. France*, appl. no. 65192/11, Judgment of 26 June 2014
- *Merabishvili v. Georgia*, appl. no. 72508/13, Grand Chamber, Judgment of 28 November 2017
- *M.H. and Others v. Croatia*, appl. nos. 15670/18 and 43115/18, Judgment of 18 November 2021
- *Milanković v. Croatia*, appl. no. 33351/20, Judgment of 20 January 2022
- *Miller v. United Kingdom*, appl. no. 32001/18, Decision of Inadmissibility of 25 July 2019
- *M.L. and W.W. v. Germany*, appl. nos. 60798/10 and 65599/10, Judgment of 28 June 2018
- *M.N. and Others v. Belgium*, appl. no. 3599/18, Grand Chamber, Inadmissibility Decision of 5 May 2020
- *Mocanu and Others v. Romania*, Grand Chamber, appl. nos. 10865/09, 45886/07 and 32431/08, Judgment of 17 September 2014
- *Mockienė v. Lithuania*, appl. no. 75916/13, Decision of Inadmissibility of 4 July 2017
- *Moldovan and Others v. Romania (No. 2)*, appl. nos. 41138/98 and 64320/01, Judgment of 12 July 2005

- *Molla Sali v. Greece*, appl. no. 20452/14, Grand Chamber, Judgment of 19 December 2018
- *Mortier v. Belgium*, appl. no. 78017/17, Judgment of 4 October 2022
- *Muñoz Diaz v. Spain*, appl. no. 49151/07, Judgment of 8 December 2009
- *Muršić v. Croatia*, appl. no. 7334/13, Grand Chamber, judgment of 20 October 2016
- *N.A. v. Finland*, appl. no. 25244/18, Judgment of 14 November 2019
- *Nachova and Others v. Bulgaria*, appl. nos. 43577/98 and 43579/98, Grand Chamber, Judgment of 6 July 2005
- *Nada v. Switzerland*, Grand Chamber, appl. no. 10593/08, Judgment of 12 September 2012
- *Naït-Liman v. Switzerland*, appl. no. 51357/07, Grand Chamber, Judgment of 15 March 2018
- *Nasr and Ghali v. Italy*, appl. no. 44883/09, Judgment of 23 February 2016
- *Napotnik v. Romania*, appl. no. 33139/13, Judgment of 20 October 2020
- *N.K.M. v. Hungary*, appl. no. 66529/11, Judgment of 14 May 2013
- *Noack and Others v. Germany*, appl. no. 46346/99, Decision of Inadmissibility of 25 May 2020
- *Nikolaishvili v. Georgia*, appl. no. 37048/04, Judgment of 13 January 2009
- *Obote v. Russia*, appl. no. 58954/09, Judgment of 19 November 2019
- *Öcalan v. Turkey*, appl. no. 46221/99, Grand Chamber, Judgment of 12 May 2005
- *Oliari and Others v. Italy*, appl. nos. 18766/11 and 36030/11, Judgment of 21 July 2015
- *Öneryildiz v. Turkey*, appl. no. 48939/99, Judgment of 30 November 2004
- *Opuz v. Turkey*, appl. no. 33401/02, Judgment of 9 June 2009
- *Osman v. The United Kingdom*, appl. no. 87/1997/871/1083, Grand Chamber, Judgment of 28 October 1998
- *Ould Dah v. France*, appl. no. 13113/03, Decision of Inadmissibility of 17 March 2009
- *P. and S. v. Poland*, appl. no. 57375/08, Judgment of 30 October 2012
- *Panaitescu v. Romania*, appl. no. 30909/06, Judgment of 10 April 2012
- *Panioglu v. Romania*, appl. no. 33794/14, Judgment of 8 December 2020
- *Papamichalopoulos and Others v. Greece*, appl. no. 14556/89, Judgment of 24 June 1993
- *Paposhvili v. Belgium*, appl. no. 41738/10, Grand Chamber, Judgment of 13 December 2016
- *Paradiso and Campanelli v. Italy*, appl. no. 25358/12, Judgment of 27 January 2015
- *Paradiso and Campanelli v. Italy*, appl. no. 25358/12, Grand Chamber, Judgment of 24 January 2017
- *Parfitt v. United Kingdom*, appl. no. 18533/21, Decision of Inadmissibility of 21 April 2021
- *Parrillo v. Italy*, appl. no. 46470/11, Grand Chamber, Judgment of 27 August 2015
- *Perinçek v. Switzerland*, appl. no. 27510/08, Grand Chamber, Judgment of 15 October 2015

- *Perovy v. Russia*, appl. no. 47429/09, Judgment of 20 October 2020
- *Petukhov v. Ukraine (No. 2)*, appl. no. 41216/13, Judgment of 12 March 2019
- *Pine Valley Developments Ltd and Others v. Ireland*, appl. no. 12742/87, Judgment of 29 November 1991
- *Polat v. Austria*, appl. no. 12886/16, Judgment of 20 July 2021
- *Provenzano v. Italy*, appl. no. 55080/13, Judgment of 25 October 2018
- *Ramazan Demir v. Turkey*, appl. no 68550/17, Judgment of 9 February 2021
- *Rantsev v. Cyprus and Russia*, appl. no. 25965/04, Judgment of 7 January 2010
- *Razvozzhayev v. Russia and Ukraine* and *Udaltsov v. Russia*, appl. nos. 75734/12 and 2 others, Judgment of 19 November 2019
- *Recognition in Domestic Law of a Legal Parent-child Relationship between a Child Born through a Gestational Surrogacy Arrangement abroad and the Intended Mother*, Request no. P16-2018-001, Advisory Opinion of 10 April 2019
- *Refah Partisi (the Welfare Party) and Others v. Turkey*, appl. nos. 41340/98 and Others, Grand Chamber, Judgment of 13 February 2003
- *Róisín Shortall and Others* v. *Ireland*, appl. no. 50272/18, Decision of Inadmissibility 18 November 2021
- *Romeo Castaño v. Belgium*, appl. no. 8351/17, Judgment of 9 July 2019
- *Saadi v. Italy*, appl. no. 37201/06, Grand Chamber, Judgment of 28 February 2008
- *Sanchez v. France*, appl. no. 45581/15, Judgment of 2 September 2021
- *S.A.S. v. France*, appl. no. 43835/11, Judgment of 1 July 2014
- *Satakunnan Markkinapörssi Oy and Satamedia Oy v. Finland*, appl. no. 931/13, Grand Chamber, Judgment of 27 June 2017
- *Savran v. Denmark*, appl. no. 57467/15, Grand Chamber, Judgment of 7 December 2021
- *Schalk and Kopf v. Austria*, appl. no. 30141/04, Judgment of 24 June 2010
- *Scoppola v. Italy (No. 2)*, appl. no. 10249/03, Grand Chamber, Judgment of 17 September 2009
- *Scoppola v. Italy (No. 3)*, appl. no. 126/05, Grand Chamber, Judgment of 22 May 2012
- *Scozzari and Giunta v. Italy*, appl. nos. 39221/98 and 41963/98, Grand Chamber, Judgment of 13 July 2000
- *Selmouni v. France*, appl. no. 25803/94, Grand Chamber, Judgment of 28 July 1999
- *S. H. and Others v. Austria*, appl. no. 57813/00, Judgment of 1 April 2010
- *S. H. and Others v. Austria*, appl. no. 57813/00, Grand Chamber, Judgment of 3 November 2011
- *Sic - Sociedade Independente de comunicaçäo v. Portugal*, appl. no. 29856/13, Judgment of 27 July 2021
- *Siliadin v. France*, appl. no. 73316/01, Judgment of 26 July 2005
- *Slovenia v. Croatia*, appl. no 54155/16, Grand Chamber, Decision of Inadmissibility of 18 November 2020
- *S.M. v. Croatia*, appl. no. 60561/14, Grand Chamber, Judgment of 25 June 2020
- *Soering v. The United Kingdom*, appl. no. 14038/88, Judgment of 7 July 1989
- *Solomou and Others v. Turkey*, appl. no. 36832/97, Judgment of 24 June 2008

- *Standard Verlagsgesellschaft mbH v. Austria (no. 3)*, appl. no. 39378/15, Judgment of 7 December 2021
- *Stec and Others v. The United Kingdom*, appl. nos. 65731/01 and 65900/01, Grand Chamber, Judgment of 12 April 2006
- *Stichting Mothers of Srebrenica and Others v. The Netherlands*, appl. no. 65542/12, Grand Chamber, Judgment of 11 June 2013
- *Streletz, Kessler and Krenk v. Germany*, applications nos. 34044/96, 35532/97 and 44801/98, Grand Chamber, Judgment of 22 March 2001
- *Stummer v. Austria*, appl. no. 37452/02, Grand Chamber, Judgment of 7 July 2011
- *S.V. v. Italy*, appl. no. 55216/08, Judgment of 11 October 2018
- *Tagayeva and Others v. Russia*, appl. nos. 26562/07 and six other applications, Judgment of 13 April 2017
- *Talpis v. Italy*, appl. no. 41237/14, Judgment of 2 March 2017
- *Terheş v. Romania*, appl. no. 49933/20, Decision of Inadmissibility of 20 May 2021
- *Terna v. Italy*, appl. no. 21052/18, Judgment of 14 January 2021
- *Torreggiani and Others v. Italy*, appl. nos. 43517/09 and others, Judgment of 8 January 2013
- *Tuşalp v. Turkey*, appl. no. 32131/08, Judgment of 21 February 2021
- *Tyrer v. United Kingdom*, appl. no. 5856/72, Judgment of 25 April 1978
- *Üner v. The Netherlands*, Grand Chamber, appl. no. 46410/99, Judgment of 18 October 2006
- *Ukraine v. Russia (Re Crimea)*, appl. nos. 20958/14 and 38334/18, Grand Chamber, Decision of Admissibility of 16 December 2020
- *Usmanov v. Russia*, appl. no. 43936/18, Judgment of 22 December 2020
- *Use of the "Blanket Reference" or "Legislation by Reference" Technique in the Definition of an Offence and the Standards of Comparison between the Criminal Law in Force at the Time of the Commission of the Offence and the Amended Criminal Law*, Request no. P16-2019-001, Advisory Opinion of 25 May 2020
- *Uzun v. Germany*, appl. no 35623/05, Judgment of 2 September 2010
- *Vallianatos and Others v. Greece*, appl. nos. 29381/09 and 32684/09, Grand Chamber, Judgment of 7 November 2013
- *Van der Mussele v. Belgium*, appl. no. 8919/80, Judgment of 23 November 1983
- *Vasiliauskas v. Lithuania*, Grand Chamber, appl. no 35343/05, Judgment of 20 October 2015
- *Vavřička and Others v. Czech Republic*, appl. no. 47621/13 and five other applications, Grand Chamber, Judgment of 8 April 2021
- *V.C. v. Slovakia*, appl. no. 18968/07, Judgment of 8 November 2011
- *V.C.L. and A.N. v. The United Kingdom*, appl. nos. 77587/12 and 74603/12, Judgment of 16 February 2021
- *Vinter and Others v. The United Kingdom*, applications nos. 66069/09, 130/10 and 3896/10, Grand Chamber, Judgment of 9 July 2013
- *Vo v. France*, appl. no. 53924/00, Grand Chamber, Judgment of 8 July 2004
- *Volodina v. Russia (No. 2)*, appl. no. 40419/19, Judgment of 14 September 2021

- *Waite and Kennedy v. Germany*, appl. no. 26083/94, Grand Chamber, Judgment of 18 February 1999
- *Weber and Saravia v. Germany*, appl. no. 54934/00, Decision of Inadmissibility of 29 June 2006
- *Williamson v. Germany*, appl. no. 64496/17, Decision of Inadmissibility of 8 January 2019
- *Yildirim v. Turkey*, appl. no. 3111/10, judgment of 18 December 2012
- *Zambrano v. France*, appl. no. 41994/21, Decision of Inadmissibility of 7 October 2021
- *Zu Guttenberg v. Germany*, appl. no. 14047/16, Decision of Inadmissibility of 25 June 2019

European Committee of Social Rights (ECommSR):

- *International Planned Parenthood Federation – European Network (IPPF EN) v. Italy*, complaint no. 87/2012, Decision of 10 September 2013
- *International Federation of Human Rights Leagues (FIDH) v. France*, complaint No. 14/2003, Decision of 8 September 2004

European Court of Justice (ECJ):

- *Achbita, Centrum voor gelijkheid van kansen en voor racismebestrijding v. G4S Secure Solutions NV*, C-157/15, Judgment of 14 March 2017
- *European Commission and Others v. Kadi*, Joined Cases C-584/10 P, C-593/10 P and C-595/10 P, Grand Chamber, Judgment of 18 July 2013
- *Google Spain SL, Google Inc. v. Agencia Española de Protección de Datos (AEPD), Mario Costeja González*, C-131/12, Grand Chamber, Judgment of 13 May 2014
- *Kadi and Al Barakaat International Foundation v. Council and Commission*, Joined Cases C-402/05 P and C-415/05 P, Judgment of 3 September 2008
- *M.A.S., M.B.*, C-42/17, Judgment of 5 December 2017
- *Rottmann v. Freistaat Bayern*, C-135/08, Judgment of 2 March 2010
- *Taricco et al.*, C-105/14, Grand Chamber, Judgment of 8 September 2015

Court of First Instance (CFI) (now European General Court) (EGC):

- *Kadi v. Council and Commission*, T-315/01, Judgment of 21 September 2005
- *Yusuf and Al Barakaat International Foundation v. Council and Commission*, T-306/01, Judgment of 21 September 2005

Inter-American Commission on Human Rights (IACommHR):

- *The Haitian Centre for Human Rights et al. v. United States*, Case 10.675, Report No. 51/96, Decision of 13 March 1997

Inter-American Court of Human Rights (IACtHR):

- *Almonacid Arellano et al. v. Chile*, Judgment of 26 September 2006
- *Artavia Murillo et al. ("In vitro fertilization") v. Costa Rica*, Judgment of 28 November 2012

- *Azul Rojas Marín et al. v. Peru*, Judgment of 12 March 2020
- *Barrios Altos v. Peru*, Judgment of 14 March 2001
- *Cordero Bernal v. Peru*, Judgment of 16 February 2021
- *Duque v. Colombia*, Judgment of 26 February 2016
- *Garífuna Community of Triunfo de la Cruz and its Members v. Honduras*, Judgment of 8 October 2015
- *Girls Yean and Bosico v. Dominican Republic*, Judgment of 8 September 2005
- *Godínez Cruz v. Honduras* (Merits), Judgment of 20 January 1989
- *Granier et al. (Radio Caracas Television) v. Venezuela*, Judgment of 22 June 2015
- *Herrera-Ulloa v. Costa Rica*, Judgment of 2 July 2004
- *Indigenous Communities of the Lhaka Honhat (Our Land) Association v. Argentina*, Judgment of 6 February 2020
- *I.V. v. Bolivia*, Judgment of 30 November 2019
- *Judicial Guarantees in States of Emergency*, No. OC-9/87, Advisory Opinion of 6 October 1987
- *"Juvenile Reeducation Institute" v. Paraguay*, Judgment of 2 September 2004
- *Lagos del Campo v. Peru*, Judgment of 31 August 2017
- *López Soto et al. v. Venezuela*, Judgment of 26 September 2018
- *Poblete Vilches et al. v. Chile*, Judgment of 8 March 2018
- *Santo Domingo Massacre v. Colombia*, Judgment of 30 November 2012
- *The Environment and Human Rights*, OC-23/17, Advisory Opinion of 15 November 2017
- *The Institution of Asylum, and its Recognition as a Human Right under the Inter-American System of Protection (Interpretation and Scope of Articles 5, 22.7 and 22.8 in relation to Article 1(1) of the American Convention on Human Rights)*, OC-25/18, Advisory Opinion of 30 May 2018
- *The Kichwa Indigenous People of Sarayaku v. Ecuador*, Judgment of 27 June 2012
- *The Obligations in Matters of Human Rights of a State that has Denounced the American Convention on Human Rights and the Charter of the Organization of American States*, OC-26/20, Advisory Opinion of 9 November 2020
- *The "Street Children" (Villagrán Morales et al.) v. Guatemala*, Judgment of 19 November 1999
- *Velásquez Rodríguez v. Honduras*, Judgment of 29 July 1988
- *Workers of the Fireworks Factory in Santo Antônio de Jesus and their Families v. Brazil*, Judgment of 15 July 2020

African Commission on Human and Peoples' Rights (ACommHPR):

- *Centre for Minority Rights Development (Kenya) and Minority Rights Groups International on behalf of Endorois Welfare Council v. Kenya*, communication no. 276/2003, Decision of 25 November 2009
- *Hossam Ezzat and Rania Enayet (represented by the Egyptian Initiative for Personal Rights and INTERIGHTS) v. Arab Republic of Egypt*, communication No. 355/07, Report of 17 February 2016

- *Interights and Ditshwanelo v. The Republic of Botswana*, communication no. 319/06, Decision adopted at the 57th regular session of the Commission (4–18 November 2015)
- *Social and Economic Rights Action Center (SERAC) and Center for Economic and Social Rights (CESR) v. Nigeria*, communication no. 155/96, Decision of 27 October 2001
- *Organisation Mondiale Contre la Torture et Ligue de la Zone Afrique pour la Défense des Droits des Enfants et Elèves (pour le compte de Céline) v. Democratic Republic of Congo*, communication no. 325/06, Decision adopted at the 57th ordinary session of the Commission (4–18 November 2015)
- *African Commission on Human and Peoples' Rights v. Republic of Kenya*, appl. no. 006/2012, Judgment of 26 May 2017
- *African Commission on Human and Peoples' Rights v. Republic of Kenya*, appl. no. 006/2012, Judgment of 23 June 2022 (Reparations)

African Court on Human and Peoples' Rights (ACtHPRA):

- *Association Pour le Progrès et la Défense Des Droits Des Femmes Maliennes (APDF) and the Institute for Human Rights and Development in Africa (IHRDA) v. Republic of Mali*, Judgment of 11 May 2018
- *Ally Rajabu and Others v. United Republic of Tanzania*, appl. no. 007/2015, Judgment of 28 November 2019
- *Lohé Issa Konaté v. Burkina Faso*, Judgment of 5 December 2014
- *XYZ v. Republic of Benin*, appl. no. 010/2020, Judgment of 27 November 2020

International Criminal Court:

- *Al Bashir* (*Prosecutor v. Omar Hassan Ahmad Al Bashir*), *Decision Pursuant to article 87(7) of the Rome Statute on the Refusal of the Republic of Chad to Comply with the Cooperation Requests Issued by the Court with Respect to the Arrest and Surrender of Omar Hassan Ahmad Al Bashir*, ICC-02/05-01/09, Pre-Trial Chamber, Decision of 13 December 2011
- *Al Bashir* (*Prosecutor v. Omar Hassan Ahmad Al Bashir*), *Decision Pursuant to Article 87(7) of the Rome Statute on the Failure by the Republic of Malawi to Comply with the Cooperation Requests Issued by the Court with Respect to the Arrest and Surrender of Omar Hassan Ahmad Al Bashir*, ICC-02/05-01/09-139, Pre-Trial Chamber, Decision of 13 December 2011
- *Al Bashir* (*Prosecutor v. Omar Hassan Ahmad Al Bashir*), *in the Jordan Referral re Al-Bashir Appeal*, ICC-02/05-01/09 OA2, Appeals Chamber, Judgment of 6 May 2019
- *Al Bashir* (*Prosecutor v. Omar Hassan Ahmad Al Bashir*), *Decision on the Cooperation of the Democratic Republic of the Congo Regarding Omar Al Bashir's Arrest and Surrender to the Court*, ICC-02/05-01/09-195, Pre-Trial Chamber, Decision of 9 April 2014
- *Al Bashir* (*Prosecutor v. Omar Hassan Ahmad Al Bashir*), *Decision under Article 87(7) of the Rome Statute on the Non-compliance by South Africa with the Request by the Court for the Arrest and Surrender of Omar Al-Bashir*, ICC-02/05-01/09, Pre-Trial Chamber, Judgment of 6 July 2017

- *Gaddafi (Prosecutor v. Saif Al-Islam Gaddafi), on the Admissibility Challenge by Dr. Saif Al-Islam Gaddafi pursuant to Articles 17(1)(c), 19 and 20(3) of the Rome Statute*, CC-01/11-01/11, Pre-Trial Chamber, Decision of 5 April 2019
- *Situation in the Islamic Republic of Afghanistan*, ICC-02/17, *Decision Pursuant to Article 15 of the Rome Statute on the Authorisation of an Investigation into the Situation in the Islamic Republic of Afghanistan*, Pre-Trial Chamber, Decision of 12 April 2019
- *Situation in the Islamic Republic of Afghanistan*, ICC-02/17 OA4, *Judgment on the Appeal against the Decision on the Authorisation of an Investigation into the Situation in the Islamic Republic of Afghanistan*, Appeals Chamber, Judgment of 5 March 2020

International Criminal Tribunal for the Former Yugoslavia (ICTY):

- *Furundžija (Prosecutor v. Anto Furundžija)*, Trial Chamber, T-95-17/1-T, Judgment of 10 December 1998
- *Kunarac (Prosecutor v. Dragoljub Kunarac, Radomir Kovač and Zoran Vuković)*, IT-96-23 and IT-96-23/1-A, Appeals Chamber, Judgment of 12 June 2002
- *Popović (Prosecutor v. Popović, Beara, Nikolić, Miletić and Pandurević)*, IT-05-88, Appeals Chamber, Judgment of 30 January 2015
- *Tadić (Prosecutor v. Duško Tadić)*, Appeals Chamber, IT-94-1-A, Judgment of 15 July 1999

Special Tribunal for Lebanon (STL):

- *New TV S.A.L. (Prosecutor v. New TV S.A.L. Karma Mohamed Tahsin Al Khayat)*, Appeals Panel, *Decision on Interlocutory Appeal Concerning Personal Jurisdiction in Contempt Proceedings*, STL-14-05/PT/AP/ARI26.1, Decision of 2 October 2014

International Tribunal on the Law of the Sea (ITLOS):

- *Dispute Concerning Delimitation of the Maritime Boundary Between Mauritius and Maldives in the India Ocean, Mauritius v. Maldives*, Judgment of 28 January 2021, Preliminary Objections

National Courts

Belgium

Brussels Court of First Instance:

- *Klimaatzaak ASBL v. Belgium*, Brussels Court of First Instance, no. 2015/4585/A, Judgment of 17 June 2021

Brazil

Supreme Court:

- Recurso extraordinário com agravo no. 954.858, Judgment of 23 August 2021

Canada
Supreme Court:

- *Balvir Singh Multani, et al. v. Commission scolaire Marguerite-Bourgeoys, et al.*, Judgment of 2 March 2006
- *Nevsun Resources Ltd. v. Gize Yebeyo Araya and Others*, Judgment of 28 February 2020
- *Re Secession of Quebec (Reference by the Governor in Council concerning Certain Questions relating to the Secession of Quebec from Canada)*, Advisory Opinion of 20 August 1998

Colombia
Constitutional Court:

- Judgment of 16 July 2004 no. C-500/14
- *Alexander López Quiroz y Marco Fidel Martinez Gaviria v. Procuraduría General de la Nación*, Judgment of 22 June 2016 no. 327/16

Costa Rica
Supreme Court (*Sala Constitucional*):

- *Guzmán v. Ministerio de Ambiente, Energía y Telecomunicaciones, Ministerio de la Presidencia*, Judgment of 30 July 2010 no. 12790

France
Constitutional Council (Conseil constitutionnel):

- Judgement of 10 June 2009 no. 580

Court of Cassation (Cour de Cassation):

- Judgments of 5 July 2017 nos. 824 and 825
- Judgment of 7 September 2021no. 868

Courts of Appeal:

- Court of Appeal of Bordeaux, Judgments nos. 20BX02193 and 20BX02195 of 18 December 2020

Administrative Tribunals:

- Administrative Tribunal of Paris, Judgment of 3 February 2021 nos. 1904967, 1904968, 1904972 and 1904976/4-1

Germany
Federal Constitutional Court (Bundesverfassungsgericht):
German Federal Court of Justice:

- Case no. 3, StR 564/19, Judgment of 28 January 2021

India
High Court of Kerala:

- *Faheema Shirin R. K. and Others v. State of Kerala and Others*, Judgment of 19 September 2019

Supreme Court:

- *Navtej Singh Johar & Ors. v. Union of India, Thr. Secretary, Ministry of Law and Justic*e, Judgment of 6 September 2018

Italy
Constitutional Court:

- Judgment of 27 June 1996 no. 223
- Judgment of 9 April 2014 no. 162
- Judgment of 22 October 2014, no. 238
- Judgment of 26 March 2015 no. 49
- Judgment of 20 June 2019 no. 194

Supreme Court of Cassation:

- *Arman Ahmed et al.*, Judgment of 28 May 2010 no. 20514
- *Ferrini v. Federal Republic of Germany*, Judgment of 11 March 2004 no. 5044
- *Medero et al. (Abu Omar)*, Judgment of 25 September 2014 no. 39788
- *I.L. v. Ministry of the Interior, Attorney General at the Court of Appeal of Ancona*, Order of 24 February 2021 no. 5022
- *T.V. v. Attorney General*, Judgment of 24 July 2019 no. 33564
- *Public Prosecutor v. Rackete* Judgment of 20 February 2020, no. 6626
- *Toldo v. Federal Republic of Germany and Italian Republic*, Judgment of 28 September 2020 no. 20442
- *M.S. v. Ministry of the Interior*, Judgment of 10 November 2020, no. 25143
- *Stergiopoulos et al. v. Islamic Republic of Iran*, Judgment of 10 December 2021 no. 39391
- *Tijani Ibrahim Mirghani Bichara & Amid Ibrahim*, Judgment of 26 April 2022 no. 15869
- *Si. Ja.*, Judgment of 15 May 2017 no. 24084

Council of State:

- *Il Tuo Viaggio s.r.l. v. Presidency of the Council of Ministers et al.*, Judgment of 29 May 2014, no. 2792

Lazio Administrative Regional Court:

- Judgment of 4 December 2017

Japan
Japanese Supreme Court:

- *Special appeal against the ruling that dismissed the appeal filed against the ruling on the division of estate*, Judgment of 4 September 2013

Kenya
Court of Appeal:

- *The Prosecutor v. Omar Al-Bashir*, Judgment of 16 February 2018

Kenyan Environment and Land Court (Meru):

- *Mohamud Italrakwa Kochale et al. v. Lake Turkana Wind Power Ltd et al.*, Judgment of 19 October 2021

Mexico
Supreme Court of Justice:

- Amparo en revisión no. 1077/2019, Judgment of 16 June 2021

Norway
Supreme Court:

- *Statnett SF et al. v. Sør-Fosen Sijte et al.*, Judgment of 11 October 2021

Republic of Korea
Constitutional Court:

- *Comfort Women* case, Judgment of 30 August 2011
- Central District Court of Seoul
- *Comfort Women* case, Judgment of 8 January 2021, case no. 2016 Ga-Hap 505092
- *Comfort Women* case, Judgment of 21 April 2021, case no. 2016 Ga-Hap 58023

South Africa
Constitutional Court of South Africa:

Kaunda et al. v. President of the Republic of South Africa, Judgment of 4 August 2004

Supreme Court of Appeal:

- *Minister of Justice and Constitutional Development and Others v. Southern African Litigation Centre*, case no. 867/15, Judgment of 15 March 2016

Spain
Supreme Court:

- *María de los Ángeles González Carreño v. Ministry of Justice* Judgment of 17 July 2018 No 1263

Switzerland
Federal Supreme Court:

- *Youssef Nada v State Secretariat for Economic Affairs and Federal Department of Economic Affairs*, No 1A 45/2007, Judgment of 14 November 2007

The Netherlands
Supreme Court:

- *The State of the Netherlands* v. *Nuhanović*, Judgment of 6 September 2013
- *The State of the Netherlands v. Mustafic-Mujic et al.*, Judgment of 6 September 2013
- *The Netherlands v. Stichting Mothers of Srebrenica et al.*, Judgment 19 July 2019
- *The State of the Netherlands (Ministry of Economic Affairs and Climate Policy) v. Stichting Urgenda*, Judgment of 20 December 2019

The Hague District Court:

- *Vereniging Milieudefensie et al. v. Royal Dutch Shell Plc*, Judgment of 26 May 2021
- *Ziada v. The State of The Netherlands*, case no. C-09-554385, Judgment of 29 January 2020

The Hague Court of Appeal:

- *Four Nigerian farmers and Friends of the Earth v. Shell Petroleum*, Judgment of 29 January 2021
- *Ziada v. Gantz*, Judgment of 7 December 2021

United Kingdom
High Court of Justice:

- *Hay*, Judgment of 10 July 2009
- *Serdar Mohammed v. Ministry of Defence*, Judgment of 2 May 2014, [2014] EWHC 1369 (QB)

Supreme Court:

- *Okpabi and Others v. Royal Dutch Shell Plc and Another*, Judgment of 12 February 2021
- *R (on the application of Begum) v. Special Immigration Appeals Commission*, Judgment of 26 February 2021
- *Sanambar v. Secretary of State for the Home Department*, Judgment of 16 July 2021
- *Vedanta Resources PLC and Another v. Lungowe and Others*, Judgment of 10 April 2019
- *Basfar v. Wong*, Judgment of 6 July 2022

Court of Appeals (Supreme Court of Judicature):

- *Abbasi v. Secretary of State for Foreign and Commonwealth Affairs*, Judgment of 6 November 2002

United States of America

Supreme Court:

- *Jesner et al. v. Arab Bank, Plc*, Judgment of 24 April 2018
- *Kiobel et al. v. Royal Dutch Petroleum Co. et al.*, Judgment of 17 April 2013
- *Nestle USA, Inc. v. Doe et al.*, Judgment of 17 June 2021
- *Obergefell and Others v. Hodges, Director, Ohio Department of Health and Others*, Judgment of 26 June 2015

Courts of Appeals:

- *Doe v. Unocal Corporation et al.*, US Court of Appeals for the Ninth Circuit, Judgment of 18 September 2002
    - *Abdullahi v Pfizer, Inc.*, US Court of Appeals for the Second Circuit, Judgment of 30 January 2009
    - *Kiobel et al. v. Royal Dutch Petroleum Co. et al.*, US Court of Appeals for the Second Circuit, Judgment of 17 September 2010

District Courts:

- *The Presbyterian Church of Sudan v. Talisman Energy, Inc*, US District Court for the Southern District of New York, Judgment of 19 March 2003

Table of UN Treaty Bodies' Comments and Decisions

Human Rights Committee (HRC):

General Comments

- *General Comment No. 22* of 30 July 1993 on Article 18 (Right to Freedom of Thought, Conscience and Religion)
- *General Comment No. 23* of 8 April 1994 on Article 27 (Rights of Minorities)
- *General Comment No. 24* of 4 November 1994 on Issues Relating to Reservations Made upon Ratification or Accession to the Covenant or the Optional Protocols thereto, or in Relation to Declarations under article 41 of the Covenant
- *General Comment No. 26* of 8 December 1997 on Continuity of obligations
- *General Comment No. 28* of 29 March 2000 on Article 3 (The equality of Rights between Men and Women)
- *General Comment No. 32* of 23 August 2007 on Article 14 (Right to Equality before Courts and Tribunals and to a Fair Trial)
- *General Comment No. 36* of 30 October 2018 on Article 6 (Right to Life)

Statements

Statement of 24 April 2020, CCPR/C/128/2

Views

- *A.S., D.I., O.I. and G.D. v. Italy*, CCPR/C/130/D/3042/2017, Views of 4 November 2020
- *Daniel Billy and Others v. Australia*, CCPR/C/135/D/3624/2019, Views of 21 July 2022
- *Elena Genero v. Italy*, CCPR/C/128/D/2979/2017, Views of 13 March 2020
- *Hebbadj v. France*, CCPR/C/123/D/2807/2016, Views of 17 July 2018
- *Ioane Teitiota v. New Zealand*, CCPR/C/127/D/2728/2016, Views of 24 October 2019
- *Portillo Cáceres v. Paraguay*, CCPR/C/126/D/2751/2016, Views of 25 July 2019
- *Yaker v. France*, CCPR/C/123/D/2747/2016, Views of 17 July 2018

Committee on Economic, Social and Cultural Rights (CESCR):

- *General Comment* No. 3 of 14 December 1990 on Article art. 2, para. 1 (The Nature of States Parties' Obligations)
- *General Comment No. 12* of 12 May 1999 on Article 11 (The Right to Adequate Food)
- General Comment No. 13: The right to education (article 13 of the Covenant), 8 December 1999-
- *General Comment No. 14* of 11 August 2000 on Article 12 (The Right to the Highest Attainable Standard of Health)
- *General Comment No. 15* of 20 January 2003 on Articles 11 and 12 (The Right to Water)

- *General Comment No. 16* of 8 April 1988 on Article 17 (Right to Privacy)
- *General Comment No. 21* of 21 December 2009 on Article 15, para. 1(a) (Right of Everyone to Take Part in Cultural Life)

Committee Against Torture (CAT):

General Comments

- *General Comment No. 2* of 24 January 2008, on the Implementation of article 2 by States parties
- *General Comment No. 4* of 4 September 2018 on the Implementation of Article 3 of the Convention in the Context of Article 22
- Decisions
- *A. v. Bosnia and Herzegovina*, CAT/C/67/D/854/2017, Decision of 2 August 2019

Committee on the Elimination of Discrimination against Women (CommEDAW):

- *Angela González Carreño v. Spain*, CEDAW/C/58/D/47/2012, Decision of 16 July 2014
- *Rosanna Flamer-Caldera v. Sri Lanka*, CEDAW/C/81/D/134/2018, Decision of 21 February 2022

Committee on the Elimination of Racial Discrimination (CommERD):

General Recommendations

- *General Recommendation No. 35* of 26 September 2013 on Combating Racist Hate Speech, CERD/C/GC/35

Decisions

- *State of Palestine v. Israel*, CERD/C/100/5, Decision of 12 December 2019
- *State of Palestine v. Israel*, CERD/C/103/R.6, Decision of Admissibility of 30 April 2021

Committee on the Rights of the Child (CRC):

- *Sacchi and Others v. Argentina*, CRC/C/88/D/104/2019, Decision of 22 September 2021

Bibliography

Websites

African Commission on Human and Peoples' Rights—https://www.achpr.org
African Court on Human and Peoples' Rights—https://www.achpr.org/afchpr
Committee Against Torture—https://www.ohchr.org/en/hrbodies/cat/pages/catindex.aspx
Committee on Economic, Social and Cultural Rights—https://www.ohchr.org/en/hrbodies/cescr/pages/cescrindex.aspx
Committee on Enforced Disappearances—https://www.ohchr.org/en/hrbodies/ced/pages/cedindex.aspx
Committee on the Elimination of Discrimination against Women—https://www.ohchr.org/en/hrbodies/cedaw/pages/cedawindex.aspx
Committee on the Elimination of Racial Discrimination—https://www.ohchr.org/en/hrbodies/cerd/pages/cerdindex.aspx
Committee on the Rights of Persons with Disabilities—https://www.ohchr.org/en/hrbodies/crpd/pages/crpdindex.aspx
Committee on the Rights of the Child—https://www.ohchr.org/en/hrbodies/crc/pages/crcindex.aspx
Economic and Social Council—https://www.un.org/ecosoc/en/home
European Commission of Human Rights—https://www.refworld.org/publisher/COECOMMHR.html
European Committee of Social Rights—https://www.coe.int/en/web/european-social-charter/european-committee-ofsocial-rights
European Court of Human Rights—https://echr.coe.int/Pages/home.aspx?p=home
https://hudoc.echr.coe.int/eng
European Court of Justice—https://curia.europa.eu/jcms/jcms/j_6/en/
European General Court—https://curia.europa.eu/jcms/jcms/p1_217427/en/
General Assembly of the United Nations—https://www.un.org/en/ga/
Human Rights Committee—https://www.ohchr.org/en/hrbodies/ccpr/pages/ccprindex.aspx
Human Rights Council—https://www.ohchr.org/en/hrbodies/hrc/pages/home.aspx
Inter-American Commission on Human Rights—http://www.oas.org/en/iachr/
Inter-American Court of Human Rights—https://www.corteidh.or.cr/index.cfm?lang=en
International Court of Justice—https://www.icj-cij.org/en
International Criminal Court—https://www.icc-cpi.int/
International Criminal Tribunal for Rwanda—https://unictr.irmct.org/
International Criminal Tribunal for the Former Yugoslavia—https://www.icty.org/
International Law Commission—https://legal.un.org/ilc/
International Military Tribunal of Nuremberg—https://avalon.law.yale.edu/subject_menus/imt.asp

P. Pustorino, *Introduction to International Human Rights Law*,
https://doi.org/10.1007/978-94-6265-563-8

Permanent Court of International Justice—https://www.icj-cij.org/en/pcij
Security Council of the United Nations—https://www.un.org/securitycouncil/
Special Tribunal for Lebanon—https://www.stl-tsl.org/en

GPSR Compliance
The European Union's (EU) General Product Safety Regulation (GPSR) is a set of rules that requires consumer products to be safe and our obligations to ensure this.

If you have any concerns about our products, you can contact us on

ProductSafety@springernature.com

In case Publisher is established outside the EU, the EU authorized representative is:

Springer Nature Customer Service Center GmbH
Europaplatz 3
69115 Heidelberg, Germany

www.ingramcontent.com/pod-product-compliance
Ingram Content Group UK Ltd.
Pitfield, Milton Keynes, MK11 3LW, UK
UKHW020242290926
15470UKWH00002B/696
* 9 7 8 9 4 6 2 6 5 5 6 2 1 *